Enchanted Island

Linden Howard

A SAPPHIRE ROMANCE

ENCHANTED ISLAND

Prologue

THE SKY SEEMED TO have been bleached of colour by the merciless sun; the sea that moved sluggishly against the Dorset coast was heavy and oily-looking; and still the sun climbed higher until the whole world seemed to stop breathing, its life sucked up into the great furnace that was being stoked in the sky.

In the little fishing village quaintly named 'Easter', nets were spread to dry, boats lolled on the beach, stranded by an ebbing tide, and the only refreshment came from the pungent smell of seaweed drying at highwater mark. The doors and windows of the white-walled cottages lining the main street had been flung open, as though the occupants were hopeful of catching a cupful of air. An old woman dozed uncomfortably on a stool in an open doorway, legs wide apart, serge skirts turned up unashamedly above her knees.

Lavinia Jessel, coming down the steep street to the quay with her two charges, hastily averted her eyes from the immodesty of the upturned skirt and tried to divert their attention; but Edith, of course, knew exactly what was in Lavinia's mind.

'Look at that dreadful woman!' she cried shrilly.

'Hush!' Lavinia said fiercely, glaring at Edith.

'Why? She *is* dreadful to show her legs like that!'

'Be quiet, Edith,' Rose Brandon said coldly. 'Don't you know that little children should be seen and not heard?'

Rose could handle Edith as poor Vinnie never could. Rose was just sixteen, tall, well-developed, with thick, wheat-gold hair, eyes the colour of forget-me-nots, and a warm, soft mouth.

Edith glared at the older girl, pursed her small, button mouth and maintained an offended silence that did not disturb Rose in the least.

In the yard of the Fortune Inn, at the bottom of the street, a dog barked once, listlessly; beyond the Fortune was the small, private jetty where a boat waited to take Lavinia and the two girls across the three-mile strip of water to the island.

The name 'Four Winds' was written on the prow of the boat; she was freshly painted, meticulously cared-for; to have hoisted sail would have been ridiculous on such a windless day, so the waiting crew would have to use oars; and though both were equal to the task, being large, ox-like men, the prospect of such a journey in the heat made them sullen and resentful.

Lavinia shared their resentment, not daring to voice it. The picnic had been Rose's idea, and Edith had insisted on being included, much to Rose's annoyance. It was Vinnie who carried the heavy wicker hamper; she hated being on the water, even on such a day as this. The movement of a boat made her feel sick, as Edith very well knew.

Edith Freemantle was the orphaned god-daughter of the Reverend Wilfrid Brandon, Rector of Easter and Tolfrey; she lived at the Rectory with Wilfrid, his wife Clara, and their daughter, Rose.

Edith was well-built with fine, drab hair, heavy features, and bright little eyes that regarded the world and its inhabitants with disdain; her one pleasure in life lay in finding and exposing other people's weaknesses for her own amusement.

Thankfully, Vinnie handed over the hamper and was helped down into the boat; she sat opposite the two girls, a small upright figure, her face pink and perspiring. She was acutely uncomfortable in her heavy dress, almost suffocated by the tight bodice and high collar, her movements hampered by the drag of her very full skirts and many petticoats. The small hard bonnet fastened under her chin did nothing to shield her eyes from the glare of the

6

sun. The girls with her wore light, muslin dresses and shady bonnets; such attire, of course, being entirely unsuitable for Vinnie, who was twenty-two, and considered herself not worth a second glance; but then, whoever gave a second glance to a governess, anyway?

The 'Four Winds' left the jetty, and two pairs of leathery, muscular arms moved rhythmically, the oars seeming to sink into the smooth sea with each thrust, then dragged clear again with such effort that sweat ran down the faces of the two men.

Vinnie felt vague pity for them, though she had little pity to spare for anyone except herself. She had been summoned to Wilfrid Brandon's study after breakfast that morning, and told that her services would not be required after the end of the month. He would see to it that she left the Rectory with a good reference; but his cousin was coming to live with them, a woman well qualified to undertake the care of young people.

Lavinia, hating him, understood; an impoverished cousin, being a member of the family, would be expected to work all hours for her bed and board, without even the meagre wages to which an outsider was entitled.

It was hardly surprising, after all, she thought bitterly; Wilfrid's meanness was a byword in the household, where his servants and womenfolk were concerned; he did not exercise such discipline towards himself — he was a man of expensive tastes.

Servants gossip; Lavinia heard bits and pieces. Wilfrid's stipend was small, but he received a very handsome allowance with which to maintain his god-daughter until she inherited a fortune on her twenty-first birthday.

So Lavinia had no heart for a picnic planned only half an hour before Wilfrid had given her notice; her head throbbed and she felt the familiar sickness churning in her stomach. No, dear God, she thought, *not* a migraine, today of *all* days!

Edith looked at her governess speculatively.

'You don't like the sea, do you, Vinnie?' she said softly.

'Are you afraid you will drown? If you DID drown, would you go right to the bottom like a stone? Right down, down, *ever* so deep? Would you, Vinnie . . . ?'

'Please,' said Vinnie desperately, '*Please*, Edith. I have a headache . . . '

She should have known better, she realised; the weakness was exposed. Edith looked happy.

'Ah, poor Vinnie!' Edith crooned softly. 'Is it *very* bad? Never mind, the sea isn't rough; perhaps there *will* be a storm, though — then it will be rough going back, won't it? Will you be sick, if the boat rocks about, and the water comes in?'

The shrill voice was like a knife turning, turning, inside Vinnie's head; she closed her eyes, wishing that Rose would silence Edith with some biting reproof; but Rose hadn't heard a word of it; her eyes were fixed steadily on the long, low green mound ahead of them.

Vinnie turned her head carefully, wincing with pain. The island: Bella Careena. She had been there only twice during her stay with the Brandons, and she hated the place; it was dark and secretive; a green jungle hiding a couple of crumbling old houses and a handful of derelict cottages.

It was not a large island; nearly three miles in length and two miles wide, and it lay like a curled cat contentedly sleeping in the sun.

It seemed an impossibly long journey; Vinnie sat, drenched in perspiration. She had felt unwell many times of late; but never so ill as this, so wretched that she longed to crawl away into some dark, cool place and shut out the thoughts that bedevilled her: *Where shall I go? What will become of me? How long before I find another position?*

Governesses were ten a penny in those days; Vinnie had no parents, no relatives at all except an indifferent, un-interested cousin far away in Norfolk. The future looked terrifying; she had never felt so alone, so destitute, in her life.

The boat glided to the small landing stage and was

secured; shakily, Vinnie stepped ashore, faced with the task of carrying the heavy hamper once again.

For the first time, Rose seemed to be aware that Vinnie was ill; she looked at the white, drawn face, and said quickly:

'Why don't you and Edith sit here, in the shade of the trees, and rest?'

'Oh *yes!*' Vinnie agreed, with a grateful sigh.

'What are *you* going to do?' Edith asked Rose suspiciously.

'I'm going to look at the little ruined chapel,' Rose retorted.

'WHY?' Edith demanded.

'Because I want to,' Rose said sweetly; but there was a curious held-in excitement about the girl today, Lavinia thought. She was impatient to be free of them both. Vinnie had seen this excitement on one or two occasions recently; and Rose, after all, was almost a woman. Vinnie felt uneasy.

'It's too far to walk on such a hot day,' Vinnie protested.

'No it isn't, dear Vinnie! I've brought my sketch book and I intend to make some sketches of the chapel. Or a peacock, if I can find one to spread his tail for me.'

'*I* want to see the chapel! I want to come with you!' Edith cried.

'Well, you're not coming!' Rose retorted firmly. 'You'll stay here with Vinnie.'

Edith began to protest furiously; Vinnie shut her eyes. If only Rose would take Edith! Then she could sit in the shade and rest, and perhaps her headache would get better. The two boatmen had gone some way along the beach on the other side of the landing stage, removed their boots and were lying on the sand, in a patch of shade cast by a tree. If they slept, Vinnie thought, she might even be able to take off her boots and stockings and cool her feet in the water. The prospect filled her with longing; but Rose, for once, was being difficult.

'Vinnie, I won't have her with me! She's a nuisance,

she'll get tired and want to come back!'

'No I won't!' Edith cried angrily. 'I *won't*! I *want* to come!'

'I don't want you.' She gave Edith a none-too-gentle shove. Edith sat down abruptly on the sand and burst into tears of rage.

Rose made her escape as fast as she could; she went, fleet-footed, through the green jungle of trees, along the overgrown paths; occasionally, she heard the screech of a peacock, a sound that made her shiver deliciously. It was a weird, unearthly cry, she thought, like that of a soul in torment.

It was quite a walk to the ruined chapel — past tumble-down farm buildings on her left, then the short cut that skirted the grounds of the beautiful old house called the House of the Four Winds, its uncurtained windows like sightless eyes looking out over the English Channel.

As she approached the chapel, her heart beat fast with excitement. The excitement became almost unbearable when she heard movement ahead of her, and saw the figure step from the green tangle of bushes into a patch of sunlight.

Her body ached with longing; her feeling for him, sweet and sensuous, was a pain that seemed to pierce every part of her.

He stood smiling at her for a moment; then he put out his hands and drew her into the ruined, roofless chapel. She felt powerless to resist him. She gloried in her feeling of weakness. She was a woman! The awareness of her own body proved that fact beyond all doubt.

'I knew you would come!' he whispered.

'I thought I wouldn't be able to, after all! Vinnie's got one of her headaches and Edith wanted to come here with me . . .'

'Hush!' he commanded. 'Hush, Rose! There is only us two, on this island, in the whole world. We are going to make our promises to one another in this chapel, and they will be binding for ever. Say to me, "I, Rose Veronice

Clara Brandon, swear to love and to cherish . . . till death do us part.'' Come on, you have to say it to me, and I have to vow to you, the words in the marriage service . . . please, Rose. Please.'

She looked at him, half-shocked, half-thrilled; she let her eyelids droop so that the fans of gold lashes lay against her pink cheeks.

'We can't say the marriage service,' she protested.

'Yes, we can. If we both mean it, nothing else matters. This place is our church! One day, Rose Brandon, we shall be married, properly married, and live here. We belong to one another, forever. This land will belong to me, and I shall never let you leave it!'

His determination scared and exhilarated her. He could persuade her to do things she did not want to do. He drew her close to him, making her say the words of the marriage service after him, making her look into his eyes as he spoke the words and she repeated them.

There was silence, as they finished; she was trembling, frightened. Now I really *do* belong to him, forever, she thought. I have made solemn promises in a holy place.

'There!' he kissed her triumphantly. 'I wish I had a ring to give you!'

'I couldn't wear it!' she pointed out.

They walked past the chapel and sat in the shade of some trees.

'My father wants me to marry Jerome Jardine,' Rose said, leaning against his shoulder, staring dreamily up at the sky.

'You can't marry *him*! He's an old man! Besides, you belong to me. How many times must I tell you, Rose?'

They sat for a while talking, but he grew restless; he felt the stir of longing for her run like a fire through his body.

'Let's go to the cave in the bay!' he whispered yearningly. 'It's not far.'

The cave, some way down the cliffs, was reached by a path; it was dim and cool there, a perfect hideaway from prying eyes.

They lay side by side, talking for a while, his arm lying carelessly across her; but the restlessness in him would not be denied. He wanted to possess her completely, to prove to them both that she was his.

Experimentally, he ran his fingers over her firm breasts. She tried to sit up, but he pushed her back.

'I must go, or Vinnie will come looking for me,' she whispered.

'She'll never find us here,' he murmured.

His lips moved over her forehead, her lips, her throat; one hand moved swiftly downwards to gather the flimsy skirts and petticoats together and push them determinedly up to her thighs.

'No, no!' she moaned, caught fast between terror and excitement; but in one lightning movement, he had covered her body with his, and she was conscious only of a wild singing in her ears, a furious clamour in her blood.

Vinnie looked at the little watch pinned to the bodice of her dress, and hastily began to repack the hamper that Edith had insisted upon opening.

Edith watched her sullenly, her voice hammering at Vinnie's nerves, bludgeoning them . . .

'Rose has been gone *ages*. I shall tell Uncle Wilfrid when we get home. I shall tell him you just sat down and did nothing, when you ought to have been looking after us. He will be angry with you . . . '

'I don't care!' Vinnie cried recklessly. 'I won't have to look after you much longer, anyway . . . thank God for that! And thank God I won't have to be near your godfather . . . '

'I shall tell him you swore and said awful things about him. I shall tell Aunt Clara, too,' Edith promised.

Getting unsteadily to her feet, Vinnie suddenly thought about The Reference. A slender lifeline, without which she would sink completely. Oh dear God, she will tell him, and he won't care that for months I have endured the hell of looking after this spoiled, wilful, unloveable little wretch . . . he will withhold The Reference . . .

The mists swam in front of her eyes, and she retched violently; Edith glared at her in utter disgust.

She said, wrinkling her nose: 'I shall tell them you were sick in front of me, on the sand, and you didn't *care*. Only drunk people are sick. Uncle Wilfrid said people who drink too much go to hell. I hope *you* go to hell, Vinnie. I hate you; I hope something nasty happens to you!'

If she hadn't felt so ill, Vinnie's sense of humour would have rescued her; not today, however. She staggered towards the trees and when she reached them, went forward slowly, holding on to the trunks for support.

'You've left the hamper on the beach!' Edith cried, outraged, as she ran after her.

'SHUT UP!' cried Vinnie, her nerves stretched and frayed to dangerous thinness. 'Damn you, SHUT UP!'

She was sobbing, fighting the pain in her head. She had to find Rose.

It was a long walk; eventually, she reached the chapel, Edith trailing after her, uttering shrill threats, promising vengeance, suggesting ways in which Vinnie might die, her voice like a needle that seemed to pierce Vinnie's brain, making a red mist dance in front of her eyes. There was no sign of Rose at the chapel; she hesitated and then went doggedly along the path towards the cliffs, driven by the same sixth sense that had urged her to find Rose before it was too late. Too late for what . . . ?

Somewhere a peacock screeched, and she jumped violently. Edith ran along the path, as it came out from under some trees near the hollow, and deliberately stood in front of Vinnie, so that the governess almost fell on top of her.

Edith was singing, a horrible little song.

> Plain Jane, out in the rain,
> Don't let her come in again.

'That's you, Vinnie. You're a Plain Jane!'

Something snapped inside Vinnie's head; she caught the child by the shoulder, and urged her angrily along the path.

'Go!' she sobbed bitterly. 'Go. Never come near me again! *Do you hear that, Edith*? Never — come — near — me — again!'

The two people lying in the cave heard the words; the moment was spoiled. Angrily, he drew away from Rose, and she sat up, shaken, smoothing down her skirts.

The path along which Vinnie was walking led towards the top of cliffs where low bushes grew; there was a gap in the bushes. Edith was running towards the gap, pausing every so often to turn her head, and poke out her tongue at Vinnie.

'Be careful!' Vinnie cried sharply. 'Edith, be *careful*!'

The child misunderstood Vinnie's sudden lunge in her direction, and ran faster, with Vinnie in pursuit. Suddenly, Vinnie caught the toe of her boot in a tree root and fell heavily. Her head struck the trunk of the tree as she fell forward and then, blessedly, there was no more pain, only oblivion, wrapping her in fold upon fold of silence; whilst Edith, looking back at her, decided that she was indeed drunk, and began to scramble down the path between the bushes . . .

'Swear it, Rose!' Wilfrid Brandon commanded fiercely. 'Swear on this bible that you will never tell another living soul what happened on the island. You have made your confession to me. That is enough. *Swear* it!'

Rose, haggard and white-faced, could only think of what she had seen: Edith, spreadeagled on the rocks at the foot of the cliffs; and Vinnie, lying on the path.

Rose began to cry; Wilfrid put his hand beneath her chin and roughly forced her face upwards until her eyes met his. His eyes were as cold as a January morning, as he held out the heavy black bible.

'I am waiting,' he told her.

'No! It is not right!'

He let go of her chin, and brought the flat of his hand in a stinging blow across her cheek; tears of pain and shame filled her eyes.

'*Why* must I swear it?' she wept.

'The answer to that is obvious. You have behaved like a common slut. You deserve a thrashing that you will never forget. No decent man would marry you, if the truth came out! *You* are going to marry Jerome Jardine!'

'I don't want to marry him!' she wept. 'I don't love him! He's *old!*'

'Love! Love!' he sneered. 'That has nothing to do with it. He will make you a good husband.'

'I won't marry him!' she said stubbornly.

The hand came relentlessly across her cheek again, making her weep afresh.

'You *will*, Rose,' he told her calmly. 'You *will* marry him. Don't tell me that you won't, because I'll not have it. As for that wretch you lay with, like a cheap little whore, you won't see *him* again. *I* shall make sure of that. Now. Take this bible in your hand and swear.'

Chapter 1

I WAS TWENTY-ONE years old when I first visited Bella Careena.

My parents were Mary and Richard Lindsay; my father was several years older than my mother and they were quiet people, kind and deeply affectionate towards me.

We lived in Bideford, Charles Kingsley's "Little White Town by the Sea"; my father had a small fleet of ships, headed by the "Devonia", that carried cargoes between

Bideford, Bristol, Cardiff, and other West Country ports.

Our house was a large one, high above the steep streets of the town, and the upstairs windows commanded a wonderful view of rooftops, and the wide sweep of the river Torridge, flowing away to the sea. My childhood was blissfully happy and secure; the house was always warm and full of books, and there were servants who devoted all their time and energy to our comfort and well-being.

My father was tall and good-looking; my mother had delicate colouring and masses of soft hair that always smelled of lavender and rosemary. There was a serenity about her that was very soothing; I remember her cool fingertips on my forehead, when I was ill, the tireless patience with which she amused me. When I was six years old, I had a daily governess, a woman who seemed very old to me, for she was well past middle-age; but she was an excellent teacher and her discipline was never harsh.

She died when I was eleven years old. She had no family, and my parents paid for her to be buried in the Higher Cemetery, with a headstone. It was quite unheard-of for well-to-do people to show such consideration to those who served them, but my mother said:

'She served us faithfully, it is no more than she deserves.'

One day a letter came for my mother. It seemed to distress her, and I know that my father tried to console her. She would not tell me anything about the letter, but some days later, my father did not go to his office: instead, he took me for a drive to Instow, where I watched a Punch and Judy show on the sands, and had tea with him in a quiet little tea-room. Then he took his watch from his pocket, studied it gravely, and said that it was time for us to return home.

I was worried about my mother, and told him so; he patted my knee, and said there was nothing to worry about. Sure enough, when we returned, she came to greet us with a smile, and seemed to be her usual calm self.

I remember the time when I was twelve, and growing

up, and my mother talked to me of life, and love.

'Never be led away by passion, Flora,' she said to me earnestly. 'For passion is a thing of the flesh only, and does not last; true love is not just a thing of the flesh, but embraces the spirit as well as the heart. I love your father dearly; as he loves me. Devotion to one another is the only true love, my child. Never forget that.'

The letters came twice between my twelfth and thirteenth year. Each time, the ritual was the same: a few days afterwards, my father would take me away from the house for the day, and my mother would seem happy when we returned. No amount of questioning from me was ever of the slightest use; they both fended my questions off very firmly.

When I was fourteen, my mother died very suddenly, following a stroke. I was shocked and utterly inconsolable for a long time; but youth is resilient — and at fourteen years old, I had to take over the reins of the household, manage the servants, and care for my father.

After my mother's death, my father spent more time with his books, and began to sell off his ships, one by one.

'I have no son to carry on with the business,' he pointed out to me on my sixteenth birthday, and when he saw my eyes fill with tears he put an arm around my shoulders, and said contritely:

'My dearest Flora, I did not mean to hurt you. You have brought your mother and myself great happiness.'

'Nevertheless, if I had been a boy, I could have been of help to you; I would have inherited the business, papa. Could not a woman do so?'

'A woman — running a business? No, my love — you manage my home with a competence that would have earned your dear mother's blessing, and that is all I ask. When I am gone, you will be well provided for; then you must beware of young men who will come courting you for your money.'

'Well, they will scarcely court me for my looks,' I replied, rather bitterly.

'Do not yearn for a pretty face, Flora,' he admonished gently. 'Rather ask for qualities of the mind and heart, for such are more enduring.'

The year I was seventeen, I was spring-cleaning my father's study, with the help of one of the maids, when I came upon a sketch book.

It was my father's; he had been a talented amateur artist, as many of the pictures on our walls bore testimony, though in his later years he had put away his brushes.

The sketchbook was full of drawings, in pencil; of trees, some of them twisted into strange shapes; of ferns and foliage and flowers, and peacocks with spread tails; of an old house and a ruined chapel.

The drawings fascinated me. On each page, in the right-hand corner, was my father's signature, the date "1855" and the words "Bella Careena".

Bella Careena. I whispered them over and over to myself and shivered, as though a cold wind had blown through the room.

At dinner that evening, I asked:

'Where is Bella Careena, papa?'

'Why do you ask, Flora?' he demanded sharply.

I told him about the sketchbook I had found.

'Where is the sketchbook now?' he asked.

'I put it on your desk, papa; it was wedged down behind some books on the shelves, and I thought . . . perhaps . . . you had forgotten it was there . . .'

My voice trailed away; I did not know what to think. I remembered the questions he had adroitly sidestepped, in my younger days — and I realized, for the first time, that the letters had ceased to come, now that my mother was dead.

I took a deep breath.

'Where *is* Bella Careena, *please*, papa?'

'It is an island,' he said flatly. 'A small, rather insignificant one.'

'Where?'

'Off the Dorset coast,' he replied reluctantly.

'The sketches that you made were — exciting,' I said.

'Exciting? What a strange word, Flora! They were perfectly ordinary drawings.' His voice had an unfamiliar sharpness, for the second time that evening.

'Did you go there often, papa?'

'No. Only a few times,' he said guardedly.

'It was before you married mama?'

'Yes; really, Flora, you ask a great many questions. It was a place with a great variety of plant and bird life; you are well aware of my interest in such things. It is only natural that I should have made sketches.'

His attitude intrigued me as I could see that he did not wish to discuss Bella Careena.

'You never spoke of the place, papa.'

'What was there to say? I visited the place on a few occasions, made some sketches of it, and never returned to it again. You are making a great mystery out of nothing,' he replied.

He would not discuss it further; but the name "Bella Careena" had fastened small tentacles around my imagination and they would not be prised free.

It took me a long time to find a map of Dorset. I had to search for it when father was away from home, and he spent more time in his study than anywhere else. However, eventually I found the detailed map that I wanted, and, sure enough, there was the island, about three miles from the coast. It reminded me vaguely of a cat curled asleep, tail folded around its paws.

I put the map back in its place, and said nothing to my father; next, I began to search for books that would tell me about the island. After a long search, I found one; it proved to be a treasure-house of information.

The place was rich in legend. In the old days, it had been a favourite hiding place for pirates, smugglers, men wanted for various crimes; it was suggested that secret black magic rites had been practised there by one of its

19

owners; it had once been the refuge of a woman whose love had deserted her; the home of a witch who had cursed the island when the owner turned her adrift from it in a leaking boat; witches could not be drowned, it was said. There was no record as to whether this particular one had drowned or not.

The tentacles began to fasten themselves even more firmly on my imagination . . .

I wanted to visit Bella Careena, and I dared not ask . . .

But the year I was eighteen I did dare. My father said shortly:

'The island is privately owned, my dear. No one just *goes* there.'

'Yet you did,' I pointed out.

'Many years ago. By invitation.'

'Whose, papa?'

'A friend of mine. I have since lost touch with him.' His face wore its most remote look.

The following year my father invited a young man called Alexander Arkwright to dine with us one evening. Mr Arkwright was in his late twenties, pleasant, personable, and an excellent conversationalist; he had recently joined his father in partnership as a solicitor. Mr Arkwright, Senior, had looked after my father's affairs for many years, and planned to retire in a year or two.

After dinner, he and my father spent a long time in the study. When I went to bed that evening, I took a despairing look at myself in the mirror.

I was frankly plain. As a child I had been gawky. As a woman, I was tall and big-boned. My hair, fine and fair when I was young, had darkened as I grew older and was an unbecoming shade of mid-brown. My eyes were blue, my brows and nose too well-defined for prettiness. I had a stubborn chin, my mouth was too large, even my skin, instead of being becomingly pale, had a healthy glow more suited to a fisherman than a refined young lady.

Mr Arkwright came to dinner several times during the

20

months that followed. One Sunday afternoon, he accompanied my father and myself on a short drive. A few days later, my father looked at me thoughtfully, and said, with a sigh:

'What is to become of you, Flora? I shall not always be here to protect you from the world.'

I did not want to be protected; I wanted freedom. I wanted to have wings, spread them, fly. To faraway places. To Bella Careena. I knew I would never rest until I had seen the place.

He stirred restlessly in his chair. 'You are almost twenty. Most young women are married at your age. Do you want to be an old maid?'

'*Yes*!' I cried defiantly; defiance was the only way I knew of hiding my shame at my lack of looks and suitors.

My father did not mention the matter again, until a few days before my twentieth birthday; then he reminded me that Mr Arkwright was a sober, industrious and trust-worthy young man.

'I do not want a husband, papa,' I said flatly.

'My dear Flora, you have become so pert and sharp, that you are already an old maid,' he said ruefully. 'You could fare worse than to marry a man who has such a grasp of financial affairs.'

But he never mentioned Mr Arkwright again, and the visits became more infrequent.

Every week, I took flowers to the grave of my mother and my governess. Sometimes my father accompanied me. The week before my twenty-first birthday, on a wild and windy October day, my father stood bareheaded beside my mother's grave, and I saw how he shivered.

'You should not be out on such a day,' I scolded gently. 'You already have a cold. Come along home, papa.'

It was the last time he ever went out. The cold turned to a pneumonia that he had not the strength to fight. My twenty-first birthday passed unnoticed. My father died a few days later, and I wept bitterly for him. I felt alone and desolate.

The funeral was over; the servants had assembled to hear the will solemnly read by Mr Arkwright. The bequests my father had made to them were handsome. The amount of money he had left took me completely by surprise. We had lived comfortably, but never luxuriously; it had never occurred to me that he was a wealthy man.

He had sold his ships, and his property, and the money had been cleverly invested; after payment of bequests, the residue was left entirely to me, in trust until my twenty-fifth birthday.

'Your father feared that you would become the prey of fortune hunters,' Mr Arkwright explained, looking down his long, aristocratic nose at the papers on his desk.

'A fate I don't propose to meet,' I retorted. 'As I am unlikely to be married for my looks, I shall doubtless remain an old maid. I am fortunate enough to have money to spend as I please, and shall not need to work.'

The corners of his mouth twitched.

'You are a very outspoken young woman, Miss Lindsay,' he murmured.

'Because I do not have to make pretty speeches to win a husband,' I replied tartly. 'Well — so my father makes it a condition that I do not inherit until I am twenty-five?'

'Yes. In the meantime, you are to receive a substantial allowance that will permit you to maintain yourself in a manner in keeping with your position. Your father has appointed me as trustee of his will. If I may suggest such a thing, it might be of benefit to you to take a holiday.'

'A holiday?' I said. 'Yes. I will think it over.'

Sorting through my father's belongings, it struck me for the first time how little I knew about my parents. My father's parents had come from Hartland; my father had been their only child, having one cousin, living in Barnstaple, and who was long since dead.

I realised that I knew even less about my mother. I knew that her childhood had been happy, and that her father had been the rector of a village on the borders of Dorset and Wiltshire. She, too, was an only child and her parents died within weeks of one another when she was in her teens, she said; and then she had gone to Bristol, where she met and married my father. I could not find her birth certificate, nor my parents' marriage certificate, and I supposed that my father had given them into Mr Arkwright's keeping.

A forgotten childhood incident surfaced in my mind when I was busy one day; I remembered a scrap of conversation I had overheard between my mother and my father.

'Dearest Richard, you have made me deeply happy all these years, and shown me an affection that many women would envy.'

'You have shown *me* loyalty and deep affection, my dear Mary. Our marriage has been a mutual delight. Do you dare to tell yourself, now, that you were second-best only . . . ?'

I did not hear the reply; now, for the first time, I wondered about the identity of the first woman in my father's life.

Two months after my father's death, I said to Mr Arkwright:

'I should like you to enquire if I may visit the island of Bella Careena.'

He looked astonished.

'I have never heard of the place!'

I told him that my father had visited there, by invitation, many years ago. He promised to make enquiries for me, and I waited, in a fever of impatience, for the days to pass.

I felt like a river that longs to meet the sea. I knew

23

nothing of life and I was anxious to learn about it; after all, I was scarcely likely to know anything of love.

Mr Arkwright wrote to the present owner of the island — a man named Jerome Jardine — stating that I would like to visit Bella Careena.

A reply came to me, written on thick, expensive notepaper and covering four pages. It was from Mrs Rose Jardine, House of the Four Winds, Bella Careena, Dorset.

'My dear Flora,' she wrote, 'I cannot possibly call you "Miss Lindsay" for, although I have never met you, I feel I know you well. I knew your father many years ago, and am saddened to hear of his death. I know your mother died a long time ago; your father wrote and told me . . .'

The whole tone of Rose Jardine's letter was friendly and solicitous. Clearly, she knew nothing of my circumstances.

' . . . Jerome, my husband, wishes me to tell you that you are indeed welcome to visit us. I add my welcome to his. Stay with us for as long as you please. Consider this as your home. Our only son, Ruan, will be twenty-one this summer, and we are making great preparations to celebrate his coming-of-age. I would be glad of your help; and you will be companion for our daughter, Bella Careena (named, as she will tell you, after our beloved island!) I am sure that you will be *very* happy with us . . .'

I had not expected such a friendly reply; it delighted me.

Alexander Arkwright called to see me that morning. I was seated at my father's desk, reading the letter for the sixth time.

'Splendid!' I said happily.

'You *will* take care, won't you, Miss Lindsay? I shall await your letters most anxiously,' he said.

I travelled most of the way in a reserved first class railway carriage, to which a dining car attendant brought a tempting tray of food. But I was too excited to eat.

Mr Arkwright had made my travel arrangements with great thoroughness. A hired coach awaited me to take me on the last stage of my journey. It was late afternoon when the driver guided the horses carefully down the steep little street to the yard of the Fortune Inn.

So this was the village of Easter, I thought, as I stepped down and looked around me with delighted eyes. I looked at the white beach, at the cliffs rising steeply on either side of the bay; and then I shaded my eyes with my hand and gazed seawards.

There it was! A dark hump on the skyline; the curled cat sleeping in the afternoon sun! *Bella Careena*. Still, for a few hours, tantalisingly out of reach, for I would not be making the crossing until the following day.

'It will be a fine day for the crossing tomorrow,' said a man's deep voice from behind me.

I turned slowly.

The stranger was bareheaded and wore a cloak — which was very old-fashioned, and entirely unsuited to the heat of the day; yet he looked right in it, somehow, for he was tall and lean; his face was not conventionally good-looking; two grooves ran from his nose to the corners of his long mouth, and there were small, fine lines around his dark, deepset eyes.

They were eyes one would not easily forget; brown and very alert beneath heavy black brows. He had a straight nose, and a defiant chin. Though he was considerably older than me, it was impossible to tell his exact age, for there were flecks of grey in the thick, springy dark hair that was one of his chief attractions.

When he smiled, I saw how white and even his teeth were; he inclined his head and his eyes measured me from head to toe. I felt acutely conscious of my drab mourning clothes — black has never suited me.

'If you are prone to seasickness,' the stranger said, 'you need have no fears.'

'How do you know I am going to the island tomorrow?' I challenged.

'You were looking at it as though you had never seen it before; as though the prospect of exploring it gave you considerable pleasure.'

'How very perceptive of you,' I said coolly.

'I, too, am travelling to the island,' he said. 'My name is Edwin Trehearne. I am going to spend the summer on there.'

'I am Flora Lindsay,' I said abruptly, extending my hand.

To my discomfiture and annoyance, he did not shake hands or bow; he took my hand in his, lifted it to his lips and kissed the gloved finger-tips. It was a very theatrical gesture and I immediately distrusted him.

'Enchanté, Miss Lindsay,' he murmured.

'Are you French?' I asked.

'My grandmother fled the horrors of the Revolution — bringing her jewellery with her, which was most sensible of her!' His voice was dry and mocking. 'My mother died when I was a baby, so Grandmère Juvenal supervised my education for some years and taught me excellent French. My father was a Cornishman, as you will guess from my name.'

At that point the innkeeper's wife came forward to greet me, much to my relief. I was well aware of Edwin Trehearne's glance following me, as I entered the inn.

I was given a bedroom under the eaves. The room was at the front and faced seawards, so I could lie in bed and look at the island.

I washed, changed into a cooler dress, took the pins from my hair and brushed it. My hair was so long, it came down to my waist, and it was very thick; as I pulled the brush through it, I leaned on the broad windowsill, and pushed open the casement window; the afternoon was very still. The boats rode lazily at anchor, as though rocking themselves to sleep on the tiny waves. The tide was coming in fast, covering the sands. In the distance, the island tantalised, beckoned; lured me like a golden-haired mermaid sunning herself on a rock.

I had never considered myself imaginative; but, dreaming on a summer afternoon, I relaxed my hold on the silver-backed hairbrush, so that it fell with a clatter down to the courtyard, right at the feet of the man standing there.

Horrified, I leaned over the sill, my hair swinging down over my shoulders. He bent and picked up the hairbrush, looked up, and smiled delightedly.

'The princess in the tower!' he cried. 'Shall I return your hairbrush, my lady? Or may I have it as a keepsake?'

'It was an accident!' I cried.

He grinned wickedly. 'You look very attractive with your hair down,' he called up softly.

His words carried clearly on the still afternoon air; I had no intention of responding to his ready impudence. I drew in my head and slammed the window shut, cheeks flaming.

A few moments later, there was a knock upon the door; a maid entered, carrying my hairbrush, with its initials on the back: F.P.L.

Her face was solemn; she was about fifteen, plump and freckled.

'With Mr Trehearne's compliments, ma'am,' she said.

The private dining-room at the Fortune was furnished with mahogany, horsehair-seated chairs and a table with a starched white cloth. I didn't have the room entirely to myself, however; the table was laid for two. Mr Trehearne joined me, handsome and dignified in formal clothes.

'It seems we are dinner companions, Miss Lindsay,' he said courteously.

'I understood that this was a private dining-room,' I replied crisply.

'A private dining-room, used by overnight guests who will be going to the island,' Edwin Trehearne replied. 'This inn is owned by the Jardines. The entire village belongs to them; *and* much of the land around it. I trust your hairbrush was safely returned, Miss Lindsay?'

'Yes, thank you, Mr Trehearne,' I replied.

'I am curious as to the intial "P" on your hairbrush. I have been speculating: Penelope. Persephone. Pandora — as you see, I have a taste for Greek Mythology. Primrose — no, that would not suit you at all!'

His smile was teasing and quizzical.

'I have no intention of telling you, Mr Trehearne,' I replied primly.

He laughed; it was a rich, full sound. All my instincts sent back warning signals to my brain. Don't trust this man. He will coax your thoughts from you, and give nothing in return.

'I know more of you than you think, Miss Lindsay, though we have not met before. Your father and mine were friends, long ago,' he said calmly.

'When?' I asked, surprised.

'They met when they were at university.'

'My father has never mentioned anyone of the name of Trehearne,' I said, frowning.

'My father,' said Edwin Trehearne, 'was Sir Marcus Trehearne.'

'Was?'

'He died some years ago,' Edwin told me. 'The friendship between your father and mine ended when they both courted the same young woman; alas, she turned down your father in favour of mine and your father was extremely upset. Your father, like mine, was a proud and stubborn man, so they never patched up the quarrel; no doubt that is why he didn't mention the name of Trehearne to you.'

'What happened to the lady in question?'

'She became the second Lady Trehearne, my stepmother.'

'How do you know I am Richard Lindsay's daughter?' I asked suspiciously.

'It seemed likely that you were, when you introduced yourself. You are going to the island. Your father was there, with mine, years ago. I knew that your father had subsequently married and gone to live in the West Country, and the innkeeper's wife told me you were coming from Bideford. Simple powers of deduction, no more!'

I looked into the teasing eyes, and told him:

'It was because I found some sketches of Bella Careena, done by my father, that I wanted to see the place.'

'I must be honest,' Edwin Trehearne said charmingly. 'Mrs Jardine wrote me that you were coming to Bella Careena, which made it even easier to guess your identity. She tells me you are to be her secretary and a companion to Bella Careena. You will find her a very generous and understanding employer, I'm sure.'

'Employer?' I stammered.

'Yes. She has told me that your father's death makes it necessary for you to find employment.'

Astounded, I struggled to hide my feelings. Alexander Arkwright had written a formal letter — a copy of which he had given me — informing the Jardines of my father's death, and saying that I would like to visit the island. Why should they have assumed I was penniless, I wondered?

I opened my mouth to correct the mistake and changed my mind. I was an heiress, a plain young woman of twenty-one. It was an unfortunate combination.

I had thought life was dull. I wanted adventure; I was the river hurrying to meet the sea. Let them all think, then, that I needed to work for a living.

With relief, I saw that the meal was about to be served.

However it was almost dawn before I slept. At half-past seven, a maidservant in crisp print brought me tea and a jug of hot water. I washed and dressed and pinned up my

29

hair with hands that shook, reminding myself that I would have to behave like a paid companion, not like Miss Flora Lindsay of Lakemba, Bideford, Devon, heiress to a fortune.

When I went down to breakfast, Mr Trehearne had already eaten his meal. I glanced out of the window, and saw him standing on the quay, looking at the island, hands clasped behind his back.

After breakfast, my luggage was brought downstairs; as I was going to the island to stay with the Jardines, I was not expected to pay for my night's stay. I looked at the little maidservant, waiting expectantly in the dining-room, and tipped her lavishly. The smile on her face made me realize for the first time the pleasures of having money to give away.

'Have you ever been to the island?' I asked.

'No, miss,' she said. 'Some of the girls from the village work there. I wouldn't care for it. I'd be feeling I was cut right off from everyone.'

The shirt-sleeved handyman carried my luggage to the private jetty, and then took Edwin Trehearne's valises, ready to be loaded.

'Good morning, Miss Lindsay,' Edwin said, strolling up to join me. 'You look excited and just a little apprehensive.'

'I feel as though I am about to embark for the other side of the world rather cross three miles of water,' I replied.

He looked at me almost sombrely.

'In a sense you are right; to go to Bella Careena is to voyage around the world.'

He took his watch carefully from his pocket, consulted it, and remarked that it was nine-forty precisely. Then he lifted his arms and pointed ahead.

'Look!' he said. 'The boat is coming!'

It was a trim little craft, cutting cleanly through the water, making arrowheads on the flat surface, and sending out ripples on either side.

The boat was painted white and blue, with a polished brass rail running around the small deck; I saw a man in a blue and white jersey, in the wheelhouse; another man, dark and swarthy, similarly dressed, balanced himself expertly on the prow, a circle of coiled rope in his hands. He spun it neatly as the boat came alongside and the rope made a noose over the iron bollard on the jetty. Then he jumped ashore and saluted us both.

I looked at the name, written on the prow of the boat: "Four Winds." I shivered as though a snowflake had brushed my cheek.

The luggage was loaded; but as Mr Trehearne turned to give me his arm and escort me on board, we heard a sudden, tremendous clatter of hooves behind us.

A closed carriage was coming at some speed down the steep little street; I held my breath, fearful of an accident, but the driver was remarkably skilled; he guided the horses expertly, checking them sufficiently to allow them to turn, and then slowing them to a more sedate trot at exactly the right moment, so that they halted only a few yards from us; their eyes were wild, their manes tossing, and they were coal-black horses such as the devil himself might have driven.

The door of the coach opened; out stepped a small, stout man, perspiring freely; by his attire, he was obviously the coachman. The man who had driven the horses so recklessly, jumped lightly from the box, put his hands in his pocket and tossed a purse full of money to the trembling coachman.

'Come, man, it wasn't such a rough ride, was it? I got us here safely — and just in time for me to join my fellow passengers!' he cried.

The coachman handed out a valise; I took a long look at the man striding, with such careless grace, towards us.

He was a man to fire one's blood, I thought.

Chapter 2

HE WAS A TALL, muscular-looking man, with the powerful litheness of a tiger. He was also extremely handsome, possessing the classic good looks found on the heads of old Greek coins. His eyes were tawny, and his hair was the same colour, worn in tight little curls over his head which was most unusual; there was an air of worldliness about him that greatly impressed me.

His voice was clear and commanding; he bowed to me, smiled at Edwin.

'Good morning, Edwin; are you, too, bound for a long holiday with Rose and Jerome?'

'Yes,' said Edwin crisply. 'Damien, this is Miss Flora Lindsay, Richard Lindsay's daughter; she is going to be Rose's secretary. Miss Lindsay, this is Damien Ashley, cousin to Jerome Jardine.'

'How do you do, Miss Lindsay?' His smile was amused. 'So Rose is to have a secretary?'

'To help with her preparations for her son's coming of age,' I murmured. 'I am also to be a companion to Bella.'

'Ah, of course.' He nodded. 'I knew your father, Miss Lindsay.'

'You, too?' I replied, astonished. 'Mr Trehearne also knew him!'

'Edwin and I spent many holidays on Easter when we were boys, and frequently visited the island,' Damien explained. 'It belonged to Jerome; my father had sold it to him. I remember that your father and Edwin's had quarrelled over a lady, and were most perturbed to find themselves staying in the same village!' He laughed, showing white teeth. 'Well, it was all a long time ago; so

32

this is your first visit?'

'Yes,' I said.

I glanced at Edwin. His expression was aloof; he seemed to have withdrawn into himself since the arrival of Damien. That was not surprising. Damien Ashley was a man who would tower over all other men, I realized.

The boat arrowed through the smooth water, leaving a foamy wake, and I watched the coast recede; the island that had been a green hump began to take shape and form before my eager eyes. As we drew nearer, I had an impression of a great many trees everywhere, of white sand, a row of cottages along the shore beside the jetty we were approaching.

Edwin pointed to the cottages, and said:

'The people who live there maintain the island, and look after Mrs Jardine and her husband.'

'It seems a very self-contained community,' I said.

'It has to be,' Damien said solemnly. 'It is a kingdom on its own, a law unto itself.'

'Nonsense!' Edwin replied sharply. 'It is subject to the same laws that govern the rest of us!'

As we approached the jetty, I saw a break in the trees; in the distance there was something that looked like a tower, and a brief glimpse of a grey church.

We drew in to a small stone jetty, identical to the one we had recently left. Edwin and Damien helped me ashore; and so I first set foot on Bella Careena.

It seemed a very silent place; the trees crowded everywhere, in a dense mass of green; at least they would give coolness and shade, I reflected.

Two conveyances waited for us, on the broad path leading from the jetty; one was an open carriage, the other a trap to take our luggage. A uniformed servant helped me into the first coach, and the two men followed. When we were seated, the servant handed me a parasol, pink and pretty.

'The sun is quite fierce, ma'am,' he assured me.

As we waited for the driver to climb on to his box, I

heard a strange sound; a soft tinkling of bells from the dense shelter of the trees beside the path. I listened, and it came again; a soft musical clash. I could have sworn I saw a flash of red under the trees. Then it was gone.

'That is probably Bella,' Edwin said, with a dry smile.

'What is she doing?' I asked, with a frown. 'Hiding from us?'

'Sizing us up, no doubt, before she makes herself known to us,' Damien replied.

The coachman flicked his whip, and the horses moved slowly forward.

I really did not need to use the pretty parasol, once we had turned from the jetty under the green arch of leaves that met overhead; they formed such a dense canopy that I was momentarily chilled; it was like driving through a tunnel with a circle of light at its far end. I wondered if the trees had ever been pruned.

The horses' hooves made no sound as they carried us along; there was only the faint creaking of the harness, and beyond that, a silence so still, so absolute, that I felt my heartbeat quicken; and then I heard the sound again, close beside us — the soft clash of bells, a movement, as twigs and leaves were brushed aside for someone to look at us.

I was annoyed, and turned my head sharply in the direction of the sound, but I saw nothing. Bella Careena was evidently amusing herself by keeping pace with the slow-moving coach and teasing us with the ghostly sound of bells.

The circle of light grew larger, much to my relief; the sun began to penetrate the thick screen, dappling the path with coins of gold, until we emerged into the full light of day.

As the path wound through a small clearing, I suddenly beheld a magnificent sight; a strutting peacock with its tail spread out in an exquisite fan of rich blue feathers, each with the eye clearly marked on the tail. As I leaned forward to admire it, the peacock suddenly gave a loud screech and flew up into the lower branches of the nearest tree, its beady little eyes looking down malovently upon us.

'What a horrible sound!' I said involuntarily.

'Indeed it is,' Damien agreed. 'This is an island of peacocks. They are almost wild, and roam the place as they choose.'

We crossed the clearing, and reached a point where the path branched away to left and right, like the two prongs of the letter "Y". The horses turned along the left-hand path.

I was facing the way we were going, and I sat forward eagerly. Again the path curved to the left and made a wide sweep around an expanse of beautifully kept lawns.

'You should close your eyes until the carriage reaches the house,' Damien teased. 'Then you will see it, as it should be seen, in all its glory. Really, the only way to approach the house is from the sea.'

I closed my eyes, as the coach turned leftwards, making a wide arc, and coming finally to rest in front of the House of the Four Winds.

'Open your eyes, Miss Lindsay!' Damien said gaily.

I opened them. I shall never forget my first sight of the house that faced south, its wide green lawns sloping down to the path where the horses stood. A long staircase of shallow stone steps led from the front of the house to this path, and the horses, from long practice, no doubt, had halted exactly at the last step.

It was more like a small castle than a house. A large, splendid building of old grey stone, with a crenellated roof, and round towers at each end. Against the many windows of its long facade, scarves of ivy lay carelessly, as though they had been blown there by the wind. At the top of the gentle flight of steps was a broad terrace, with a stone balustrade, and great stone urns were placed along the terrace at intervals, each urn foaming over with brilliant fuschia tassels. In the centre of the terrace, a door was being slowly opened, and two figures stepped out; a

35

tall, grey-haired man and a younger woman. They did not come down the steps, but waited at the top for us, and I thought suddenly: they are like royalty, waiting to receive their guests.

'Well?' said Damien softly.

'It is so *beautiful*!' I whispered. 'This is another world.'

The steps were wide enough for three of us to walk abreast, and so we made our way upwards towards the couple waiting on the terrace.

Even on such a hot day, there was no great effort involved in mounting the steps to the terrace, so shallowly were they cut; as we neared the top, another figure stepped from the French doors that took the place of windows on the ground floor, crossed the terrace, and stood beside the waiting couple.

He was a boy of about twenty, tall, good-looking, with thick gold hair. He was taller than the other two beside whom he stood, and he held himself proudly.

'Ruan has grown into a handsome young man,' Damien said, with satisfaction. 'No doubt he is looking forward to his coming-of-age, and all the celebrations that will attend it.'

As we reached the terrace, the woman suddenly left her husband's side, and came forward, hands outstretched, as though the desire to welcome us had won the battle over dignity.

It was towards *me* that she looked; it was to *me* that she came, and to my astonishment she seized my hands, so that I dropped the parasol, letting it fall with a clatter on the top step. There were tears in her eyes; her voice was deep and husky. Her soft lips brushed my cheek.

'My dearest child!' she whispered, 'Welcome to Bella Careena! I am so happy that you are here!'

I was astonished at the warmth of her greeting towards a young woman whom she did not know, and whom she believed to be near-penniless and in search of employment. She must have been very fond of my father, I thought.

Rose Jardine was the most beautiful woman I had ever seen; she was tall and well built, with a full bust, narrow waist, and curving hips. Her hair, thick and deep golden in colour, like ripe corn, was elaborately dressed high above her face. She did not have the fashionable lily-pale look, but the sun had touched her skin only very gently, for it was the texture of a ripe peach and faintly sunwarmed. Her mouth was soft and full and her eyes were the bluest I have ever seen. The thick lashes, the finely-arched brows, the rounded chin and the long neck had been perfectly fashioned, as though by a master craftsman. She wore a delicately tucked and ruffled dress of pink; it had frills at the neck and elbow length sleeves; the skirt was caught up into a bustle at the back. Her shoes exactly matched her dress; I saw the gleam of gold at her throat, and on her slender wrist.

It was not fair that one woman should possess so much beauty, I thought dismally; I was acutely aware of my own plainness; this woman, so softly and prettily curved, carried her height beautifully. *I* was big-boned; at that moment I felt gawky, and very dowdy, in my hot black mourning attire.

'Rose,' said Damien plaintively, 'I swear we are invisible to you. Have you no welcome for us?'

She laughed, and apologised prettily, offering each of them a soft, perfumed cheek.

'Damien, I am delighted to see you. You did not say when you could come, and I imagined Irene would be with you.'

'She will be here soon,' he told her. 'She had last-minute affairs that delayed her; as for me, I could not wait to exchange the heat and noise of London for this Paradise!'

Rose smiled at Edwin.

'You, Edwin? Are you tired of all your responsibilities?'

'How can I be otherwise, when you offer such an attractive alternative, my dear Rose?' he said charmingly. 'Gloucestershire cannot compete with this incomparable island. Your proposition was most tempting: squander a summer here, you said. I owe myself a long holiday; and I have left a good man in charge of my affairs.'

Rose turned to me and said:

'Come, Flora; Ruan and Jerome are waiting to meet you.'

Rose was tall for a woman; Jerome was more than six feet in height, a man who dwarfed us all, broad-shouldered, upright, with rugged features, and brown eyes that were friendly, belying the severity of his mouth and cragginess of his face. His hair was silver grey, brushed high above his forehead and then falling back in deep waves. One hand rested on a silver-topped walking-stick.

I realized that he was much older than his wife; but when he smiled, his mouth lost its severity. His voice was clear and resonant.

'Welcome to Bella Careena, Miss Flora Lindsay!' he said; and, in spite of Damien's jest about "King Jerome" I thought that Jerome Jardine had a very regal bearing at that moment.

Ruan Jardine resembled his mother more than his father. His thick, springy hair was the same golden colour, his bright hazel eyes looked at me with interest; he had his mother's well-defined features and generous mouth. I thought him a pleasant and very personable young man.

'Welcome to the island,' he said to me.

'There is one member of the family missing,' Jerome Jardine told me wryly. 'Isabella has chosen to absent herself. She prefers to see before she is seen. She has no doubt made herself well aware of your arrival and journey here.'

'Isabella?' I queried.

'She was christened Isabella Serena Catherine,' Rose told me. 'As a child she could not manage the "Isabella", so what more natural than that she should shorten it to Bella and then add "Careena" after her beloved island? You'll meet her soon enough, Flora. At this moment, I am sure you need rest and some refreshment.'

She put her hand on her husband's arm; I saw the look of love and tenderness that flashed between them as they led the way into the house. We followed them, the servants bringing up the rear, with the luggage.

Other servants waited in the big cool hall, with its carved furniture, and faded old wall hangings.

Rose spoke to Damien.

'Will you stay here until Irene joins you? As you have come earlier than I anticipated, Seawinds is not quite ready for you,' she said to him.

'In that case I shall be delighted to accept your hospitality,' he told her.

She signalled to one of the servants and said that Mr Ashley would occupy the east tower suite. The suite in the west tower was to be Edwin's, I gathered.

I felt a light touch on my arm; Ruan was smiling at me.

'I think you'll be good for Bella,' he murmured.

'You make me sound like a dose of medicine!' I protested.

'I don't mean to; it's just that she hasn't any young company, except me, and I have been kept busy now that my father isn't in good health. She only has Nanny Radford, her old Nurse; Nanny has been with Bella ever since she was born.'

'Are you looking forward to your coming-of-age?' I asked him.

He sighed.

'I'm not sure I'll enjoy all the fuss. Still, the first of September is several weeks away yet.'

He went across to speak to one of the servants. Jerome said to me:

'I liked your father, Flora.'

I shook my head, puzzled.

'You all knew him: you — Mr Trehearne — Mr Ashley. Yet he never mentioned any of you to me.'

'It was a long time ago; twenty-five years. I didn't know him well, more's the pity. He rented a house for a couple of months, near where I was living, and it was a casual acquaintanceship, I suppose. We had a few meals together, at the Fortune, and discussed books and ships. Was his marriage to your mother a happy one?'

'Very happy,' I said.

'I'm glad to hear it,' he said.

'Did you ever meet my mother, Mr Jardine?'

'Jerome, my dear Flora — Jerome, not "Mr Jardine". We want you to consider yourself one of the family.'

He didn't answer my question, for Rose came over to me at that point.

'I will take you to your rooms, Flora,' she said, for all the world as though I was the most honoured guest of all.

She led me across the great hall, over grey flagstones, whose coldness was softened by several old eastern rugs; at each end of the hall, I saw twin, shallow staircases, curving upwards to a long gallery from which led many doors. We went up the stairs together.

'I thought you would prefer to be at the back of the house,' she said, opening a pair of double doors with a flourish. 'You have sea views from the front; but I think the sea looks empty and lonely. I believe you would prefer to have a view of the island.'

The room was large, airy and prettily furnished; it was a sitting-room, with comfortable chairs, a well-filled bookcase, plants, a writing-desk: a door led from it to a bedroom, with a great four-poster bed, splendidly draped in blue velvet.

The deep-set windows looked out over treetops. I saw the tower of an old church, not far from the house; it was the one I had seen from the boat. Away westwards, towards the Devon coast, the island seemed to curve up fairly steeply. I had tantalising glimpses of sun-speckled water, and ahead of me was the mainland, a hazy purple ribbon in the distance. The view immediately below me was delightful; lawns unrolled like green velvet towards a small marble temple, with a cupid on top of the round cupola; I glimpsed the tantalising shimmer of a lake in the distance; there were massed bushes of rhododendrons, fuchsia, many plants whose names I did not know.

I looked eastwards, at the ruined tower some distance from the house; I had seen it from the boat.

'What is that?' I asked Rose, pointing.

'The Folly,' she said lightly. 'There are two such follies on the island. The other is a very delightful cottage in the grounds where Bella lives with Nanny Radford. When you and Bella have come to know one another, then perhaps you will live in the cottage with her.'

'Why does Bella live apart from you?' I asked.

'Oh, it is not apart, not in *that* sense! I love my daughter dearly; her affection for me has never been in doubt! It is simply that she is a strange child, coming now to womanhood, and wanting to have, as she put it, "a little house of her own, amongst the trees." This island is a strange place, you will find; haunted, some say. It casts its own spells, and they are very potent. I want *you* to love it, also. I want you to stay. It is *right* that you should be here!'

'Why?' I asked, still nonplussed.

'Oh, Flora, dear child!' She caught hold of my arm and looked almost pleadingly into my face. 'Don't vex yourself with questions. *I* want you to be here. Let that suffice.'

'Did *you* know my father?' I asked.

'Yes. The year I was sixteen. Afterwards, when he married and moved away, we lost touch.'

I said, with some exasperation:

'Whenever I seek to know more about my parents, I find closed doors.'

'Perhaps one should not look for keys to every door, Flora.'

'It is natural to be curious concerning one's parents.'

'Whatever it is you wish to know, *I* cannot tell you,' she answered. 'Do you have happy memories of them?'

'Yes. Very happy ones.'

'Then you are lucky. My father was hard and unloving; he punished me severely for the smallest misdemeanour. My mother suffered from a number of ailments: fatigue, migraine, "turns" — all of which seemed to necessitate her spending most of her time in a darkened room. The years I have spent with Jerome have been very happy. Nothing changes here. I don't like change.'

'I would have thought it was inevitable in life,' I pointed out.

'Oh, Flora, how old and wise you sound. Like — ' she stopped abruptly.

'Like whom?' I pressed.

'Vinnie,' she said. 'She was my governess. Well, now, Flora, this is to be your home for as long as you wish. You must not look upon Jerome or myself as your employers. You are one of us.'

I was at Bella Careena under false pretences. Why didn't I tell the truth, then? Perhaps because I wanted to be accepted on my own merits, to prove myself capable of earning a living, even though I didn't need to do so.

She kissed my cheek, and said:

'I'll have some hot water and a cool drink sent up to you. Then you can rest until lunchtime. Did you have a comfortable night at the Fortune?'

'Oh, yes,' I told her. 'I met Mr Trehearne there.'

'His father, Sir Marcus Trehearne, designed all the gardens on the island. Jerome asked him to do so because he had laid out the grounds of his house in Gloucestershire so beautifully, and he was an authority on plants, as well as being an artist. You will enjoy seeing his workmanship; especially the Grottoes. Hs was a man with a vivid imagination.'

'Mr Ashley told me that *his* father once owned the island,' I said.

'Yes, it's quite true — the island belonged to Damien's father, once. He found the place an encumbrance. Jerome is a generous man, Flora; he insisted that Seawinds should be kept as a home for Damien whenever he wished to come here. It's at the other end of the island.'

She crossed the room; at the door she paused and said:

'They come every summer; Damien, and his wife, Irene.'

Chapter 3

I SPONGED AWAY staleness and heat in silk-soft water.
A maid unpacked my luggage and put away my clothes.

The room seemed suddenly airless, the silence hot and
heavy. I was supposed to be in mourning for my father.
Would the Jardines think it odd if I wore a light-coloured
dress? Probably not; this was not Bideford, where the
conventions had to be observed.

I settled for a dress of cream voile, with lavender-
coloured ribbons and an edging of lace at the neck and
sleeves, fastened my hair behind my neck and splashed
lavender water liberally on my hot forehead.

It was nearly lunch-time; I went out of the room, along
the gallery to the top of the stairs and looked down.

A young girl stood in the hall, hands clasped behind her
back; she was staring upwards, and her glance met mine
gravely. She did not smile nor move.

I knew at once who she was.

I went slowly down the stairs, and as I reached the
bottom step, she walked across to me, still clasping her
hands behind her back. She looked me over from head to
toe.

This tall, slim girl could have passed for sixteen. Her
hair was much darker gold than her mother's; it was thick
and curly, was drawn back from her face, and fastened
with a large bow on the nape of her neck. Her eyes were
the same brilliant blue as her mother's.

'Are you Flora Lindsay?' she asked.

'Yes,' I said.

She held out her hand.

'My name is Isabella Serena Catherine Jardine,' she

told me gravely. 'I do not like the first three names at all, and the fourth is unnecessary because everyone here knows that I am the only daughter of Mr and Mrs Jardine. My real name is "Bella Careena", the same as the island. I *am* the island. I am exactly like it. Do you understand me, Miss Lindsay?'

'Not really,' I admitted frankly.

'It doesn't matter. Soon you *will* understand. I know this island better than anyone else. I shall show it all to you. We will begin this afternoon. If you are going to stay here for a time, you must know your way around.'

I looked into the blue eyes and found them cold, and I realised that Bella did not share her mother's pleasure in my arrival.

'Are you a good walker?' she demanded, in a tone of voice that said she rather doubted the fact.

'I am considered to be so,' I said mildly.

'I will lend you my parasol,' she said. 'It is made of scarlet silk, shaped like a pagoda, and has bells hanging around the edge; when the bells tinkle, the sound is very pretty.'

'Is that the sound I heard this morning?' I asked.

'No. You heard the tinkling of the bells sewn on my dress.'

I looked, with raised eyebrows, at the simple, unornamented white dress she was wearing, and she frowned impatiently.

'I wasn't wearing *this* dress. Nanny Radford is deaf and short-sighted, so I sewed bells on some of my dresses — then she could hear me and know I was safe. I put red ribbons on, too, because red shows up best when people can't see. I've always done it, for her; well — I rather like it, anyway. Ruan says it's childish, at my age, but I don't care what he thinks.'

'Why did you hide away from me this morning?' I asked.

'I wanted to see what you looked like,' she replied coolly.

'I trust I met with your approval!' I said tartly.

She said calmly: 'I don't need a governess, and I've never had one. Mama and Papa taught me everything. I can read, write, paint and sew, speak French and German and play the piano. I also know how to conduct myself in company, and be agreeable to people. So there is no need for you to teach me *anything*, Miss Lindsay.'

I tried to hide the twitching of my lips.

'You may call me Flora,' I said.

'Thank you. There really was no need for you to come here, you know.'

'I came at your mother's invitation; she, at least, has welcomed me,' I retorted. 'It is neither kind nor polite of you to make me feel unwelcome.'

She said calmly: 'I don't wish to make you feel unwelcome, but there is something I must tell you: I do not intend to leave this island yet, and I shall not do so until I am ready. I hope you will not try to persuade me that it is for my own good that I should leave here. I wonder why mama was so anxious to have you here? She has talked of nothing else for days. One would imagine you were the daughter of her oldest friend, yet I have never heard your name mentioned until a few weeks ago.'

I wondered if she was jealous; but the sudden arrival of Edwin put an end to further conversation, and she ran joyously to him.

'Uncle Edwin! I hope you are going to stay for a long time.'

She flung her arms round his neck, kissed him and raced upstairs; he looked quizzically at me.

'You look cool and elegant,' he told me. 'Black doesn't suit you at all.'

'I'm in mourning for my father,' I said.

'No one observes the conventions here. I am still trying to fit a name to the tantalising letter "P" on your hairbrush. So far I've made no progress. Don't tell me, or you will spoil the game!'

'It's a great deal of nonsense about nothing!' I retorted.

'Ah, I have it! *Phyllida*! *Pepita*? No, you do not look sultry enough for a "Pepita". Ah well! It is not every man who has an acquaintance with a lady's hairbrush! It suggests all kind of scandalous liaisons!' he replied solemnly.

A latent sense of humour awoke in me, and made me laugh, unwillingly.

I saw approval in his glance.

'We *are* making progress, after all,' he murmured.

'What a man of moods *you* are, Mr Trehearne!' I replied lightly. 'Early this morning, you seemed quite — sombre.'

'Perhaps because I foresaw that you were coming under a spell . . . '

'The spell of the island?'

'No. A spell as potent, however, and even more dangerous. I refer, of course, to Mr Damien Ashley. His reputation for spell-casting is well known.'

He went coolly on his way, leaving me furious and struggling for words.

I walked towards the open door and stood looking at the crinkled blue sea, trying to find some breath of air. There was none. The glitter of the sun on the water was fierce and unrelenting.

Ruan found me standing there, when he ran up the steps and crossed the terrace, some minutes later.

'Flora? You've met Bella?' he asked.

'Yes. Your sister wants nothing of the outside world, it seems,' I told him. 'Do you feel the same complete affinity with the island that she feels?'

'Oh, Bella is a law unto herself — like the island. She's strange. "Fey" is the word, I think. It's different for me; I have been away to school, *and* abroad. I studied Art in Italy. For such a small country, it is packed with treasures: paintings, sculpture, architecture; a feast of beauty.'

'You sound as though your heart is there still!' I teased.

'Flora — I may call you that, mayn't I? — you have guessed the truth. Bella Careena can never be *my* world!' He spoke with great passion. 'Mama says my father must not know that. It would distress him.'

'He will have to know one day; men must follow their own paths in life,' I argued.

'And women?' he asked, with a smile of gentle amusement.

'Oh, they are not so fortunate, as a rule!' I replied lightly.

There were seven of us for lunch in the big, cool dining room: Jerome and Rose, Ruan and myself, Damien, Edwin and Bella. Over lunch, Bella told her mother that she proposed to take me on a tour of the island during the afternoon. Rose shook her head.

'My darling child, it is *much* too hot for such an expedition.'

I saw the look of disappointment on Bella's face; but the greatest surprise was the look that Jerome gave his wife.

It was a look of such blinding love and tenderness that I felt I had trespassed by witnessing it; I had never before seen love between husband and wife so clearly expressed; for Rose smiled across the round table at her husband, and it was a smile that accepted and returned in full measure the great love he had for her.

'You cannot expect poor Flora to walk so many miles in this heat!' Ruan was protesting to his sister.

'*I* can do it!' Bella retorted, in genuine surprise.

'For such a delicate-looking young lady, you are as strong as a horse,' Ruan teased his sister.

'We shall *all* go,' Rose said, unexpectedly. 'Except you, Jerome. You must rest, as the doctor has ordered. We are *not* going to walk, however; we shall travel in two open carriages.'

I had no hat suitable for such an outing; well — if the conventions were unobserved here, as I had been told, it would not matter if I went hatless, I decided. A maid brought the scarlet silk parasol to me, with great ceremony, telling me that Miss Bella had sent it. It was very pretty and the bells sang softly as I moved it.

I decided to wear my gold locket; my mother had possessed little jewellery, never caring for adornments, with the exception of this gold locket set with seed pearls and hanging from a fine gold chain. Inside was the only photograph I possessed of my mother, not a very good one, for it did not do justice to her delicate colouring; but I liked the tale of the locket: when Grandfather Lindsay was courting my grandmother, who lived in Bristol, he often sent presents by boat to the Welsh Back at Bristol, instructing my grandmother to call on the Captain and collect these love tokens. The locket had been an engagement present.

I showed it to Rose, just before we left the house, and told her the tale.

'What a lovely story!' she said.

I opened the locket and showed her the photograph; she studied it intently for several seconds.

'So that is your mother, Flora?' she remarked, at last.

'Yes.'

'Did you love her very much?'

'Of course.' The question surprised me. Rose straightened, smiled, and said it was time we were leaving.

We split into two groups; Damien escorted Rose in the first carriage, with Ruan, Bella, Edwin and myself in the second one. Ruan remarked, laughingly, that as Dowte, his mother's coachman, was very deaf, his mama and Damien could talk as freely as they pleased.

The carriages took the path along which we had come that morning, until we reached the place where it joined the main path; then the horses plodded back towards the small landing stage, and, when we were halfway there, the carriages stopped.

The little bells on my parasol clashed softly together, as the four of us stepped down. Rose and Damien made no move; Damien waved his hand languidly, and said:

'We shall sit here in this patch of shade, whilst you explore the Folly. I am in no mood for climbing steps on such a day, and neither is Rose.'

The Folly stood in a small clearing at the end of a footpath that wound under an arch of tree branches. The "ruined" tower was of a type that had been popular in the previous century, when gardens were often most romantic affairs. There was an arched door, and two empty windows, like eye-sockets.

Ruan told me: 'The island was once jointly owned by two brothers, Charles and Barkeley Selwyn, who fell out with one another. Charles built The House of the Four Winds, on *his* part of the island, and Brother Barkeley was furious; he said it was far superior to Seawinds — which is now Damien's house — and, of course, that *is* true. So the disgruntled Barkeley built himself a tower high enough to overlook the grounds of Charles' house that he coveted so much!'

It was not a new story. I had heard versions of it before; I watched Bella Careena, running ahead, not seeming to feel the intense heat, and Edwin following her at a more leisurely pace.

'So now Mr Ashley owns Seawinds?' I said.

Ruan nodded. 'Damien's father, Sylvester Ashley, was first cousin to Jerome's father, Caspar Jardine. Sylvester was the sole owner of Bella Careena, but he couldn't be bothered with the place, and considered it a liability. My grandfather Jardine made a lot of money out of the Napoleonic Wars, you know; for men in the field of battle need provisioning and clothing and they must be well supplied with weapons. My grandfather was a shrewd man, and probably undercut his competitors for tenders to supply all the needs of the troops; he ended up with a comfortable fortune, and he wanted the island; Sylvester was only too glad to sell it to him; he preferred to spend his time in London amongst the ladies and the gambling salons and he had lost a great deal of money. I believe he drove a hard bargain with Caspar Jardine, and asked far more than Bella Careena was worth, for all the buildings had fallen into disrepair and no one was living there. It must have been a desolate place, but grandfather saw it, in his mind, as it is today: it was to be his kingdom. It seems as though there was some kind of curse on the place, though.'

A curse; it sounded interesting. I looked at him expectantly, as I furled my tinkling parasol, and bent my head to enter the low arch that led to a flight of stone steps.

The steps were only wide enough to take one person at a time, and I went ahead of Ruan. Bella's laughter floated back to me, sweet and clear, followed by the resonant sound of Edwin's voice.

'Tell me about the curse,' I said to Ruan.

'It was said that strange fertility rites were performed in a grove of trees, and black masses were held by a renegade monk who lived in the ruined chapel; they say his ghost still haunts the place.'

I paused, to look out of a narrow window; the blood was pounding in my ears, and I felt giddy; though we had not accomplished half the climb, we were both out of breath, and Ruan was glad enough to rest whilst he finished the tale.

'Grandfather Jardine brought a young bride here; they had one son, my father, who was born on the island. There was a big christening party, and a boatload of people came over from the mainland, but a storm blew up, the boat capsized, and several of them were drowned; and Grandmother Jardine died, suddenly, that same day, of a seizure. We were intruders, you see; the curse was working! Grandfather left the island in the hands of an agent and went back to live in Dorset; he was absolutely desolate at the death of my grandmother, for theirs was truly a Romeo-and-Juliet romance, I am told. Grandfather lived another thirty years, and though my father often visited the island, he never settled here; not until he married my mother. That was twenty-three years ago. He was thirty-eight then.'

I made some rapid calculations and said in astonishment:

'Then your father is now sixty-one years old!'

'Yes,' he agreed. 'Twenty years older than my mother.'

In silence, we finished the climb up the corkscrewing stairs; when I reached the top, my heart was hammering, and my legs felt like jelly.

The space on which we stood was only just wide enough to hold the four of us, and the stone parapet was barely waist high. I looked down on a green sea of treetops; I could see the girdle of bright blue water around the island, the houses by the jetty, the farmhouse on the other side of the jetty, where toy-like cows moved slowly in the heavy heat.

'Isn't it beautiful up here?' Bella Careena said happily.

'Yes,' I replied, with an effort.

Edwin looked sharply at me.

'Don't you like heights, Flora?' he asked.

'Not very much,' I admitted; it was an understatement. The ground seemed to draw me, as though urging me to lean over, too far, so that I would fall . . .

I battled with nausea; Edwin's voice was even sharper.

'You should not have come,' he said. 'Why didn't you say you didn't like heights?'

'To give in to one's fears is cowardice,' I told him.

Bella looked at us with interest. 'Poor Flora!' she said softly. 'It is easy to be frightened here. There are curses on this island . . . This is a witch-tower. Years ago, it was the home of a witch who was turned adrift in a boat . . . '

'It was not! Barkeley Selwyn built it,' Ruan retorted.

'Don't be frightened, Flora,' Bella Careena said softly. 'You won't fall. Look at the view; isn't it beautiful?'

'Yes,' I said briefly.

'You haven't looked properly.' She tugged at my sleeve insistently. 'Look, there's a peacock — see that flash of blue? The peacock frightened you this morning, when it screeched, didn't it? Peacocks sound almost human when they cry out.'

'For Heaven's *sake*!' Edwin rounded angrily on her, and Ruan jerked his sister's hand from my arm. The double rebuke made her eyes fill with tears, and she turned away tossing her head.

'Let's go below,' Edwin said; I heard the exasperation in his voice. I put my hand to my throat; I felt as though I was going to choke.

I was glad to reach the bottom of the tower; Edwin went in front of me, Ruan behind me, while Bella brought up the rear.

As we walked back to the carriage, Ruan and Edwin lagged behind, talking so quietly together that I could not hear their conversation. Bella walked beside me. I opened the parasol, shielding my face, listening to the tinkle of the bells, a sound that suddenly seemed eerie.

'I can tell you all about the island,' Bella assured me, watching me closely. 'Ruan doesn't really know much, neither does Uncle Edwin. *I* have seen a book that tells everything.'

'Where?' I asked; and her face became secretive.

'I won't tell you. It's in a secret place. It's all true, though. About the smugglers, and the people who hid here so they wouldn't be captured and killed, and the wicked monk. It's quite creepy, you know, on stormy nights; when the wind is in the trees, it sounds like the voices of all the people who ever lived here, calling to each other.'

'Are you trying to frighten me?' I demanded.

Her eyes were guileless.

'Of *course* not, Flora! Why would I do such a thing?'

'So that I shall go away from the island, perhaps.'

'If you did so, mama would be most upset. She would be angry with me for frightening you. She says you belong here; I heard her tell papa so; but you *don't* belong, Flora, you DON'T! You weren't born here, as I was. You aren't part of the island, as *I* am. Even Ruan isn't part of it, though *he* was born here. Only ME . . . !'

I did not know what to make of her extraordinary

remarks. I was still trying to puzzle them out when we reached the carriage where Rose sat, very upright, but looking pale and fatigued. She smiled, and the smile seemed to be an effort.

'Did you enjoy the view from the top of the tower?' she asked me.

'Flora suffers from vertigo,' Edwin answered crisply.

'Do you feel quite well, dear?' Rose asked. 'Or do you wish to return to the house?'

'I'm well enough now that I'm on the ground again,' I said, trying to make light of it.

I was acutely aware of Damien's eyes upon me; tawny eyes, full of warmth; the sun, slanting through the trees, gave burnished richness to the tight curls that clustered over his head. I had never seen such a handsome man, nor one so full of vitality. There was an extraordinary magnetism about him, as though he silently drew me towards him.

My heart lurched wildly. Vainly, I tried to steady its wild beating; how fatally easy it would be to fall completely under the spell of Damien Ashley. What would it be like to be loved by him . . . ?

I knew nothing of the love between a man and a woman. My mother had warned me never to be led away by passion, insisting that devotion between two people was the only true and lasting love. Passion brought children into the world, but it was something that only a man should feel, not a woman. Passion, in a woman, was immodest, she declared.

I thought of passion as a fever; a wild tumult, a madness of the heart, a craving for the touch, the look, the nearness, of just one person.

I pulled my thoughts back to the ground. Damien had a wife, a woman called Irene.

I gathered my trailing skirts in my hand as the coachman helped me to my seat.

We set off at a sedate pace, and when we reached the landing stage, Ruan pointed out the farm to me.

'It covers a big area, as you see,' he said. 'It supplies us with all our vegetables, eggs, milk, butter and cheese. It's managed by the Cleggs, and their two grown-up sons.'

On the right of the landing stage was another path that I had not noticed earlier that day. The carriages turned along this path, and soon we were passing the backs of a row of cottages that faced towards the mainland. Each cottage was trim and well-kept, with its own vegetable plot. Ruan explained that the cottages were occupied by retired servants, and by families of servants who still worked at the House of the Four Winds as well as at Seawinds; he was obviously proud of the fact that his father cared for his tenants and made their well-being the most important part of his administration.

'There's another cottage,' Bella Careena said importantly. 'It's on the edge of a wood, hidden by trees. Laurie Perkins lives there. He's odd, because he likes to be alone and doesn't care for people. He has a little forge where he shoes the horses. He keeps the rifles clean, too, and sharpens the arrows.'

I stared at her in sudden consternation; Ruan shook his head at me, and smiled reassuringly.

'No one does any hunting here, Flora. It's forbidden, anyway. The arrows are for sport — archery is a great favourite with mama and papa, though papa indulges less often these days. The rifles are also for use on targets and clay pigeons only!'

We left the cottages behind and the scenery became wilder and more beautiful; we passed an ornamental pool and a tiny Grecian temple standing on a rise above massed purple rhododendron bushes and wild fuschia. Looking closely about me, I realised that what appeared to be a delightful artlessness was, in reality, the result of careful planning. We rode through a grove of birches, and beyond it was a tiny rock-girdled pool with a stone figure of a girl standing in a niche above it; tasselled fuschia tumbled in a cascade around her.

I exclaimed over it with such pleasure that Ruan

ordered the coachman to stop, so that I might step down and admire it more closely.

'Edwin's father designed it so,' he explained. 'An island made into a garden.'

'Not a formal garden,' Edwin told me, 'but with some parts of it left wild and unspoiled. The most interesting gardens, like the most interesting people, are constructed on that principle, wouldn't you agree, Flora?'

Bella frowned and said crossly:

'Why do you talk in riddles, Uncle Edwin?'

'My dear child, I do not talk in riddles. When you are old enough, you will discover the sense of what I say.'

'Tell Flora about the grottoes your father designed,' Bella commanded Edwin.

'She is about to see them for herself,' Edwin reminded her.

'We'll go to the Shell Grotto, up above Neptune's bay, first of all,' Bella said, with a touch of imperiousness.

'Mama does not care for that place,' Ruan pointed out.

'But we *must* go there! It's my favourite! Mama can sit in the carriage and talk to Damien.'

'Is there something sinister about this particular grotto?' I asked.

Bella shrugged; she was obviously dying to tell me the tale.

'There was an accident there, years ago, before Ruan and I were born. Mama came here for the day with her governess, Lavinia Jessel, and a little girl called Edith Freemantle, who lived with mama's parents. Edith was playing on the cliffs above the grotto — it's the only place where the cliffs are really high — when she fell over and was killed. Mama found her; she had been sitting, sketching, in the ruined chapel nearby.'

Ruan shook his head at his sister.

'Mama hates to be reminded of that time; no wonder. It must have been a great shock for her,' he pointed out.

'Where was the governess when Edith was killed?' I asked.

'She was ill, or strange in the head, or something,' Bella replied. 'Miss Jessel — Vinnie, as they called her — wasn't looking after Edith as she should have been, and it was all hushed up afterwards. She was sent away in disgrace.'

'That hardly seems fair if she wasn't responsible for her actions,' I pointed out.

Bella had already lost interest in the fate of the governess.

'There's the Grotto of the Peacocks to see,' she told me, 'that's between the church and the house; then there's the Grotto of the Four Winds, which is near the house; and, right at the other end, beyond Clegg's Farm, is mama and papa's very private Sun Grotto.'

'Aren't you forgetting the fifth grotto?' Ruan teased.

'No,' said Bella shortly, as though she did not want to discuss the subject.

'Where is the fifth grotto?' I asked.

'No one knows. It has never been found,' Edwin replied calmly. 'I have spent a great deal of time searching for it. I shall search for it until I find it.'

I wanted to ask why, but Bella Careena was looking at Edwin with a curious expression on her face, and I decided to save my questions until later.

I knew that I was falling under the spell of the island; yet I had a strong feeling that there was a sinister quality that ran like a dark river beneath all its beauty and strangeness. Perhaps it was because of its history, I thought: there had been plenty of tragedy and violence here.

The ground rose gently upwards as we approached the western end of the island; we rode through leafy tunnels and under beech trees, down aisles of dark, pointed firs, through groves of slender birches, past sturdy oaks. We passed a tiny waterfall, a natural spring tumbling between rocks; and then we reached a clearing beyond which was a grassy plateau. On the plateau stood a white house facing the mainland.

'That's Seawinds,' Bella told me.

It was not so large nor so grand as the House of the Four Winds, but it looked very gracious, with a terrace all around it, and stone urns at each corner, filled with scarlet geraniums.

I looked at it, and thought of Damien living there with Irene; my heart felt like lead.

The island was criss-crossed with small paths, apart from the main paths which were like roads, well-made, able to take the coaches without difficulty.

'I know every path on the island,' Bella told me proudly.

Everywhere, we came upon peacocks, flashes of blue-green amongst the trees; arrogant birds, with an unearthly sound to their screeching, their bright little eyes proclaiming us intruders in their domain. Away to the left, half-hidden by trees, I saw the ruined chapel.

'That's where the monk lived,' Bella said, her eyes never leaving my face. 'He was terribly wicked; not like a *proper* monk. He offered up human sacrifices; at night, he still walks about the island . . .'

'Don't talk such utter rubbish!' Ruan said curtly. 'What are you trying to do — frighten Flora? Drive her away?'

She didn't answer him; she sat with downcast eyes until we had travelled a short way along a path that seemed to end in cliffs. We came to a group of trees, and there, in the shade, was the coach containing Rose and Damien. Our coach pulled in behind the first one, and we all got out.

'We're going to look at the Shell Grotto,' Bella told her mother.

'I shall not come with you,' Rose said quietly. 'Do be careful, all of you.'

'The path isn't dangerous, mama,' Ruan told her gently. 'It's steep, in places, and we have to watch our step, that's all. Edwin and I will take care of the girls.'

'I am going to return to the house,' she told us. 'The heat has given me a headache.' She gave Damien a small, strained smile. 'There's really no need for you to accompany me, Damien; Dowte can take me back.'

Dowte turned the horses and set off for the House of the

Four Winds. The rest of us went to the cliff top, and I saw the path — steep, stony, but — as Ruan had said — not dangerous if one was reasonably sure-footed. It was a fair drop to the beach, and a spine of rocks poked through the sand of the secluded little bay.

Ruan and Edwin went first, then Bella and I followed, with Damien bringing up the rear. Some way down the path, I saw a cave, with a broad, rocky ledge in front of it. It was easy enough to step from the path to the ledge; the path went on, past the opening, right down to the beach.

'This way,' Ruan said, holding out his hand.

I stepped into the cave, my heart beating fast.

'Well?' said Damien softly.

I instantly hated the place; unreasonably, for it had been marvellously adapted to make a natural grotto; a pattern of shells, stones and sea-smoothed glass had been inset into the walls to make a mosaic. Stones and shells had been carefully and painstakingly matched; the result was a picture of a sea-serpent, with a mermaid riding on his back; the eyes of the serpent and of the mermaid had been made of pieces of glass that glittered in the sun.

'It looks beautiful by moonlight,' Bella Careena whispered. 'Then the eyes glitter, the moon sparkles on the sea and the ghost of poor little Edith walks along the beach.'

'You're frightening Flora again,' Ruan said angrily. 'You're obsessed with ghosts and legends and all the silly gossip about this island.'

She looked angrily at him.

'Gossip? You forget that this is where Edith died!' she cried.

'It was a long time ago,' Damien said placatingly. 'Stop bickering, both of you.'

'Why did your father build a grotto here, after such an accident?' I asked Edwin curiously.

'He didn't create *this* grotto. The mosaic work was done by the Selwyns,' Edwin told me.

'Was Rose very attached to the child who was killed?' I asked.

'No,' Damien told me. 'She was rather an unpleasant little girl, by all accounts. The whole thing was hushed up by Rose's father; I heard that he put Miss Jessel into a private nursing home.'

'Of course he did,' Edwin replied smoothly. 'He inherited a vast sum of money that would have gone to Edith had she lived. He didn't want any scandal attached to her death. Poor Vinnie!'

'Let's go,' I said, shivering. 'It's damp and chilly in here.'

I was glad to be out in the comforting warmth of the sun again. As I stepped into the carriage, Bella Careena looked at my neck, and said:

'What has happened to the locket you were wearing when we left the house, Flora?'

Hastily, I put my hand to my throat. The locket had gone. Horrified, I groped for the chain.

'I've lost it!' I whispered, stricken.

Chapter 4

'IT MUST BE FOUND at once,' Ruan said. 'You *could* have dropped it in the grotto; I'll go and look.'

'Perhaps it fell on the beach,' Bella said.

'I'll look on the beach,' Edwin said.

'*I* will return to the tower,' Damien said to me, with a reassuring smile. 'Don't worry, Flora. I am sure we shall find your locket.'

I turned my back on the coachman, and fumbled inside my dress; I shook out my skirts and even investigated the inside of the parasol. In vain.

'Are you *very* worried?' Bella asked, watching me as I searched.

'Naturally,' I said shortly. 'Would you not be concerned if you had lost something of great sentimental value?'

'Strange things happen here,' she murmured.

'Such as?'

'Well, like people losing things; odd accidents. Not recently, but long ago. Now they are happening again. Perhaps you are not meant to be here at all.'

'Why do you dislike me so much?' I challenged her.

'I don't!' she muttered, red-faced.

'Yes you do, Bella Careena. I came here at your mother's invitation, to help her with preparations for Ruan's coming-of-age, and to be a companion to you.'

'I don't *need* a companion!'

'Your mother evidently thought otherwise.'

'I like to be by myself!' she cried angrily.

'I understand that; so do I — often; but you must see that it is not good for *anyone* to be alone all the time.'

'I have mama for company — Edwin, Ruan, Damien; papa, when he is well enough. Nanny Radford. *Lots* of people.'

'I ought to tell your mama that you do not want me to be your companion. You should have told her so yourself when she first suggested it.'

'I *did* tell her! She wouldn't listen to me. When she had your letter, she was *so* excited!'

'Because she enjoys having visitors, I daresay.'

'If you're just a visitor, why did she say you belonged here?' Bella Careena demanded.

'I don't know, Bella Careena. I looked forward to coming here. I have wanted to see this island ever since I saw some sketches of it in my father's book. I have no intention of staying here for good.' We walked to the shade of a tree, and sat there. She leaned back on her elbow, plucking at blades of grass.

'I don't want to go away from this island,' she muttered. 'If I had my way, I would stay forever.'

'I don't think that would be a good idea, Bella; you

should see what the world outside is like.'

She turned her back towards me, and stared up at the sky. It seemed a very long time before I saw Ruan and Edwin walking back towards us.

They shook their heads sympathetically.

'There is no trace of the locket in the grotto,' Ruan told me. 'Edwin searched the beach thoroughly, and found nothing. Perhaps Damien will have better luck.'

'It could have got wedged in a rock or something,' Bella pointed out.

'I shall come back to search again, if Damien is unsuccessful,' Ruan assured me.

It was some time before Damien returned, looking downcast.

'I am sorry, Flora,' he said ruefully. 'I have searched the tower, the steps, the ground at the bottom; and there is no trace of your locket.'

'Don't worry, Flora,' Ruan said reassuringly. 'Mama will instruct the grooms and the servants to search for it; the locket cannot be lost, merely mislaid.'

Bella looked at me gloomily, and said:

'I suppose you don't want to see the Peacock Grotto, now?'

'Of course I do,' I replied, hiding my anxiety behind a smile.

We got into the carriage; the path wound inland, through a miniature forest of tall firs, crowding so close that they shut out the light, giving us a few moments of blessed coolness before we entered a clearing surrounded by sweet-scented, flowering shrubs.

The Grotto of the Peacocks was in the centre of the clearing; a stone temple, with paintings of peacocks on the walls, and a map of the island made in mosaic work on the floor. A stone bench ran around the inside of the walls.

'This was a birthday present from mama to papa,' Bella told me. 'Edwin's father engaged an artist to paint the walls.'

'An artist of great skill,' Edwin conceded, with satisfaction. Everywhere, on the island, was evidence of his father's work; it was surely Edwin who had a right to feel he belonged here, I reflected.

It was only a short walk from the Peacock Grotto to the square-towered church.

The church was old and tranquil, as churches should be; around it the grass was kept neatly trimmed, and on the leaning tombstones I could trace the names of previous owners of the island, as well as servants and estate workers, all their graves neatly kept, and some with wild flowers growing on them.

There was a large tomb in one corner of the little churchyard; it had cherubs' faces carved on one side, and an angel stood on the top, with bowed head. The stone had been mellowed and worn by time, but the inscription on one side was clear enough.

Bella Careena read the words aloud:

> *Now will I make fast my heart unto yours this day; so that my heart shall be as a ship that is anchored in a quiet harbour, nor shall it venture upon the high seas again; but be forever made fast by this, our troth.*

As Bella Careena finished speaking, the silence was complete; the sun burned in the hot blue sky, the five of us seemed locked fast in a spell, charmed to sleep like the courtiers in the old fairy tale.

Ruan broke the spell; he said:

'This is Ann Churnock's tomb; she lived here alone, in the seventeenth century. Some say her true love deserted her, and never kept his promise to marry her; other records state that he was a Royalist killed in the first battle of the Civil War, in August 1642. Whatever the truth of it, after his death, she cut herself off from the world and lived here with only one servant. She made it her business to protect the wild life of the island, and she made lists of all the plants and flowers, and herbs and trees.'

We went into the little church, to which the preacher came every Sunday, when the weather permitted, to take a service. It was cool and dim inside, with heavily-carved pews, two stained glass windows depicting the Creation and the Resurrection, in rich, jewel-like colours; and a splendid marble effigy of a knight in armour lying beside his lady.

'We don't need the carriage now,' Bella Careena said. 'We can walk to my house from here, easily.'

So the carriage was dismissed and we all walked to the cottage in the grounds of the House of the Four Winds.

It was very much a Hansel-and-Gretel sort of cottage, with ornate woodwork and a small balcony; it was secluded, being half hidden by a thick clump of tall firs.

Nanny Radford appeared as we reached the carved door of the little cottage.

She was a small, upright woman, with a faded look about her, as though she had been pressed between the leaves of a book for years, and forgotten. Hair and skin seemed to be the same shade of grey, but her eyes were bright; when Bella Careena introduced us, Nanny Radford put out a hand, and the fingers lay, dry and cool, in mine for a moment.

'We're tired and thirsty, Nanny,' Bella Careena said. 'Please ask Anne to bring us a tray of tea.'

Nanny was not so deaf as poor Dowte; she nodded and went into the house, calling for the servant.

'Come and see *my* house, Flora,' Bella commanded. 'Mama says you are going to come here and live with me.'

'To stay with you,' I corrected firmly. 'I am not going to spend the rest of my life here.'

The furnishings of the house had the same light delicacy as those at Four Winds. There was an airy freshness about it that I found delightful. Bella showed me the room that was to be mine. It had a balcony, and when I stepped on to it, the trees made everything outside so dim and cool that I could have been standing under the sea.

'We'll look at the Grotto of the Four Winds tomorrow,' she said suddenly. 'It's hot and we've wasted a lot of time looking for your locket.'

She looked at me to see if I was going to rebuke her for her rudeness; when I did not reply, she said, more amiably:

'I shall ask mama if I may show you the Sun Grotto. A stream runs into the Grotto, which is really a cave, and there is a pool there in which mama and papa used to bathe. The water is icy cold, though, and papa must not bathe there with her, any more. It is bad for him.'

We went downstairs to have our tea on the lawn outside the cottage. I did not see Nanny Radford again until we were leaving; she nodded approvingly at me, as I lingered behind the others, to hear her words.

'Good thing you're here, Miss Lindsay. That child needs young company. I can see to her creature comforts, same as always, but her mind is beyond me. She's a strange soul; no real malice in her, mind. Never given me a ha'porth of trouble. Too imaginative, though; you'll bring her to earth.'

'I'm only staying for the summer,' I told her.

'Eh?' She chuckled drily. 'We'll see. If Mrs Jardine wants you to stay for ever, you will.'

Damien and I walked back to the house together; Ruan had an errand to attend to at one of the cottages, and Edwin and Bella walked well ahead of us. I watched her, this tall, good-looking girl, and the tall good-looking man beside her, his springy dark hair flecked with grey.

'A handsome couple!' Damien murmured wickedly in my ear.

'She is still a child,' I protested, shocked. 'Edwin is old enough to be her father!'

'Such alliances have been known to work well; in a few years, Bella Careena will be a woman,' Damien reminded me.

'I suppose so; after all, Rose is twenty years younger than Jerome,' I said.

'She should not have married him!' Damien said. 'She was not meant to be shut away here with an old man. She is lively, beautiful, gracious; she has wit and style.

She would be an asset to any London drawing-room.'

'But Rose insists that she is very happy here. I imagine that this is a kind of Paradise for both of them.'

'Nonsense; Jerome keeps her prisoner,' Damien replied coolly.

'Would you like to live here always?' I asked.

'I should like this to be my Kingdom — yes,' he admitted.

'This island would have been yours if your father had not sold it to Jerome's father,' I said impulsively.

'Yes, I am sorry that my father sold the island — but of what use are regrets? Jerome has been kind enough to give me Seawinds as my own domain here.'

'You like staying here?'

'Very much.'

'And — your wife? Does she share your pleasure in the island?'

'No. Irene prefers London. She is a restless creature and likes a social life.'

'Have you no family?' I asked.

'No. Irene lost a child, a daughter. She was ill for some time afterwards. She did not wish to have other children.'

His face looked as though it had been cut from steel.

'Flora,' he said, abruptly. 'Sooner or later you will discover the truth. I prefer to tell you myself: my marriage to Irene is not a happy one.'

'I am sorry,' I whispered inadequately.

'Few marriages are what they seem to be on the surface,' he replied drily.

I looked at him fleetingly as we walked close together, shoulders almost touching. The tawny eyes were bright and hard; his mouth had harshness in every line at that moment; yet I had never found his magnetism so compelling as I did then.

'You must have loved your wife when you married her,' I said, with a sigh.

His smile was bitter.

'According to Irene, I married her for her money. She

told me so, on our honeymoon. It is true that I had little money of my own, and she was very rich; an unfortunate situation, but not an impossible one, I thought. Also on our honeymoon, she informed me that she had married me because, at twenty-six, she was already an old maid, and did not wish to die without a wedding-ring on her finger.'

'How could she say such things?' I protested, horrified. 'No marriage could flourish in such a cruel climate!'

'I should not have mentioned such things to you, but your sympathy loosed my tongue,' he told me drily.

We walked the rest of the way in silence. We reached the house and began to walk up the shallow flight of steps to the terrace; I heard Damien draw a sharp breath, and followed the direction of his glance.

A woman, who had been sitting on the terrace, stood up suddenly, shading her face with a parasol.

'*Irene!*' he murmured, astonished.

She stayed where she was, as still as a statue; I had time to note every detail as we slowly came closer to her.

Irene Ashley was small and slender; she was expensively dressed in cream silk which did nothing for her pale skin, light-coloured eyes and fawn-coloured hair. She was a colourless creature, as colourless as clear water; the more so in contrast to Damien with his powerful build, his air of vitality, his bright gold hair and unusual eyes.

'Irene!' He made no move to embrace her. 'I understood that you intended to remain in London for several days to clear up matters that needed your attention!'

'I *have* attended to them, more quickly than I expected to, my dear Damien.' Her voice was as quiet as her personality. 'There were — certain documents needing my signature.' The smile was edged with faint malice, as though she was enjoying herself. 'I have been at pains to safeguard the little money I have left,' she added.

'*Irene!*' he said curtly. 'You show a deplorable lack of good manners in embarrassing Miss Lindsay thus!'

She turned, giving me a long, assessing glance.

'Ah; so *this* is Miss Lindsay, the new governess.'

'I am not a governess,' I replied calmly. 'I am here to assist Mrs Jardine in preparing for her son's coming-of-age, and to be a companion to Bella Careena.'

Her delicate eyebrows rose.

'A very odd child. I am sure you will find her a handful. So you are not a governess, but an employee of the Jardines, nonetheless.'

'If you wish to put it that way,' I said, disliking her more with every minute that passed.

Colour stung her face, making her look less like a wax doll. I felt the air crackle with the anger that raced between us.

'Miss Flora Lindsay's father was a friend of the Jardines,' Damien told his wife, his voice smooth and cold as marble.

'Really?' She turned an indifferent shoulder towards him and smiled sweetly at me. 'I have to tell you, Miss Lindsay, that Mr Jardine wishes to see you in his study. I am sure you should not keep him waiting.'

As I walked across the terrace, I heard her say, in a high, clear voice:

'I understand that Seawinds is not ready for us, and that we shall be staying here for a day or two . . . how pleasant!'

I was shaking with anger, as I stepped into the big, book-lined study that was so like my father's; I composed myself with a great effort.

Jerome greeted me warmly; I thought what a fine-looking man he was, with his thick waves of silvery hair, and the piercing dark eyes set in the craggy face.

'Flora, my dear! I hear you have had the misfortune to lose your locket,' he said, full of concern.

'The news has indeed travelled quickly,' I replied, surprised.

'Edwin told me moments ago; and so I asked Irene if she would send you to me as soon as you reached the house.'

I filled in the few details I had concerning the loss of my locket; he listened intently.

'I will have those places searched thoroughly. I am sure it will be found. Edwin said it was of considerable importance to you, because it contained your mother's photograph,' he said.

'The only one that I possess.'

'It *shall* be found,' he insisted. 'Well, my dear — how do you like our beloved island?'

'Very much. It is beautiful; its legends are fascinating.'

'Do you think you would be happy living here permanently?' he asked.

His scrutiny was so intense that I moved uneasily.

'It is, perhaps, too soon to say,' I replied cautiously.

'Ah; you are wise to reserve judgment at this stage! Remember, though, that your happiness is important to Rose; and, therefore, to me.'

'Why?' I asked bluntly.

'Because I liked and respected your father, and now you are alone in the world,' he replied.

'I know that you and Rose have been very happy here,' I said.

'Yes.' He nodded. 'We were married in the little church here, when she was eighteen and I was thirty-eight; many predicted that the age gap between us was too great, but we have confounded the doubters! Our summer idyll has lasted for twenty-three years. When Ruan marries and brings his wife here, I hope that they — and their children — will be blessed with such happiness as Rose and I have known.'

I thought that he looked tired and grey as he leaned back in his chair.

'Is there a doctor living on the island?' I asked him.

'No. If anyone is ill, we send the boat to fetch Dr Samuels from Tolfrey. Rarely is the weather so rough, or the fog so thick, that the boat cannot make the journey; in any event, Mrs Clegg is highly skilled in medical matters and I swear she is as good as any doctor. Now, Flora, there remains the question of your salary . . . '

When I tried to stammer a protest, he waved my words away with a smile.

Upstairs in my room, I wrote a letter to Alexander Arkwright, having been told by the maid who looked after me that the mail was taken across to the mainland every afternoon at four o'clock.

I gave Alexander only the briefest details, telling him I had been most kindly received and was being well looked after; then I took my father's sketchbook from the small writing case of his that I had begun to use since his death, and thumbed through it.

The drawings took on a new life; I recognised one of the trees near the church, bent into a curious shape, like a figure crouching to spring. There was a peacock, the facade of the ruined chapel which I had yet to see, the folly with its ivy-covered walls, and Seawinds.

I left the sketchbook on the dressing table whilst I made preparations for dinner. I wished I had a trunkful of pretty clothes. Instead, I had to make do with a lavender muslin gown trimmed with violet ribbons; I felt as dowdy as any governess or paid companion.

When I went downstairs, Edwin was at the bottom of the staircase, watching my descent.

'I think I shall call you Philomena,' he said lightly. 'It suits you.'

'Do let me put you out of your misery . . . ' I began.

'No,' he retorted. 'I have no wish to be put out of my misery. I wallow in it. I am like these young ladies who happily enjoy the pangs of unrequited love!'

Rose did not put in an appearance at dinner. Jerome seemed perturbed and said if her headache persisted, he would summon Dr Samuels in the morning.

Irene acted as hostess, very graciously, sitting small and upright in her carved chair, and treating me with great condescension.

Edwin and Irene seemed to get on very well, I noticed. She responded with a show of animation to his enquiries as to her health and the state of London, yet she was aloof and cool when she spoke to her husband.

Jerome mentioned the fifth grotto, asking me if I knew the story of it; when I shook my head, he said:

'Edwin's father decided to build it as a special tribute to Rose. He would not tell me any of the details. She was quite excited; she loved surprises. Sir Marcus had the island to himself for several weeks, whilst Rose and I were in London; he wrote and told us, just before we returned, that it was finished; but when we landed, we discovered, to our distress, that Sir Marcus had been taken ill. He never recovered consciousness.'

I looked at Edwin; his face was impassive. His eyes met mine, and he said:

'As a result of my father's sudden death, the location of the grotto remains a secret. He wrote me, once, concerning it, just before he was taken ill, saying that he considered it his finest piece of work. That is why I am so anxious to discover its whereabouts.'

'Couldn't the workmen have told you?' I asked.

'The men — there were three of them — had finished their work and gone, by the time we returned,' Jerome pointed out. 'They were not local men; I had no way of tracing them. There was also an artist specially commissioned by Sir Marcus, but I did not know his name.'

Bella Careena stared down at her plate, frowning. The thought occurred to me that perhaps she alone, amongst all of them, knew where the grotto was to be found, and did not intend to reveal her knowledge.

I was tired out by the events of the day and glad enough to go to bed. I fell asleep almost at once, but awoke, some time later, to find the room full of light.

Rose was standing by the dressing table, holding my father's sketchbook in her hand, turning over the leaves very slowly; she wore a loose wrapper, her beautiful hair lay like cloth of gold about her shoulders, and her face was like ivory. On the dressing table beside her was the oil lamp she had carried into the room.

As I sat up in bed, she turned and smiled faintly.

'Are you feeling better?' I asked.

'A little.' I sensed the effort behind the smile. 'I am sorry, Flora, dearest, I did not mean to disturb you — I came to satisfy myself that you had been made comfortable, and I saw the book. I could not resist looking at the sketches. How well I remember your father's love of making drawings, and his skill with a pencil . . . '

'Your eyes are full of tears,' I said slowly.

She made no reply; instead, she picked up a small box lying beside the lamp, and handed it to me.

'I have brought you a gift, Flora; I intended to leave it by your bedside for you to find when you awoke.'

She handed me the box; it was made of leather; when I opened it, I saw a locket lying on the velvet pad. It was a much more elaborate one than the locket I had lost — it hung from a thick chain, and was heavily chased.

'For you,' she said softly. 'I know that it cannot replace the one you have lost, but I should like you to have it. It belonged to Caspar Jardine's mother.'

'It is beautiful!' I stammered. 'But — I — cannot . . . it is too valuable . . . '

'Nonsense. I *want* you to have it, my dear,' she said emphatically.

'I am sure that my own locket will be found.'

'Then you will have two lockets!' She smoothed back the hair from my forehead, as though I was no older than her daughter.

'Wear it, Flora. Enjoy it, as young people should enjoy pretty things,' she said, adding: 'Your father's sketches are very good . . . '

'When I first saw them, I knew I had to come to the island,' I told her. 'It was a strange compulsion that I cannot explain.'

'Have you been disappointed in our island, Flora?'

'No. I love it.'

'As I do. Everything here is perfect; unchanging!' she whispered, with a vehemence that surprised me. 'You may say that nothing changes, but here time walks more slowly than anywhere else in the world. I felt so safe here!'

'You speak in the past tense,' I said. 'Do you no longer feel safe?'

She hesitated; I thought how pale she looked, how sad she seemed. With an effort, she said:

'So long as I have Jerome, and we have the island and our children, *nothing* can hurt us! I know that! Ruan is young and restless; he will not be content to stay here always, and I don't want Jerome to be burdened with that knowledge until it is absolutely necessary — he has such plans for Ruan, such ideals for the future of the people who live here. Bella, now, is different; she has no wish to leave. I hope you two will be great friends.'

She bent and kissed me.

'Goodnight, Flora, dear,' she whispered.

I did not wear the locket next morning; it was rather too elaborate a piece of jewellery to accompany the simple gown I wore.

I breakfasted alone in the small morning-room; Bella Careena stepped into the room as I was finishing my meal. She wore a simple white dress, on the bodice of which had been sewn several bows of scarlet ribbon; the hem was hung with silver bells that clashed softly as she moved.

'You look very attractive,' I told her.

'I have seen a picture of Ann Churnock,' she told me unexpectedly. 'She wore a dress like this, with bells on it, so that the birds and animals could hear her coming to feed them.'

'Oh? Where is this picture?'

A secretive smile edged her lips.

'I can't tell you that,' she said. 'Come along, Flora. It's

a lovely day, much too nice to stay indoors.'

A familiar figure appeared in the doorway; it was Damien, the sun making a golden halo of his thick curls. My heart leapt at the sight of him.

He wished us good-day, and said to Bella Careena:

'You cannot appropriate Flora for a whole day. I am going to take her rowing on the lake this afternoon.'

'By yourself?' Bella asked disapprovingly.

He looked amused.

'Irene doesn't like the water — you know that. She wants to try her skill at the archery butts, and — on this island, at least — no one is required to provide a chaperone.'

Excitement ran like quicksilver in my veins at the prospect of an afternoon spent exclusively in Damien's company. Bella Careena looked taken aback; Damien smiled at her, and said:

'Your papa proposes to give you a French lesson this afternoon, I understand. You must be educated as befits a young lady about to take her place in society.'

'I am not going to take my place in society!' she replied stormily.

'Be that as it may, your papa expects you to present yourself at his study after lunch,' Damien retorted, unperturbed.

She ignored him.

'Let's go to the Sun Grotto, Flora,' she said. 'I have mama's permission. You are favoured, for she rarely allows anyone to go there.'

Damien touched my arm lightly as I passed him.

'I shall look forward to this afternoon,' he told me.

Just beyond the house was a gate set in thick shrubbery; on the other side was a grassy clearing where targets had been set up for archery practice. There was a small building, no more than a shed, where folding chairs were stacked, together with bows and arrows. The shed was locked.

'You need very strong wrists for archery,' Bella told me

knowledgeably. 'Papa used to be quite good, though Ruan prefers a rifle, like Damien. Edwin is quite good at archery, but it's my mother and Irene who are best of all; isn't that strange? They often have competitions.'

Beyond the archery butts was the rifle range, again with its small outbuilding. I noticed the padlock on the door, and Bella Careena told me:

'Laurie Perkins has the key; my father is very strict about keeping guns and arrows locked up. We haven't got a gunroom in the house — it's been made into a sitting room for mama.'

The path along which we walked ended in a small headland, where bushes grew, and gorse hung out its yellow banners, together with the paler gold of wild tree lupins; the path narrowed and became sandy as it wound between the bushes and then sloped down to a deserted sickle of beach.

'This is mama and papa's most private grotto,' Bella Careena announced importantly.

Once again, natural surroundings had been used. There was a wide-mouthed, shallow cave just high enough for a tall man to stand upright inside it; it was empty except for two stone seats; right in the centre was a natural rocky pool, fed by a silver stream of water that trickled into it from the back of the cave and overflowed to form a small rivulet that ran down the beach.

'Mama and papa used to come here to bathe early in the mornings,' Bella Careena explained. 'That's why no one else is allowed here. Mama says it's lovely when the sun rises, and shines right into the cave. Come!' She dipped her hands in the water that filled the shallow pool and splashed her face with it.

'You do it,' she said solemnly.

'What on earth for?' I asked, astonished.

'It might make you beautiful. I call this The Pool of Venus,' Bella Careena told me.

I put my hands in water so cold that it made my wrists ache, and then I splashed the icy drops over my face.

On the way back to the house, we looked at the last grotto: it was in a clearing near the house, a marble temple, with a pagoda-like roof, and the sides open to the wind and weather that blew up the Channel. There was a stone seat in the centre of the temple, and four statues stood facing different ways: the North Wind, an old man with a craggy face and a wild mane of hair; the East Wind, a young man with his head lifted as though to the morning; and I was surprised that the South and the West Winds had been depicted as women, which was most unusual: the South Wind reminded me of Rose, a summer creature with rounded limbs and a serene face; she looked straight across the sparkling blue waters of the English Channel; whereas the West Wind was a plump, more mature-looking woman, her tranquil gaze fixed on the hazy outline of the Devon coast.

I was entranced.

'This is the work of a very gifted sculptor,' I said.

'Oh, yes; it was for mama's second wedding anniversary, so it had to be just right,' Bella Careena pointed out.

The whole island had been made into a bower for Rose, so dearly had Jerome Jardine loved her, I thought.

'I hope you have enjoyed yourself,' Bella added, with a return to her usual aloofness.

'Very much, thank you.'

'Mama said that I was to look after you.' She sounded piqued.

I sighed.

'Bella, I do want us to be friends. Will you believe me when I say I have no wish to try to get you to leave here?'

'Ruan said your coming was the thin end of the wedge.'

'No. I shall go away from here at the end of the summer.'

'If I grow to like you, I shall not want you to go,' she said candidly.

I laughed, highly amused.

'Thank you, Bella! It's a great comfort to know that!'

I found my locket, just before lunch.

I had gone for a walk to the Peacock Grotto, because I wanted to study its paintings more closely than I had been able to do on the previous day.

It was very quiet; much too quiet, everywhere, except for that occasional ugly screech, heard in the distance. I had the uncanny feeling that I was being followed, yet when I turned my head sharply, there was absolutely no one in sight.

As I stepped into the grotto, I completely forgot my intention of studying the paintings and the map; for my eyes caught a gleam of gold under the stone seat that edged the walls . . .

I bent and reached for the gold. It was my locket. I straightened, holding it in my hand, looking at it with tears in my eyes.

The chain was broken; that had probably happened when I lost it. The locket that dangled from the severed chain looked as though it had been flattened by a heavy heel.

Deliberately, I wondered bitterly? Of course. How else? Not only was the delicate gold marked, the tiny pearls crushed, but the photograph of my mother was missing.

Rose and her son were standing in the hall, talking, when I returned to the house; silently, I held out the locket on the palm of my hand.

'Oh, my dear!' Rose picked it up, distressed. 'Where did you find this?'

'In the Peacock Grotto.'

'It seems to have been deliberately damaged,' Ruan said, examining it.

'The photograph has been taken out!' I said bitterly.

'*Who* has done this?' Rose whispered. '*Why*?'

'I don't know,' I said wearily. 'Someone must dislike me very much.'

'That's ridiculous,' Ruan said sharply. 'Leave it with

me, Flora; I will see if I can have it repaired next time I go to the mainland.'

'It's beyond repair,' I told him.

'There is a jeweller in Dorchester who does the most skilful repairs,' he told me gently. 'Don't despair until you have seen what he can do. I wish I could restore the picture of your mother; that, alas, I cannot do.'

Nevertheless, I was touched by his kindness.

At lunch, Irene said:

'Dear me! It all seems most odd and inexplicable. Poor Miss Lindsay loses her locket and someone treads on it; furthermore, the picture of her mother has been removed. *Is* all this true, Miss Lindsay?'

'Quite true,' I said distantly, meeting her bright, mocking eyes that reminded me, startlingly, of the eyes of the peacock I had seen that morning.

'A most unpleasant occurrence,' Jerome said shortly. 'I should like to find the culprit.'

'Naturally,' Irene agreed. She smiled across the table and said:

'I understand that my husband is taking you rowing on the lake this afternoon?'

'Yes,, I said.

'I prefer dry land to water. I shall test my skill at the archery butts. I am out of practice, but you would be astonished if you knew the strength in these frail-looking wrists, Miss Lindsay!' she answered.

I looked at her thin wrists; at the long, white fingers, heavy with rings; and, finally, at the face, calm, smiling, watchful . . .

Damien and I walked from the house to the lake.

'I share Rose's distress at the accident to your locket,' Damien said.

'Bella talks of curses and ghosts,' he added.

'I am sure that both exist only in her imagination.'

'Oh, the island has quite a violent history; I once read that deeds of violence and great tragedies breed ghosts in the minds of those who are finely attuned to such things!'

'*I* am a very practical young woman!' I assured him.

'Not too practical, I hope,' he teased.

The lake was like a mirror; it was not very large, and on the far side of it, willows trailed green fingers in the water, as though to cool them. One of the boats had been taken from the boathouse and made ready for us; there was a seat in the stern with a cushion placed in readiness for me. Damien stepped into the boat and helped me down, holding me firmly. His nearness made my breath catch painfully in my throat, and my heart beat wildly.

Damien rowed well, with strong, sure strokes; a couple of wild ducks skimmed the surface of the water and veered away seawards; overhead two gulls dipped and soared and uttered their strange, harsh cries.

'Ruan does not share Bella Careena's all-absorbing passion for this island,' I said drily.

'Ruan is a young man, with his life before him; it would not be right for him to be incarcerated here,' Damien said briskly.

He rowed across to the far side of the lake.

'We'll leave the boat here and walk in the woods,' he said.

I gave him my hand as I stepped from the boat; his fingers closed very firmly on mine; and then something came hurtling across the lake with a thin, whistling noise; I heard the hiss of air as it almost brushed my cheek. In the nick of time, Damien ducked, still keeping hold of my hand, and the speed of his movement made the boat rock wildly.

The whistling noise stopped suddenly, followed by a piercing. inhuman scream that made my blood run cold; the boat almost capsized as I tried desperately to scramble ashore. Damien lifted me bodily from my feet, and for a split second, I lay against his broad, powerful chest.

shaken and terrified. I heard a horrible, strangled sound from the trees behind us.

'What was it?' I whispered.

'An arrow,' Damien replied grimly; he helped me up the bank, until we stood on firmer ground. He glanced over his shoulder, briefly.

'Don't look, Flora,' he commanded.

It was too late; I had already seen the dead peacock lying beneath a tree, an arrow embedded in its bright, beautiful plumage.

I felt giddy and nauseated; Damien held me close as I bent my head, shivering, remembering that he had told me the place was a bird sanctuary.

'We'll go to Seawinds,' he told me. 'However, first we'll pay a visit to Laurie Perkins' forge. It's only just across the lake, near the boathouse. He is responsible for the safe custody of the guns and arrows.'

His jaw was hard; he kept hold of my arm very firmly, as we skirted the path that led around the lake; within a short time, we had reached a rather secretive-looking cottage, and beside it, a small forge.

Damien rapped at the door of the cottage; there was no reply. We went into the forge; the fire was low, the bellows idle. A couple of horseshoes had been nailed to the walls. The smith's implements lay beside the nearly-dead fire, together with some pieces of fancy wrought iron. On a bench, I saw four arrows. Beside them was a bow, which would be used to test the sharpness of the arrows once they had been sharpened.

'Surely Laurie Perkins must know that Jerome would be extremely angry with him for killing a peacock?' I said.

'Perhaps the arrow was aimed at me,' Damien replied shortly.

'Who would do such a thing?' I demanded, in shocked disbelief.

'I don't know.' He shrugged. 'Perhaps it was meant to frighten me.'

'You could have been killed!' I whispered.

'Would it have mattered very much to you, Flora?' Damien asked softly.

Before I could reply, we heard the sound of footsteps on the path outside; a shadow darkened the doorway.

He was a man of about thirty, short, well-muscled and stocky; he had a shock of wild black hair, a broad, tanned face, and wore working clothes.

'Lookin' for me?' he asked.

Chapter 5

DAMIEN LOOKED SHREWDLY at the figure in the doorway.

'How many arrows did you bring here to sharpen, Perkins?' he asked.

'Five — sir.'

I didn't like Laurie Perkins' manner; there was no deference in it.

'There are four arrows here,' Damien pointed out.

'Then it seems one's bin taken, don't it?' Perkins replied smoothly.

'Someone shot an arrow at me, as I was stepping from the boat,' Damien told him. 'It missed me; it has killed a peacock.'

'There's bad luck, then,' Perkins replied impassively. 'At least, so 'tis said. Kill one of them birds, and no good will follow on it. Who done it, sir?'

The bold black eyes stared unwinkingly at Damien.

'Dammit, man, I might have been injured! So might Miss Lindsay!' Damien cried angrily.

'Or killed, sir. Them arrows has all bin sharpened. I'm about to test 'em,' Perkins answered.

'Whoever loosed the arrow could, only have done so

from a bow,' Damien pointed out.

'Well, sir, there's the bow, as you see.' Perkins pointed to the beach. 'Someone must 'ave bin nippy to try a spot o' target practice and then put the bow back, for I ain't been gone more 'n 'ar an 'our.'

'Where were you?' Damien demanded.

'At *your* 'ouse, Mr Ashley, *sir*!' The voice was frankly surly. 'Mrs Jardine sent for me. There's something wants doin' to one o' the latches on the garden door. She's there, now, sir, why don't you check for yourself, and you'll see I'm speakin' the truth? I've better things to do, Mr Ashley, than try me skill with them arrows except on the proper target; and better respect for Mr Jardine than to go killin' 'is peacocks!'

He stood aside pointedly for us to leave; I saw the tightness of Damien's mouth, and I could still feel Perkins' eyes on my back as we walked out of the forge.

'Do you think he was lying?' I whispered, as soon as we were out of earshot.

'Hardly likely. How could he have sprinted back and returned the bow?'

'Who would have a grudge against you?' I asked, still unhappy.

'I don't think it was meant for either of us,' he answered. 'Not in the sense of being a lethal weapon, anyway; someone was trying to annoy or frighten us.'

We passed into the dimness of a tiny forest of trees, Damien walking so close to me that his shoulder touched mine, but I could not recapture the pleasure I had previously felt in the afternoon and the company.

The trees thinned; we came upon Seawinds, doors and windows open to sun and fresh air. We went straight to the sitting room and found Rose, giving instructions to a servant.

She looked surprised to see us; when she had dismissed the servant, Damien told her what had happened. I saw disbelief and horror on her face.

'You cannot seriously think it was Perkins!' she said.

'He *is* telling the truth. I came over here to see that all was in order for you and Irene to move in; and I gave him instructions about the latch.'

'Where is Mrs Ashley?' I asked.

'I left her at the butts, with Edwin.' Rose looked at me, troubled. 'Ruan has gone fishing with one of the Clegg boys, Jerome is working in his study on the farm accounts. There is only one person I cannot account for; Bella Careena has been missing all the afternoon. She didn't go to Jerome for her French lesson and when he sent one of the servants to look for her, she was nowhere in the house or cottage. Nanny declares there has been no sign of her since before lunch.'

'I'll look for her,' I offered.

'How will you know where to look?' she asked doubtfully.

'I don't know; I'll try the Shell Grotto first.'

'Will you have some tea before you leave, Flora?'

I shook my head. Damien said he would take tea with her; as I was leaving the house, Rose said unhappily:

'I think perhaps we could keep the incident of the peacock from Jerome. It will only anger and distress him to know what has happened.'

'Of course,' Damien agreed, at once. 'It was probably an unpleasant practical joke that could have had dire consequences. Let's forget the whole business.'

I took the path to the grotto. Ahead of me was the gap in the bushes that led to the beach path; away to my left I glimpsed the ruined chapel that I had not yet explored, and I wondered suddenly if Bella Careena had gone there.

A narrow earth track led under the trees to the chapel; it was not far away, but when I came upon it, I shivered, disliking the place. It was very silent; there was no bird-song, no sign of life; only crumbling walls, netted in ivy, with gaps where there had been windows and doors, and no roof.

82

I returned to the cliff-path, and stood at the gap in the bushes looking below me. I was nimble-footed enough to climb down to the beach without fear of mishap, but my dislike of heights affected me strongly and I wished there was someone with me.

'Bella Careena!' I called. Only the soft shush-shush of the waves on the sands answered me; but I thought I heard another sound — the faint tinkling of bells.

I took a long, steadying breath, and tried not to think of poor little Edith, whose untimely death had made Wilfrid Brandon rich, and sent a distracted governess almost out of her mind. Carefully, I made my way down the path until I came to the rocky ledge.

She was there; sitting at the cave entrance, arms crossed around her knees. She smiled happily at me, and patted the sun-warmed stone beside her.

'Come and look at the sea, Flora,' she said. 'I am waiting for the sun to come round and light up the mermaid's eyes, and make the sea-serpent look like a real one.'

I was angry with her.

'You heard me call, yet you did not answer,' I accused. 'People have been looking for you! Here you are, comfortably tucked away enjoying yourself, when you are supposed to be having a French lesson with your father!'

She sighed.

'Oh, Flora, don't be governess-y! I know papa will be cross, he'll lecture me, and I shall have to do extra French for a penance.'

'So this isn't the first time you've played truant?'

'Of course it isn't! Everyone plays truant sometimes. DO sit down, just for a minute, please, Flora.'

I sat down, reluctantly; the roof of the cave overhung the ledge sufficiently to give a welcome shade.

'Why aren't you with Damien?' Bella Careena asked.

I hesitated; she saw my hesitation and pounced.

'Something happened; what?'

'Damien and I were rowing on the lake when someone

shot an arrow across and killed a peacock, close to us.'

Her eyes were like saucers.

'It's terribly unlucky to kill a peacock! It brings down a curse on the island.'

'Don't be silly!' I cried, exasperated; the afternoon that had begun so happily had ended in disaster, and — following upon the discovery of my broken locket — it was all too much for me. I felt wretched.

'Perhaps the peacock was killed by the person who broke your locket,' Bella said reflectively.

Her eyes were on the horizon; below us the blue waters of the bay preened themselves in the sunshine, and tiny white waves spread their lace along the beach; but I had little heart for the beauty all around me.

'There is a serpent in every Garden of Eden,' Bella said matter-of-factly.

'Who told you that?' I asked.

'Edwin; last time he was here. I told him that mama and papa call this place their Garden of Eden and that's when he made the remark about the serpent.' She gave me a very childlike scrutiny, adding:

'Ruan likes you, doesn't he?'

'So you say. I've been here scarcely two days and he hardly knows me,' I pointed out.

'Ruan will have to find a wife soon. I heard papa tell mama it was time Ruan thought seriously about getting married; mama laughed and said the choice was a bit limited, here on the island; then, soon afterwards, mama invited you here,' she answered.

I stood up, brushing my skirt with a hand that shook a little.

'Come along, there's a good girl. It isn't fair to worry your mama, and she has no idea where you are.'

Reluctantly, Bella rose to her feet; the beach suddenly seemed very far below me, and I put my hand to my forehead as the horizon dipped and swayed in front of me.

Bella caught my arm in a firm grip.

'I forgot. You don't like heights, do you? You *do* look

pale, Flora; it's all right, you're quite safe. You won't tumble over like poor, silly, Edith Freemantle did. Perhaps it was punishment on her — she was so horrid to poor Vinnie, the governess. I'd hate to be a governess or a companion; it's just a sort of servant, really. Mama said she never wanted to see *anyone* treated as poor Vinnie was. I wish it hadn't happened here, because now mama doesn't like this part of ths island a bit. That's because *she* was the one who found poor Edith . . .'

I wasn't thinking about Edith and her unfortunate governess; I was reflecting, for the first time, that I had never actually seen my birth certificate even though I knew when and where I had been born.

Probably Alexander Arkwright had it, safely locked in his office with my father's will, and a number of other personal documents.

I decided to write and ask him — if it was in his possession — to send it to me.

When Bella and I reached Seawinds, Damien had already left there to return to the House of the Four Winds.

Rose was in the sitting-room; she looked at her daughter with a mixture of relief and annoyance.

'Go straight home to papa, Bella, and tell him you are sorry you played truant. You know he isn't well; it was wrong of you to worry him so.'

She looked mutinous.

'Can't I wait here until *you* go back?' she muttered.

'No!' said Rose sharply. 'You have really been very naughty, Bella. You can walk home, as a punishment. When you reach the house ask one of the servants to send Dowte with the carriage. Off you go, now!'

Her voice brooked no argument; Bella Careena shrugged philosophically, and left the room. Rose pushed the heavy masses of wheat-gold hair away from her forehead, and looked at me sombrely.

'Flora, there is something I have not told anyone. A

secret I have kept to myself for weeks. I *cannot* tell my family. It would be a relief to tell *you*!'

'Your confidence is safe with me,' I promised.

Her eyes were full of tears.

'Jerome has a serious heart condition; the specialist whom he consulted in London told me that my husband could expect to live a couple more years, at the most.'

'Are you certain of this?' I stammered, appalled.

'Absolutely. The consultant left me in no doubt; the decision, he said, was mine: whether or not to tell Jerome and our children the truth. I made my decision. I don't regret it; even though I know that the strain of too much excitement, any serious over-exertion, or a sudden shock, would undoubtedly prove fatal to my husband.'

'Do you think that Jerome suspects?' I asked uneasily.

'No. He has been told to rest and take life more quietly, and not overtax himself, or his heart will protest vigorously. It has not been easy for him to accept physical restrictions, you know. He has always been an active man.'

'Should you not tell Ruan?' I asked.

'I have considered it; and decided not to do so. It will make him unhappy, and that fact will soon be apparent. Jerome would soon ferret the truth from him.'

'What about the coming-of-age celebrations? They will put a strain on Jerome,' I pointed out.

'*I* shall see that he doesn't overtax himself. I will learn to be even more vigilant that I am now,' she replied, almost ferociously. 'Jerome would be bitterly disappointed, as well as suspicious, if Ruan was not given a splendid welcome to his new status. As for Bella — it would be cruel and pointless to tell *her* the truth; no, Flora — let them all have two years unclouded by sorrow for what will come after!'

'You will find it a heavy burden,' I told her.

'My shoulders are strong. It is a comfort to talk to you.'

'Will you tell Damien and Irene?' I asked.

'No!' she said sharply. 'I do not want them to know!'

'What about Edwin?' I asked.

There was a moment's gentleness in her face.

'Edwin? Yes, a dear friend, Flora, one who could be as understanding as you have been; but I needed to confide in a woman, for who else will understand the nature of my problems half so well? It would distress him very much; he has known Jerome and myself for many years. Let him remain in happy ignorance until the time comes. You see, Flora, I have been selfish in burdening only you!'

'Perhaps I'm better equipped than anyone else,' I told her. 'My mother and my father have both died within the last few years, as you know.'

She nodded, her eyes suddenly full of blue fire.

'Jerome is the one man I have ever truly loved. A man of tenderness and strength, humility and passion. I was a child when I married him, and he was already middle-aged; but he has taught me all I know of every aspect of love between a man and a woman.'

'Love will give you strength to live through the next two years,' I told her.

'One day, *you* will love as I do, Flora. We are alike. There is great capacity for passion tucked away behind the quiet facade of yours!'

'My mother distrusted passion,' I said.

A curious expression crossed her face.

'Was she — a *cold* woman, Flora?' she asked hesitantly.

I shook my head.

'By no means; warm, affectionate, kind; but passion was of the flesh only, she said devotion to one another was the only true love.'

'There *must* be passion, in the love between a man and a woman, Flora. One day, you will understand that.'

I thought it best to change the subject. 'Will Ruan stay here for the next two years?' I asked. She nodded.

'He will stay, Flora. Because I need him here, because Jerome needs him. After Jerome's death, he may do as he pleases, go where he will. It will not matter to Jerome — or to me — then.'

I did not wait for the carriage to collect me from Seawinds. I walked alone, back to the House of The Four Winds. I had a great deal to think about; Rose's news had shocked me greatly, and saddened me. Yet Jerome Jardine would have been the first person to admit that his life had been full and happy.

Before I dressed for dinner, I sat down at my desk and wrote to Alexander Arkwright.

The matter of the arrow was kept from Jerome; at dinner that evening he asked me if I had enjoyed my afternoon, which seemed to greatly amuse Irene. It was a cold kind of amusement; I distrusted her.

After dinner, Jerome went to his room, accompanied by Rose; Damien challenged Ruan to a game of chess and Bella Careena had to return to the cottage to read an hour's French.

The night was so warm that I decided to walk in the grounds. The moon was coming up, silvering the sea with a touch of phantom light. I walked round to the back of the house; the conservatory was in darkness, and I peered through the window. It was like a green jungle inside, the plants pushing against the glass as though trying to escape into the outdoors. The curtains in the study were undrawn, and I could see Ruan and Damien engrossed in their game of chess, looking very companionable.

Two hands came out of the darkness from behind, and fastened themselves firmly on my shoulders. I screamed aloud.

A familiar voice said in my ear:

'Ah! It wasn't fair to startle you, but you should not be alone on such a night!'

I whirled on him so fiercely that his hands were wrenched from my shoulders; I was furiously angry.

'Do you usually spring upon people in the dark?' I choked.

'Oh, come,' Edwin Trehearne said mildly, 'I didn't

spring upon you. But perhaps I should have given warning of my approach. It is a fine night; I was going to ask you to walk with me.'

'No thank you!' I retorted.

'Alas! I am not Damien!' he said, with mock dismay.

'That is a mischievous and impertinent remark!' I cried angrily.

'I make no apologies!' His smile was wicked, his teeth gleamed whitely. 'I am merely trying to warn you not to let your heart run away too far and fast.'

'I need no warnings; I am quite capable of managing my own life!'

'There are times when I doubt that, Flora Belle!'

'This is a ridiculous conversation, Edwin Trehearne!'

'I find you interesting,' he replied softly. 'I like your independence, your lively mind. Bella Careena tells me she hopes you will marry Ruan; that will *never* do. He is a boy!'

'*You* are too old for me!' I retorted.

I could have bitten out my foolish, impetuous tongue. It was a cruel remark and I had not meant it. His reaction surprised me.

'Ah yes, Flora! I am seventeen years older than you are; but think of the pleasure that Rose and Jerome have found in one another, despite the difference in their ages! Damien is forty-one, I believe; yet you look upon him with favour. What does he possess that I lack?'

The mockery was savage; without warning, he pulled me close and kissed me, a hard, fierce kiss on my lips. I was outraged; to kiss me like that, as though we were lovers, or, at the very least, engaged to be married! It was unforgivable.

I was shivering when he released me, and he laughed.

'No gentleman would behave as you do!' I told him angrily.

'What *is* a gentleman, Flora? A man who conducts himself circumspectly on all occasions? Is that all there is to it?'

89

He disappeared into the darkness, leaving me thoroughly confused, my lips throbbing, my body still trembling.

In the morning, I told Rose that I was ready to move in to the cottage with Bella; she seemed delighted.

'Oh, Flora, I am glad you have made the decision — that is an excellent idea. You will be good for her; I like to feel she has someone sensible near her, now that Nanny is growing old.'

If Bella was pleased concerning my decision, she did not say so. One of the servants carried my luggage to the cottage, and Nanny Radford expressed her approval of the move.

Bella sat on the edge of the bed, watching me unpack my possessions.

'I hope you are not going to keep an eye on me all the time,' she said flatly.

'I've no intention of doing so,' I replied briskly. 'I'm going to be busy helping your mama.'

'I like being by myself.'

'You can have plenty of solitude. You won't come to any harm here, on this island.'

'Oh, you're wrong, Flora! All kinds of strange things happen here. People have disappeared. Besides — look what happened to your locket; *someone* did it. Someone shot at you with the arrow. Sometimes I feel eyes watching me, you know.'

'You need to keep a tight hand on that imagination of yours,' I told her. 'Your mama is expecting you at the house this morning; the dressmaker has arrived from Tolfrey with some materials to be made up for you.'

Bella looked bored, but she slid from the bed, and went across to the house.

That afternoon, I watched Rose and Irene practise their skill with bow and arrow. A small crowd of us gathered; the servants were permitted to watch and they all thoroughly enjoyed the occasion.

Watching them, I realized the strength needed in those fragile-looking wrists, and saw the steadiness of aim, the sharpness of eye that both possessed. The arrow was fitted to the bow; drawn back with care and a deadly stead-fastness of purpose. No one moved or spoke; we all seemed to be holding our breath. Not even the peacocks screeched, as the arrow was loosed to go winging cleanly through the air and find targets set up at the end of the butts.

Rose had won. The silence was broken by a small cheer. She smiled at Jerome, who was sitting in a camp chair beside Damien.

The two men took over; Edwin won. Damien shrugged ruefully and congratulated him. Irene came across to me.

'I hope you have enjoyed watching the game,' she said graciously.

'Very much. Who taught you?'

'A tutor who was once here, a friend of Jerome's. I play when I am in London; I enjoy the sport.'

She sat down beside me. I smelled light flowery perfume. I looked again at the bony wrists and long, delicate-looking fingers. As though she knew what I was thinking, Irene leaned towards me, and encircled my wrist with her fingers.

The strength of the grip made me wince. It caused me intense pain though I would not cry out.

When she released her grip, I said:

'I wonder who shot the arrow that killed the peacock? Or have you not heard about it?'

'I have heard, Miss Lindsay. Rose has a little con-spiracy afoot to keep it from Jerome who might be upset about it. How absurd! It was not a good shot; after all, I don't think it was the peacock who was the target, do you?'

'You are not seriously suggesting that the intention was to kill one of us?' I retorted.

'It seems like it, you must admit, Miss Lindsay.'

Her voice was careless, as though the subject had ceased

to interest her. She lifted her hand to pat her hair and the diamonds in her ring glittered as coldly as the glass eyes on the wall of the Shell Grotto.

'*I* should like to kill my husband,' she said coolly.

I stared at her, aghast.

'You should not say such things — especially to someone you regard as an employee, Mrs Ashley,' I told her.

'Touché!' Irene was delighted; she threw back her head and laughed, showing small white teeth. 'Damien knows how much I hate him and finds it amusing. He drags me here, to be with him, when he knows that I am bored with this place and with the people in it who believe they are living in a fairytale that has a happy ending. How stupid, how dull they are!'

Chapter 6

ROSE TOLD ME that Irene and Damien would be giving a party at Seawinds, and afterwards, there would be a return party at Four Winds.

She looked critically at my only evening dress, of pale lilac, and said:

'There is not time for Miss Hyams to make you something in time for Irene's party, alas; however, there are gowns in my wardrobe that I have not yet worn. I will have one of them altered to fit you.'

I stammered embarrassed protests which she waved away, smiling.

'Accept the loan of a gown as a token of gratitude from me Flora. Your presence here gives me pleasure, as well as comfort.'

Bella suggested a picnic tea in the Peacock Grotto.

'It's cool there,' she said. 'You know the peacock that was killed? Laurie Perkins said we could use the feathers to decorate the walls. That's a good idea.'

I shivered. It sounded macabre.

The weather was still very hot; Nanny Radford supervised the packing of a picnic basket, but after half an hour in the grotto, Bella grew bored; she wanted to show me things I had missed on my tour of the island: a little tombstone, half-buried in ivy, dedicated to the memory of "Redwings" a favourite horse.

'That was my first horse,' she said. 'Do you ride, Flora?'

'No. I've never learned.'

'Then you must,' she said, leading me on to a little natural hollow by the banks of a stream; just above the water, almost hidden by ferns, was a little, weatherbeaten stone statue of a Cupid, a chip in one wing, his sightless eyes turned towards us; beyond it, at the end of a small grove, was a round, rustic summerhouse with a thatched roof. The door creaked eerily on its hinges when Bella lifted the latch. Inside, it was empty, smelling of dust and dead leaves.

'You can follow the stream all the way back, you know,' she said.

'Back to where?'

'The grotto.' She sat down, pulling off shoes and stockings.

'I'm going to paddle back along the stream, Flora. It's quite safe, it only just comes over my ankles. Coming? Or are you going to walk back along the path?'

'I'll follow the path,' I said. I couldn't be bothered to strip off my stockings, and, anyway, I wanted to be alone with my thoughts.

'See you at the grotto!' she cried.

I stood there watching her until she was out of sight. Silence washed peacefully around me, broken only by the sound of running water.

Once again, I had the feeling that I was being watched;

93

I turned, and looked over my shoulder. A figure stepped on to the path, and my heart leapt.

I saw a tall, muscular man with a thick cap of tawny curls; a sensual lift to his mouth; classic good looks of a profile on a Greek coin; an air of vitality about him, of great power, of strength like a tiger's.

'Flora!' he called, holding out his hands.

I went to him, my heart clamouring furiously; I felt helpless, as though I was drowning, and did not want to save myself.

He put his arm around my shoulders.

'Come!' he whispered.

He led me to the little summerhouse, smiling as the latch protested at being lifted again. Inside, he gently put his hands on my shoulders and drew me to him. All about us was the warm dusty silence, as he bent his head and kissed me.

It was not a hard kiss such as Edwin had given. It was a slow, warm, exploring kiss that gradually increased in intensity. His lips fastened more firmly on my willing mouth; I was held so close, I could feel his heartbeats.

Never be led away by passion, my mother had said. Words, words! Words to be tossed like leaves on the wind; words that rose and whirled around me like a flock of birds. Passion was a slow fire running in the veins, glowing with terrible intensity, as heartbeats became faster and more uneven, limbs more willing.

Suddenly, he let me go. I felt a bitter disappointment, even whilst I recognised his wisdom in releasing me.

'I make no apology,' he said arrogantly. 'You are truly wonderful, Flora. A woman, not a girl. A woman of warmth, loving and giving. When I first saw you on the quay, I thought you looked like a seabird, wild and free and proud. I have the bird in my hand, but I have to open my hand and let it go for a little while. Do you understand?'

'Yes,' I said, with a sigh. *For a little while*? I wondered at those words.

His voice was harsh when he spoke again:

'I am leaving Irene. I have told you, my marriage is at an end.'

'You will still be tied to her.'

'No.' He drew a deep breath. 'We will not talk of things on such a day as this.'

'I must go,' I said flatly. 'Bella Careena will wonder what has become of me.'

'Tell her that you were lost. After all, is that not true?' His smile was wry.

Briefly, he laid a cool, dry hand against my hot cheek. I saw the longing in his eyes; I wanted him; I knew that he wanted me. We had no future, for divorce was unthinkable. At summer's ending, I must leave Bella Careena and never return.

Perhaps Damien read my thoughts; he bent his head, and told me:

'The summer is young, yet.'

He kissed me again, gently, without passion. Then he lifted the latch and we went outside.

I was up early next morning. For the first time, I wore the locket Rose had given me. It was heavy on its gold rope, the locket hanging almost to my waist. Like mine, there was a hinge on it, but when I opened the locket, there was no photograph inside.

Ruan didn't notice the locket until we were in the boat together; I was watching the island smudged into a blue-green haze on the horizon, wondering if its spell would seem less potent, once I was free of it; and I heard his sharply drawn breath and turned my head towards him. He was looking nonplussed.

'Who gave that to you, Flora?' he asked.

'Your mama; why do you look at me so?'

'It is odd that she should have given you that particular piece of jewellery.'

'She did so when I lost my own locket,' I told him.

95

'I have your locket with me; I shall instruct Mr Gilford, at the Fortune, to take it into Dorchester for me, in order that it can be repaired. Flora, the piece of jewellery that you are wearing is a family heirloom.'

Embarrassed, I said stiffly:

'Then I will return it to your mother when my own is repaired.'

'No, no, you don't understand.' He came and sat beside me, his face gentle and oddly amused. 'You mustn't think of handing it back; she would be very hurt.'

'Is there something else special about it besides the fact that it is an heirloom?' I asked.

'Yes.' He spoke reluctantly.

'Well?' My voice was tart. 'Is it cursed? Is *that* it? Curses seem to grow along with trees on your island.'

'No, it's not cursed. Don't be cross,' he coaxed. 'It's just that this locket belonged to my great-great grandmother, and, by tradition, it is handed down to the bride of the heir to Bella Careena.'

I was silent, my embarrassment growing; I had to look up, at last, and I met his eyes reluctantly. He was still smiling.

'Perhaps mama was being a little premature,' he said wickedly. 'I *do* rather like you, Flora. I thought perhaps you'd say you liked me, too. Don't look so unhappy. I'm teasing. Flirting with you; hasn't anyone ever done that before?'

'No,' I admitted.

'You're not like most of the women I have met,' he told me. 'They all have their sights firmly set on Holy Matrimony.'

'What other career is there for a woman, unless she has private means?' I argued.

'None, I suppose.' He pursed his mouth thoughtfully. '*You* have to work for your living, Flora; whatever you are, governess, companion, it cannot be an easy life.'

This was dangerous ground; I changed the subject.

'Your mother and father are very happy,' I murmured.

'Their devotion to one another makes a clear statement that a good marriage is a great gift.'

'Yes,' he agreed. 'Mama is content to stay on the island because papa loves it there. Bella Careena is much too involved with the island; at her age, she should be eager to sample the world outside.'

'You told her I had come to take her away from the island!' I accused.

His grin was boyish.

'Oh, I teased her about that, and she took it seriously! Papa is not well, nor is he a young man. I shall stay on the island because of that; but not willingly, Flora; and when I marry, I shall not expect my wife to be content with such a narrow life.'

I sensed his restlessness, his impatience. I looked back at the island. It would never put a spell on Ruan Jardine, I reflected.

'I want to travel all over the world,' he said, with a sigh.

'Then you should not think of marriage,' I retorted. 'Women do not take kindly to wandering around the world with all their possessions in a dress basket. They like to put down roots.'

'Edwin once said that wise men never marry at all,' Ruan told me.

'How cynical; is that why *he* never married?'

'He once told me he was too busy to look for a wife,' Ruan replied. 'He has great estates to look after, in Gloucestershire and Somerset.'

'With no son to inherit them!' I retorted.

'Well — Edwin is a romantic, you know. He told my father that he had never met a woman he wanted to marry. He would not marry simply to produce heirs.'

There was a bustle of activity at the quay when we arrived. Fishing boats were putting out to sea, children were playing on the sands. At the Fortune, casks and barrels of beer were being unloaded; mats were spread over the garden walls of little cottages that straggled up the main street.

It was a pleasant day; Ruan knew everyone, and at each cottage we visited we were received with great deference. As Rose had assured me, there were plenty of willing volunteers for the task of helping with the coming celebrations. My list was full by lunchtime.

We ate lunch in the cool dining-room of the Fortune; fresh salmon, tiny new potatoes, strawberries picked that morning, thick yellow cream. It was a very pleasant and leisurely lunch.

'I *have* enjoyed today,' I told him.

'Good!' His smile was boyish, with a hint of the maturity yet to come. He leaned forward and looked closely at the oval of gold swinging from its chain against my dress.

'It does suit you, Flora,' he murmured.

I was tired when I returned to the island that evening; the day had been exhausting, as well as delightful. There was no sign of Bella when I reached the cottage.

'Miss Bella has gone for a walk on her own,' Nanny told me. 'Mrs Jardine called and left presents upstairs for you.'

Upstairs, on my bed, were more gifts from Rose; a very pretty dress of ivory silk, tucked and flounced and cut low on the shoulders. There were touches of colour in the skirt, where it was caught up by tiny posies of velvet pansies, amethyst, purple, yellow. A knot of amethyst velvet ribbons trailed long streamers from the bodice. There was a pair of shoes to match the gown and a narrow leather box lying on the bed.

I opened the box, with trembling fingers; inside was a necklace of small, perfectly-matched pearls. The richness of their sheen, their milky depths, proclaimed that they were real.

There was also a note from Rose.

'Dear Flora, please accept these gifts, with my blessing. Wear the dress and the pearls this evening.'

I was deeply troubled; the more so, because Rose believed me to be penniless and, out of a loving generous heart, wanted to share some of her beauty with me.

The little maid came to help me dress; when I was ready, I looked in the mirror, and saw her face reflected there as well as mine. She looked impressed, and admiring.

'Oh, miss, you *do* look lovely!' she said.

Damien was standing in the hall when I reached Four Winds. His tawny eyes were suddenly full of a fire like the sun . . .

'Flora!' he said softly. 'You look very beautiful.'

'You flatter me,' I murmured.

'Indeed I do not. I wish that *I* could have taken you to the mainland today, instead of Ruan.'

'It would not have been right!' I whispered.

'What is right and what is wrong when two people desire one another?' he demanded. 'If life comes with hands outstretched, offering gifts of joy, are we to dash them from her hands and turn our backs? Opportunities are precious, life is fleeting; yesterday we were young, tomorrow we shall be old. Remember that, Flora. One day you and I will bathe from the Sun Grotto in the early morning.'

'It is not possible,' I replied, trembling.

'All things are possible, if one wishes them to be. Ah, Flora — you are like most women! You fear what you most desire!'

His eyes danced, his voice was mocking, his smile teased me, drew my heart even closer to his . . .

Our conversation was interrupted by the sudden entrance of Bella, dressed for dinner; she came up to me, and said:

'Mama has made you a present of the gold locket that is given to the bride on the day she marries the heir to the island!'

'How do you know that?' I asked, as calmly as I could.

'I went to your room to look for you, and it was lying

99

there on the dressing table.' Her eyes were accusing. 'Are you going to marry Ruan? Is that why you came here?'

I drew a deep breath and said:

'I shall marry whom I choose — *when* I am ready to be married!'

There was a grim expression on Damien's face; he said nothing more, as the three of us went across the hall to the drawing-room.

I tried to put the incident out of my mind. I thanked Rose for her gifts of the gown and shoes and pearls, and she told me, happily, that she found pleasure in giving.

As the day of the party approached, there was a great bustle of activity on the island; in the late afternoon, the guests began to arrive, and extra boats had been hired to bring them over.

The guest-list was a long one. A band had been hired. Several coaches took the people from Four Winds over to Seawinds. It was exciting to drive under the trees, with the stars sparkling in the sky above, the sound of laughter, the rhythm of the horses' hooves all around me; the night air cool against my cheeks, when we came suddenly upon Seawinds, ablaze with lights, the sound of music coming through the open windows.

Irene stood beside Damien, in the hall, receiving the guests. He looked aloof and formal; Irene was more nondescript than ever in a gown of pale-green silk; she seemed weighted down by the jewels at her throat, on her hands, encircling her wrists. Her smile for me was as cold as a winter morning, her greeting perfunctory.

I danced with Edwin; he was an expert dancer, to my surprise. I was clumsy, never having learned to dance.

'You must learn to relax,' he told me. 'Let me guide you. You don't like to be guided, do you, Flora Lindsay?'

I looked sharply at him. There was no way of guessing his thoughts. His dark eyes sparkled, his hold was firm.

'Forget him, Flora!' he whispered. 'No happiness can

come from such a liaison as you and he contemplate. There will be no lasting joy in the thoughts and feelings *you* entertain for him!'

'You do not know what I think or feel!' I retorted angrily.

'I know better than you imagine. It is all such a waste. You are infatuated!'

'As always, you talk impertinent nonsense!' I choked furiously.

We did not speak again, and I was glad when the dance ended.

Jerome sat in a splendid carved chair with a scarlet leather seat, watching his wife with open admiration. She was beautiful in yellow silk, with touches of emerald velvet, and rarely left him alone for long, but came over to speak to him after every dance.

I danced next with Damien, aware that Irene's eyes followed us.

'I have missed you, Flora,' he said. 'You have deliberately hidden yourself away from me.'

'No. I have been busy. There is a great deal for me to do.'

'I shall keep my promise: one day, we will bathe from the Sun Grotto,' he told me.

'You know it is a private place.'

'The Jardines do not go there, now. No one will see us; we can go early, before the sun rises. It will be our secret.'

I was kept busy helping Rose with preparations for a return party at the House of the Four Winds. There was to be a treasure hunt; she would not tell me anything about it; it was something that she and Jerome always planned together, for the amusement of their guests.

On the night of the party, Four Winds was full of flowers. A buffet had been set out in the big supper room adjoining the Ballroom, the band had been re-engaged, the rooms made ready for the overnight guests. Bella

Careena was full of the second party, having had a taste of gaiety at Seawinds.

We paired off for the treasure hunt, which was the high spot of the evening. Edwin Trehearne was my partner.

'Ah, poor Flora!' he mocked gently. 'It is not at all to your liking, is it?'

It was a calm, beautiful night, the sky bright with stars, a welcome little breeze blowing in from the sea. From the grounds around the House of the Four Winds came the laughter and triumphant shouts of the searchers as they unearthed clues, and went on to the next one. The servants had placed lighted oil lamps at intervals around the grounds, and the effect was extremely pretty, especially as some of the lamps had coloured glass in them.

I suddenly did not want to be with Edwin; let him look for the treasure on his own, I thought. I had seen Damien with Irene, and I was full of despair, bewilderment, the misery that inevitably follows great elation and happiness when one is in love.

I found myself near the Grotto of the Four Winds. I was wearing a shawl of the same colour as the dress, and I turned it up so that it covered my head as well as my shoulders, not wanting to catch a chill.

The moon lit the statues eerily. There was the South Wind, the sculpted woman who reminded me of Rose, the basket of flowers on her arm; the West Wind, with her corn-sheaf, facing towards Devon, the East Wind looking towards the Sun Grotto.

I sighed, staring out to sea; I heard a faint movement behind me, and I at once thought of Damien; he had come here to find me; he had escaped from Irene, we would have a few minutes alone together.

In a moment, he would call my name; I would turn and he would come to me and put his arms around me.

So I waited, and held my breath, hearing again the faint

movement behind me; then I could bear the suspense no longer.

'Damien?' I whispered, as I turned.

The sixth sense that warned me of impending danger sprang to my defence with split-second timing. I was looking at the statue of the God of the North Wind, and even as I looked into the hard, craggy face, I saw it move forward, with a curious grinding movement. Its face seemed to rush swiftly towards mine; it was six foot high, and stood on a small marble plinth.

Instinctively, I sprang aside — only just in time; there was not a hair's-breadth between me and the falling statue as it crashed to the stone floor; its arm caught me a sharp glancing blow on the shoulder that sent me sprawling.

I screamed aloud with pain and terror. I saw a figure, no more than a moving shadow, melt into the bushes that grew near to the temple. The statue had broken in falling, and part of the arm that had struck me lay nearby, looking like a dismembered limb. I began to sob, as I got to my feet; my shoulder was throbbing, and I realized how near I had been to death.

At that moment, a figure appeared suddenly, beside the statue of the South Wind. It was Edwin. He stared down at the broken statue, and, as he lifted me to my feet, his hands were surprisingly gentle.

Chapter 7

I SAT IN THE drawing room at the House of the Four
Winds, sipping the brandy that Edwin had insisted upon
giving me; it was like fire and I choked on it, but gradually
I stopped trembling so violently, and felt the blood move
in my veins.

'That's better!' he said, with great satisfaction; he
closed the door firmly against the sounds of revelry
outside. Only a few people knew what had happened; we
collected a handful of curious stares as Edwin helped me
into the house and sent a servant in search of Rose.

My shoulder still throbbed where the falling statue had
caught it; there was a mark on the skin that would be a
bruise tomorrow. Edwin's fingers were firm and cool as
they moved over the bare flesh of my shoulder.

'You've been lucky!' he said. 'A few more inches to the
left and you would have received the full force of the falling
statue; it could have killed you!'

I heard anger in his voice; Rose came into the room,
looking horrified.

'Irene says that one of the statues in the Grotto of the
Four Winds has fallen over!' she said. 'That is not
possible! The statues have stood firm on their bases for
years!'

'It didn't fall,' I said bleakly. 'Somebody deliberately
pushed it towards where I was standing.'

'Flora might have been killed!' Edwin told her grimly.
His eyes were like flints.

Troubled, Rose stared down at me.

'I cannot believe it!' she whispered.

'I was wearing your pink dress,' I told her. 'I had a

shawl over my head. I am as tall as you are, and it is quite dark outside.'

Suddenly, she put her hands over her face; the slender, exquisite white hands on which Jerome's jewelled tributes sparkled. It was only a brief surrender to horror; but when she took her hands away, her face was full of despair.

'It is absurd!' she cried. 'No one would wish to kill me! *Or* you!'

'You were my partner,' I said accusingly to Edwin. 'Where were you?'

'Looking for you, my dear Flora,' he retorted. 'You had conveniently lost me.'

'We cannot keep this from Jerome,' Rose said wearily. 'He will be furious!'

'Naturally.' Edwin's voice was dry. 'There are a good many people here tonight; many of them young and high-spirited. Yet, I would scarcely have thought that any of them had such a cruel taste in practical jokes. The only alternative is to suppose that someone wished you — or Flora — deliberate harm.'

'*Could* it not have been an accident?' she pleaded.

'Not unless there was an earthquake, my dear Rose,' he retorted, cynically.

'Jerome will be upset that the statue was broken, apart from anything else; he used to call himself the North Wind, and say that I was his South Wind.'

A reminiscent smile curved her lips briefly, though her eyes were unhappy.

'Did you see anyone near you?' Rose asked me.

'I heard someone move, behind me. I thought I saw someone running away, afterwards,' I told her.

'We were all out-of-doors,' Rose said. 'Even Jerome. We were both on the terrace, watching the others.'

I stood up determinedly, stilling the queasiness in my stomach. I was prepared to believe anything except that someone had tried to kill me.

'I am ready to return to the party,' I said.

Edwin offered his arm.

'It is suppertime. Let us go.'

A splendid buffet had been laid on long tables in the supper room. The white cloths had been decorated with pink velvet ribbons and trails of greenery; a magnificent silver centrepiece held a huge cascade of crimson roses, with petals like silk.

Everyone crowded around me, wanting to know what had happened, and to enquire if I was recovered. I told them all that there seemed to have been some kind of an accident. Jerome did not put in an appearance, for which I was glad; Rose appeared, halfway through supper, and said that Jerome was exhausted, and resting in the library. She seemed worried about him.

Damien came up to me, demanding to know what had happened; I heard his sharp, angry intake of breath.

'Who did such a thing?' he asked ferociously.

'I don't know. I wish I did. I thought it was . . . you . . . coming . . . ' my voice died away. He shook his head, a bitter expression on his face.

'Had *I* been there, such a thing would never have happened,' he told me curtly.

Irene came across the room to me; her eyes were bright and excited in her small, pale face.

'I hear you have had a most unpleasant experience, Miss Lindsay,' she said.

'Yes. I was fortunate to escape the more pressing attentions of the God of the North Wind,' I answered drily.

'How brave you are to make light of it! *I* should have been terrified!' She gave an affected little shiver as she smiled at her husband; it was a cold little smile.

'Where were *you*, Damien, when this happened?' she chided.

I saw a muscle twitch in his cheek.

'I was searching for you, Irene. We were partners in the treasure hunt, if you remember.'

'Ah! We were careless, to have lost one another in such a fashion!' she replied.

She murmured something about hoping I had recovered, and reminded Damien that the next dance was theirs.

I stood beside Edwin, under the crystal chandeliers; looking at the pretty women in their dresses like flowers, at the men, handsome in evening dress.

'What are you thinking about?' Edwin asked me.

'I am wondering if one of them tried to kill me,' I said.

'Do you find it a sobering reflection?'

'Very,' I replied drily.

He laughed, showing strong white teeth in his craggy face.

'You have courage, Flora,' he said admiringly.

Bella Careena sat on the end of my bed, wearing a long white nightgown; her feet were bare, and she was brushing her hair with long, slow strokes.

'It's the Curse of the Peacocks again,' she said. 'That's why the statue nearly fell on you.'

'Nonsense!' I said firmly.

'Oh yes, you always say that!' She looked angry. 'This monk who once lived here — his name was Alfrec de Bressard. He was supposed to be a good man and a hermit but he held black masses. You could hear screams and cries, over on the mainland, and anyone landing here was never seen again. Well, *he* killed a peacock — the peacocks were wild, they always lived on the island and no one was supposed to touch them.'

'Where did you read this?'

'In the fifth grotto,' she said calmly.

She had my interest, at last; she knew it, and looked triumphant.

'You're not going to tell me where it is, are you?' I said resignedly.

'Of course not. I shall probably never tell anyone. It's my secret.'

'Edwin wants to find it,' I told her. 'Surely you'll tell him?'

She shook her head, lips pressed together. After a pause, she said:

'When Alfrec killed the Peacock, there was a great storm on the island; trees were blown down, and the waves came right up over the chapel. He was swept away and drowned. It's a bit like the legend of lost Atlantis, isn't it? Thousands of years ago, there was this beautiful place, Atlantis, full of people who became evil. So, one day, a great wave came out of nowhere, drowning the island and everyone in it. Sailors say you can hear the bells of Lost Atlantis, ringing sometimes, at the bottom of the seas. Lost Atlantis whispers, in a foam of bells, ice-cold and clear . . . '

Her voice died into silence; in spite of my belief that I should put a gentle rein on her imagination, I was intrigued by her words.

She smiled at me, an enigmatic smile as she slid from the bed. 'I hope you sleep well, Flora,' she murmured.

'I intend to; I have had enough excitement for one night.'

Unexpectedly, she kissed my cheek. It was the first spontaneous gesture she had made towards me.

'Goodnight, Bella,' I said. 'Have I at last convinced you that I have no intention of trying to persuade anyone to send you away to the mainland?'

'I think so,' she replied sedately.

In spite of my assurances that I was going to sleep well, I found it impossible to do so; I sighed wearily, got out of bed and went to the window.

Gently, I eased up the window, and leaned on the sill, listening intently; the night was still, but not quiet. It was full of small, soft rustlings and movements, as though the wild creatures had taken over and were going about their business undisturbed by humans; this was another life, an alien one; the one that Anne Churnock had cared for and protected.

The moon was high, printing black and silver shadows, sharp and clear, bathing the whole place in luminous light. Somewhere an owl hooted, and was answered by another owl. I thought of Damien, at Seawinds, and an unbearable loneliness ached within me. This was a night made for lovers.

I saw a movement in the grassy clearing below my window, and saw a figure step from a patch of deep shadow. I recognized him at once; tall, lean, craggy, the moonlight putting silver flecks in the dark hair. He stepped forward until he stood beneath my window, looking up at me, an impudent smile on his face, his eyes gleaming in the moonlight.

'Could I but sing, I would serenade you, Flora. I have a repertoire of French songs taught me by my grandmother, but they are slightly saucy, and not suited to a young lady's ears . . . '

'Hush!' I hissed furiously. 'You will wake the household.'

'I doubt it. Put on a wrapper and walk with me in the moonlight.'

'Certainly not!' I said, scandalized.

Edwin's soft laughter rippled up to me.

'Then put on a sedate dress, but don't fasten your hair; it becomes you better hanging loose over your shoulders. You look like the Queen of the Night, and I am reminded of a young lady who once threw her hairbrush at my feet, and then demanded it back again.'

In spite of my annoyance, my lips twitched. I stifled a laugh, and saw the pleasure in his face.

'I am making progress,' he called up softly. 'You no longer dislike me as much as you did.'

'You are ridiculous,' I scolded. 'Why are you out so late, when everyone else is in bed?'

'I have been to the Grotto of the Four Winds, with a lantern.'

'What on earth for?'

'I wished to examine the place, in view of what happened tonight,' he replied.

I leaned even farther out of the window.

'Did you find anything there?' I asked.

'Nothing that gives me reason to suppose the statue toppled from its plinth of its own accord. I tried the other statues. They stand firmly on their pedestals, though a good, hard push would send them over.'

'Do you have a list of suspects?' I asked, trying to hide my uneasiness.

'Alas, no. I shall consider the matter, as I walk by myself in the night. I am glad you are safe, my dear Flora — glad, in spite of your cold heart and indifference towards me!'

He laughed, swept a graceful bow, and blew me a kiss with his fingertips before he walked away.

Next day, Jerome sent for me; he looked grey and exhausted.

'I have heard what happened last night,' he said. 'I am deeply disturbed and very angry. I should have been told about it at the time.'

'Rose was anxious that you should not be distressed.'

'Distressed? Of course I am! Had I known of the incident yesterday evening, I would have questioned everyone present.'

'It would have spoiled the party,' I pointed out gently. 'Besides, no one would have owned up.'

'You could have been severely hurt!' he retorted.

'I wasn't, though; so please don't upset yourself any longer. It is over. Perhaps it was one of the young men in the party from the mainland, playing a silly joke.'

'Well, it was certainly no one from the island, I am sure; not guest or servant. The whole episode has left an un- pleasant memory,' he replied curtly.

'Then let it be wiped away,' I coaxed.

He shook his head, looking dissatisfied. Later that day two men came over from the mainland to take the statue away for repair. When they had gone, Rose and I walked down to the grotto; it didn't look the same without the proud God of the North Wind in his usual place.

'Jerome,' Rose said softly, tears in her eyes.

I looked at her enquiringly, and her smile was tremulous.

'Jerome, the God of the North Wind. There is a space where he should be. It seems like an omen!'

'Nonsense!' I told her firmly. 'The statue will be back as good as ever.'

'Oh, Flora!' she said, with a sigh, 'you *are* such a comfort!'

Later that morning, Rose asked me, looking hurt, why I did not wear the locket she had given me, and I told her.

She laughed gently.

'My dear, I think it would be delightful if you and Ruan entertained an affection for one another!'

'You cannot arrange such matters!' I protested.

She slid a hand through my arm as we walked together on the terrace.

'I'm not trying to arrange anything. I merely said it would be delightful.' She bit her lip, as though wondering whether to say anything more, and added:

'Forgive me, Flora. I don't wish to pry — but I cannot help noticing the looks that pass between you and Damien sometimes. You are — very much drawn towards him?'

'Yes,' I admitted reluctantly.

'I have seen, also, the way he looks at you. If there is mutual affection between you, then I beg you, Flora, to fight it with all your strength. It cannot bring you any happiness. Surely you must realize that? He is Irene's husband.'

In the afternoon, Bella and I went to the beach just below the house. I bathed there, for the first time in my life, and found the cold shock and the buoyancy of sea-water an exhilarating and delicious experience.

Bella swam with me, laughing at my efforts to float and to master the more complicated swimming strokes that she managed with such ease; she was like a porpoise in the water.

Afterwards, when we had dressed, we sat on the beach together. I was barefoot, my damp hair hanging about my shoulders. I had never enjoyed myself so much in all my life.

Bella did not like to sit still for very long; she ran down to the water's edge, letting the wavelets cream around her ankles. I leaned against a smooth slab of weathered rock and shut my eyes. I scarcely heard the sound of footsteps scrunching softly over the shingle bank behind me until a shadow fell between me and the sun.

I sat up at once, my eyes wide open. Damien was smiling down at me. Hastily, I tried to cover my ankles, but he shook his head, as he dropped down beside me.

'Don't do that, Flora; you have such pretty ankles,' he said.

Our shoulders touched; I thought my heart would break with the violence of its beating. I looked at Bella Careena, walking away from us, still at the water's edge.

'We have so little opportunity to talk together these days,' Damien said softly.

'We meet quite often,' I murmured.

'That is not what I meant, and you know it, Flora. I wish the summer was over; then Irene would return to London.'

'*I* shall go back to Bideford,' I replied.

'No, Flora,' he said softly. 'Stay with me here, when summer has gone. You will not find it dull, I assure you.' A strange smile curved his mouth. 'We shall do as we please, then, you and I; it will be — most entertaining. You will be mine, one day, Flora. Not Ruan's.'

'Why does everyone assume I am Ruan's property?' I demanded angrily.

'Because of the locket. It was most unwise of Rose to give it to you.'

112

'Do you hate Irene?' I asked slowly.

'No, my dear; hatred achieves nothing. Revenge may be born of hatred; but revenge must find and feed upon opportunity if it is to survive.'

'Revenge?' I echoed, looking at him in bewilderment. 'Do you then wish to be revenged upon her?'

'No!' He shook his head, his face enigmatic. 'I merely stated a fact. You and I will keep our tryst, yet, at the Sun Grotto; on that day, I shall make you mine, Flora!'

'For a woman to lose her honour . . . ' I began.

He laughed very softly; the light made a shining nimbus of his hair, reflected the fire in his eyes.

'The conventions mean nothing to those who desire one another, who long for one another, and wish to be one!' he told me gently.

He walked away, without another word; I bent my head to hide my tears.

I met Edwin in the library before dinner that evening; I had gone there in order to choose a book to while away night hours when sleep would not come.

He turned from the bookcase, a slim, leather bound volume in his hand. The lamplight made his craggy face look sharp and mocking, frosted the silver threads in his thick dark hair. His eyes rested on me approvingly.

'Ah, Flora Belle,' he said gaily. 'Are you in search of distraction? Can I recommend a little light reading?'

He held out the book he had been holding.

'Try this book, if you are interested in the island. It is full of stories and legends. Alas, it does not tell me where the fifth grotto may be found.'

I did not tell him that Bella knew the answer; I would sooner have bitten out my tongue.

'What is its importance to you, apart from the fact that your father created it?' I asked.

'It contains treasure, my dear,' he replied blandly.

'Golden ingots? Diamonds, rubies, emeralds?' My

voice was as light as a snowflake.

'No. Treasure of a less substantial kind. Something that my father wrote. If ever I find the grotto, I may show it to you. It depends.'

'On what?'

'On you,' he said deliberately. 'You are a strange young woman. Wilful and capricious.'

'You don't really know me at all!' I retorted, furious at his cool assessment of me.

'True. Perhaps I never shall. It is for you to decide.'

His eyes met mine challengingly. I shrugged and turned towards the bookcase.

'You have not asked me, recently, what the initial "P" stands for, on my hairbrush,' I said.

His reply infuriated me.

'I have decided to abandon the game; it is much too taxing in this hot weather.'

After dinner that evening, as I was returning to the cottage alone, I heard Rose talking to someone. I could not tell who it was; I was passing a small room at the end of the terrace, and the French doors were open to let in a little air, though the heavy curtains inside were pulled across.

Her voice was low and angry.

'*I* choose who shall come here, and I have decided that Flora shall stay here! It is her right, and my reasons are nothing to do with you. Remember, I am still Mistress of this island . . . '

I spent the rest of the evening in my room; puzzling over such a strange remark. There had been no answer, and though I had paused, I heard only the sharp slam of a door as though someone had left the room angrily.

It is her right; it is her right.

It made no sense at all; I had no rights on this island, so far as I knew. I thought uneasily of the locket, the gifts she had given me, and wondered greatly.

114

Beneath all the golden loveliness of this island, the undercurrents ran dark and deep; people had secrets; whilst all the time their thoughts and their feelings were at variance with the facades they presented to one another.

It was a new experience for me; life had never been complex, nor had my relationships with other people caused me uneasiness until now.

Perhaps I should not have left Bideford at all, I reflected sadly; I should have burned my father's sketchbook, turned my back on my desire to see this place for myself; now its spell was upon me and the lives of its inhabitants were inextricably tangled with my life.

The boat went over to the mainland next morning, and returned with the mail. The little servant, Ann Jones, brought one letter to me as I was sitting in the garden checking lists for Rose.

The letter bore the Bideford postmark and Alexander Arkwright's writing sloped neatly across the envelope. I put the lists aside, and, with trembling fingers, I opened the envelope.

I read his covering note; my birth certificate was enclosed as requested, and he trusted that I was enjoying my stay on the island.

I spread the birth certificate out and studied it carefully. Date and place of birth, sex of child, father's name, name and maiden surname of mother.

Name and maiden surname of mother: written clearly in bold, beautiful copperplate. 'Lavinia Mary Lindsay (née Jessel).'

Chapter 8

I SAT THERE for a long time, the certificate in my hand. I read the details several times; then I put it back in the envelope.

It was cool in the shade of the big tree, and there was no sound, save the soft sigh of the wind. Bella had gone for a fitting with the dressmaker; indoors, I heard little Anne Jones singing tunelessly to herself as she worked; and I remembered that Nanny Radford was in the house, too.

She was alone, in her small sitting-room, stitching at a torn dress of Bella Careena's; there was a pile of mending on the table beside her.

She put down her sewing, looking pleased to see me.

'Sit down then, Miss Lindsay. Too hot to be out of doors, on a day like this. It'll give you freckles, all that sun, and turn your skin to leather.'

'Nanny,' I said, loudly and clearly, 'tell me about the day that Edith Freemantle died. All that you can remember.'

She peered at me, surprised.

'What do you want to hear that old tale for?'

'I've only heard bits and pieces. I'm — curious.'

'Ah. Well, it was a terrible time and no mistake.' She sat back in her chair, letting the sewing drop into her lap. 'Never thought Miss Rose 'ud want to come and live here, after the accident, but I reckon Mr Jardine must have won her round. You know something? It was your father who took charge of everything, after it happened.'

'He didn't tell me that,' I said slowly.

'Maybe he thought the old story would upset you. Long before you were born, wasn't it? It was a day like this one;

the sun like a furnace and not a bit of relief from the heat. I was nursemaid to Miss Edith, then, and a nastier, more spoiled child you've never come across. She was an orphan and heiress to a lot of money. Mr Brandon, Miss Rose's father, was her legal guardian. Mean? Huh!' Nanny made a gesture of utter contempt, and continued:

'As for Mrs Brandon, she was a poor creature, and no mistake. Always ailing, or whining about something. What a household it was, and the only ray of sunshine was Miss Rose. Different, *she* was; had a nice nature. The governess, Miss Jessel — Vinnie, as she was called — *she* found Edith a right handful, poor soul. Always making trouble for the servants, that child was.'

'Did *you* like Miss Jessel?' I asked, watching her closely.

'Oh yes. Quiet little creature, always friendly and anxious to please, and tried to do her best for Edith, but she was no match for the child; and Mr Brandon didn't have time for Vinnie, neither. Took it out on her whenever he was in the mood; treated her like a servant; he was always saying a governess thought herself a cut above a servant and gave herself airs; and there was Mrs Brandon, expecting her to be a lady's maid, as well; fetch this, carry this, do that . . . ah, poor soul, she had a wretched life of it!'

I bowed my head, feeling the tears sting my eyelids; Nanny glanced curiously at me.

'Anything wrong, Miss Lindsay?'

'The heat,' I lied.

'Just like it was then. The picnic on the island was Miss Rose's idea. Mr Jerome owned the place, then, and he let them all come and go as they pleased. He let Mr Lindsay go there sketching, too.

'Next to sketching, he liked sailing. A nice man he was, too; *very* fond of Miss Rose, and she was fond of him. *Everyone* liked Miss Rose.'

Nanny fell silent, remembering, no doubt.

'The day of the picnic . . . ' I prompted.

'Well, poor Miss Jessel wasn't well, and half out of her

mind with worry, because Mr Brandon had given her notice . . . he had a cousin coming to live with them who could look after Edith's lessons. Miss Jessel hadn't nowhere to go, and she said jobs like hers weren't easy to come by; she told me so, that morning. She looked sick enough to be in bed, I told her, not to be going out in the sun . . .

'I was down at the Fortune; Mrs Finney, who was living there then, was a friend of mine. I saw Mr Lindsay come back from a sail and tie the boat up; I remember thinking how hot and bothered he looked, had to use the oars, because there wasn't no wind, not a drop, and Mrs Finney called out to him to come and have a cool drink . . . he said he'd be glad to . . . he looked all in, I remember . . .

'We were all sitting in the window of the Fortune when we saw the boat coming back from the island, with Abel Carter and his brother rowing like mad, and something up, you could tell. When the boat came in, there was Miss Rose, in a terrible state, and they had Edith's body in the boat — that gave me a right turn — and poor Miss Jessel lying in the bottom, moaning and crying and saying things that didn't make sense and every few minutes she'd go right off again, and then she'd come to . . . *dreadful* it was. Miss Rose was hysterical and your father took charge of everything, quietened her down, got poor Miss Jessel into the Fortune, sent for Mr Brandon and the doctor, and tried to comfort Miss Rose and find out what had happened.

'Mr Brandon wouldn't have Miss Jessel back at the house when he heard what had happened. I reckon that was cruel of him; still, I heard afterwards she'd been sent to be nursed privately somewhere, I suppose he reckoned he could afford *that*.'

Nanny's voice was sour with sudden cynicism. I thought of the blazing heat of a sweltering afternoon, a dead child and a half-conscious woman, and Rose in a state of shock, in a boat gliding through summer seas, away from the island. I shivered, and felt goose prickles

118

along my arm, as though I had been there, part of the dreadful happenings.

'Well, it all came out afterwards,' Nanny said. 'Miss Rose had been sitting near some ruins, sketching, and Miss Jessel had been on the beach looking after Edith. Miss Rose said she didn't know anything was wrong, she heard a couple of screams and thought it was the peacocks; they were half-wild; nasty birds they are. Miss Rose said when she had finished sketching she started off for the beach, and found the governess lying under a tree, moaning and crying and saying she'd lost Edith. She had a great lump on her forehead and said she'd had a fall; then poor Miss Rose found the child, lying on the rocks, with her skull fractured, and the tide coming in.'

I felt dreadfully sick; my head was swimming, and nausea filled me. I could see it clearly, the waves lapping at the spreadeagled figure of the child who had fallen down to the beach.

'Edith must have fell awkward-like,' Nanny said, shaking her head. ' 'Tain't all that much of a drop, they said, but she hit the rocks.'

'Where were the boatmen?' I asked.

'Oh, *them* two!' Nanny said, with great scorn. 'Fast asleep, near the jetty; waiting to row the party back, they said, and just dozed off . . . Well, there 'twas. The curse of the island, Miss Bella calls it. Carelessness, *I* say. If you're looking after a handful like Edith, you can't afford to let up, not for a minute. I spoke up for Miss Jessel; said she hadn't been right when she left the house, she'd looked ill to me. All I got for my pains was being told to mind my own business by Mr Brandon. It was all kept very quiet, Miss Jessel got the blame, and the Brandons didn't want any fuss made. It did *him* a lot of good. My word, didn't his style of living change after that! He neglected the church; in the end he gave it up for good. Rich? *He* had money to spare, all right, with Edith Freemantle dead.'

'Where was he, that afternoon?'

Nanny grinned wickedly at me, showing yellow teeth.

'Now, Miss Lindsay, you're not thinking wrong things, I hope? He was in his study, preparing his sermon, and there were plenty to prove it; and Mrs Brandon was lying down with one of her migraines; the doctor called to see her, there was a couple of the maids in the house. Mr Jerome had gone to Dorchester; Sir Marcus was busy working on some sketches he'd made for the gardens. Young Master Edwin was away in the fields somewhere; you know what boys are. Master Damien went sailing; he was staying with Mr Jerome, like he often did.'

'What happened to Miss Jessel after she left the nursing home?' I asked.

Nanny shook her head and looked blank.

'Never heard nothing more about her. Miss Rose used to worry a lot, I know. Said she had been treated shocking. Maybe she could tell you.'

Miss Rose used to worry a lot. She would have been glad, I thought, that poor little Miss Jessel had married Mr Richard Lindsay, even though she had been second-best then, for my father had loved the woman Marcus Trehearne married. I knew, now, the identity of the woman who had visited us at Bideford on the days when my father took me out.

Little Lavinia Jessel had covered up her tracks very well; made sure that her daughter knew nothing of the past; but she was *not* to blame, I thought angrily! What happened was not her fault! Wilfrid Brandon used her cruelly and then disposed of her, hushing up the incident for fear a scandal would affect his inheritance. Anger burned within me, fiercer than the sun's heat; anger against Edith. Against Wilfrid.

Rose had been troubled and unhappy, knowing there had been injustice done; she had wanted to make amends, and found a way of doing so when she believed I had been left without means following the death of my father.

It explained so much; yet I had a feeling that only half of the jigsaw puzzle was complete.

'Sure you're feeling quite well, Miss Lindsay? You *do*

look pale. I should go and lie down if I were you,' Nanny said.

I rose stiffly to my feet.

'Thank you,' I said. 'I will.'

I drew the curtains against the sun; my head throbbed, and I lived every moment of that afternoon as my mother must have lived it, ill, unhappy, desperate. No wonder she had shown such compassion for the woman who had been *my* governess!

I kept remembering how I had felt the day I had first gone to the Shell Grotto. I recalled the cold prickling of my skin, the throbbing of my head, my intense revulsion for the place. I wished that my mother had talked to me of what happened, then. She must have suffered a severe nervous breakdown afterwards — and no one had cared, except my father — and Rose.

Jerome and Rose knew what had happened that day; Damien and Edwin also knew the tragic events that took place on the island; but did any of them, except Rose, know I was Vinnie's daughter?

Jerome would certainly know, I reasoned; Rose would not have kept any knowledge from the man she loved so much. Did Edwin and Damien also know? Or Ruan — had be been told about me?

The taking of the photograph from my locket now had a new significance. It was an old photograph; anyone who had known Lavinia Jessel would recognise her; and *I* had announced to everyone that the picture in the locket was that of my mother.

The more I thought about it, the more confused I became. The first sharp shock had dulled into an ache of misery for my mother.

I decided to say nothing to Rose yet concerning my discovery.

On my way from the cottage to have lunch at the House of the Four Winds, I met Ruan.

'Hello, Flora! You look very cool and charming.' His smile was suddenly wicked. 'I am glad to see you are wearing the family heirloom; mama *will* be pleased.'

'There's nothing special in acknowledging your mother's kindness by wearing her gift,' I retorted.

'Ah, dear Flora, you disappoint me!' he murmured teasingly. 'Mama would look most favourably upon a romantic attachment between us!'

'*I* have not been consulted in the matter!' I replied, tossing my head.

'But you *do* like me, don't you?'

'Yes,' I said.

'I like *you*; now that's a good beginning, I think.'

I looked into the candid, laughing eyes; here was a good-looking man with a great deal of charm, I thought. It would be easy, perhaps, to fall in love with him were it not for Damien.

'You are a tease,' I told him lightly.

'I am not teasing, I assure you,' he said, trying to look solemn.

I was thrown into a sudden panic. Too much was happening to me, all at once. I had not yet recovered from the shock of discovering the identity of my mother.

His voice was playful; his smile was still teasing, but there was no laughter in his eyes.

During lunch, I watched Rose carefully; only a very close observer would have seen the look of strain on her face. Only I knew the cause; every hour, every day was precious to her; each beat of the clock brought her nearer to the time when Jerome would no longer be with her, and I could guess what agony she suffered because of that knowledge. The long, hot summer was taking what little strength he had left. There were questions I wanted to ask; but I had to be discreet.

122

I spoke to Damien; I found an opening for the subject when I walked over to Seawinds that afternoon with a message from Rose to Irene.

I saw him along the path that led from the Shell Grotto; I waited, and when he saw me waiting, he came quickly towards me, delight in his face; impetuously, he caught me in his arms beneath the shade of the tree, holding me close, kissing my eyelids, my cheeks, my mouth, until I pulled away, gasping for breath.

'Still so timid?' he murmured, eyebrows raised. 'One day, Flora, I will teach you the meaning of passion. Don't tell me that such a day will never come, for I will not listen to you. It *will* come, Flora; it will!'

'I shall never consent to becoming your mistress,' I told him firmly.

He smiled, and changed the subject.

'Where are you going?' he asked.

'To Seawinds.'

'So am I; we'll walk together. I have been down to the beach, below the Shell Grotto. It is the most secluded of all the beaches. I like to swim from there '

'Neptune's Bay? That is where Edith fell to her death.'

'My dear Flora, I am not superstitious,' he said, with a touch of sharpness. 'It happened a quarter of a century ago. People would have forgotten about it by now, if only Bella didn't keep the story alive.'

'I doubt if the governess ever forgot what happened that day,' I pointed out. 'Did you know her?'

'Scarcely at all; she was a quiet, nondescript little creature, engaged to look after Edith Freemantle and totally unfitted for the task. *I* kept out of Edith's way. The day she was killed I was sailing along the coast and didn't return until evening.'

His voice warned me not to pursue the subject; clearly, he found the memory distasteful. It was obvious that *he* did not know Vinnie was my mother.

Irene was walking in the grounds of Seawinds when we arrived; she looked like a ghost of summer in her white, floating dress, her face pale beneath her shady hat.

I gave her the message, anxious to be away; her eyes seemed to pierce right through me. When she smiled, it was a travesty of a smile, merely a weary lifting of the corners of her mouth as though she found life an unpalatable jest.

'I know you think you are in love with Damien,' she said calmly, as though she was giving the day's orders to the housekeeper. 'He pretends to love you; he does *not*. He is incapable of love. When he has had you, used you and done with you, he will forget that you ever existed.'

I said nothing, because I did not know what to say. The smile became contemptuous; she put out a slender, waxen-looking finger and touched the locket at my throat.

'You should settle for Ruan,' she said scathingly. 'What a prize for a penniless governess! For that is all you are: a penniless governess!'

The irony of her description struck me so forcibly that I hated her, for a moment; the hatred passed, to be replaced by something curiously like pity.

'You are a fortune hunter,' she added. 'Ruan's mama dotes on you; I cannot think why, but she seems to think you would make Ruan an excellent wife. Ruan would be an easy conquest for you, wouldn't he? A wealthy husband — and *my* husband at a discreet distance, ready to rescue you from the boredom you will feel sooner or later — because Ruan is a mere boy; and you, Flora Lindsay, will demand a man, with full-blooded passions . . . '

'You have my word that I have not been your husband's mistress, nor do I intend to be,' I replied.

'Liar!' she said venomously.

'Believe what you choose,' I said; I walked away and left her, resisting the temptation to look back.

Well, I would make sure there was no more guilt on my part; I would avoid Damien. If I did not do so, I would be drawn down into a whirlpool of emotions that would engulf me.

The feeling grew within me that the golden days were ending; that we were all moving helplessly towards some terrible and tragic climax. I said nothing to Rose; she had burdens enough as it was. There were times when she seemed exhausted, completely drained of energy; yet her smile never faltered; her love for Jerome shone clearly through all that she said and did.

So many times, the words were on the tip of my tongue: *I know I am Vinnie's daughter.*

Perhaps I should tell Jerome, I thought; still I hesitated. I had a great desire to know all about the affair of Edith Freemantle; and the small thought nagged, like a toothache in my mind, that something was still withheld from me, some knowledge still denied me.

Often, when I walked about the island, I was certain that I was followed; but I could not find out who followed me, I was never quick enough to see who walked only a short distance from me; the island was a perfect place for anyone bent on a game of stalking.

Sometimes Bella walked with me; but lately she had taken to going off on her own a great deal. She was writing her own history of the island, she said, and took a large exercise book and pencil with her, hiding away in one of many secret places that only she knew.

I was glad to be alone, although my thoughts were poor company; so, walking in the green coolness of the trees on a scorching afternoon, I came to the end of the little grove of trees leading to the niche where the Cupid stood.

On the flat-roofed rock that made a natural seat at the feet of Cupid, Jerome and Irene were sitting together.

His arms were around her, her head was on his shoulder. I could not clearly see the expression on Jerome's face, but he stroked her hair gently, and spoke softly to her.

Stunned, I stood behind a concealing tree, watching them; after a few moments, Irene lifted her head and looked at Jerome. Her face was streaked with tears; I heard her voice, clear and accusing.

'Flora is having an affair with Damien! You must have seen that, Jerome! You must have seen how they look at one another!'

I did not hear his reply, but I saw him shake his head; and the words she flung back to him were angry.

'You are Master here, Jerome! You can send her away. I tell you it is true, and I will not tolerate it . . .'

Again he spoke quietly to her. She dabbed at her cheeks with a scrap of lace, and stood up, jerking away angrily from his protective embrace, as she twitched her skirts into place.

I turned and fled.

I sat in my room at the cottage, trying to read and unable to concentrate. I felt cold, in spite of the heat of the day; my hands were shaking, my thoughts would not be quiet.

My love for Damien would bring disaster upon us both if I did not leave the island soon, I realized.

The time had come for me to approach both Rose and Jerome, tell them the truth about myself, and admit to having witnessed the scene in the woods.

The following afternoon I came upon Rose and Jerome in the conservatory taking tea together. They sat side by side, on chairs of wrought iron, and the tea tray, with its silver appointments, was set in front of them on a low table. Rose looked very beautiful in a pale dress the colour of hyacinths that set off her lovely eyes and rich, wheat-coloured hair to perfection; one slender, white hand with its jewelled fingers held Jerome's hand, as he sat beside her, looking pale and tired, but relaxed.

They looked up and smiled when they saw me; Jerome got to his feet, and told me to summon a servant to bring fresh tea.

He glanced at the heavy gold locket I wore, and said mildly:

'I hear there has been speculation because my wife gave you a family heirloom. Only tradition says it is destined for a Jardine bride. You must make up your own mind, Flora; as I did. As Rose did.'

I met his penetrating look calmly.

'I like Ruan very much,' I said quietly. 'I think he is a fine young man; I have no feelings other than those of warm friendliness towards him.' I turned to Rose. 'Does that disappoint you?' I asked frankly.

'Only a little,' she admitted, with a smile. 'It would be lovely to have you as a daughter-in-law, Flora; but, as Jerome says, we all make up our own minds on such matters. When Ruan marries, there will be other jewels to hand down to his bride. The locket was an especial gift to you — from me.'

As soon as the fresh tea had been brought, Jerome said briskly:

'Now, Flora; what troubles you?'

'I must leave here soon,' I said as calmly as I could.

'*Leave?*' Rose looked incredulous. 'Why, Flora? *Why?* Are you not happy with us?'

I drew a deep breath; it was going to be far more difficult to tell them about Damien than to tell them I knew my mother's identity, I realized.

So I told Jerome of the scene I had witnessed in the woods between him and Irene. I saw Rose grow even more pale, so that her face was devoid of all colour, and she glanced sharply at Jerome, who sat impassively.

Rose looked at me; there were tears in her eyes, and her voice was so soft that I scarcely heard the words.

'It isn't true, is it, Flora?' she begged piteously.

'It *is* true that I have very strong feelings for Damien,' I said, staring down at my hands clasped, trembling, in my lap. 'He also entertains strong feelings for me. I have behaved foolishly and indiscreetly, but I have not misconducted myself in the way Irene believes. I feel that it is best for me to return to Bideford, where I shall be out of touch with him, and learn to forget him.'

Forget him? Never, I thought! I looked up and saw the terrible anguish in Rose's face.

'My dear Flora, you have no idea how unhappy I am to know that this situation has arisen,' Jerome said sadly.

'You *do* believe that I have not misconducted myself with Damien? That there have been no more than words and kisses between us — even though that, in itself, is a matter for shame on my part?' I whispered.

'Yes, I believe you. Irene is overwrought; Damien plans to leave her.'

'If her marriage has been so unhappy, surely that will please her?' I replied.

'You must surely be aware of the social stigma a woman suffers when her husband leaves her,' Jerome pointed out.

Rose lifted her head; I saw both fury and fear in her face.

'He shall not stay here?' she whispered. 'He shall *not!*'

'He is the owner of Seawinds,' Jerome reminded her quietly. 'Whatever we may feel about his conduct towards Flora, my dearest, we cannot compel him to leave the island.'

'Exactly,' I said briskly, 'It is best that *I* should leave. I have seen the island; I have been happy here, and shall take away pleasant memories with me. There is one more thing that I must tell you. I requested my solicitor to send my birth certificate, and he did so. I know that I am Lavinia Jessel's daughter.'

Rose was the first to break the silence. She asked, very quietly:

'What made you suspect the truth?'

'Your — great affection for me. I *wondered*, greatly; then it occurred to me that my mother had always been reticent about her youth.'

'She did not want you to know,' Jerome said heavily. 'She went to great lengths to keep it from you because she was a proud and sensitive woman. There was an account of the accident in the newspapers, and when Wilfrid Brandon made it clear to everyone that he blamed her entirely for what happened, she suffered agonies of mind.'

'My father was a hypocrite,' Rose said, with intense

bitterness. 'Poor, poor Vinnie!' She bent her head, crying softly. 'I wanted so much to make it up to her. I traced her to the nursing home. Richard — your father, Flora — was shocked and distressed about it all; he showed her great compassion and understanding.'

'Did he marry her from pity?' I asked.

'No.' The tears were still falling, and I saw the almost iron grip of Jerome's fingers on hers. 'The first woman in your father's life was Sara Trehearne, who married Edwin's father. Caring for your mother healed the wound for Richard.'

'When Richard and your mother were married in Bristol, I attended the ceremony, at your father's request,' Jerome told me. 'Rose kept in touch with your mother; she even went to visit her occasionally.'

I smiled tiredly.

'I knew. She wouldn't let us meet, would she, Rose? In case I discovered the truth. If only she had told me; I would have understood.'

'Would you?' Jerome asked drily. 'You were only fourteen when she died. She was very happy with your father. She said her marriage had brought her contentment, peace of mind and a beloved daughter. She needed nothing more.'

I felt a tightness within my throat, a heavy weight behind my eyelids; I said gently to Rose:

'You were kind to my mother; for that, you have my gratitude, always.'

She was tensed; taut and nervous, as though she held on to her self-control with immense difficulty.

'If I had stayed with Vinnie, that day, the accident would not have happened,' she whispered forlornly.

'My mother would not wish you to blame yourself,' I assured her.

She smiled; a tired little smile that ended on a sigh.

'She told me , often, that I should not feel guilty; but if *only* I had seen that Vinnie was not fit to look after Edith,' she answered sadly.

'It is all over. I'm glad I know the truth about my mother,' I told her. 'Does anyone else know it?'

Out of the small silence, Jerome said quietly:

'Yes. Edwin. His father was always anxious to patch up the old quarrel with your father, and wrote, many years ago. The letter was not answered. He was worried, and had some enquiries made, as a result of which he discovered the truth. He told Edwin; but Edwin is aware that your mother wished you to remain in ignorance, and he would never betray her.'

So Damien did not know. Nor Irene. Nor Bella and Ruan. Well, none of it was important, now; I had one last task to fulfil.

'You thought I was in need of employment, when my father died,' I said.

'Yes,' answered Rose, 'though your home seemed comfortable enough to me, I knew nothing of your father's finances, nor did I ever expect your mother to discuss them with me. I assumed you were left without means when your father died. It is not an unusual situation.'

'I have not been honest with you,' I said frankly. 'My father was a rich man — I did not know the extent of his wealth until his death. You assumed I was penniless, and I did not correct the mistake because I wanted to come here on my own merits, not as an heiress. It was cheating, though; you pay me a generous wage, which I must return.'

For the first time that afternoon, Jerome really smiled.

'My dear child, I am delighted to know you are provided for; as for your wages, you have earned them. Keep them!'

'Dear Flora, I do not want you to leave here,' Rose said, still looking unhappy.

'It is for the best,' I insisted firmly.

'Stay a little longer,' she urged. 'A week or two.'

I bent my head, lost; ashamed of my weakness.

'Another two weeks, then,' I whispered, vowing not to be alone with Damien.

'Never let the past make you unhappy,' Jerome told me. 'Your mother put the past behind her and found happiness; as, one day, you will.'

'I shall never marry,' I told him.

'Why on earth not?'

'Because I shall be wooed for my fortune, not for my face,' I replied.

'You underestimate yourself, dear Flora,' Rose told me.

The events of the day had exhausted me; I pleaded a headache and asked to be excused from putting in an appearance at dinner. I went to the cottage and Anne brought a supper-tray to my room.

Bella Careena came to see me, with some eau-de-cologne; she looked concerned and I realized how much I was going to miss her; from uncertain beginnings, we were progressing towards a good friendship, and I hoped Rose would not tell her daughter, until the last possible moment, that I was leaving the island.

'Mama says you are not feeling well,' said Bella, patting cologne on to my throbbing temples.

'It's the heat,' I said, with a smile.

'I should go to bed, if I were you,' she said briskly, as though I was the child, and she was the adult. 'You'll feel better in the morning.'

I smiled at her, wished her goodnight, and decided to take her advice; but I could not sleep, and tossed in my bed most of the night.

I didn't want any breakfast, though I made a pretence of eating some, under the watchful eyes of Bella and Nanny Radford. Afterwards, I went for a walk to the folly.

I went into the church and sat there, staring up at the stained glass window; I could find no peace, and I knew it was my own fault. I came out into the sunshine again, and read the lovely inscription on the tomb of Ann Churnock.

I didn't want to return either to the House of the Four Winds or to the cottage. The desire to be out-of-doors with my thoughts had never been so strong. I walked on past the cottage, past the house, and came to the clearing where the folly stood.

The door was open; a figure stood at the top, staring at the tall firs that reached to meet the sky; when he saw me, he leaned over the stone parapet and cupped his hands around his mouth.

'Come up, Flora! Come and see what I see!'

'No!' I called back.

'Ah, I forgot; you dislike heights; but you will be safe with me.'

The voice was teasing, tantalising; Edwin was leaning over, beckoning, and I was tired of my own company.

It wasn't such a long climb, after all; I took it slowly, refusing to think about the height of the tower. I thought about other things; preparations for Ruan's celebrations, already far advanced. The flowers planned, the caterers' menu approved, dust sheets being taken from furniture in rooms not used, the whirr of a sewing machine as Miss Hyams worked against the clock; and I would not be here to see any of it.

Edwin waited at the top, an unfathomable expression in his eyes.

'Well done, Flora. I said you had courage!'

'What is it you see from here?' I asked impatiently.

'Look!' he said, standing close to me, and pointing upwards. 'Look at the tip of that fir. What do *you* see?'

'Only a bird,' I told him, disappointed.

'A sparrowhawk; it is not every day that one sees a sparrowhawk.'

I looked again; it was a large bird, sitting motionless against the blue sky; slowly it turned its head in our direction, and I saw the bright, searching eyes, the cruelly curved beak. There was something repellent about it, and I shivered.

'There is a nest of young sparrowhawks in the tree,' Edwin told me. 'The father hunts for food, and carries it back in his claws.'

'I don't like birds of prey,' I told him.

'In their way, they are fascinating, Flora. They wait and they watch, and nothing deflects them from that waiting and watching; when they are ready, they swoop, silently, on their prey.'

'Some defenceless bird or mouse, I suppose.'

'That is nature; nature is cruel.'

I felt sick; and suddenly giddy. The panorama of the island was spread around me, like a great carpet; trees, buildings, church tower, the two houses and Bella Careena's cottage, the blue girdle of water encircling it all and the green hump of the mainland.

Edwin put an arm about my shoulders, gripping me so tightly that I could not move away. Behind me was the winding stair; in front of me, a long drop to the ground. The parapet was only waist-high; I was afraid, and fought it back. I would not let Edwin Trehearne see fear in my face.

'Isn't it a beautiful sight?' he murmured.

'Yes,' I said quietly.

'From here, you can see it all, the whole island, the people coming and going about their business. You must never be afraid of heights — or depths, Flora. The view from the heights is always wonderful; as for the depths, they teach us to climb up to the sun.'

'Are you trying to tell me something?' I asked him.

'Perhaps. A riddle for you to read. Are you bored? Shall I entertain you instead with stories of the escapades of my French grandmother, who outwitted her enemies and donned a dozen different disguises along the route of her escape to England? Perhaps this is no time for frivolous tales. You look sad, Flora Belle!'

I looked up into the face so near my own; there was no mockery in it, though his brown eyes were alert and watchful.

'You know who I am,' I said.

'Indeed I do. You are Miss Flora P. Lindsay, who does not intend to satisfy my curiosity about her middle name.

You are a stubborn, self-willed, courageous, unpredictable young woman, who is just beginning to discover what life is all about.'

'That isn't what I meant. You know that I am Lavinia Jessel's daughter.'

'Yes,' he said calmly. 'How did *you* come upon the truth?'

I told him; he listened in silence. Finally, he said:

'I was a boy of thirteen when it happened, Flora. I didn't know your mother well, but I met her a few times, and I felt sorry for her. It was natural that she should want you to be kept in ignorance about the events of that terrible day. Remember, the knowledge was kept from you for the best of reasons. Now you know; and it is in the way you accept such things that you either enrich or impoverish your life.'

'I know little enough about life, yet,' I admitted wryly.

'True. You are now being given the opportunity to learn. Before you know life, you must know yourself; and your heart. You must first learn to separate love from mere infatuation.'

'You think I am merely infatuated with Damien, don't you?' I cried bitterly.

'I *know* that you are. No one can help you; it is a jungle through which you must hack your own way.'

'Oh wise Edwin, who has never felt the need of a woman's love!' I retorted bitterly.

'Who told you that?' His voice was dangerously quiet.

'Ruan. He says you have never needed a wife.'

'That is true. I have not been celibate, like a monk, Flora.' His voice was still soft. 'I have had mistresses; enjoyed women's bodies as well as their minds, but never lied to them with pretences of love, and never treated them badly.'

'And never truly loved?' I cried triumphantly.

'You are wrong, you know; I love *you*. Much good will it do me. Have your victory, Flora!' His voice was suddenly savage. 'I shall not speak of this again. Enjoy Damien

134

whilst you may; he reminds me of the sparrowhawk, who watches and waits, with infinite patience, for the right moment to swoop on his prey!'

Angrily, I pulled free of his encircling arm. He did not love me; he mocked me.

He was a stranger; hard, ice-cold. He went ahead of me down the stairs, and I followed, my legs trembling. I felt utterly exhausted.

In spite of my vow not to be alone with Damien, there came a time, two days later, when I could not avoid him. It was just before dinner, at Four Winds; he was alone in the drawing-room when I arrived, standing with his back to the room, hands clasped behind him, as he stared out into the velvet night.

My heart beat fast; the blood thundered in my pulses, as he turned and smiled at me.

'*Flora*!' He came across, holding out his hands; when I stood helpless before him, not attempting to touch those outstretched hands, he frowned and said softly:

'You have been avoiding me; why?'

'You know why,' I stammered. 'To meet will only make an impossible situation worse.'

'Someone has been talking to you,' he said shrewdly, his eyes narrowing. 'Rose, perhaps?'

I shook my head, saying nothing. I thought he looked like one of the statues in the Temple of Four Winds come to life. I knew that if he commanded me to come away with him, I would have gone to the edge of the world and beyond.

His smile was warm and slow; it hinted at possibilities I dared not consider, at a future I could not contemplate.

'Only be patient,' he said softly. 'Be patient and trust me.'

'I am going away,' I told him, with all the strength I could muster.

'When?'

'In a little while. It is best,' I said.

'It is nonsense!' he retorted. 'Stay for Ruan's coming-of-age celebrations! *Then* we shall see if you want to leave the island!'

'I don't understand,' I stammered.

'You will understand everything, one day.' Gently, he stroked my cheek with a fingertip, adding:

'I tell you, Flora, that soon, Irene will have no part in our lives. Only be patient for a little while longer. Bella Careena is about to add one more chapter to its strange history, and I want you to be there to see it!'

Chapter 9

ROSE SAID THAT if she had decided to stay with Vinnie on that fateful day, Edith might not have died; had she done so, it is probable that I would never have come to the island, at all. Fate hangs by very slender threads; and had I not got up earlier than usual, a couple of days after my strange conversation with Damien, then the ending to my own story might well have been different.

The night had been clammy; the east was still pearl grey when I arose from my bed, dressed, and decided I needed to walk in the fresh air, before anyone was about.

I let myself quietly out of the house; it did not much matter which direction I took: north, east, south or west. I walked aimlessly for a little while, and when I saw Damien, he was ahead of me, beyond the trees that shielded me, walking due east in the direction of the Sun Grotto.

I cannot say what utter madness possessed me, then, making me follow him. I was lost to all thoughts of modesty or dignity; I forgot my vow I had made to myself.

I only knew that I wanted to be alone with him, for one last time. Such was the strength of my feelings for him that I cared for nothing except my own desires.

I wondered if he went alone to the Sun Grotto every morning, hoping that I would join him; the thought made my heart leap. I decided I would follow him, surprise him, sit and talk with him awhile; I tried to imagine his delight when he saw me . . .

Perhaps, in my heart, I believed in the promise he had made that Irene would not always come between us, that there would be happiness in the future; though how he could hope to keep such a promise, I did not know . . .

I knew that I *had* to talk to him; now, before I left the island for ever.

The trees thinned out as he reached the little headland that led to the Grotto. Now there were only stunted bushes, growing low to the ground, crouched against the skyline.

I thought how splendid Damien looked; he was casually dressed in silk shirt, riding breeches and boots. I hugged to myself the thought of creeping up to surprise him, calling his name softly, seeing him turn.

He walked to the tip of the little headland, and then dropped down slightly on to the beach below. Soundlessly, I sped along the sandy little path between the furze and bushes, until I was right above him.

I looked down on a tall, well-built figure, a head of bright curls; Damien sat on a flat slab of rock near the grotto entrance, looking relaxed, as he stared out to sea. The sun was not yet up, the sea was like wrinkled grey silk; the tide was going out, and showed the wet, ribbed sand, where a couple of seagulls strutted, looking for food.

I knew a moment of pure delight; a delicious, feminine sense of power in watching whilst he remained unaware of my presence.

As I edged closer to the very edge of the low cliff, and drew breath to call his name, I saw his head jerk sharply to the right, as though he had seen someone.

He rose to his feet; still with a leisurely air, as though he had all the time in the world, and turned towards the figure walking along the wet sand at the water's edge, towards him.

I recognised her at once; it was Rose.

She walked slowly, as though she was very tired; her golden hair fell loosely about her face; she wore a plain, dark dress and her shoulders drooped. She was quite unlike the regal figure who had stood beside her husband on the terrace of the House of the Four Winds, welcoming me . . .

Damien laughed and held out his arms to her; crouched against the bushes, I stared at her in utter disbelief.

Rose stopped dead, just out of reach of his arms; she glanced at him scornfully.

'Have you no welcome for me, dear heart?' he mocked softly.

'None,' she said flatly. 'I asked you to meet me here because it is the one place where there is no possibility of our being overheard. Unless, of course, you have an assignment with Flora?'

His teeth showed white in his handsome face; he threw back his head and laughed.

'Flora? She is too timid to turn her desires into reality!' he retorted. 'She loves me to distraction, my dear Rose, but fears both herself and the conventions!'

'She is merely infatuated with you, though she does not know it, yet,' Rose retorted.

'You are wrong, Rose. She has a great and consuming passion for me. It would be easy to seduce her, but the time has not yet come. When that time does come, it will be an enjoyable experience, for us both. I find her desirable. A woman of spirit. Very like you, my love. Shall we go into the grotto to discuss whatever it is you are so anxious to talk to me about? *Shall* we, Rose? And then make love there, as we did all those years ago?'

'You are vile!' she choked. 'You spoiled the grotto for me!'

138

'You did not think so, then. You were ardent and willing, on the day you conceived Ruan!' he jibed.

'With your son in my womb, I knew I hated you!' she retorted fiercely, pushing back the bands of hair from her face. 'The spell you had over me was broken, then! Would to God I had never let you know he *was* your son! At least he does not resemble you in any way! How I hate you still!'

'Pity and hatred are both akin to love!' he replied, laughing.

'Don't harm Flora, please,' she said quietly.

'Ah! If I did, you would bear double guilt, wouldn't you? I know very well whose daughter she is, Rose. It was *I* who found the locket, and recognised the photograph.'

'Was it you, also, who damaged it and threw it into the grotto?' she demanded angrily.

'What else did you expect me to do? Return it to her? I was too furious, Rose. Furious that you should have brought Vinnie's daughter here. It was indiscreet of you; if she asks too many questions, you might decide, in your folly, to answer them; and that would never do.'

I saw a peculiar expression cross her face, gone in an instant. I stayed immobile, my body numb, my mind alive, raging in agony, disbelief and horror . . .

'Now. Why did you ask me to meet you here today?' he demanded curtly.

I saw her steady herself with an effort; when she spoke, her voice was so low that I could only just catch the words.

'I have come to beg you not to announce to everyone, at Ruan's coming-of-age Ball, that you are his father!'

'You can't cheat me of the pleasure I have waited so long to taste!' he retorted. 'I told you, long ago, that one day I would revenge your rejection of me. You broke the vows we made.

'That is absurd. We were sixteen years old, hardly more than children.'

'We made vows,' he insisted, eyes narrowed. 'I wanted you, Rose; you and the island. The island was Jerome's, but I promised myself I would get it back from him one day; but you married *him*, a man old enough to be your father! You didn't love *him*!'

I heard the sneer in his voice; but the look on her face as she answered, set her apart from him in a way that nothing else could have done.

'No, I didn't love him, then. It grew slowly, through the years; it began to grow after Ruan was born when I suffered agonies of guilt, seeing Jerome's delight in the child he thought was his son. You know nothing of love and everything of passion.'

'You rejected me; damn you, Rose! You let your father send me away, like a beggar. *You* had money, position, the island that should have been mine — and *my* son. I had — *Irene*!' He laughed derisively.

'You married her for her money and squandered it!' Rose replied evenly.

'Squandered it? No. I made prudent investments with the money I persuaded her to part with, and they have served me well. I may not be able to match Jerome's wealth, but I am, as they say, "comfortably placed". Whereas Irene is almost penniless; a reversal of fortune that causes her some distress.'

'You *are* evil!' she said. 'You've heaped terrible humiliation on Irene!'

'As I will upon Jerome!' he cried triumphantly.

'No, Damien! His heart is not strong. The shock could prove fatal!'

'I told you, the day I arrived here for the celebrations, that I would take the revenge I'd always promised myself!' he retorted.

'What good will it do you? Ruan will hate you!'

'You, too, my dear. Who will hate you most, I wonder — Jerome or Ruan?'

He was supremely arrogant; utterly self-assured. Rose's voice was quiet and controlled.

'Jerome means more to me than anyone else in the world. There is one way in which I can stop you from making your announcement.'

'Tell me!' he jeered.

'Years ago, my father made me take a solemn oath on his bible. He made me swear that I would never tell a living soul what really happened on the afternoon that Edith died. I have never broken that vow; but I *shall* do so, if you hurt Jerome. I shall make public the fact that *you* killed Edith!'

I thought I had suffered all the shocks my mind could bear. I was wrong; but I felt curiously detached, as though I was watching a play on a stage. Damien Ashley had killed Edith Freemantle . . .

'Do you imagine anyone will be interested after twenty-five years?' he jeered.

'The authorities will listen with great interest to my tale.'

'And discount it; you have no proof, no witnesses. It will sound like the petty spite of a woman who has been publicly denounced as a whore!'

'They *will* listen,' she replied determinedly. 'I shall *make* them listen to me! You *did* kill her, Damien; you know you did!'

'It was an accident!' he flung at her.

'It was *not*! She came down to the grotto and saw us there, and started shouting that she would tell papa. You pushed her . . .'

'She was taunting us, just as she taunted Vinnie. You were hysterical! All I wanted to do was get rid of her . . .'

'You climbed down afterwards, and saw that she was dead, Damien. You told me you were going to get away in your boat, and come back to Easter that evening as though you had been sailing all day. You climbed up and saw poor Vinnie lying on the path, and said we were lucky, that no one would ever know the truth.'

'How well you remember it all! However, your threat is empty, Rose. Even if you are believed, you must produce proof; and you have none.'

I saw, in her face, the realization that he was right; the tears ran down her cheeks. She looked at him imploringly.

It shocked me to see Rose beg for mercy from this man.

'Please don't hurt Jerome!' she pleaded.

'Jerome! *Jerome!*' he cried savagely. 'Do you think I care about *him*! He's had his precious island all these years, but it is *my* son who will inherit it! You told me that you were Mistress of Bella Careena when I said that you had no right to invite Flora here! Did you plan that she should marry Ruan — to spite me?'

'No!' she replied. 'I did not. To me, Ruan *is* Jerome's son, not yours!'

'I will decide whom Ruan shall marry,' Damien said coolly. 'I shall control his future, on this island.'

'You are mad!' she told him contemptuously. 'Ruan has a will of his own!'

'I am his father!' It was a triumphant hymn, coming from Damien's lips, on the still morning air. 'Irene will go back to London; when Jerome is dead, and Bella has gone away — and *I* shall see to it that she leaves here — then you may stay or go, as you wish. Perhaps I will let you live at Seawinds. Flora, if she chooses, shall live with me at the House of the Four Winds.'

'Oh, God!' she whispered, bowing her head. 'Truly you are mad, Damien!'

'I have waited so long!' he said, softly and yearningly. 'All these years. You thought I had forgotten, didn't you, Rose?'

She stared at him, for a moment; then she turned and walked swiftly along the beach. Her head was still bowed, her bright hair lay like a shawl over her shoulders.

I was jerked sharply back to reality by the realization that Damien would probably return by the way he had come to the grotto, and find me there.

I scrambled quickly to my feet, the skirt of my dress caught fast on a thorny branch. Frightened, I bent and tugged it free, tearing the material. I left a scrap of the material hanging on the bush, as I began to run, crouching low, not looking back until I came to the place where the path entered the belt of trees.

From the shelter of the trees, I looked back; there was no sign of Damien; however, I didn't slacken speed. I went on, under the green boughs, and across the clearing where the tower stood sentinel. Involuntarily, I glanced upwards, but there was no sign of the sparrowhawk, the bird that waits for the right moment before swooping down silently on its victim.

Head bent, my feet carrying me as fast as my laboured breath would allow, I made for the cottage. It was still very early, and no one was about as I went up to my room. I collapsed on the bed, shivering, sobbing for breath. The morning was still grey and the sun had not risen in the east; it was hidden behind a thick bank of humid cloud.

The golden days had come to an end.

The tears ran down my cheeks. I suddenly hated Rose, I hated Damien, and most of all I hated my own stupidity and the fact that Edwin Trehearne had been right in his assessment of me.

I was composed when Bella Careena came to my room. I had learned in the past hour what Rose had long before learned: that it is possible to contain terrible anguish within oneself and present a calm, unruffled surface to the world.

At breakfast, Nanny Radford said:

'Mr Jardine's had a nasty fall, I hear. Got up early this morning and slipped in his bedroom. Mrs Jardine was there; no bones broken, thank goodness, and he's a bit shook up. Hurt his back. Bruised it, he said, and he won't let Mrs Jardine send for a doctor. Stubborn, that one . . . '

After breakfast, Bella Careena insisted on going straight to her father. I followed slowly. The air was thick and cloying, and the heavy sky seemed to press down upon me like an iron weight. My hands and face were damp with perspiration, every movement was an effort, and my clothes clung to me most uncomfortably.

Though I knew that I moved and spoke normally, I was still in a state of shock. When I saw Damien standing on the terrace of Four Winds, I could scarcely breathe. I

143

forced myself to walk slowly towards him, to look at him, and wish him good-day.

He smiled charmingly.

'Flora, you don't look yourself,' he said.

'I am very well, thank you.'

'There will be a storm,' he said, looking up at the sky.

He stood as still as one of the statues in the Temple of the Four Winds; only a little wind, blowing in from the sea, lifted the thick gold curls on his forehead.

'I hear that Jerome has met with an accident,' he added.

'Yes. I am going to Rose now,' I told him.

He made no attempt to detain me as I moved past him. I had been hot; now I was so cold that I felt as though I was encased in a sheet of ice. I went upstairs, and met Rose outside Jerome's room.

I asked her how he was.

'He's resting,' she said. 'He wrenched his back, and refuses to have Dr Samuels. He'll have to stay in bed for a few days.'

I said heavily:

'I want to talk to you, please, Rose.'

'Come to my sitting room,' she said. 'Bella Careena and Ruan are with Jerome. They'll keep him amused for half an hour.'

Half an hour? Was that long enough to tell her how much I despised her for a silence that had lasted twenty-five years and robbed my mother of her good name?

She sat upright on a green velvet chair, hands folded in her lap, and I sat opposite her. I saw the way her fingertips moved restlessly, as though they would not be quiet.

'The air is so still that it seems as though the world has stopped breathing,' she said. 'Flora, something is wrong; what is it?'

'This morning, I followed Damien to the Grotto of the Sun,' I told her flatly. 'I hid behind the bushes to surprise him, and then you came. I heard everything that passed between you. You let my mother be blamed for Edith's death all these years, yet you knew Damien had killed her!'

'Oh, dear God!' she whispered brokenly. 'Oh, Flora, I am sorry!'

'*Sorry?*' I said scornfully.

Her head was bent; her fingers plucked at the material of her skirt, and her voice shook.

'You do not know the anguish and guilt I have suffered through the years, Flora,' she whispered. 'If you knew, you would not condemn me. I believed it to be the price I paid for my happiness with my husband. There *were* times when I forgot . . . '

'*Forgot?* You didn't really care about my mother . . . !'

'Oh yes, I did, Flora! I have *always* cared. I went straight to my father and told him the truth. He wasn't angry because I had disgraced myself, being found by Edith in a compromising situation with Damien; oh no! He was afraid that if there was any scandal or suspicion attached to Edith's death, he wouldn't get a penny of her money. He said if anyone discovered the truth he would see to it that Damien was charged with murder and spent a lifetime in prison. I was sixteen years old, Flora. I believed him. He made me swear a solemn oath.'

'That oath wasn't binding, under the circumstances!' I retorted scornfully.

'I believed it to be so, Flora.'

'Perhaps you were so infatuated with Damien that you were afraid of what would happen to *him* if the truth was known!' I said bitterly.

She lifted her head and looked at me; there was sorrow, but no anger, in the beautiful blue eyes.

'Yes. I *was* infatuated. Even after I married Jerome at my father's insistence. Until the day, two years after our marriage, when Jerome was away, and Damien came to the island for the first time since it all happened. Three weeks later, when Jerome returned, I knew I was pregnant. If only I had not hurled the truth at Damien then, telling him I never wanted to see him again! Ruan doesn't resemble him, even in features; but he *is* Damien's son, and that has been another burden of guilt that I have carried.'

'You should have told Jerome the whole truth then!' I said.

'It is easy to be wise in maturity. I didn't know what to do! All these years, it has seemed as though Ruan was truly Jerome's son. Damien married Irene, and I believed, then, that the whole unhappy business was ended.'

'Why was Damien on the island the day that Edith died?' I asked.

'He knew we were going for a picnic. My father disapproved of our friendship so we used to meet when we could, in secret. It seemed so wonderful, so exciting, then. Damien sailed his boat to the bay . . . you heard what he said: we made vows in the chapel, then we went to the cave. I heard Edith coming along singing her silly rhyme about Plain Jane out in the rain . . . Vinnie hated it . . . I heard Vinnie shout at her, and Edith was laughing . . . then Edith came down the path and ran into the grotto . . . Damien was about to . . . make love to me, and he was furious with her . . . It *was* an accident, I suppose . . .'

She looked piteously at me. All the hate ran out of me. My mother wouldn't have wanted me to feel bitterness towards Rose, who had been a sixteen-year-old girl, trapped like a fly in a spider's web of deceit that had wound its threads more tightly around her through the years. She had been at the mercy of one man's obsession and another man's greed, and had paid dearly for both.

'Did you try to kill Damien?' I asked suddenly.

She looked dumbfounded.

'Never! Why?'

'I was thinking of the arrow shot at us, when we were on the lake; and of the falling statue . . . but then, you would have *seen* it wasn't Damien, but me, in the temple . . . oh, I don't understand . . .'

'If I say that I wish with all my heart and soul that Damien *was* dead, you will think I am wicked, I suppose?'

146

'Wicked? No, Rose. It's a perfectly natural wish, even if it's morally wrong. You're caught in a trap.'

'Of my own making!' she said, with intense bitterness. 'I would not willingly have forfeited your friendship, Flora.'

'You haven't forfeited it. I don't hate you. Hatred belongs to people like Damien, who feed it . . . what is to be done, though? If Damien keeps his promise, the shock of knowing the truth will kill Jerome. But will you do as you told him you would, and tell the truth about the day in the Shell Grotto?'

She lifted a weary, tear-streaked face.

'You heard what he said! I have no witnesses, no proof! Oh, Flora, every day the threat that Damien has made comes closer, and every day I pray for a miracle!'

'If Jerome loves you as much as you say he does, then he will forgive you for what happened,' I told her gently.

'He will forgive, Flora; but the damage will have been done and if the shock should prove too great for him, as well it may, of what use will forgiveness be to me?'

I heard the wretchedness of her cry. I went over to her, put my arms around her, and said that there was time yet to find a solution. She didn't believe me, but at least I felt she was comforted a little.

When I went downstairs, Damien was still on the terrace, walking up and down. He looked at me sharply as I stepped out into the air.

'There is thunder in the distance, and I can smell rain,' he said. 'Let us hope the storm blows itself out today and does not spoil tomorrow's festivities.'

'What festivities?' I asked.

'The yearly fair at Easter and Tolfrey. It's quite a big affair. All the servants who can be spared will attend. Ruan is going. The boat will take them over tomorrow morning and bring them back late tomorrow night,' he said.

I turned and almost ran from him. Halfway across to the cottage, I looked over my shoulder. He was still standing on the terrace, watching me.

The storm broke in all its fury an hour later. In the stillness that preceded the storm I felt a quality of menace about the island; the sleeping cat, curled in the sun, was wide-awake, claws out.

The rain came, pattering heavily through the trees; and then the wind that comes before a storm, making the trees toss their heads wildly, like restive horses. Lightning cut the clouds apart as it flew, jagged and brilliant, from end to end of the sky; the thunder raged above us, and the sea raced angrily inshore, the waves white-capped. Bella Careena enjoyed it, Nanny Radford was frankly terrified.

It lasted for a couple of hours, then the thunder rolled away over the Dorset coast, and the rain stopped; but the sky remained ominously heavy.

I performed several small services for Rose and for Nanny Radford; I stood patiently whilst Miss Hyams fitted my gowns, and all the time an idea was growing, taking shape, becoming feasible . . .

I did not want to go to dinner that evening at the House of the Four Winds, but Rose pleaded with me to put in an appearance.

'I shall be glad of your support, Flora,' she told me wistfully. 'It is becoming daily more difficult to hide what I feel . . .'

I had three hours before I needed to dress for dinner; it was long enough.

Damien had said scathingly to Rose that her testimony against him would be useless because she had no witnesses and no proof; but my letter to Alexander Arkwright would be a report of facts that I had overheard in the Sun Grotto, and would state, in detail, the admission that Damien had made about Edith's death.

In my letter, I said nothing about Rose's reason for

being in the Shell Grotto on the day Edith died, nor did I mention the circumstances surrounding Ruan's conception. I cherished a hope that those facts might never be made public — even though it was a faint hope.

I told Alexander Arkwright that I had discovered my mother's identity, and wished to clear her name, hence the reason for my letter; I instructed him that enquiries and investigations were to be made with all speed, and also informed him that Mr Damien Ashley was not aware that I knew of his part in Edith's death.

My real reason for the letter went much deeper; investigations would mean that Damien would undoubtedly have to leave the island before the coming-of-age celebrations began. Rose would have to back up my evidence, but who would condemn her for keeping silent for so many years after she had sworn, on oath, never to reveal the truth? The fact that she now had to reveal it would undoubtedly only evoke feelings of sympathy. Jerome would be shocked; but the shock would be less than the discovery of his wife's infidelity.

The idea I had mulled over all day seemed to me to be bold and clever; certainly it would take Damien by complete surprise. Let him shout to the world, *afterwards*, that Ruan was his son! The world would look upon it as a desire for revenge, the tables would be neatly and completely turned and disaster might yet be averted; or so I believed.

When at last, I was satisfied with the letter, I folded it, put it in an envelope and sealed it firmly. Tomorrow, I thought, it will be on its way to Bideford.

Chapter 10

I HAD LITTLE APPETITE for dinner that evening. There were seven of us: Rose and Edwin, Damien and Irene, Bella Careena, Ruan and myself.

We dined indoors; the weather was cooler, with a wind blowing in from the sea; lightning still flickered far out across the water and thunder grumbled in the distance.

Both Damien and Ruan were attentive to me, and I managed to maintain conversation of a light-hearted nature that didn't tax me too much.

As for Irene, she surprised us all by her animation. She who was usually so pale and so quiet, had a feverish gaiety about her.

'Damien, my dearest, why do you not join me at the butts more often? With a little practice, your skill with the arrows would almost match mine!' she said gaily.

'I have no desire to match your skill at archery, my dear Irene,' Damien retorted smoothly. 'I prefer a gun.'

'Ah yes!' she murmured. 'The flight of a bullet or the flight of an arrow — what is the difference, if the target is the same? The purpose of both is to kill.'

'Not on this island!' Rose said firmly.

'So we practise for a killing we shall never make. A sad waste of talent, I think,' Irene replied.

'Whom do you wish to kill?' Edwin asked her, with interest.

Her eyes were wide, brilliant, and unfocussed.

'Why, no one, Edwin. I merely say it is a waste of talent if weapons are not used for the purpose for which they were intended!' she replied.

'Did you kill the peacock?' Bella Careena asked bluntly.

There was dead silence. Rose looked reprovingly at her daughter, Ruan was aghast.

'Yes,' Irene replied. 'I killed it.'

The silence was electric. I saw the look on the faces of the two servants who were waiting with the serving dishes; Irene seemed to enjoy the attention she was causing.

'I was going to Seawinds,' she said gaily. 'As I came near Laurie's forge, I remembered you and Miss Lindsay were going to spend an afternoon on the lake, Damien. I was going to ask Laurie for an arrow and a bow, but he wasn't there, so I took them. I saw you getting out of the boat with Miss Lindsay, and I wanted to frighten you. No, that isn't true; I wanted to kill *you*, Damien. After all, you have many times wished *me* dead, and stated so; is that not true?'

The silence was terrifying; I could hear the drumbeats of my heart in my own ears.

Rose made a valiant attempt to retrieve the situation; she looked appalled.

'Irene, you must not say such things! You are ill . . . '

'*Ill?*' Irene shook her head, laughing. 'No, I am not, Rose. I am *well*!' She turned to me, and gave me a smile of unearthly brilliance. 'Dear Miss Lindsay, you have no *idea* what a narrow escape you had on the night of the party. You were waiting in the Temple of the Four Winds for my husband, were you not?'

'No!' I whispered, furious and horrified.

'Ah, but you *were*! The temptation was not to be resisted. To kill you or to frighten you . . . it made no difference . . . Have I not said before that you would be surprised at the strength in these wrists and arms, Miss Lindsay? I am not soft and weak as Damien would like to think!'

Edwin sprang to his feet with such speed that he overturned his glass of wine. The glass shattered and a stain spread across the white cloth.

'Flora could have been killed!' he said, his face white with anger.

'Exactly what I have said, my dear Edwin . . . '

With immense dignity, Rose stood up.

'Irene, you *are* ill; much more ill than you realize. You must return to Seawinds and go to bed . . . you need to be properly cared for . . . '

Irene shook her head, smiling; her smile had a vague quality, and I felt chilled. Damien's face was like granite. He stood up, and said curtly:

'Come, Irene.'

Irene rose to her feet; she shook off Damien's arm, smiled again, wished us all goodnight, and informed her husband that she was quite capable of making her own way back to Seawinds.

However, Damien insisted upon accompanying her. The carriage was brought to the door, and one of the servants was sent to the farm for Mrs Clegg. Rose instructed two maids to clear away the rest of the meal. No one had any appetite.

It was a silent party that gathered in the drawing room. Coffee was served to us, and the servants left us alone. Only then did Rose speak.

'Poor Irene!' she whispered. 'How dreadful. Oh, how *dreadful*!'

'A mental breakdown,' Edwin said shortly. 'Caused by Damien's treatment of her, I imagine.'

'It's the curse of the peacocks,' Bella Careena declared.

'Oh, Bella, that's stupid nonsense!' Rose cried sharply.

Edwin stood up and said calmly:

'It has been a distressing evening. I suggest that an early night would be of benefit to us all.'

Rose nodded, relief in her face.

'The boat will leave at eight o'clock tomorrow morning,' she said. 'As you are going to Dorchester on business, Edwin, you may like to take the early boat. It will cross again at noon, with the rest of the servants who are going to the fair.'

'Will the mail go out as usual, at four o'clock?' I asked.

'Not tomorrow. It will go at eight — and again at noon.'

'I have a letter,' I said. 'I should like it to be on its way as soon as possible.'

'Then have it here by half-past seven for Hawkins to put in his satchel,' Rose told me.

I had a restless night. The thought that Irene had tried to kill me was so incredible that I found it difficult to believe. But I knew that Edwin was right. Damien, by his treatment of his wife, had lit a fire that had smouldered on and finally burst into flame.

I was up and dressed by seven o'clock next morning. It was raining hard and the skies were pewter-coloured. I felt sorry for the servants who were going to the fair. They had all looked forward to the outing, and only the older ones, like Nanny Radford, did not want to go.

I put on a cloak and turned up the hood; with my precious letter hidden under the cloak, I stepped out into the rain that was driving in relentlessly from the sea.

I did not expect to see Damien; but he was there, sheltering under the trees just beyond the house; I stared apprehensively at him; but there was nothing in his face to alarm me as he came up to me and said:

'I'm on my way to Clegg's farm; Mrs Clegg was good enough to spend the best part of the night with Irene.'

'How is Irene?' I asked, staring straight ahead, as I walked swiftly towards the house.

'Sleeping soundly. Mrs Clegg gave her a sedative. Irene's behaviour has been odd recently, and I have feared something like this might happen.'

I did not answer him; I hated him and had no desire to talk to him.

He insisted on coming to the house with me. My hands were shaking as I took the letter from my cloak and thrust it hastily into the big leather satchel lying on the table. I felt cold sweat break out along my forehead; Damien was standing in the hall talking to Hawkins.

By ten o'clock, it had stopped raining, though the skies remained heavy and there was a strong sea running.

Dr Samuels came over when the boat returned from its eight o'clock trip, and went straight to Seawinds.

Later I saw Rose; she told me that Dr Samuels had called on her after his visit to Seawinds, and had stated that Mrs Ashley seemed quite rational and had apologised profusely for her behaviour of the previous evening, saying that she had drunk a great deal of wine before coming to the House of the Four Winds.

I stared at Rose.

'It isn't true,' I said.

'No, it isn't. Dr Samuels seemed convinced, though. I believe he thought we were making a great fuss about nothing.' She looked uneasily at me. 'I repeated what Irene had said. He laughed and told me it was a highly dramatic piece of fantasy for which, undoubtedly, an excess of wine was responsible.'

Irene was being very cunning. I didn't like it. I wished the day was over, that Ruan and Edwin were back on the island. I felt isolated, and it was not a pleasant feeling . . .

Dr Samuels had left a supply of powders which were to be given to Irene if she became over-excited. He declined Rose's offer of lunch, and went back to the mainland at noon with the rest of the island servants.

Jerome was still confined to his bed. Dr Samuels had seen him and advised a further period of rest. Rose, Bella Careena and I had lunch together, and we were a silent trio; even Bella Careena seemed to have lost her usual good spirits. No one had seen Damien since he had come to the house with me, early that morning.

The wind rose after lunch it blew in sharp, squally gusts that gradually reached gale force as the tide turned and began to race in, breaking into great plumes of foam all along the shore.

At five o'clock, Rose said grimly:

'If this weather continues, the boat won't be able to come back this evening.'

154

I felt a terrible sense of loneliness. I wanted the boat to come back, I wanted Edwin, who had said "I love you" to a woman who hadn't listened . . .

'What will they do?' I asked.

'Oh, they'll stay at the Fortune, quite comfortably,' she told me.

The violence of the storm was terrifying. I thought it would lift the house and carry it bodily away. Bella Careena listened to the noise of the gale howling outside with a dreamy look on her face.

'The bells of Lost Atlantis are ringing under the sea,' she said.

'It's a pretty story, but I'm in no mood for your fancies,' I told her wryly.

'You're safe here,' she assured me. 'Quite safe.'

It was an evening on which the darkness would come early; the clouds were very low in the sky, racing in with the swollen seas.

After tea Bella Careena went upstairs to play chess with her father.

'I'll go back to the cottage,' I told Rose. 'Nanny Radford doesn't like being left on her own, especially when the weather is bad.'

Nanny was pleased to see me; she had lit a fire in her small sitting room, and was huddled over it, declaring that she had caught a cold and no wonder, the way the weather changed.

At seven o'clock, she went to bed; I looked out of the window at the lights burning in The House of the Four Winds, and wondered how long it would be before Bella Careena returned. The wind seemed to have dropped a little, I reflected thankfully. Perhaps the boat would get back.

When I heard the knock at the door, some time later, my heart missed a beat; Bella Careena would not have knocked . . . I opened the door.

Damien stood there; for a moment, I thought I was going to suffocate. This man, so tall, so handsome, had sent a child to her death, and held a woman to ransom for her folly . . . and a little while ago I had believed I loved him with all my heart.

'What is it?' I asked.

There was not a vestige of a smile on his face; he stared sombrely at me.

'It's Irene,' he said. 'She's very ill. I gave her a sedative this afternoon, but it seems to have had no effect. She's in a fever and delirious. There are only two elderly servants in the house, so I'm going to Clegg's farm for Lucy. Will you go to Seawinds, Flora? I can scarcely ask Rose.'

I looked at him suspiciously. I didn't trust him; but what harm could come to me, with two servants and Lucy Clegg in the house? Who else was there? At Four Winds there was only an elderly man, sick and confined to his bed, a girl of fourteen — and Rose. The island was shorn of its usual staff; Ruan and Edwin were away.

Nevertheless, I felt distinctly uneasy.

'It's a long walk in this weather, even if I take the short cuts,' I told him.

'Then wait here until I return with Lucy Clegg,' he said shortly. 'Though I would prefer that you went straight to Irene. I am desperately worried about her, in view of what happened last night.'

He turned and strode away, towards Clegg's Farm.

I fetched my cloak; I listened at Nanny's door; she was sound asleep. I scribbled a note for Bella Careena, telling her where I had gone, and let myself out of the cottage.

There was still plenty of daylight left; I hated walking under the trees, for it was dark there, but I made my way as fast as I could in the direction of Seawinds, remembering all the short cuts that Bella Careena had showed me.

I avoided looking at the ruined chapel; from there it was a short walk to the wide path that led to the Shell Grotto. I had to cross the path, pass under a short tunnel of trees, and then I would come out at the back of Seawinds.

He was waiting for me; at the end of the tunnel. He stepped into my path and his arms went around me like a vice. I screamed again and again, but the sound was borne away on the wind, and, somewhere, a peacock screamed in answer.

He hadn't been near Cleggs Farm! He had come back here, to wait for me!

I struggled fiercely against him; he held me closer, laughing. In the tunnel of trees, no one could see us.

'Why?' I panted furiously. '*Why*, Damien?'

'Because you are dangerous, Flora Lindsay. You wrote a letter, a very damning letter. I've read it with interest; and destroyed it. I've spent a lot of time watching you, Flora, ever since you were at the Sun Grotto!'

So he had seen me; he knew that I had all the information I needed to condemn him. My heart sank like a stone to the bottom of the pool.

'You weren't quick or clever enough!' he said contemptuously. 'I saw you running away; I found a piece of material on the bushes, torn from your dress. I asked Bella Careena what you did yesterday after tea. She said you were busy writing a letter. *That* interested me; so I watched again this morning, and saw how anxious you were to hide your letter away in the safety of the satchel that Hawkins took to the jetty. There was very little in the satchel, when I examined it — which I did, the moment you had left the house.'

I had failed; the bitterness of failure ousted every other feeling for a moment. Damien had won, he would create havoc worse than anything the storm could bring.

'Curiosity is a fine servant and a bad master, Flora,' he told me. 'It served me well, you must agree!'

'You can't keep *me* silent!' I cried defiantly. 'I know the truth! I shall tell it . . .'

'No. You will be dead by the time they start looking for you,' he said calmly.

Horror filled me, and a frantic desire to escape from that vice-like grip, to run and run . . .

He only held me tighter; his voice was almost playful.

'On such a night, who will be surprised that there is a casualty of the storm?'

I bent my head back as far as it would go, glaring at him.

'I left a note for Bella Careena, telling her I was going to Seawinds,' I told him.

'It will be some time, yet, before she finds it. It won't unduly alarm her, for she will think you are at Seawinds. When they come looking for you, *I* shall be there, with Irene whom I have not left unattended. Who can disprove my story? In years to come, Bella Careena will spin another pretty tale to prove that the island is cursed; and you, Flora, will be *dead*!'

He turned me round with such violence that I almost over-balanced and pinned my arms behind my back in an agonisingly painful grip until tears ran down my cheeks. He thrust me in front of him, forcing me to walk back along the tunnel to the path that led to the Shell Grotto.

'Vinnie's daughter!' he cried. 'What a fitting end for the daughter of the governess! I would have made you my mistress! We should both have enjoyed that; but your curiosity will sign your death-warrant!'

I knew what he intended to do, for he was forcing me to stumble in front of him along the path leading to the Shell Grotto; the path my mother had once walked, looking for Edith. I heard the hiss of waves below us.

'Will you kill a second time?' I cried bitterly.

'Yes! With so much within my grasp, do you suppose I shall let you cheat me of victory? When you are dead, only Rose will know what happened to Edith, and her testimony is worth *nothing*!'

I sent up a last fierce, desperate prayer. I never really believed, until then, that prayers are sometimes answered.

'*Damien*!' The voice was high, clear and commanding.

He had the presence of mind to spin me round with him, as he turned.

I saw her standing on the path, smiling; a small woman, neatly dressed, the hood of a cloak almost covering her fawn-coloured hair. She wore a quiver of arrows that gave her a medieval look, as though she had stepped from an old painting. She carried a bow, to which she was carefully fitting an arrow.

'*Irene!*' he shouted angrily. 'You are ill . . . I left you sleeping . . . '

'So you thought, my dear Damien. I decided that to-night would be a good time for a peacock hunt.'

'*A peacock hunt!*' he said, astounded.

'Yes. I have six arrows. Laurie has gone to the fair . . . he wasn't at the forge when I went there a little while ago, so I took a stone and broke his window. I wanted the bow and some arrows for the hunt. I shall hunt the peacock; a beautiful bird, vain, arrogant. I shall bring him down, in all his pride and beauty, and see his plumage trail in the dust.'

She spoke quite calmly; but in the dying light, I could see the glitter of her eyes.

I heard Damien laugh.

'If you shoot that arrow, my dear Irene, it will kill *Flora!*'

'Very well. I shall kill the peahen first,' she retorted. 'Your mistress — and then *you!*'

'I am *not* his mistress!' I cried furiously.

'Yes, you are, Flora. *You* are the reason he intends to stay here instead of returning to London with me. I have suffered years of humiliation and tonight it will be at an end; my aim will be the better for my memories!'

Damien held me in a powerful grip from which I could not free myself; standing there, only a few yards from Irene, I was a certain target.

I tried to duck; from somewhere, I found a strength I did not know I possessed. My arms were almost wrenched from the sockets, and I screamed at the top of my voice. The sound put Irene off her stroke for an instant, and it gave me fresh heart; frantically, I wriggled from side to side trying to free myself, and the fury of my movements caused Damien to shift his position.

The arrow was ready; Irene had only to release it from the bow. I thrust myself forward as far as I could, at the same time kicking backwards through clinging skirts. It was a superhuman effort.

It worked; I went to the ground, and Damien came down on top of me, cursing furiously. He was a heavy man, and I was winded completely for a few seconds; but I rolled away, bruised, grazed, muddied from the wet, slippery ground — but alive.

Damien got to his feet; the arrow whistled past his head, just missing him. He crouched low, ready to make a lunge at Irene, as she fitted the second arrow. He measured the distance between them and then hurled himself at her.

He missed her by a fraction of an inch, though she dropped the arrow. She let it lie where it fell; she took another and, instead of fitting it to the bow, held it in her hand, and lifted it above her head like a spear.

I felt sick; I hated Damien, but I had no wish to see him killed. I saw the deadly purpose in her face; the horror in his, as he clawed at her skirts, trying to pull her down; but she remained just out of reach, arrow poised, waiting.

The moment seemed like eternity. Damien suddenly lost his nerve. He rolled away from her along the path, then scrambled wildly to his feet and backed away; I believe he suddenly thought of the Shell Grotto, knowing that if he could reach it he would have the advantage of Irene; he crouched low, running towards the top of the path; the second arrow sped from the bow as he reached the top and began to scramble down.

For the second time it just missed him; but it unnerved him. The rain had made the path slippery, haste and fear made him clumsy. He slipped; floundered, and regained his balance; slipped again and hurtled headlong down to the beach where waves hissed and foamed over the rocks.

I closed my eyes against the whirling kaleidoscope of sand, sea and sky. I saw Irene walk to the end of the path and look down with an air of detachment. I thought of the sea clawing at Damien, carrying him away. I thought of the eyes of the mermaid and the sea-serpent; ice-cold, like Irene's; glittering, like Irene's as she turned to me, and smiled.

'I have four arrows left,' she said. 'I shall not waste them, Flora! The sea has taken the peacock; now for its mate!'

Irene was mad. Stiffly I scrambled to my feet. I was taller than she was, but I doubted that I had her strength. She picked up her bow; went back and picked up the arrow she had dropped, whilst I thought furiously.

'If you are going to hunt me,' I said, 'then you must give me at least a few minutes start. Those are the rules; where is the sport in taking a sitting target? You have to *prove* your skill . . . '

She looked at me thoughtfully, head on one side; then she laughed happily.

'Don't be silly, my dear Miss Lindsay. You must think I am mad to be taken in by such a suggestion. If you have a few *minutes* you will easily elude me and that would never do. I will give you ten seconds . . . '

I turned and ran as though the Devil himself was at my heels. I was running level with the cliffs and the beach, but I had turned westwards, not eastwards. I was heading for the westernmost tip of the island, a place to which I had never been.

Inevitably, I came to the trees again; the blessed, friendly trees, growing thickly together in a small plantation of firs that hid me from Irene's eyes. An arrow sang past me, and was lost in the green gloom; she was finding it more difficult to aim at a moving target in a poor light than to send her arrows at a fixed target on a sunny afternoon.

She had three arrows left; if I could elude them until daylight ran out, then I would be safe.

The trees began to thin; I avoided using the little paths, because it was safer to keep away from them; nevertheless, the next arrow barely missed my head, and, during a lull in the wind, I heard Irene's laughter.

Two arrows left; no more trees to shelter me. I was on open ground, running up a rise, with Seawinds away on my right. I thought of trying to make a detour to the house, and decided against it; she would trap me there.

I reached the top of the rise, went over it and collapsed, sobbing, into a small grassy depression on the other side. My breath cut painfully through my lungs; I lifted my head cautiously, and saw Irene standing where the trees ended — waiting.

Hopelessly, I looked around me. The slope descended gently to open turf, with no paths and only a few stunted bushes. The land was so narrow here that I could see the water on either side of me, and, ahead of me, white spray broke over a low headland.

Directly in front of me, on the tip of the island, only a few yards from the headland, was what seemed to be a long, low stone building.

Irene was still waiting at the edge of the trees. There was no way back for me, and she knew it. Ahead was the unfriendly sea. Seawinds was behind me, away to my right, and I could never reach it unseen.

There might be somewhere to hide in the stone building. I slithered down the slope and raced towards it, wondering why it had no doors or windows; when I finally reached it, I discovered that it was a tomb, similar to Anne Churnock's. There was a name carved on it that I could not read.

The turf was uneven, there appeared to have been a small landslide, disturbing the ground and damaging the landward end of the tomb, for there was a gaping hole, bricks spilled everywhere, and a thick wooden door hanging from its hinges. It occurred to me, fleetingly, that it could not be a very old tomb if it was built of bricks.

If I stayed in there until it was quite dark, I could then make my way back across the island to Four Winds, I thought, as I crawled into the hole. I could taste the salt spray on my lips; the waves were very near, but at least they wouldn't come this far.

I don't know what I expected to find inside; certainly not a flight of steps, down which I hurtled to a stone floor.

I lay there stunned; there were two oblongs of greyish light in the wall above me, and the sea sounded very loud. I could see nothing else in the thick gloom.

I was very battered and bruised, exhausted and aching in every limb, but at least I was safe for a while. It was a comforting thought to take down into the soft darkness that lapped around me . . .

I drifted hazily between consciousness and unconsciousness; when I finally roused myself with a surpeme effort, it was pitch dark.

I put out my hand anf found smooth stone. I rose unsteadily to my feet and carefully felt my way around the wall. The inside of the tomb seemed much bigger than one would imagine from the outside.

I steeled myself against finding some grisly remains; I moved slowly, keeping against the wall, feeling with my hands, until I came to the place where I had seen the oblongs of greyish light; they were still there, faint relief from the deep gloom around me.

I put up my hands; to my astonishment, my fingertips felt glass, thick and smooth. I went on probing with my fingers until I found what I thought was a catch. When I tugged it, the glass slid back, the sea sounded as though it was all around me and the night air whistled more coldly than ever.

Beyond the glass, my hands encountered iron bars. I could see the white caps of waves and a few faint stars above them.

The oblongs were two gratings, made to admit light and air, protected by reinforced glass. I was glad enough to close them, for reaction had set in and I was shivering. I still couldn't see my surroundings; cautiously I put my hands in front of me, sweeping imaginary half circles as I shuffled forward.

I almost bumped into a low table, with a book on it. The table seemed to be carved; beside it, there was a carved stool. I made another much more exciting find; a stone ledge on which I could feel the outline of a lamp. Beside the lamp, I discovered a couple of tapers and a box of matches.

I almost wept with relief . . . if there was oil in the lamp . . . !

I wasted half a dozen matches. I crouched, trying to shield the fragile flame from the draught coming down the steps, and I thought I should never get the taper alight. Then, when I finally had the lighted taper in my hand, I had to lift the glass chimney and turn up the wick. My fingers shook so much that I could scarcely hold the taper to the wick; and after I had lit the lamp I had to replace the glass chimney before the flame dipped and went out.

I made it! I had the flame safely sheltered in its glass prison, and I turned up the wick as far as it would go.

I lifted the lamp high and looked around me. I was in a large stone chamber, roughly circular. There were paintings on the walls; murals of fish and sea-animals, mermaids and dolphins, strange seaweed forests, all done in brilliant colours. There was a map of the island stuck on the wall, and made entirely of small shells. On one wall was written: "The Grotto of Atlantis".

This was the fifth grotto. Bella Careena's secret place. I drew a deep breath of pure pleasure, forgetting that I was tired and muddied, and that my arms ached intolerably.

I went across to the table and looked at the book. It was composed of several sheets of thick paper fastened between two covers of carved wood. I lifted the top cover and read aloud from the fly-leaf.

'A history of Bella Careena, by Marcus Trehearne.'

It began with the tale of the first invaders, centuries ago, who had found a floating forest, once part of the mainland, and had thought it was Paradise . . .

It had been written by hand in beautiful copper-plate, a long and detailed history; I turned the pages at random.

There was a painting of Ann Churnock, with bells sewn to her dress, and a flat basket full of grain on her arm; birds and animals bordered the page. There was an account of Alfrec de Bressard's exploits that made me shiver, an account of the quarrel between the Selwyns; a history that went right up to the day that Caspar Jardine had bought the island from Sylvester Ashley.

Finally, I found the poem at the end of the book. Marcus Trehearne had written it.

LEGEND

Lost Atlantis whispers
In a foam of bells, ice-cold and clear,
From towers of amethyst,
Beneath unfathomed seas.
Along broken streets of pearl
Lonely echoes linger,
And in sleeping gardens, no leaf
Stirs on sunken tree, nor breeze
Ruffles smooth ribbon of fronded weed.
To silken melody
Her shattered cities of turquoise
And coral, gleam iridescent
In slender twist and curl of spire
Undulating through shadowed deep.
Her courtyards are dim
With the hush of centuries,
And old palaces of emerald and jade,
Receive again their Kings;
Around her singing fountains,
Full-skirted dancers
Sway like clustered sea-anemones.

Sea-mist winds a silver shroud,
On silent valleys and hills;
From secret harbours, ghostly ships
Ride out across the seas,

To amber cities of the sun,
And rainbow worlds of fantasy.

Lost Atlantis lies
In a vault of emerald, shrouded
In jewels for the splendour
Of her story; remembered
Only where these echoes linger, lonely
On the evening air,
Bells, iee-cold and clear,
Ringing down the centuries,
From the towers of amethyst.

I have never forgotten that night when I stood in the Grotto of Atlantis, reading Marcus Trehearne's poems, whilst outside the sea sang to itself in the darkness and the wind grumbled away in the distance.

I closed the book. I came out of yesterday back to the present, and the sudden realization that the lamplight might give me away to Irene, if she was still watching and waiting, somewhere.

I was confused; I couldn't imagine how long I had been in the grotto though it seemed to have been hours. I turned the wick of the lamp down low, and, with the words of the poem still in my mind, went cautiously up the short flight of stone steps to peer through the gap.

Seawinds seemed to be ablaze with lights; far more than I had seen when I ran from the sheltering trees. Though the sea was still wild, the night was calmer; but I doubted very much if the boat had come back from the mainland.

I sat on the top step, wondering what to do; I was deathly tired; the comfort of a soft bed and hours of dreamless sleep seemed the most precious thing in the world.

When at last I saw lights that moved, I thought it was an illusion; they danced up and down, goblin lights in the night, and as they came nearer, I panicked, remembering Irene . . . until I heard the voices.

'Flora . . . Flora . . . !'

Voices? Ah, there was but one voice!

I stood up.

'Edwin!' I cried. 'Oh, *Edwin!*'

When he reached me, yards ahead of the others, the reaction was so great that I burst into tears. I could not stop, even when he put down his lantern and held me in his arms, rocking me back and forth like a baby.

'Hush . . . Flora, dearest, hush . . . you are safe . . . '

My face was against his shoulder; his arms were strong and gentle. I felt his chin against the top of my head.

'Irene . . . ' I whispered.

'It's all right, Flora. We're going to get you home, now. I thought we'd never find you. There's a boatman in Tolfrey who deserves a medal. He brought Ruan and I over in his boat, and it's not a journey I want to repeat in a hurry. I was worried, so desperately worried about you, though I didn't know *why* . . . '

'I've got something to show you,' I said.

I had to wait whilst he sent Ruan and the rest of the search party back to Seawinds for a horse and trap; then I took his hand and led him down into the grotto.

Mine was the sheer joy of seeing the wonder in his face, as he looked at the paintings on the walls and read the poem in the book.

'This is the treasure I've looked for,' he told me. 'My father told me before he died that the fifth grotto was his greatest achievement; and you have found it for me . . . '

I leaned my head against his shoulder.

'I am so glad. Edwin . . . it's for — Perdita.'

'What is?' he asked, puzzled.

'The "P" on the hairbrush . . . it's from Shakespeare and it means the lost one.'

There was a long silence; very gently, he kissed my forehead. Then he said:

'I don't think you're lost now, though, are you?'

'No, Edwin; but I am very, very tired. Everything else must wait until tomorrow . . . '

I don't remember much about the journey back to The House of the Four Winds. I remember that Rose was there, and Bella Careena . . . I remember brandy that burned my throat, someone washing away the mud from my face and hands, cool fingers tending the bruises and scratches . . . then a soft bed, and sleep, deep, dreamless . . .

When I awoke, the sun was shining; the clouds had gone and the sky looked as though it had been rinsed and hung out to dry; the wind was no more than a skittish breeze in the treetops.

Rose was sitting by the window, cheek resting on her hand. She looked very tired; when I spoke her name, she turned her head and came across to sit on the bed. I realized she had been crying.

'Jerome?' I asked fearfully.

'Sleeping. What happened last night was a great shock, but he has taken it well.'

'Irene?' I whispered.

'She is very ill; in a coma. They found her hiding in the Shell Grotto . . . she said she was waiting for Damien . . .'

I saw the horror in Rose's eyes; the Shell Grotto; truly it was cursed, I thought.

Rose added: 'It's been such a nightmare. Bella Careena stayed late playing chess with her father, and then suddenly Edwin and Ruan and a few of the menservants arrived . . . I was so surprised, especially when Edwin said he had been worried about you. We went to the cottage and found your note; then Edwin and Ruan went straight to Seawinds. The two servants there had barricaded themselves in their rooms, frightened because Irene had behaved so strangely, saying she was going to hunt peacocks. They said she wasn't sane . . . we didn't know what had happened to *you*, and Edwin said he was going to tear the island apart to find you . . .'

I told her what had happened; I began with the letter and the trap Damien had set.

'How strange life is,' she said, shaking her head. 'You wrote that letter, hoping to make things easier for me . . . *you*, Vinnie's daughter; and I let Vinnie be blamed all these years . . .'

'Don't talk about it, Rose. I did it for Jerome, too — because you two have so much love for each other, and it's a rare thing, love like that . . .'

'There will be investigations,' she said tiredly. 'The police will come.'

'Of course; after that, it will all be over. Whatever you have felt, through the years — remorse, guilt, regret — will be done with, forever.'

'How young you are to be so old and wise!' she said.

Bella Careena came to me later that morning.

'So you found my secret grotto, Flora?'

'By accident. It was a refuge. It may have saved my life. I didn't even know the tomb was there, until last night.'

'It isn't a real tomb,' she told me. 'It's got Alfrec de Bressard's name carved on it, and it says in the book that there was a real tomb, once, but it was washed into the sea. It's a vault made out of rock, and there are two gratings; I found the slits, high up in the rock face above the beach. Then I looked at the brick tomb, the one the Selwyns put there, after the old one was washed away, and I thought: there must be a way in. It was easy!' she said, with a superior air. 'I found a big bunch of keys hanging on a nail in the church porch and one of them fitted the door. *Anyone* could have found it; but no one ever goes to that part of the island. It's like the Shell Grotto: haunted.'

'Oh, Bella Careena . . . !' I began; but she frowned.

'You shouldn't laugh at me, Flora. Some places are haunted on this island: the Shell Grotto, the ruined chapel; Alfrec's tomb. So I bet Edwin's father thought *that* was a safe place to make the fifth grotto. It's my favourite of them all.'

'Mine too,' I said.

'You wouldn't have got in if the storm hadn't made a bit of a landslide near there,' she pointed out. 'Wasn't Edwin's father clever? The men who went there weren't really workmen at all, they were artists; the Grotto was already made, of course. It's all in the book. I suppose you didn't read it?'

'Some of it; I read the poem.' I sighed. 'Edwin saw it all.'

'*I* wouldn't have told him where it was,' she said calmly. 'People have to find places like that for themselves . . .'

During the next few days, it seemed that there were strange men everywhere on the island. Men in plain clothes, men in uniform, asking questions. I answered them truthfully, without telling them that Damien had trapped me, nor did I mention the letter. I merely said he had asked me to go to Seawinds because he was worried about Irene . . .

So I kept back some small part of the truth, and I do not regret my silence. The truth would not have helped Damien, whose body was washed up some weeks later along the Hampshire coast; nor would it have helped Irene, who never came out of her coma.

Dr Samuels told the police that he had been sent for on account of Irene's strange behaviour; and the statement of the servants at Seawinds bore out his testimony. Poor Irene! I felt great pity for her. Life had treated her unkindly, and given her little cause for happiness.

Rose insisted on telling Edwin the whole story from beginning to end; so only he and I share her secret, and Ruan and Bella Careena will never know it, thank Heavens.

On the night he asked me to marry him, I told Edwin the truth about my inheritance; he laughed, kissed me, and made a characteristic reply.

'I don't want one penny of your money, my love. Do what you please with it. You can use it to spread happiness where there has been misery, ease the burden of poverty; educate; improve the lot of others. Money is a great treasure, you'll find!'

Epilogue

JEROME JARDINE LIVED FOR nearly three years after that summer. When he died, Rose told me that they had been the happiest years of her life, years of perfect tranquillity and peace of mind, and the joy in one another that only two people deeply in love can know. Even now, six years after his death, some of that happiness remains with her.

Bella Careena left the island when her father died.

'It is time for me to go,' she told me. 'Ruan is going to travel. I don't think he'll settle in the island, even when he marries. Mama doesn't want to stay any longer, of course. Alfrec de Bressard's tomb has been bricked up, and the grotto will be secret for ever now, though I'm giving Edwin his father's book. It is time for me to see the rest of the world, but I shall always know that the island was mine, more than anyone else's, that I am part of it in a way I can never explain.'

Bella Careena and her mother have travelled far and wide since then and they write to us of strange and wonderful cities, half way across the world. Ruan is married and living at the other end of England.

I hope some day that Bella Careena will fall in love and marry, though she may never go back to the island. I hope she will be as happy as Edwin and I are, today, living quietly in Gloucestershire with our twin sons and baby daughter.

Perhaps none of us will ever return; Edwin says it is

better that we should not do so; but I think of the island often, when I am lying awake at night.

The servants have all gone from Bella Careena; there is no one there now, except a caretaker and his wife, and a couple of gamekeepers. I think of the wind walking in the trees. I think of the inscription on Anne Churnock's tomb: *Now will I make fast this day my heart unto yours*. Edwin has had those words engraved on a locket for me.

I think of the Shell Grotto, and the figures with their eyes of glass; of the secret and lovely Grotto of Atlantis, the peacocks strutting everywhere, uttering their weird, unearthly cries, spreading out their exquisite feathers.

I think of these things; then I sigh and turn restlessly, until Edwin, knowing what I am thinking, takes me in his arms, tells me that only today and tomorrow are important, not yesterday.

I know he is right; but my memories live with me still, especially on nights when the wind that blows over our quiet fields seems to smell of the sea.

LASER APPLICATIONS

Volume 3

CONTRIBUTORS

M. BASS

DAVID CASASENT

D. CHEN

R. M. DWYER

H. HASKAL

JAMES A. MCCRAY

P. D. SMITH

LASER APPLICATIONS

Edited by MONTE ROSS

McDonnell Douglas Astronautics Company
St. Louis, Missouri

VOLUME 3

ACADEMIC PRESS   New York San Francisco London   1977
A Subsidiary of Harcourt Brace Jovanovich, Publishers

ACADEMIC PRESS, INC.
111 Fifth Avenue, New York, New York 10003

United Kingdom Edition published by
ACADEMIC PRESS, INC. (LONDON) LTD.
24/28 Oval Road, London NW1

LIBRARY OF CONGRESS CATALOG CARD NUMBER: 79–154380

ISBN 0–12–431903–3

PRINTED IN THE UNITED STATES OF AMERICA

CONTENTS

Lasers in Medicine

R. M. DWYER and M. BASS

Optical Data Storage

H. HASKAL and D. CHEN

LIST OF CONTRIBUTORS

Numbers in parentheses indicate the pages on which the authors' contributions begin.

M. BASS, Center for Laser Studies, University of Southern California, Los Angeles, California (107)

DAVID CASASENT, Department of Electrical Engineering, Carnegie-Mellon University, Pittsburgh, Pennsylvania (43)

D. CHEN, Honeywell Corporate Research Center, Bloomington, Minnesota (135)

R. M. DWYER, Department of Gastroenterology, University of California, Los Angeles, Harbor General Hospital, Torrance, California, and Center for Laser Studies, University of Southern California, Los Angeles, California (107)

H. HASKAL, Department of Electrical Engineering, Tufts University, Medford, Massachusetts (135)

JAMES A. McCRAY, Department of Physics and Atmospheric Science, Drexel University and the Johnson Research Foundation, University of Pennsylvania, Philadelphia, Pennsylvania (1)

P. D. SMITH,* Department of Physics and Atmospheric Science, Drexel University and the Johnson Research Foundation, University of Pennsylvania, Philadelphia, Pennsylvania (1)

* Present address: Laboratory of Technical Development, National Heart, Lung & Blood Institute, National Institutes of Health, Bethesda, Maryland 20014.

PREFACE

In this, the third volume, we have articles on optical data storage, lasers in medicine, lasers in molecular biology, and devices for coherent optical processing. The diversity of laser applications is apparent, as two chapters relate to the impersonal world of machines and automation, dealing with information handling and processing, and two relate to life and biological processes.

Dwyer and Bass deal with the practical possibilities of lasers in surgery and related medicine. The laser is finding use in head and neck work, neurosurgery, burn surgery, stomach ulcers, and other surgical uses besides the well-known ophthalmological applications. Dwyer and Bass treat the subject of optical design for lasers in surgery as well, identifying the requirements and subtleties that make for a well-designed surgical laser system.

McCray and Smith deal with the laser as a tool to increase understanding of biological processes at the molecular level, to aid in biological research, and to elucidate biochemical and biophysical processes.

Optical data storage is treated by Haskal and Chen. Holographic storage, videodisk systems for home entertainment, and some massive computer memories are applications resulting from work in optical data storage technology. Haskal and Chen treat the general areas of optical data storage, discuss optical recording materials and techniques, components for optical data storage, and review optical recording systems.

Coherent optical processing is an area which, together with optical data storage, has held great promise for a long time, yet has seen applications grow slowly due to the limited components and technology. Casasent treats the system considerations and includes in detail the critical unique devices necessary to make coherent optical processing successful in application. Emphasis is placed on real-time recyclable spatial light modulator input devices and spatial filter materials. The most promising transducers for use in optical processing are presented in detail.

Laser applications have matured in the past few years, as we see from the applications discussed here, but, more important, as we see in our daily lives. The optical price scanner in the supermarket, laser use in eye surgery, the coming of the videodisk for home TV playing, fiber optics telephone links, are some results of the work that has been covered in the past and present in these volumes.

It is our intent that the work presented in this serial publication aid those involved with laser applications to further its vast potential. It is our wish to bridge the gap between research and practical application by treating subjects in sufficient depth to allow the engineer to design products and systems, using the material here as a starting base.

MONTE ROSS

CONTENTS OF PREVIOUS VOLUMES

LASER APPLICATIONS

Volume 3

APPLICATION OF LASERS TO MOLECULAR BIOLOGY

James A. McCray and P. D. Smith[1]

Department of Physics and Atmospheric Science
Drexel University and the Johnson Research Foundation
University of Pennsylvania, Philadelphia, Pennsylvania

I. Introduction

In this article the term molecular biology will be used in its most general sense; that is, interest will be in an understanding of biological processes at the molecular level. This requires knowledge of the optical spectra of biomolecules and the measurement of the time dependence of the various biochemical and biophysical processes in which these molecules are involved as well as structural information about these molecules. Many of these processes, such as electron transfers and

[1] Present address: Laboratory of Technical Development, National Heart, Lung & Blood Institute, National Institutes of Health, Bethesda, Maryland 20014.

1

molecular conformation transitions, occur very rapidly; thus their study with conventional light sources has been difficult. Collecting Raman spectral data has also been hard because of the lack of an intense cw monochromatic light source.

The advent of the laser in 1960, however, changed this picture dramatically. The introduction of Q-switched solid state lasers was of particular importance. In 1962 at the Sixth Annual Biophysical Society Meeting in Washington, D.C., Britton Chance and Heinz Schleyer (1962) of the Johnson Research Foundation at the University of Pennsylvania reported their results of the application of a liquid-nitrogen-cooled ruby laser, which was constructed in their laboratory, to the study of electron transfer in photosynthetic algae. The details of this work were published in 1963 in the paper "Activation of Electron Transfer in a *Chlamydomonas* Mutant by Light Pulses from an Optical Maser" (Chance *et al.*, 1963). Since that time there have been many applications of lasers to molecular biology, and some of these will now be considered in detail.

II. Laser Activation of Photosynthesis

A. CYTOCHROME C AND CHLOROPHYLL

In order to be able to understand the application of lasers to photosynthesis it is necessary first to describe the types of biomolecules involved and their interactions. Basically, light energy is absorbed by chlorophyll and subsequently converted into energy associated with electron transfer. One of the major macromolecules involved in both photosynthetic and mitochondrial electron transfer is called cytochrome c. This large molecule (molecular weight 12,400) is one of the immense number of molecules present in living systems called proteins. All proteins are made up of one or more long chains of amino acids, along with some smaller molecular groups. As shown in Fig. 1 amino acids consist of a central carbon atom with an amino group ($-NH_2$), a carboxyl group ($-CO_2H$), a hydrogen atom ($-H$), and one of several side groups ($-R$). Two amino acids may combine in a specified way by giving off a water molecule (H_2O) and forming a peptide bond. Since the combined molecule is still an amino acid with a free amino group and a free carboxyl group, further condensation may take place, the result being a long polypeptide chain. Table I illustrates different amino acids that exist in nature. The table shows, for example, that the side chains may place a positive or negative charge at any point along the chain or

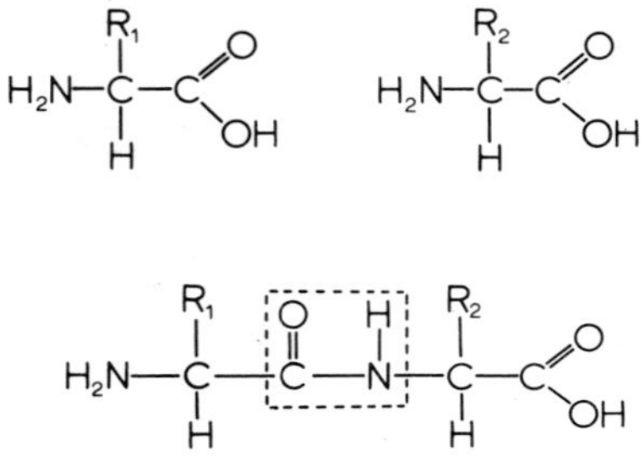

Peptide Bond

FIG. 1. Structure of amino acids and the peptide bond.

neutral group or groups of atoms which may participate in intra- or interchain bonding, such as hydrogen bonding, disulfide bonding, or aromatic side chain contact bonding. Most proteins in nature contain various combinations of about 20 different types of amino acids. It is evident then that the number of possible proteins is enormous. Cyto-

TABLE I

TWENTY AMINO ACIDS THAT MAKE UP MOST OF THE PROTEINS IN NATURE[a]

[a] In most cases only the side chains R are shown.

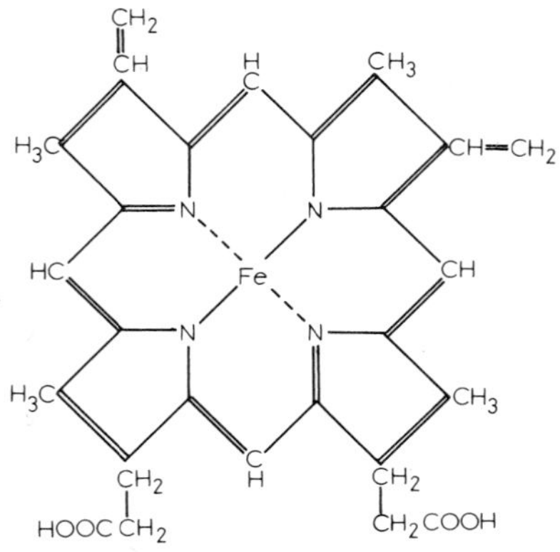

FIG. 2.   Heme groups (protoporphyrin IX).

chrome c has amino acids in a single polypeptide chain which wraps itself around a planar group of atoms, basically a modified heme or iron porphyrin group.

This group (shown in Fig. 2) consists principally of alternating single and double bonds in a closed loop that contains both carbon and nitrogen atoms. In the center of this group is an iron atom which is the

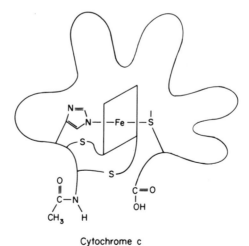

Cytochrome c

FIG. 3.   Simple schematic of cytochrome c with polypeptide chain wrapped around the hemelike group. The square with Fe^{2+}, viewed at an angle, is meant to represent the heme group.

heart of the molecule since the basic function of cytochrome c appears to be that of an electron transfer device, with the iron atom alternating between a Fe^{2+} ferrous state and a Fe^{3+} ferric state. A picture of the cytochrome c molecule with an indication of the way in which the modified heme group is bound to the polypeptide chain is given in Fig. 3.

Chlorophyll molecules are also metalloporphyrin complexes but they have a different planar arrangement and a magnesium atom at the center instead of iron. Bacteriochlorophyll, which is found in photosynthetic bacteria, is shown in Fig. 4. The exact arrangement of molecules in a photosynthetic system is still not known, but basically many of these "bulk" chlorophyll molecules are arranged in planar arrays with a "trap" chlorophyll molecule at some point in the system. Photons are then absorbed by bulk chlorophyll molecules, and the energy then migrates around the system in the form of excitation energy until it is trapped at a reaction center chlorophyll. This latter molecule is oxidized very rapidly, presumably by an adjacent iron sulphur protein. Subsequently this reaction center chlorophyll molecule oxidizes one or more adjacent cytochrome c molecules thereby initiating photosynthetic electron transport. By studying the rate of oxidation of cytochrome c it is possible to investigate part of the molecular mechanism involved in the early stages of photosynthetic electron transport.

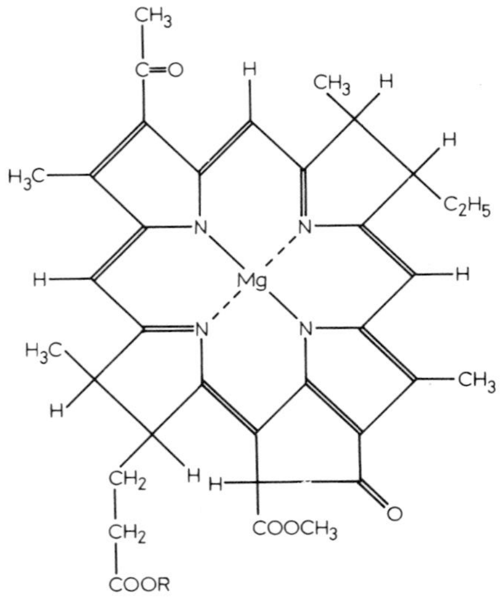

FIG. 4. Bacteriochlorophyll.

B. EXPERIMENTAL TECHNIQUES

1. *Ruby Laser Activation*

An ideal way to study cytochrome c oxidation is to have a narrow pulse of light impinge upon a photosynthetic sample and then to measure directly the oxidation of cytochrome c. However, the half-times for cytochrome c oxidation for many species of plants, algae, and bacteria are very fast at room temperatures so that it was difficult to study directly this process with conventional light sources. When the successful operation of a ruby laser was announced by Maiman in 1960 (Maiman, 1960), Britton Chance and his colleagues at the Johnson Research Foundation began work on the construction of a liquid nitrogen vapor-cooled ruby laser which they were subsequently to use in the study of photosynthetic electron transport in algae. The wavelength (694 nm) of the ruby laser was ideal for this work because it fell right on one of the major absorption peaks of chlorophyll a. In this first work the ruby laser was used in the burst mode with an overall duration for the group of spikes of about 0.8 msec. The macromolecule, which was oxidized in less than 20 msec in this case, was thought to be a cytochrome of type b.

The development of the Q-switching technique made it possible to study the oxidation of cytochrome c in a photosynthetic bacterium that appeared to have a very fast rate—too fast to be measured with the system described above (Chance and Schoener, 1964). A rotating prism Q-switched ruby laser (TRG, Inc.) activation system with 10 nsec 0.5 J pulses at 694 nm with appropriate spectrophotometric measuring instrumentation was first reported by Chance and DeVault (1964) and described in detail in 1966 (DeVault and Chance, 1966). The experimental setup used is shown in Fig. 5. The half-time for oxidation of cytochrome c in the photosynthetic bacterium Chromatium was found to vary from about 2 μsec at room temperature to about 2.3 msec at 100 K. A very significant finding of this work was that below 100 K the rate of oxidation was found to be essentially temperature independent (see Fig. 6). This result suggested that some type of quantum mechanical tunneling may be involved in electron transport at low temperature.

There have been numerous studies of photosynthetic electron transport in which Q-switched ruby lasers were used (see, e.g., Hildreth *et al.*, 1966; Parson, 1967; Hildreth, 1968; Ke *et al.*, 1968; Kihara and Chance, 1969; Kihara and Dutton, 1970; Siebert and DeVault, 1970; Dutton and Jackson, 1972; Prince *et al.*, 1974). These include laser systems with various types of Q-switching such as rotating prism,

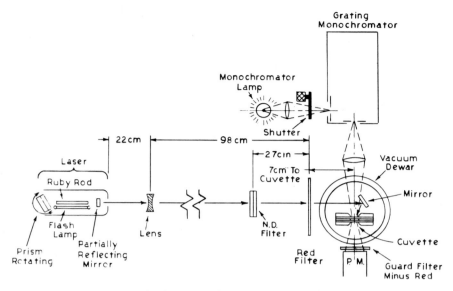

FIG. 5. Typical laser activation setup with spectrophotometric readout. From DeVault and Chance (1966).

Pockels cell, and passive dye. The Pockels cell Q-switched dual laser activation system of Parson (1967) and the high rate repetitively pulsed ruby laser used by Witt (1967) are novel variations of the standard laser activation system described above.

2. Detection of Cytochrome c Oxidation

As indicated in Fig. 5 light of variable wavelength and weak intensity is allowed to impinge upon a sample of solutions of bacterial whole cells or subcellular particles called chromatophores which contain the photosynthetic apparatus, in particular cytochrome c. The absorption spectra, determined principally by the porphyrin rings of the cytochrome c macromolecules, are also dependent upon the oxidation state of the iron, i.e., whether it is oxidized (Fe^{3+}) or reduced (Fe^{2+}). Figure 7 illustrates this and shows that the number of cytochrome c molecules oxidized at any given time can be calculated by using the finite extinction difference $\Delta\epsilon = \epsilon_{ox} - \epsilon_{red}$ between the oxidized and reduced species. If light scattering is small compared with absorption then the change in transmission of the sample can be used to follow the time dependence of the oxidation process. Initially the cytochrome c molecules will all be

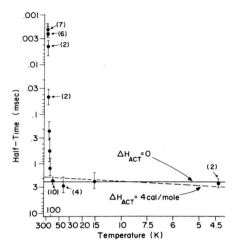

FIG. 6.   Arrhenius plot of temperature dependence of the rate of laser-induced cytochrome oxidation in the photosynthetic bacterium *Chromatium*. From DeVault *et al*.
(1967).

reduced so that by Beer's law the light detected by the photomultiplier
will be

$$I_r(l) = I_0 e^{-2.3\epsilon_{\text{red}}C_T l} \tag{1}$$

where I_0 is the measuring light impinging upon the sample, ϵ_{red} the
extinction coefficient of the reduced species in millimolar^{-1} centime-
ter^{-1}, C_T the total heme (or cytochrome c) concentration in millimolars,
and l the path length in centimeters. During the reaction we will have
both oxidized and reduced species so that Beer's law becomes

$$I(l, t) = I_0 e^{-2.3[\epsilon_{\text{red}}C_{\text{red}}(t) + \epsilon_{\text{ox}}C_{\text{ox}}(t)]l} \tag{2}$$

A constraint, however, exists because a given heme must be either
oxidized or reduced.
    Thus

$$C_{\text{red}}(t) + C_{\text{ox}}(t) = C_T \tag{3}$$

Equation (2) then becomes

$$I(l, t) = I_0 e^{-2.3[\epsilon_{\text{red}}C_T + \Delta\epsilon C_{\text{ox}}(t)]l} \tag{4}$$

where

$$\Delta\epsilon = \epsilon_{\text{ox}} - \epsilon_{\text{red}} \tag{5}$$

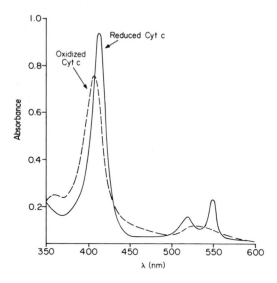

FIG. 7. Optical spectrum of oxidized and reduced cytochrome c.

Hence

$$I(l, t) = I_r(l)e^{-2.3\Delta\epsilon C_{ox}(t)l} \qquad (6)$$

The experimental quantity measured will be a voltage proportional to the difference $\Delta I(l, t)$ in light intensity seen by the photomultiplier at any given time compared (in a difference amplifier) to that seen initially.

$$\Delta I(l, t) = I(l, t) - I_r(l) \qquad (7)$$

If these voltages are measured under the same gain conditions then one has

$$\frac{\Delta I(l, t)}{I_r(l)} = e^{-2.3\Delta\epsilon C_{ox}(t)l} - 1 \qquad (8)$$

The time dependence of cytochrome c oxidation is then found from the expression

$$C_{ox}(t) = \frac{1}{2.3l\Delta\epsilon} \ln \left[\frac{1}{1 + \dfrac{\Delta I(l, t)}{I_r(l)}} \right] \qquad (9)$$

The above description may also be written in terms of the "absorbance change" (optical density or O.D. change)

$$\Delta A(l, t) = A(l, t) - A_r(l) \tag{10}$$

where

$$A(l, t) = \log_{10}[1/T(l, t)] \tag{11}$$

and

$$T(l, t) = I(l, t)/I_0 \tag{12}$$

is the transmittance of the sample.

From Eqs. (10), (11), (12) and (1) and (2) we see that

$$A(l, t) = [\epsilon_{red}C_{red}(t) + \epsilon_{ox}C_{ox}(t)]l \tag{13}$$

$$A_r(l) = \epsilon_{red}C_T l \tag{14}$$

and

$$\Delta A(l, t) = \Delta\epsilon C_{ox}(t)l \tag{15}$$

For small changes in intensity

$$\Delta A(l, t) \simeq \frac{1}{2.3} \frac{\Delta I(l, t)}{I_r(l)} \tag{16}$$

Figure 8 shows an oscilloscope trace of the result of a typical experiment where cytochrome c oxidation follows laser activation.

3. *Photosynthetic Bacteria and Liquid Dye Laser Converters*

While the absorption spectrum for chlorophyll a is in the visible, the absorption spectrum of bacteriochlorophyll is in the near IR (see Fig. 9).

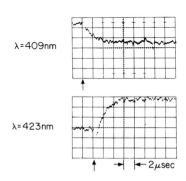

λ=409nm

λ=423nm

←2μsec

FIG. 8. Cytochrome c optical absorption change in the photosynthetic bacterium *Chromatium D*. From Seibert and DeVault (1971).

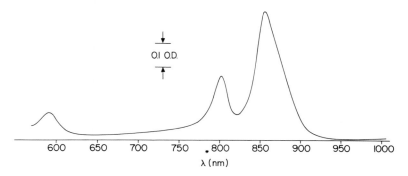

FIG. 9.   Absorption spectrum of the photosynthetic bacterium, *R. gelatinosa*. From T. Kihara (personal communication).

When liquid dye lasers were discovered (Sorokin and Lankard, 1966) it became possible to use a *Q*-switched ruby laser to pump various cyanine dyes in dimethyl sulfoxide (DMSO) in order to convert the ruby energy into a pulse at higher wavelength. Wavelengths of 710 to 1060 nm have been obtained (Miyazoe and Maeda, 1968) and used to excite various photosynthetic bacteria at their absorption peaks (Chance *et al.*, 1970; Dutton *et al.*, 1971; Kihara and McCray, 1971, 1973). Figure 10

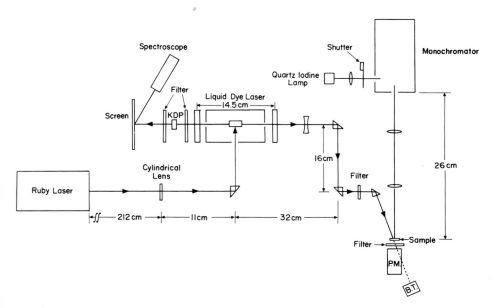

FIG. 10.   Ruby laser light activation system with liquid dye laser wavelength converter.

illustrates a ruby laser excitation system to which a liquid dye laser wavelength converter has been added. As an example of a typical situation, the output of a liquid dye cavity containing the dye 3,3'-diethyl-2,2'-thiatricarbocyanine-iodide in DMSO is at 860 nm and is 100 mJ when excited by a 700 mJ ruby pump. By absorbing photons at an absorption peak a lower intensity excitation source is needed and hence a small laser artifact is present.

III. Laser Photolysis of Ligand–Hemoprotein Complexes

A. Myoglobin and Hemoglobin

Myoglobin is also a single subunit protein with molecular weight 17,000 that consists of amino acid residues forming a globin polypeptide chain. This chain is also wrapped around the heme group but in such a way that the sixth coordinate position of the iron atom is free (Fig. 11). Small molecules (called ligands), such as molecular oxygen (O_2), carbon monoxide (CO), and nitric oxide (NO), can enter an open pocket and

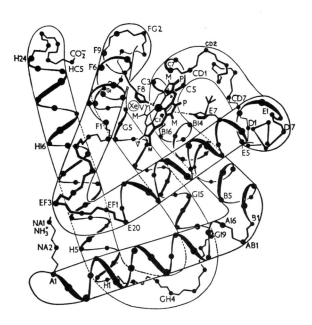

FIG. 11.   Structure of the protein myoglobin. From Dickerson (1964).

bind reversibly to the Fe^{2+} state iron. Myoglobin is a muscle protein and can provide storage sites for oxygen.

The optical absorption spectra of deoxy-(no ligands) and carboxy-(CO) myoglobin are shown in Fig. 12. The spectra are again determined mainly by the heme groups with Soret and visible absorption peaks. A reaction of CO with deoxyhemes may be followed by using the extinction change $\Delta\epsilon = \epsilon_{co} - \epsilon_{deoxy}$ at, for example, 436 nm.

Hemoglobin is the oxygen carrier protein of molecular weight 64,500 and is found in red blood cells. It is a tetramer; that is, there are four subunits of two different types called α's and β's (see Fig. 13). The α subunit contains 141 amino acid residues, and the β subunit 146. Both fold around a heme group and are very similar in shape to myoglobin.

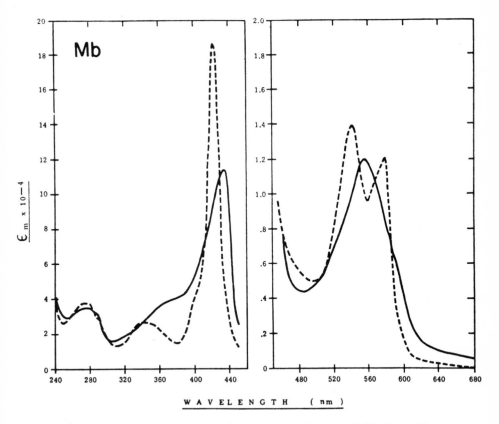

FIG. 12. Optical absorption spectra of deoxy- and carboxymyoglobin. From Hardman *et al.* (1966).

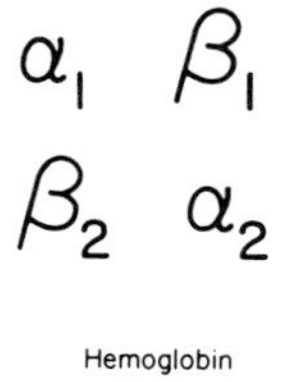

$$\alpha_1 \quad \beta_1$$

$$\beta_2 \quad \alpha_2$$

Hemoglobin

FIG. 13.   Simple schematic of the hemoglobin tetramer. Each subunit is very similar to myoglobin.

Now, however, with four open heme groups each hemoglobin molecule can bind four diatomic molecular oxygen molecules. The tetramer has at least two different conformational states (three-dimensional relative configurations of the subunits), and this leads to a type of "cooperativity" in ligand binding so that it is easier to bind ligands to a tetramer which already has several ligands. The absorption spectra of the hemoglobin complexes are very similar to those of myoglobin. One of the major goals of research in this area is to determine the mechanism of action of hemoglobin by studying the rates of ligand binding to the hemes and the conformational changes involved. The results may then be correlated with the detailed X-ray structure data reported by Perutz and his associates (Perutz, 1968, 1969, 1970; Perutz et al., 1968).

B. EXPERIMENTAL CO PHOTOLYSIS SYSTEMS

1. Ruby and Frequency-Doubled Ruby Laser Systems

When light of appropriate wavelength impinges upon a sample containing ligand–hemoprotein complexes, such as carboxymyoglobin or oxyhemoglobin, photons are absorbed by the heme group with the result that the ligand dissociates from the hemoprotein. The subsequent reassociation of the ligand and hemoprotein may then be followed spectrophotometrically in this premixed condition. The ideal light source for this type of photolysis (or photodissociation) experiment would be a short, high energy light pulse. The applicability of a Q-switched laser to this situation is apparent. However, a further condition is that the wavelength of the laser output match one of the absorption peaks of the ligand hemoprotein complex. When the 700 mJ, 30 nsec ruby laser (694 nm) was tried for the photodissociation of carboxymyoglobin and other CO hemoprotein complexes, the amount of photolysis was very low. Staerk and Chance (1969) therefore attempted photolysis with the 347 nm frequency-doubled output of a Lear Siegler ruby laser. The experimental setup used is shown in Fig. 14. The laser was Q-switched with a saturable filter (pumped uranyl glass) and the second harmonic crystal used was potassium dihydrogen phosphate (KDP). Although the heme absorption coefficient is greater at 347 nm than at 694 nm, the low quantum efficiency for second harmonic conversion (a few millijoules output) offsets the expected advantage. However, relative CO-recombination half-times (in milliseconds and measured under comparable conditions) were obtained for several hemoproteins including myoglobin (2.3), horse radish peroxidase (310), turnip peroxidase (140), cytochrome c peroxidase (640), and cytochrome oxidase in pigeon heart mitochondria (43), and cytochrome oxidase extracted from pigeon heart mitochondria (30).

2. Frequency-Doubled Neodymium Glass Laser

The second harmonic (530 nm) of the neodymium glass laser (1060 nm) falls within an absorption peak (β-band) of most hemoproteins. This fact and the larger conversion efficiency available (as compared with ruby) lead to the use of this system for CO laser photolysis. In Chance's laboratory a 40 nsec, and 1 J Lear Siegler neodymium glass laser with rotating prism Q-switching and temperature controlled ammonium dihydrogen phosphate (ADP) doubling crystal (20–100 mJ at 530 nm) was used for the study of carbon monoxide binding at high CO pressures to hemoglobin in solution (Anderson et al., 1970) and in the crystalline state (Reed et al., 1971).

Alpert et al. (1974) used a very high energy Q-switched neodymium glass laser (Compagnie Générale d'Electricité type V D 230) consisting of an oscillator and two amplifiers which when frequency-doubled gave

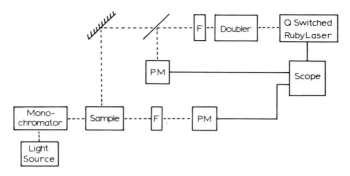

FIG. 14. Frequency-doubled ruby laser flash photolysis system. From Staerk and Chance (1969).

a 50 nsec output at 529 nm with energy ranging from 0.1 to 1 J to study CO photolysis of several normal and modified hemoglobins. They measured spectral changes that followed in the first 300 nsec and observed a primary transient species which they believe may correspond to a modification of tertiary structure of the protein subunits.

3. *Liquid Dye Laser*

With the discovery of liquid dye lasers (Sorokin and Lankard, 1966) it became possible to consider tunable laser photolysis sources. It happens, however, that one of the most efficient dye–solvent systems used (Rhodamine 6G in ethanol) has an output at about 585 nm which falls within another absorption peak (α-band) of many hemoproteins. Consequently the 0.5 μsec, 200 mJ cylindrical flash lamp pumped (Furumoto and Cecone, 1970) liquid dye laser has been used for CO photolysis of hemoproteins without tuning.

Recently Austin *et al.* (1974) have used a 0.5 J Rhodamine 6G-methanol liquid dye laser to photolyze carboxy- and oxymyoglobin at low temperatures (down to 20 K) and have observed nonexponential behavior at long times. From this data they have been able to deduce the form of the activation energy spectrum for carbon monoxide binding to myoglobin. One unique feature of their experiment is an analog-to-digital converter and storage electronic system which is controlled by a logarithmic clock. This allows them to monitor ligand binding over a range of nine decades of time.

C. Cytochrome Oxidase

1. *Mitochondria and Electron Transport*

For many years Chance and his collaborators at the Johnson Research Foundation have been studying the very basic problem of molecular energy transduction in mitochondria with the use of spectrophotometric, electrooptic, and magnetic resonance techniques. This work along with contributions from other groups has lead to the identification of a large number of membrane bound macromolecular components such as dehydrogenases, iron-sulphur proteins, and cytochromes. One of the major goals of this work is to determine the molecular mechanism involved in the coupling of electron transport and oxidative phosphorylation. In this process nicotinamide adenine dinucleotide (NADH) is oxidized to NAD^+, O_2 (molecular oxygen) is reduced to two molecules of H_2O (water), and PO_4^{-3} (phosphate) is

NADH$\rightarrow$FP$\rightarrow$Co Q$\rightarrow$Cyt b$\rightarrow$Cyt $c_1$$\rightarrow$Cytc$\rightarrow$Cyt a $\rightarrow$Cyt $a_3$$\rightarrow$$O_2$

FIG. 15.   Mitochondrial electron transport chain.

combined with adenosine diphosphate (ADP) to form energy rich adenosine triphosphate (ATP) which is then used as the energy source in many energy requiring biochemical reactions. Figure 15 illustrates the presently known composition of the mammalian mitochondrial electron transport chain.

Since the terminal macromolecular complex, cytochrome oxidase, has a hemoprotein (cytochrome A_3) that combines with O_2, it is possible to block the membrane bound oxidase with a minimum amount of CO, rapidly mix the mitochondria with oxygen in solution, and then fire a laser to photodissociate the CO so that oxygen may rapidly react with the oxidase. The various absorption changes observed may be identified with the different macromolecular complexes within the membrane and their relative ordering in the chain may be determined. Both the frequency-doubled neodymium glass and more appropriately the Rhodamine 6G–ethanol liquid dye laser have been used by workers in Chance's laboratory to study the function of cytochrome oxidase (Chance and Erecińska, 1971; Erecińska and Chance, 1972; McCray and Anderson, 1972). Junge and DeVault (1975) have used linearly polarized laser light to produce linear dichroism in mitochondria containing cytochrome oxidase.

2. *Turbidity and Dual-Wavelength Detection*

In studying biological preparations, the sample is frequently turbid and the spectroscopic changes small. Chance (1951) developed the technique of dual wavelength spectrophotometry to work with these small absorbance changes in the presence of background scattering. The essential features of the apparatus are shown in Fig. 16. A single high intensity light source is focused on the entrance slits of two monochromators M_1 and M_2 which are set for wavelengths λ_1 and λ_2. The two monochromatic beams are alternately focused onto the sample cell by means of the vibrating mirror (60 Hz). The light passing through the cell is collected by the measuring photomultiplier; a fraction of the input beams to the sample cell is monitored by a reference photomultiplier to compensate for intensity fluctuations of the light source. Phase sensitive detection at 60 Hz is used to reduce noise.

Cowles (1965) has analyzed the dual wavelength technique of measuring small absorbance changes. If I_{01} and I_{02} are the intensities of the two

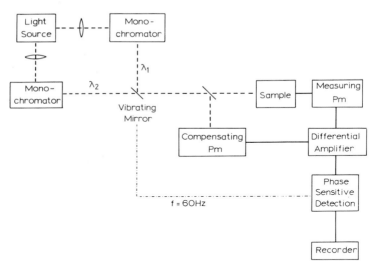

FIG. 16. Double beam spectroscopic apparatus. The high intensity light is incident on the two monochromators producing wavelengths λ_1 and λ_2. The vibrating mirror allows each wavelength to impinge on the sample alternately. The photomultiplier output is fed through a differential amplifier and phase detector and displayed on a recorder. The compensating pm corrects for source noise.

input beams, and I_1 and I_2 the intensities of the emergent beams falling on the measuring photomultiplier, then

$$A_1 = -\log(I_1/I_{01})$$
$$A_2 = -\log(I_2/I_{02})$$
(17)

If the photomultiplier has a linear response and the initial photomultiplier voltages are set equal to the reference voltage V_{ref}, then for small absorbance changes

$$\Delta V/V_{\text{ref}} = 10^{-\Delta A_1} - 10^{-\Delta A_2}$$
(18)

For mixture of two components in the sample, concentrations C_1 and C_2, the absorbance change for unit path length is given by

$$\Delta A_1 = \alpha_{11}\Delta C_1 + \alpha_{12}\Delta C_2$$
$$\Delta A_2 = \alpha_{21}\Delta C_1 + \alpha_{22}\Delta C_2$$
(19)

where α_{ij} are the molar absorbitivities at the two wavelengths.

In the important case where C_1 and C_2 are the concentrations of two interchangeable substances, and λ_2 is an isosbestic wavelength the above expressions reduces to

$$\Delta V/V_{\text{ref}} = 10^{-\alpha_1 \Delta C_1} - 1 \tag{20}$$

or for small changes

$$\Delta V/V_{\text{ref}} = -2.31\alpha_1 \Delta C_1 . \tag{21}$$

Thus for small absorbance changes a linear recording device may be employed. However, the effects of scattering have been neglected.

If the two wavelengths are close together such that the scattering changes at each wavelength are the same ($\Delta \tau$), then the expression for $\Delta V/V_{\text{ref}}$ is modified to the form

$$\Delta V/V_{\text{ref}} = 10^{-\Delta \tau}(10^{-\Delta A_1} - 10^{-\Delta A_2}) \tag{22}$$

so that light scattering changes cause a change in the sensitivity only.

D. Cytochrome P450 and Tryptophan Oxygenase

In myoglobin and hemoglobin the diatomic molecule, molecular oxygen (O_2), is bound reversibly at the heme sites. However, at the heme site of cytochrome A_3 of the macromolecular hemoprotein complex, cytochrome oxidase, molecular oxygen is not bound reversibly but instead the diatomic molecule is activated, split into two parts, and finally reduced to two molecules of water (H_2O). There are two other possible operations that might be performed on molecular oxygen by macromolecular complexes. One of these is the function performed by mixed function oxygenases such as cytochrome P450, which is found in microsomes. Here a hemoprotein activates molecular oxygen, splits it into two parts but then converts only one oxygen atom to water. The other oxygen atom is inserted into a substrate molecule in the form of a hydroxyl group (—OH). This process is very important for the detoxification of molecules foreign to the living system. The macromolecule is called cytochrome P450 because it is a cytochrome whose CO-complex is a pigment with a Soret absorption band at 450 nm. This absorption is anomalous in that most other CO–hemoprotein complexes have Soret absorption bands in the region 420–430 nm. Carbon monoxide recombination with this cytochrome system has now been studied by using a 455 nm, 1 J, 1 μsec laser output of a 7-diethylamine-4-methylcoumarin-ethanol liquid dye laser.

A second type of operation that may be performed on molecular oxygen by a hemoprotein complex is carried out by dioxygenases which activate O_2, split it into two parts, and then insert both oxygen atoms

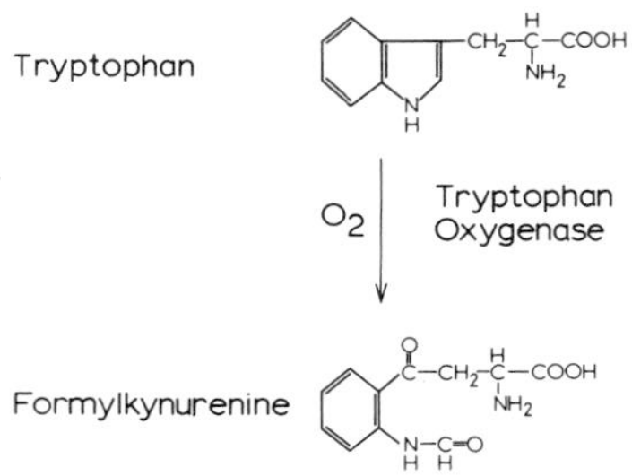

Tryptophan

O_2 | Tryptophan Oxygenase

Formylkynurenine

FIG. 17.   Fixation of oxygen by the enzyme tryptophan oxygenase.

into a substrate molecule. A good example of this is tryptophan oxygenase which catalyzes the reaction shown in Fig. 17. The enzyme is a tetramer with two heme groups and two copper atoms (see Feigelson and Brady, 1974). The carbon monoxide recombination kinetics and allosteric properties of a bacterial tryptophan oxygenase enzyme have been studied with the use of the 585 nm, 1 J, 1 μsec output of a Rhodamine 6G-ethanol liquid dye laser (Feigelson *et al.*, 1973).

E. OXYGEN PHOTOLYSIS

One of the major difficulties in the experimental study of oxygen binding to hemoglobin has been that the kinetic "on" rate constants are very high; thus the reaction is too fast to be studied fully with the use of a stop-flow mixing apparatus. It was also not possible to perform such studies with a conventional (for example a xenon flash) photolysis light source because the quantum efficiency was too low to produce significant photolysis (Gibson and Ainsworth, 1957). High energy, short pulse width, tunable liquid dye lasers now make it possible to perform such experiments. McCray (1972, 1974) has described a dual liquid dye laser system that can produce full photolysis (greater than 95%) of the oxyhemoprotein complex of human hemoglobin. This system utilizes two cylindrical flash lamp–pumped Rhodamine 6G-ethanol liquid dye lasers which each have 1 J, 1 μsec outputs at 585 nm. These lasers are operated in the fundamental Gaussian mode and a portion of the center part of each beam is allowed to impinge, from opposite directions, upon a cuvette containing the hemoglobin sample (see Fig. 18). The recombination rates of oxygen combining with deoxyhemes now can be studied in the microsecond time range, and the process is followed by using the extinction difference $\Delta\epsilon = \epsilon_{oxy} - \epsilon_{deoxy}$ at 436 nm to count the number of

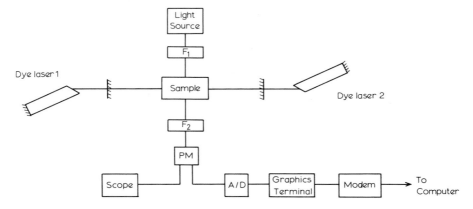

FIG. 18. Experimental setup for laser photolysis of oxyhemoglobin. The two-dye laser outputs are focused on the sample cell. A high-intensity lamp is used for monitoring the sample. The photomultiplier records the spectral changes occurring and the output is displayed either directly on an oscilloscope or alternatively after a/d conversion sent over a modem link to a computer for on-line analysis. An interface board is part of the graphics terminal which is also used to communicate with the computer. F_1 = heat filter, F_2 = interference filter.

hemes that have bound oxygen. The transmission changes that occur on low and medium photolysis levels are shown in Fig. 19.

At lower levels of photolysis various distributions of triply, doubly, and singly liganded tetrameric species are produced. The triply liganded species (for HbA in phosphate buffer) are in the quaternary R-state and bind oxygen vary rapidly, while the doubly and singly liganded species make a very rapid conformational change, immediately after photolysis, to the quaternary T-state with subsequent rate-limiting slow ligand recombination. As the laser intensity is increased, more of the doubly and singly liganded species, as well as the completely unliganded species, are produced and these tetramers rapidly convert to the quaternary T-state. Since the T-state reaction "on" rate is slow, more slow phase would be expected for a higher laser intensity. Figure 19 illustrates this, where the application of both laser pulses to the sample of oxyhemoglobin leads to a much greater slow recombination. Experiments of this type are being used to understand better how the conformational states of the tetramer are involved in the molecular mechanism of oxygen binding to hemoglobin.

Alpert *et al.* (1972) have reported 30% photolysis of oxyhemoglobin complexes with the high-energy 529 nm second harmonic output of a neodymium glass laser system.

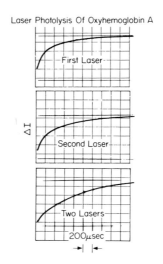

FIG. 19.   Optical transmission changes representing oxygen recombination kinetics to hemoglobin following either single or double laser flash photolysis of oxyhemoglobin.

IV. Resonant Raman Spectroscopy

In recent years considerable interest has developed in the application of Raman spectroscopy to the study of biological molecules. In view of the large amount of information already available for many of these molecules from techniques such as X-ray diffraction, nuclear magnetic resonance, electron spin resonance, spectroscopy, etc., one might be tempted to ask: What additional information can Raman spectroscopy provide? This section will outline the principles and techniques involved in the particular aspect of Raman spectroscopy that has found wide biological application, and will illustrate them with examples from the rapidly expanding literature in this field. A recent comprehensive review of the subject has been done by Spiro (1974).

Raman spectroscopy in general received a tremendous stimulus in the 1960s when high power density laser sources became available. It is the field of resonant Raman spectroscopy, however, that has been applied to the biological world.

In normal Raman spectroscopy the exciting light falls in a nonabsorbing region of the molecule under investigation. In resonance Raman spectroscopy the excitation wavelength lies within the absorption profile of the molecule of interest. A coupling occurs between the characteristic electronic and vibrational transitions of the molecule resulting in an enhancement of certain of the vibrational modes associated with Raman scattering. Indeed the scattering intensity for these modes is several orders of magnitude greater than for normal Raman spectroscopy. However, the real power of resonance Raman spectroscopy in biology is not fully realized until it is appreciated that the very chromophore giving rise to the electronic transition, as well as the vibrational modes that are thus enhanced, is frequently the biologically interesting active site of the molecule. Resonance Raman scattering thus provides a probe of this site, or, more specifically the vibrational modes associated with the active site. The information obtained is specific to the site itself; very little, if any, contribution is attributable to the complex distribution of atoms that form the framework which surrounds the chromophore. Of particular significance in the interpretation of the data obtained from resonance Raman spectroscopy is the fact that since water is a poor Raman scatterer an aqueous environment can be used. The molecule is therefore in a "natural" state and in addition the concentrations (10^{-3}–10^{-5} M) normally used are typical of those used in other studies of biomolecules.

A. RAMAN SCATTERING

The Raman process involves the inelastic scattering of an incident photon by a molecule, the frequency of scattered light being shifted from that of the incident light by a quantum associated with a molecular transition of the molecule of interest. The most important of these transitions is concerned with the vibrational motion of the molecule. Stokes scattering occurs when the incident photon loses energy and the molecule is raised to an excited vibronic state; the reverse process where the scattered photon has a higher energy is known as anti-Stokes scattering.

Classically Raman scattering is associated with an electric moment **P** induced in the scattering molecule by the electric field **E** of the light, so that $\mathbf{P} = \alpha\mathbf{E}$, where α is the molecular polarizability; in general α is a tensor quantity. Placzek's paper (Placzek, 1934) introduces his polarizability theory and discusses the quantum mechanical theory associated with Kramers–Heisenberg–Dirac. The quantum mechanical result for the induced electric moment matrix element P_{nm} is (see, e.g., Woodward, 1967).

$$P_{nm} = \frac{1}{h} \sum_r \left(\frac{M_{nr}M_{rm}}{\nu_{rn} - \nu_0} + \frac{M_{nr}M_{rm}}{\nu_{rm} + \nu_0} \right) \cdot E \qquad (23)$$

where h is Planck's constant, n and m are the initial and final states, respectively, r is an excited state, ν_{rn}, ν_{rm}, M_{nr}, M_{rm} are the corresponding frequencies and transition moments, respectively, and ν_0 is the incident frequency.

The intensity of the scattered light is given by

$$I_{nm} = \frac{64\pi^2}{3c^2} (\nu_0 + \nu_{nm})^4 P_{nm}^2 \tag{24}$$

where c is the velocity of light, and $(\nu_0 + \nu_{nm})$ is the frequency of the scattered light.

In resonance Raman scattering the frequency of the incident light approaches that of an electronic transition, i.e., as ν_0 approaches ν_{rn}. As $(\nu_{rn} - \nu_0)$ becomes small, P_{nm} is subject to preresonance enhancement and eventually $(\nu_{rn} - \nu_0)$ becomes very small (not zero due to the inclusion of a damping factor to allow for a finite electronic linewidth). At this point the first term of the equation is dominant and determines the greatly increased intensity of the Raman lines associated with resonance Raman spectroscopy.

B. EXPERIMENTAL TECHNIQUES

As indicated above, in resonance Raman spectroscopy the excitation source overlaps the absorption band of the molecule under study. Lasers provide an ideal source. They have the high power densities required to observe Raman spectra, and they also are available at many frequencies within the visible spectrum. In addition, tunable cw dye laser sources are now available with power levels of a few hundred milliwatts and a tuning range between 420 and 700 nm. The majority of the work in the biological field has been done using various lines from argon (e.g., 458, 488, 514), argon/krypton, helium-cadmium (442), and helium neon lasers (633). For example, these lines in the hemoproteins lie either within the Soret region or within the $\alpha\beta$ absorption region, and thus different Raman frequencies will be enhanced in each region.

The major problems associated with illuminating the sample in an absorbing region are localized heating, photodissociation of the sample, and fluorescence background signal which can easily mask the weak Raman signal. The fluorescence problem is particular to each individual system studied though many biological systems have effective inherent quenching mechanisms; for instance, in oxy- and deoxyhemoglobin the fluorescence background signal is not very large. However, in methemoglobin [Fe (III)], serious interference of the background signal is encountered. In cases where this occurs various agents may be used to quench the fluorescence provided they do not react chemically with the sample itself. In the case quoted potassium iodide has been found to eliminate effectively the fluorescence problem. Localized heating and disintegration of samples can be reduced by using the rotating cell technique developed by Kiefer and Bernstein (1971). However, in some instances the illuminating light is so intense that photodissociation of the sample can occur; for example, carbon monoxide is easily removed from carboxyhemoglobin under high light levels. Thus the experimenter must be aware of the intrinsic properties of the molecule under study.

A typical experimental arrangement is shown in Fig. 20. The sample is contained in a holder, either of the rotating cell type discussed above or more usually in less exotic arrangements, such as capillary tubes typically 1 mm in internal diameter. The laser output is focused on the sample and the scattered light is collected by a lens system and focused on the slit of a double monochromator. A plasma spike filter is usually inserted to reject spurious lines from the laser. Analysis of the polarization dependence of the scattered light is performed prior to entry into the monochromator by a Polaroid disk; the scattered light is then scrambled to eliminate errors due to the inherent polarization properties of the double monochromator. The monochromator scans the frequency shift region of interest and the output is recorded on a cooled photomultiplier. The amplified signal is discriminated against spurious signals. The outputs of the frequency drive and the ratemeter are displayed on the x–y axes of a chart recorder, and the Raman spectrum displayed.

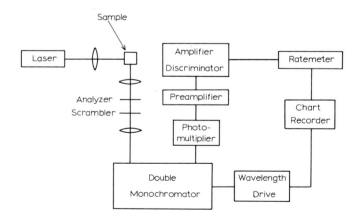

FIG. 20.   Laser Raman experimental setup.

Typical scan rates are 10–100 cm^{-1} min^{-1}, peak positions accurate to 2 cm^{-1} with an instrumental linewidth of 10 cm^{-1}.

C. APPLICATIONS

The application of resonance Raman spectroscopy to the study of biological molecules is a mixture of two approaches. On the one hand, a complete interpretation of the various lines in terms of the various vibrational modes of the chromophore is undertaken. On the other, a more empirical approach is taken where a particular line is used to indicate the "state" of the molecule. This second approach although useful is, however, susceptible to misinterpretation.

As a group of molecules the hemeproteins have been widely studied using the resonance Raman technique. The chromophore responsible for the characteristic electronic absorption spectra of these molecules (see Fig. 12) is the heme group, or more specifically iron protoporphyrin IX (shown in Fig. 2). The absorption is attributed by Gouterman (1959) to π–π^* transitions of the porphyrin ring. In resonance Raman, a coupling occurs with the in-plane stretchings and deformations of the porphyrin ring, and these vibrational modes are resonantly enhanced. These vibrational modes will thus be sensitive to structural alterations associated with the porphyrin ring. As indicated earlier the degree of enhancement of a scattered line is dependent on the region of the spectrum in which the exciting light falls. Raman spectra of deoxy-oxy hemoglobin (Spiro and Strekas, 1974) are shown in Fig. 21 under conditions where the incident light is in the Soret (457.9 nm) and the $\alpha\beta$ region (514.5 nm). The Raman lines observed have been analyzed assuming D_{4h} point group symmetry; the vibrational modes that will be resonance-enhanced in the $\alpha\beta$ region are the A_{1g} [$\delta < 3/4$ polarized-inactive (Perrin et al., 1969)], B_{1g}, B_{2g} ($\delta = 3/4$, depolarized) and A_{2g} ($\delta > 3/4$, inverse polarized) where δ is the polarization ratio defined as

$$\delta = I_\perp / I_\| \tag{25}$$

where $I_\perp$ is the intensity of the scattered light with its polarization perpendicular to the incident light, and $I_\|$ the intensity of the scattered light with its polarization parallel to the incident light. The light scattered in the Soret region are A-type and are totally symmetric. Indeed, the observation by Spiro and Strekas (1972a) of inverse polarized lines for ferrocytochrome c and hemoglobin was the first experimental observation of this effect predicted by Placzek's theory (1934)

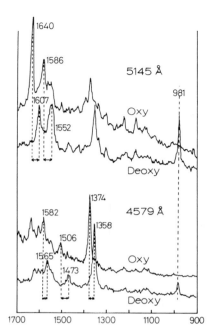

FIG. 21. Resonance Raman spectra of oxy- and deoxyhemoglobin illuminated in the Soret region, 451 nm, and the $\alpha\beta$ region, 514.5 nm (see Fig. 12). The solutions were 0.68 and 0.34 mM on a heme basis for oxy- and deoxyhemoglobin, respectively. The latter solution contained $(NH_4)_2SO_4$ and this is responsible for the 981 cm^{-1} band $v_1(SO_4^{2-})$. The frequency shifts for corresponding bands are marked by arrows. Instrumental conditions: slit width 6 cm^{-1}. Laser power of 25–50 mW was used to record the spectra. From Spiro and Strekas (1974).

that the scattering tensor becomes asymmetric as the excitation radiation approaches a resonant transition.

Early spectral studies (Strekas and Spiro, 1972; Brunner and Sussner, 1973) of hemoglobin were able to detect frequency shifts for certain lines in the spectra when the hemoglobin was oxygenated or deoxygenated (see Fig. 22). The interpretation of these spectra is associated with the fact that the iron atom moves out of the plane of the nitrogen atoms when hemoglobin becomes deoxygenated (Perutz, 1970). This movement causes a lengthening of the Fe—N bonds and a doming of the porphyrin ring, and as a consequence, changes the vibrational modes associated with the C—C conjugated ring that are enhanced. A similar investigation is concerned with the spin state of the iron atom. Perutz (1970) has postulated that the spin state of the iron acts as the trigger mechanism

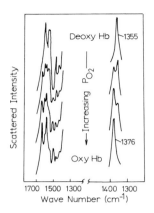

FIG. 22. Resonance Raman spectra of hemoglobin in the region 1300–1700 cm^{-1} at various oxygen partial pressures P_{O_2}. The shift of the band at 1355 cm^{-1} to 1376 cm^{-1} upon oxygenation is clearly seen. From Brunner and Sussner (1973).

for the tertiary conformational change of hemoglobin occurring on ligand binding. Hoard (1971) showed that in high spin compounds the iron is out of the plane, 0.8 Å in Fe(III), and 0.3 Å in Fe(II); this is in contrast to low spin Fe(II) where the iron is planar.

In addition a similar movement of the iron occurs from Fe(II) (planar) to Fe(III) (out of plane) oxidation states for the same spin state, presumably due to the different size of the ionic radius. Yamamoto et al. (1973) made a comparative study of hemoblobin and its derivatives in a variety of oxidation and spin states. They identify a band between 1356 and 1361 cm^{-1} characteristic of Fe(II), and a band between 1370 and 1378 cm^{-1} characteristic of Fe(III) for the various hemoproteins: a second set between 1584 and 1566 cm^{-1} is characteristic of the low and high spin configuration, respectively. On the basis of these comparisons they asserted that the iron exists in the low spin ferric structure in oxyhemoglobin, i.e., $Fe^{3+}O_2$. The same conclusion was reached by Spiro and Strekas (1974) in a similar investigation. This is in agreement with the infrared stretching frequency characteristic of superoxide found at 1104 cm^{-1} by Barlow and co-workers (1973), and with the model proposed by Weiss (1964). Pauling (1964) and Griffith (1956) had proposed the alternative structure of $Fe^{2+}O_2$ (low spin), and Gray (1971) had proposed $Fe^{4+}O_2^{2-}$.

Cytochromes are hemoproteins associated with electron transport in the electron chain, the final step being cytochrome oxidase donating its electron to oxygen which subsequently forms water. As indicated earlier cytochrome oxidase is complex, consisting of two components, cyt a and cyt a_3, the latter reacting with molecular oxygen. In addition the heme groups are associated with copper atoms which undergo Cu(II), Cu(I) transitions during electron transport to oxygen. Salmeen *et al.* (1973) using helium-cadmium excitation at 442 nm have obtained the resonant Raman spectra of this hemoprotein. In the reduced state they were unable to detect any differences due to nonequivalent hemes. However, in the fully oxidized state they suggest the possibility of observing nonequivalent hemes, a and a_3. Correlation of these studies with other techniques may provide an insight into the mode of action of cytochrome oxidase. Cytochrome c, however, is more fully character-ized, receiving its electron from cytochrome b and donating it to cytochrome a mentioned above. Several observations of cytochrome c have been made (see, e.g., Spiro and Strekas, 1972b), the results being typical for hemoproteins. Adar and Erecinska (1974) have exploited the variation of resonance enhancement with frequency of the incident light to study the resonance Raman spectra of succinate cytochrome c reductase. By varying the wavelength of the exciting light they were able to distinguish between the b- and c-type cytochromes of succinate cytochrome c reductase. At 514.5 nm both c and b cytochromes were observed. However at 568.2 nm predominantly b-type cytochromes were observed due to the overlap of the exciting light with the α absorption band.

A further example of using the frequency dependence of the reso-nance enhancement is the work of Lutz and Breton (1973) on chloro-phyll a, chlorophyll b, and carotenoids in chloroplasts. Using 10 excitation wavelengths between 442 nm (helium cadmium) and 515 nm (argon ion), they were able to produce selective amplification of each component relative to the other two. In fact the noncoincidence of the electronic absorption allows a different wavelength zone to be optimum for each component. Thus below 450 nm chlorophyll a is enhanced, between 450 nm and 475 nm chlorophyll b, and above 475 nm the carotenoid spectra are predominant (see Fig. 23).

Now that tunable dye lasers are becoming readily available, more experiments of selective enhancement are bound to be forthcoming. Lewis (1973) using a 30 mW dye laser pumped by a chopped argon ion laser obtained spectra between 550 and 1700 cm^{-1} of dark adapted bovine rhodopsin without causing significant cis-trans isomerization of the retinylidene moiety. This cis-trans isomerism is the primary photo-chemical act of vision. The spectra were obtained using an incident wavelength at 583 nm (see Fig. 24). A comparison "off resonance"

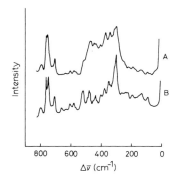

FIG. 23. Resonance Raman scattering of chloroplasts under different illumination conditions. (A) Chloroplasts illuminated with 442 nm helium-cadmium excitation at room temperature with resonance enhancement of chlorophyll a. Resolution 8.5 cm⁻¹. (B) Chloroplasts illuminated at 458 nm argon excitation with enhancement of chlorophyll b. 50K. Resolution 8 cm⁻¹. From Lutz and Breton (1973).

spectra at 630 nm is shown. These results clearly show the power of being able to tune to resonance, and in particular Rimai *et al.* (1971) using a fixed frequency Ar^+ laser were only able to detect two bands at 1520 and 1550 cm⁻¹ for the lumirhodopsin product of rhodopsin at −70°C. The spectra of Lewis are at physiological temperatures.

The field of resonant Raman spectroscopy is only a few years old in the biological context and already the literature is large and rapidly expanding. The purpose of this section was to outline the areas in which resonance Raman has been applied and to illustrate that under suitable conditions meaningful spectra can be obtained and interpreted.

V. Laser-Induced Fluorescence

The measurement of fluorescent lifetimes is an important technique in biology. The interest lies not only in the energy transfer processes occurring after excitation of some specific molecule but also in the fact that fluorescent molecules are used as probes of the system, for example, to monitor the local environment surrounding a probe embedded in a membrane.

Merkelo *et al.* (1969) used a mode-locked He-Ne laser to measure the fluorescence decay of chlorophyll a in the green alga *Chlorella pyrenoidosa*. They obtained a value of 1.6 nsec in agreement with 1.4 nsec measured by the phase shift technique. The experimental setup is shown in Fig. 25. The helium neon laser oscillates with a fundamental inter-

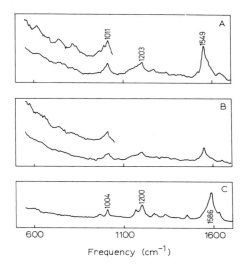

FIG. 24.   Tunable dye laser excitation of dark adapted bovine rhodopsin. (A) Resonance Raman spectra recorded with dye laser excitation at 683 nm (30 mW) step size 0.1
nm, time at each step 1 sec. Insert with time at each step of 3 sec. (B) Same as (A) with
incident radiation at 630 nm. This spectrum is not as resonantly enhanced as that in (A).
Upon illumination of the sample the resonance Raman spectra, 565 nm excitation,
recorded in (C) shows no bands in the 550–950 cm⁻¹ region. From Lewis (1973).

mode frequency separation of 102.207 MHz, the average output power
being 10 mW, the average mode-locked power being a few milliwatts.
For direct measurements the output was incident on the sample cuvette
and the fluorescence was measured at right angles using optical filters
and a RCA 7102 photomultiplier. The output was displayed on a

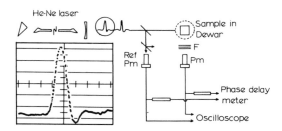

FIG. 25.   Apparatus for measurement of fluorescent lifetimes. This apparatus allows for
direct measurement of the fluorescent lifetime of the sample excited by the mode-locked
helium-neon laser, and for measurement using the phase delay technique. From Merkelo
et al. (1969). Copyright 1969 by the American Association for the Advancement of
Science.

sampling oscilloscope. These results can be compared to those obtained by the phase delay technique. The reference photomultiplier samples the laser output and the phase meter is nulled using calcium carbonate suspended in the sample cuvette. The phase-delay introduced by the sample can then be obtained. As indicated above the two techniques are in good agreement.

Mar *et al.* (1972) using the above techniques measured the fluorescence decay of chlorophyll a in various algae, under conditions where photosynthesis was inactive either by cooling to 77 K or in the presence of 3-(3,4-dichloropheryl)-1,1-dimethylurea which poisons the system. They obtained for Chlorella a value of 5×10^8 sec^{-1} for the radiationless decay of the excited molecule assuming that the intrinsic fluorescence lifetime of chlorophyll a is 15.2 nsec. Govindjee *et al.* (1972) at the same laboratory using a mode-locked argon ion laser (56 MHz at 488 nm) measured the lifetime of the excited state of bacteriochlorophyll in various photosynthetic bacteria.

In an attempt to isolate the rate-determining step of oxygen binding to hemoglobin, Alpert and Lindqvist (1975) utilized the property of oxygen as a triplet state quencher to probe the rate of oxygen diffusion into the heme pocket. In iron-free porphyringlobin and iron protoporphyrin IX, the triplet state was populated by nanosecond excitation using a 30 nsec pulse of frequency-doubled Nd^{3+} laser.

The decay was measured at 470 nm in aerated and deaerated solutions (see Fig. 26). The first-order rate constant k for the decay process is found to be 1.6×10^9 M^{-1} sec^{-1} for the free porphyrin and 1.8×10^8 M^{-1}

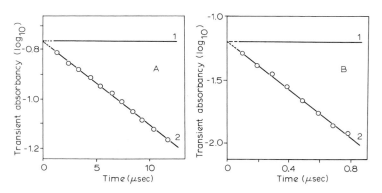

FIG. 26. (A) Decay of triplet porphyrin-globin in deaerated (1) and aerated (2) solution, measured at 470 nm after laser excitation, at equal laser energy. (B) Same as (A) for triplet decay of protoporphyrin IX. From Alpert and Lindqvist (1975). Copyright 1975 by the American Association for the Advancement of Science.

sec^{-1} for the porphyrin-globin. The "protecting" effect of the globin is interpreted as being due to the insertion of the porphyrin into the heme pocket of the globin. The significance for the binding of oxygen in hemoglobin is that these rates are an order of magnitude larger than the known binding rate constants of oxygen to hemoglobin. It would therefore appear that the rate-limiting step is not the rate of penetration of oxygen into the heme pocket.

VI. Laser Doppler Scattering

Another area the laser has opened up for study is the measurement of the time dependence of dielectric constant fluctuations. These fluctuations modulate the scattered laser light giving rise to a broadened frequency spectrum. The scattered light may also be considered to be emitted by molecules that are moving because of their Brownian motion and hence give rise to frequency-shifted light. From the spectral broadening, it is possible to obtain translational and rotational diffusion coefficients, and with the use of the Stokes–Einstein relation information may be obtained about the mass and shape of the molecules. A number of good reviews on laser Doppler scattering have appeared (see, e.g., Ford, 1972; Ford *et al.*, 1973; Benedek, 1969; French *et al.*, 1969).

The scattering of light from different parts of the medium is coherent and leads to a Bragg law diffraction formula. Pecora (1964, 1965, 1968) theoretically treated light scattering from particles undergoing Brownian motion and predicted a Lorentzian line shape for the spectral distribution of the scattered light with a life half-width

$$\Gamma = \frac{16\pi^2 n^2 D \sin^2(\theta/2)}{\lambda_0^2}$$

where λ_0 is the incident wavelength, n the index of refraction of the solvent, θ the forward scattering angle, and D the translational diffusion coefficient.

Experimentally these scattered linewidths have been very difficult to measure since they may be of the order of 10 Hz. The incident light has a frequency of the order of 10^{14} Hz and the sharpest optical filter, the Fabry–Perot etalon, has a resolving power $\nu/\Delta\nu$ of about 10^7. Hence, optically the narrowest linewidths that may be resolved are of the order of 10^7 Hz. In order to overcome this difficulty, "radio" techniques such as the superheterodyne principle have been extended into the optical region so that a modulated difference frequency signal is obtained in a frequency region in which the narrow lines involved may be resolved. Figure 27 illustrates the basic idea in this type of spectrometer. Optical scattering from a Teflon wedge produces the local oscillator which is then mixed in a square law detector with light scattered from the solution to produce low frequency beat signals which are then put into an audio frequency spectrum analyzer. For this technique the laser used should be operating only in the axial TEM_{00} modes. It was found (Ford and Benedek, 1965; Ford et al., 1969) that the local oscillator was not needed as the scattered light may be allowed to beat with itself in order to produce a low frequency spectrum. In addition the Weiner–Khintchine theorem gives the power spectrum of the scattered light as the Fourier transform of the autocorrelation function of the scattered light which is defined as

$$C(\tau) = \langle E(t)E^*(t + \tau)\rangle = \lim_{T\to\infty} \frac{1}{T} \int_{-T/2}^{T/2} E(t)E^*(t + \tau)dt$$

Thus the autocorrelation function may also be measured directly with the use of an electronic autocorrelator. Figure 28 illustrates a typical experimental setup for a self-beating spectrometer.

An example of the data obtained from such experiments is shown in Fig. 29 where the scattering spectrum linewidth is plotted against $|\bar{\kappa}|^2$ where

$$|\bar{\kappa}| = 2|\bar{k}| \sin(\theta/2)$$

is the magnitude of the scattering wave vector and $|\bar{k}| = 2\pi n/\lambda_0$. The

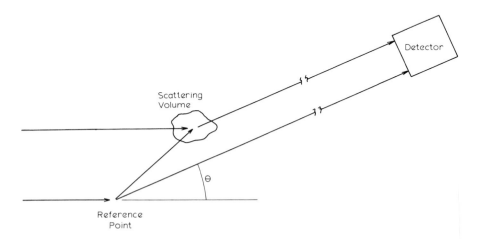

FIG. 27.   Scattering geometry for laser Doppler scattering.

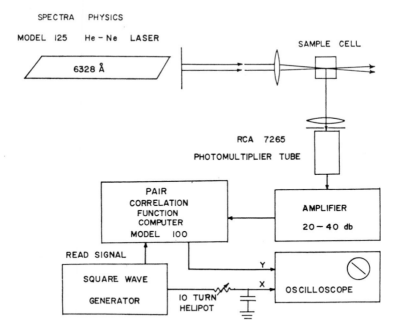

FIG. 28. Experimental setup for self-beating laser spectrometer. From Ford *et al.* (1969).

molecular system studied in this case (Ford *et al.*, 1969) was a poly-α-amino acid poly-γ-benzyl-L-glutamate (PBG) in various solvent composition of 1,2-dichloroethane (DCE) and dichloroacetic acid (DCA). The fact that the Doppler scattering is sensitive to the molecular shape may be seen from Fig. 30 which illustrates a helix-random coil transition.

Laser Doppler scattering has been used to study rotational diffusion in the macromolecules lysozyme (Dubin *et al.*, 1971) and tobacco mosaic virus (TMV) (Wada *et al.*, 1971); long wavelength internal modes of vibration of flexible molecules such as F-actin which is a muscle protein (Fujime, 1970; Fujime and Ishiwata, 1971), *E. coli* ribosomes (Hocker *et al.*, 1973; Gabler *et al.*, 1974), and *in vivo* blood flow velocity (Tanaka and Benedek, 1975). Many more examples will be found in the reviews cited above.

VII. Applications of Picosecond Pulses

A new area of investigation of biological molecules is the application of the mode-locked laser to study picosecond spectroscopy. Busch *et al.*

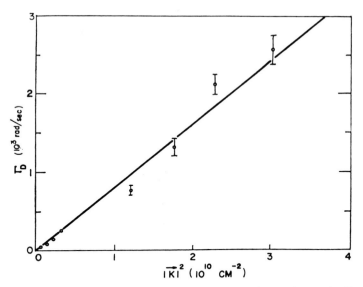

FIG. 29. Half-width of scattering spectrum as function of scattering angle. From Ford *et al.* (1969).

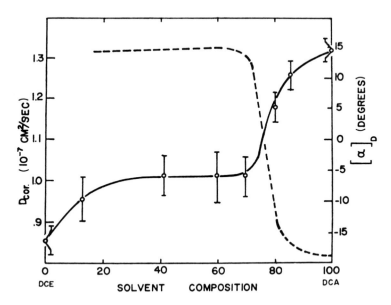

FIG. 30. Diffusion constants of PBG in DCA-DCE as function of composition. From Ford *et al.* (1969).

(1972) used the second harmonic of a mode-locked Nd^{3+} glass laser to study the formation and decay of prelumirhodopsin. Prelumirhodopsin is an intermediate that is thought to be formed as a result of the primary photochemical step in the geometrical isomerization of the polyene chromophore following photoexcitation of bovine rhodopsin (see, e.g., Wald, 1968). Using an experimental arrangement similar to that discussed below, they determined a rise time for the formation of prelumirhodopsin of less than 6 psec and an exponential decay of the transient intermediate species with a lifetime of 30 nsec, supporting the view that prelumirhodopsin is the product of the primary photoprocess. Netzel *et al.* (1973) used an experimental arrangement shown in Fig. 31 to measure the kinetics of reaction centers containing bacteriochlorophyll. Here a single mode-locked pulse is extracted from the pulse train of a Nd^{3+} glass laser using a laser triggered spark gap. The single pulse is then amplified before passing through a phase matched KDP crystal producing the second harmonic at 530 nm. After passing through a flash lamp rejection filter the 1060/530 nm laser pulse is focused into a long cell containing water where stimulated Stokes and anti-Stokes Raman scattering occurs. This produces a continuum (in the 864 nm spectral region) synchronous with the laser pulse. A beam splitter followed by a 1060 nm rejection filter separates the 530 nm light and 864 nm continuum

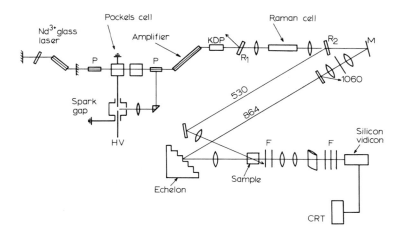

FIG. 31. Experimental arrangement to measure the picosecond kinetics of bacteriochlorophyll containing reaction centers from *Rhodopseudomonas spheroides* R-26 chromatophores. (P) polarizers, (R_1) dielectric reflector at 864 nm for rejection of laser flash lamp emission, (R_2) dielectric reflector at 530 nm, (M) mirrors, (F) filters. From Netzel *et al.* (1973). Copyright 1973 by the American Association for the Advancement of Science.

into two beams. The 530 nm light passes directly to the sample cell. The 864 nm light is incident on a series of aluminized glass slides stacked to form an echelon, thus producing a series of pulses 6 psec wide. These pulses are used to monitor the changes produced in the sample cell by the 530 nm light. Temporal and spatial overlap of the pulses in the cell was checked using transient birefringence of CS_2 by the 530 nm light. The events occurring in the cell were recorded at 864 nm using a silicon vidicon and multichannel analyzer, and the results were displayed on an oscilloscope.

Figure 32 shows the results obtained when the 530 nm and 864 nm light are present, the sample cell containing 15 μM reaction centers isolated from *Rhodopseudomonas spheroides* R-26. From the carbon disulphide experiments overlap of the 530 nm and 864 nm light occurs at the 7th "echelon" segment and thus this is defined as $t = 0$. The 864 nm light is absorbed in the first six segments, partial bleaching occurring in the seventh and full bleaching by the eighth segment. The bleaching of the bacteriochlorophyll band at 864 nm by the 530 nm light is thus complete 7 ± 2 psec. Thus the first steps in photosynthesis have been observed. A clear interaction between the bacteropheophytin (excited by the 530 light) and the bacteriochlorophyll band at 865 nm is thus clearly demonstrated. The same group (Kaufmann *et al.*, 1975) has recently reported on the reaction center bacteriochlorophyll oxidation.

Using a mode-locked Nd^{3+} laser, Seibert and Alfano (1974) used the 1.06 μm and KDP frequency-doubled 0.53 μm output to study photosys-

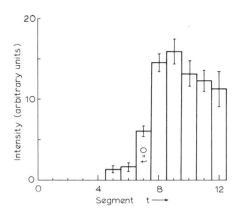

FIG. 32.   Histogram of normalized intensities as a function of segment position. 6 psec/segment. From Netzel *et al.* (1973). Copyright 1973 by the American Association for the Advancement of Science.

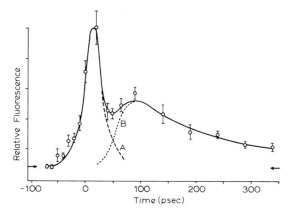

FIG. 33. Time dependence of fluorescent emission from spinach chloroplasts at 685 nm after excitation by a 4 psec pulse of 0.53 μm. Monochromator bandwidth 6.6 nm; total chlorophyll concentration 35 gm/ml. (A) is an extrapolation of the first peak and (B) represents the difference between the solid curve and (A). The arrows indicate the background level. From Seibert and Alfano (1974).

tem I and II fluorescence in spinach chloroplasts. The 0.53 μm output induces the fluorescence in the sample. This is analyzed at variable delayed times using the 1.06 μm beam to produce transient birefringence in a CS_2 cell through which the induced fluorescence is observed. The instrument has a resolution time of 10 psec. At 685 nm two peaks are observed in the fluorescence (see Fig. 33) with a minimum intervening. The first peak 15 psec after the flash is associated with the components of photosystem I and has a lifetime of 10 psec, the second peak 90 psec after the flash being associated with photosystem II and having a characteristic lifetime of 210 psec in spinach chloroplasts. The 90 psec delay is attributed to energy transfer between accessory pigments such as carotenoids and chlorophyll a.

REFERENCES

Adar, F., and Erecińska, M. (1974). Arch. Biochem. Biophys. 165, 570.
Alpert, B., and Lindqvist, L. (1975). Science 187, 836.
Alpert, B., Banerjee, R., and Lindqvist, L. (1972). Biochem. Biophys. Res. Commun. 46, 913.
Alpert, B., Banerjee, R., and Lindqvist, L. (1974). Proc. Natl. Acad. Sci. U.S.A. 71, 558.
Anderson, N. M., Reed, T. A., and Chance, B. (1970). Ann. N.Y. Acad. Sci. 174, 189.

Austin, R. H., Beeson, K., Eisenstein, L., Frauenfelder, H., Gunsalus, I. C., and Marshall, V. P. (1974). *Phys. Rev. Lett.* **32**, 403.

Barlow, C. H., Maxwell, J. C., Wallace, W. J., and Caughey, W. S. (1973). *Biochem. Biophys. Res. Commun.* **55**, 91.

Benedek, G. B. (1969). "Polarisation, Matter, and Radiation," p. 49. Presses Univ. France, Paris.

Brunner, H., and Sussner, H. (1973). *Biochim. Biophys. Acta* **310**, 20.

Busch, G. E., Applebury, M. L., Lamola, A. A., and Rentzepis, P. M. (1972). *Proc. Natl. Acad. Sci. U.S.A.* **69**, 2802.

Chance, B. (1951). *Rev. Sci. Instrum.* **22**, 634.

Chance, B., and DeVault, D. (1964). *Tag. Bunsenges.* May.

Chance, B., and Erecińska, M. (1971). *Arch. Biochem. Biophys.* **143**, 675.

Chance, B., and Schleyer, H. (1962). *Biophys. Soc. Annu. Meet. Abstr., 6th, Washington, D.C.* No. FC9.

Chance, B., and Schoener, B. (1964). *Biophys. Soc. Annu. Meet. Abstr., 8th, Chicago* No. FD9.

Chance, B., Schleyer, H., and Legallais, V. (1963). *Stud. Microalgae Photosyn. Bact., Univ. Tokyo* p. 337.

Chance, B., McCray, J. A., and Bunkenburg, J. (1970). *Nature (London)* **225**, 705.

Cowles, J. C. (1965). *J. Opt. Soc. Amer.* **55**, 690.

DeVault, D., and Chance, B. (1966). *Biophys. J.* **6**, 825.

DeVault, D., Parkes, J. H., and Chance, B. (1967). *Nature (London)* **215**, 642.

Dickerson, R. E. (1964). *In* "The Proteins" (H. Neurath, ed.), 2nd Ed., Vol. 2, p. 603. Academic Press, New York.

Dubin, S. B., Clark, N. A., and Benedek, G. B. (1971). *J. Chem. Phys.* **54**, 5158.

Dutton, P. L., and Jackson, J. B. (1972). *Eur. J. Biochem.* **30**, 495.

Dutton, P. L., Kihara, T., McCray, J. A., and Thornber, J. P. (1971). *Biochim. Biophys. Acta* **226**, 81.

Erecińska, M., and Chance, B. (1972). *Arch. Biochem. Biophys.* **151**, 304.

Feigelson, P., and Brady, F. O. (1974). "Molecular Mechanisms of Oxygen Activation" (O. Hayaishi, ed.), p. 87. Academic Press, New York.

Feigelson, P., Brady, F. O., and McCray, J. A. (1973). *J. Biol. Chem.* **248**, 5267.

Ford, N. C. (1972). *Chem. Scr.* **2**, 193.

Ford, N. C., and Benedek, G. B. (1965). *Phys. Rev. Lett.* **15**, 649.

Ford, N. C., Lee, W., and Karasz, F. (1969). *J. Chem. Phys.* **50**, 3098.

Ford, N. C., Gabler, R., and Karasz, F. (1973). *Adv. Chem. Ser.* **125**, 25.

French, M. J., Angus, J. C., and Walton, A. G. (1969). *Science* **163**, 345.

Fujime, S. (1970). *J. Phys. Soc. Jpn.* **29**, 751.

Fujime, S., and Ishiwata, S. (1971). *J. Mol. Biol.* **62**, 251.

Furumoto, H. W., and Cecone, H. L. (1970). *IEEE J. Quantum Electron.* **6**, 262.

Gabler, R., Westhead, E. W., and Ford, N. C. (1974). *Biophys. J.* **14**, 528.

Gibson, Q. H., and Ainsworth, S. (1957). *Nature (London)* **180**, 1416.

Gouterman, M. (1959). *J. Chem. Phys.* **30**, 1139.

Govindjee, Hammond, J. H., and Merkelo, H. (1972). *Biophys. J.* **12**, 809.

Gray, H. B. (1971). *Adv. Chem. Ser.* **100**, 365.

Griffith, J. S. (1956). *Proc. Roy. Soc., Ser. A* **235**, 23.

Hardman, K. D., Eylar, E. H., Ray, D. K., Banasak, J., and Gurd, F. R. N. (1966). *J. Biol. Chem.* **241**, 432.

Hildreth, W. W. (1968). *Biochim. Biophys. Acta* **153**, 197.

Hildreth, W. W., Avron, M., and Chance, B. (1966). *Plant Physiol.* **41**, 983.

Hoard, J. L. (1971). *Science* **174**, 1295.
Hocker, L., Krupp, J., Benedek, G. B., and Vournakis, J. (1973). *Biopolymers* **12**, 1677.
Junge, W., and DeVault, D. (1975). *Proc. Int. Meet. Soc. Chim. Phys., 27th, Thiais, Fr.*
Kaufmann, K. J., Dutton, P. L., Netzel, T. L., Leigh, J. S., and Rentzepis, P. M. (1975). *Science* **188**, 1301.
Ke, B., Vernon, L. P., Garcia, A., and Ngo, E. (1968). *Biochemistry* **7**, 311.
Kiefer, W., and Bernstein, H. J. (1971). *Appl. Spectrosc.* **25**, 500.
Kihara, T., and Chance, B. (1969). *Biochim. Biophys. Acta* **189**, 116.
Kihara, T., and Dutton, P. L. (1970). *Biochim. Biophys. Acta* **205**, 196.
Kihara, T., and McCray, J. A. (1971). *Biophys. Soc. Annu. Meet. Abstr., 15th, New Orleans,* Vol. 11, p. 34a.
Kihara, T., and McCray, J. A. (1973). *Biochim. Biophys. Acta* **292**, 297.
Lewis, A. (1973). *J. Raman Spectrosc.* **1**, 473.
Lutz, M., and Breton, J. (1973). *Biochem. Biophys. Res. Commun.* **53**, 413.
McCray, J. A. (1972). *Biochem. Biophys. Res. Commun.* **47**, 187.
McCray, J. A. (1974). *Eur. Electro-Opt. Market Tech. Conf., 2nd, Montreux,* p. 74.
McCray, J. A., and Anderson, N. (1972). *Fed. Proc., Fed. Am. Soc. Exp. Biol.* **31**, 886.
Maiman, T. H. (1960). *Nature (London)* **187**, 493.
Mar, T., Govindjee, Singhal, G. S., and Merkelo, H. (1972). *Biophys. J.* **12**, 797.
Merkelo, H., Hartman, S. R., Mar, T., Singhal, G. S., and Govindjee (1969). *Science* **164**, 301.
Miyazoe, Y., and Maeda, M. (1968). *Appl. Phys. Lett.* **12**, 206.
Netzel, T. L., Rentzepis, P. M., and Leigh, J. S. (1973). *Science* **182**, 238.
Parson, W. W. (1967). *Biochim. Biophys. Acta* **131**, 154.
Pauling, L. (1964). *Nature (London)* **203**, 182.
Pecora, R. (1964). *J. Chem. Phys.* **40**, 1604.
Pecora, R. (1965). *J. Chem. Phys.* **43**, 1562.
Pecora, R. (1968). *J. Chem. Phys.* **49**, 1036.
Perrin, M. H., Gouterman, M., and Perrin, C. L. (1969). *J. Chem. Phys.* **50**, 4137.
Perutz, M. F. (1968). *Harvey Lect.* **62**, 213.
Perutz, M. F. (1969). *Proc. Roy. Soc., Ser. B* **173**, 113.
Perutz, M. F. (1970). *Nature (London)* **228**, 726.
Perutz, M. F., Muirhead, H., Cox, J. M., and Goaman, L. C. G. (1968). *Nature (London)* **219**, 131.
Placzek, G. (1934). *In* "Handbuch der Radiologie" (E. Marx, ed.), Vol. VI, Part 2, p. 205. Akad. Verlagsges., Leipzig.
Prince, R. C., Cogdell, R. G., and Crofts, A. R. (1974). *Biochim. Biophys. Acta* **347**, 1.
Reed, T., Bunkenburg, J., and Chance, B. (1971). "Probes of Structure and Function of Macromolecules and Membranes. Vol. II: Probes of Enzymes and Hemoproteins," p. 335. Academic Press, New York.
Rimai, L., Giu, D., and Parsons, J. L. (1971). *J. Amer. Chem. Soc.* **93**, 1353.
Salmeen, I., Rimai, L., Gill, D., Yamamoto, T., Palmer, G., Hartzell, C. R., and Beinhert, H. (1973). *Biochem. Biophys. Res. Commun.* **52**, 1100.
Seibert, M., and Alfano, R. R. (1974). *Biophys. J.* **14**, 269.
Seibert, M., and DeVault, D. (1970). *Biochim. Biophys. Acta* **205**, 220.
Seibert, M., and DeVault, D. (1971). *Biochim. Biophys. Acta* **253**, 396.
Sorokin, P. P., and Lankard, J. R. (1966). *IBM J. Res. Dev.* **10**, 162.
Spiro, T. G. (1974). *In* "Chemical and Biological Applications of Lasers" (C. B. Moore, ed.), Vol. 1, pp. 29–70. Academic Press, New York.
Spiro, T. G., and Strekas, T. C. (1972a). *Proc. Natl. Acad. Sci. U.S.A.* **69**, 2622.

Spiro, T. G., and Strekas, T. C. (1972b). *Biochim. Biophys. Acta* **278,** 188.
Spiro, T. G., and Strekas, T. C. (1974). *J. Amer. Chem. Soc.* **96,** 338.
Staerk, H., and Chance, B. (1969). *FEBS. Lett.* **3,** 287.
Strekas, T. C., and Spiro, T. G. (1972). *Biochim. Biophys. Acta* **263,** 830.
Tanaka, T., and Benedek, G. B. (1975). *Appl. Opt.* **14,** 189.
Wada, A., Ford, N. C., and Karasz, F. E. (1971). *J. Chem. Phys.* **55,** 1798.
Wald, G. (1968). *Nature (London)* **219,** 800.
Weiss, J. (1964). *Nature (London)* **203,** 83.
Witt, H. T. (1967). *Fast React. Primary Processes Chem. Kinet., Proc. Nobel Symp., 5th*
    p. 81.
Woodward, L. A. (1967). *In* "Raman Spectroscopy" (H. A. Szymanski, ed.), pp. 1–43.
    Plenum Press, New York.
Yamamoto, T., Palmer, G., Gill, D., Salmeen, I. T., and Rimai, L. (1973). *J. Biol. Chem.*
    248, 5211.

RECYCLABLE INPUT DEVICES AND SPATIAL FILTER MATERIALS FOR COHERENT OPTICAL PROCESSING

David Casasent

Department of Electrical Engineering
Carnegie–Mellon University
Pittsburgh, Pennsylvania

I. Introduction

Coherent optical data processing has captured the imagination and attention of many researchers. This interest is due to the potential advantages of optical processors compared to digital or other analog

43

systems. An optical processor is a two-dimensional system in which all points in the input plane of a lens are operated on in parallel. This is in contrast to other processors which are inherently serial and which require extensive duplication of circuitry or components to achieve parallel processing. Coherent optical processors can also inherently perform Fourier transforms, correlations, and convolutions on two-dimensional data.

Many applications for these operations have been described in several survey articles (Vander Lugt, 1974; Stroke, 1972), special issues of journals (*IEEE Trans. Comput.*, 1975; *Proc. IEEE*, 1977; *J. Soc. Inf. Disp.*, 1974; *Opt. Eng.*, 1974), and elsewhere in the present series of volumes. Perhaps the major interest in optical computing lies in the high data throughput possible. The above operations can be performed in parallel on two-dimensional data at processing rates that can approach the speed of light and are limited only by the input and output transducers and the rate at which data can be placed in the system.

In most coherent optical processors, data is recorded on photographic film. This is neither a real-time nor a reusable transducer. If a viable coherent optical processor that even approaches the throughput possible is to be realized, replacements must be found for photographic film. The need for real-time, reusable, light modulators capable of spatially modulating coherent light has been apparent for many years. Many devices and materials have been suggested as such replacements for film. A survey of the most promising transducers including their operating principles and performance specifications is the subject of this chapter. Applications of many of these devices will be emphasized. Many of these devices and materials have their origin in the field of noncoherent projection displays (IEEE *Trans. Electron Devices,* 1973) and as mass storage media for digital data (*Appl. Opt.,* 1974; *RCA Rev.,* 1972). Electroded transducers exhibit low resolution and are principally of use as page composers (Roberts, 1972) in mass optical storage applications and are thus not included. Volume and magnetooptic storage materials are likewise of primary use in archival and binary storage applications.

The scope of this survey is restricted to devices that have been used as input devices and spatial filter materials in coherent optical processing. Only reusable and quasi-real-time two-dimensional transducers are considered. Even with these limitations, the magnitude of available results and literature on candidate devices and materials is enormous. Only the major and most recent references on the representative transducers are thus included. The true limitations, performance, and additional development work required for those transducers that are well documented and that have seen extensive use by diverse researchers are well known. These facts should be realized in comparing newer devices and materials to the more well known ones. All transducers to be discussed are in such various stages of research and development and are intended for such widely different applications that direct comparisons of present device specifications can be misleading. Furthermore, no universal set of specifications and device characteristics is appropriate for all applications and transducers.

II. Optical System Configurations

Thorough treatments of the Fourier transform and correlation properties of various optical systems exist (Goodman, 1968). The basic coherent optical frequency plane correlator is shown schematically in Fig. 1 and the joint transform (Weaver and Goodman, 1966) correlator in Fig. 2. These two optical configurations are used extensively with real-time transducers. Several features and desirable properties of the input devices and spatial filter materials can be deduced from a brief analysis of these configurations. Plane P_0 in Fig. 1 is the input plane. If its transmittance is proportional to $f(x_0, y_0)$, the Fourier transform $F(u, v)$ of $f(x_0, y_0)$ is formed in plane P_1 by lens L_1. The coordinates (x_1, y_1) of P_1 are related to the spatial frequency variables (u, v) by $x_1 = u\lambda f$ and $y_1 = v\lambda f$, where f is the focal length of L_1 and L_2 and λ is the wavelength of the input laser light. Capital letters (e.g., F and G) will be used to denote the Fourier transforms of the associated small letter spatial functions ($viz.$, f and g).

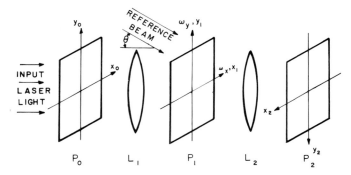

FIG. 1. Conventional frequency plane coherent optical correlator. P_0 is the input plane, P_1 the Fourier transform plane, and P_2 the output or correlation plane. L_1 and L_2 are Fourier transform lenses.

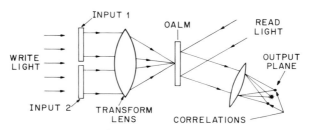

FIG. 2.   Joint transform (or dual in-line) coherent optical correlator.

While much information on the input data can be deduced from an analysis of the Fourier transform plane, the more powerful correlation and convolution operations can also be optically synthesized. If F is interfered with a plane wave reference beam $A_0 \exp(-j2\pi ay_1)$ at an angle θ as shown in Fig. 1 [where $a = (\sin \theta)/\lambda$], an intensity sensitive material at P_1 will record four terms, two of which are

$$F_H = (A_0 F^*/\lambda f) \exp(-j2\pi ay_1) + (A_0 F/\lambda f) \exp(j2\pi ay_1). \qquad (1)$$

If two of the terms in the transmittance of P_1 are given by Eq. (1) and if the transmittance of P_0 is proportional to a second spatial function $g(x_0, y_0)$ [whose transform is $G(u, v)$], then the amplitude of the light distribution leaving P_1 is given by G times Eq. (1). The contents of plane P_2 will contain the transform of this product and hence the correlation and convolution of f and g centered at $x_2 = 0$ and $y_2 = \pm a\lambda f$, respectively.

A large angle θ must often be used to insure an adequate separation of terms in plane P_2. This increases the spatial carrier frequency that the material in P_1 must resolve. With $\theta = 15°$ and $\lambda = 514$ nm, 800 line/mm resolution is needed in P_1.

The correlation of two spatial functions can also be realized using the joint transform optical correlator shown schematically in Fig. 2. The two input functions to be correlated, $f(x_0, y_0)$ and $g(x_0, y_0)$, are placed side by side in P_0 of Fig. 2 and separated by a center-to-center distance $2a$. The transmittance of P_0 can be described by

$$f(x_0 - a, y_0) + g(x_0 + a, y_0). \qquad (2)$$

The amplitude distribution incident on P_1 in Fig. 2 is the Fourier transform of Eq. (2) formed by lens L_1,

$$F(u, v) \exp(jua) + G(u, v) \exp(-jua). \qquad (3)$$

If the modulus squared of Eq. (3) is recorded by an optically sensitive material at P_1, the transmittance of P_1 will contain four terms, one of which is $F^*G \exp(-j2ua)$. The read beam shown in Fig. 2 is modulated in reflection by the transmittance of P_1. The Fourier transform of the modulus squared of Eq. (3), formed at P_2 by L_2 contains the desired correlation of f and g centered at $x_2 = 2a$, $y_2 = 0$.

Other optical configurations exist, but the systems in Figs. 1 and 2 have been used extensively with real-time transducers. If both functions to be correlated are similar in size, the spatial frequency resolution requirements for the material used at P_1 will be higher if the optical system of Fig. 1 rather than the one in Fig. 2 is used. The material at P_1 must be able to resolve a spatial frequency resolution of seven and six times that of the input (for the systems in Figs. 1 and 2, respectively). If the filtering function is narrower than the other function, the spatial frequency resolution requirements for the P_1 material are 25% less if the system in Fig. 1 rather than Fig. 2 is used. The required resolution for both systems is less than for the case when both functions are comparable in size (Nisenson and Sprague, 1975).

The joint transform system of Fig. 2 has less stringent alignment problems than the system of Fig. 1. A transform plane material at P_1 that is read out in reflection is indicated in Fig. 2. This system can easily be modified to accommodate a transmission readout material at P_1. The configuration in Fig. 1 can likewise be modified to incorporate a reflex-mode readout material at P_1. These considerations are important since many transducers require different wavelengths for reading and writing; and many are written on from one side and read out in reflection from the opposite side. These arrangements reduce the interaction of the readout light on the stored data. The optical configuration of Fig. 2 avoids many of the wavelength scaling problems that would arise with such transducers. This system is also more practical for use with transducers at P_1 that do not exhibit storage and for applications in which data must be simultaneously written on and read from P_1.

The joint transform correlator is also more practical when lower resolution materials are used at P_1. In the frequency plane correlator, low resolution P_1 materials require the use of small reference beam angles θ. This is accomplished by including a beam splitter between L_1 and P_1 in Fig. 1. The system in Fig. 2 requires the use of two input transducers and a third one at P_1. Furthermore, the read wavelength for the two input devices must equal the write wavelength for the P_1 material. This requirement is not compatible with the operation of many existing transducers. Such practical considerations must be realized in such systems.

III. Device and Material Considerations

A. CLASSIFICATIONS

There are two major types of transducers: those that are optically sensitive and those that are electronically addressed. Optically sensitive materials can be addressed in three ways: (a) by a scanning, modulated and focused laser beam (point-by-point addressed material); (b) by a spatially modulated noncoherent optical wave (noncoherent-to-coherent optical converters); or (c) by recording the holographic interference of a reference beam and a Fourier transform pattern (holographic recording material). The input signal for an electronically addressed transducer can be applied either: (a) by a scanning and modulated electron beam (electron-beam addressed device), or (b) by an electroded matrix deposited on the transducer (electroded device).

Optically addressed materials generally exhibit higher resolution than electronically addressed devices. This generally occurs because a laser beam can usually be focused to a smaller spot size (containing adequate energy) than an electron beam. Total resolutions of 32×32 seem to be a practical limit for electroded structures, whereas electron-beam addressed transducers have exhibited 40 line/mm resolution. Practical limits on laser beam deflectors generally result in comparable (or slightly higher) resolutions for point-by-point optically addressed devices. Holographic recording materials and optical-to-optical converter transducers exhibit far higher resolutions. The recording materials used at P_1 are generally always optically sensitive since a higher spatial resolution is always required than for the input transducer. Both electron-beam addressed and optically addressed devices are useful as the input P_0 plane transducer.

The transducers can also be distinguished by the material used, the modulation involved, or the type of recording produced. In this chapter, deformable devices, liquid crystal structures, and transducers using the Pockels electrooptic effect will be discussed. Rather than include only a few words on each of the many candidate materials and devices, emphasis will be given to the more documented and promising transducers that have seen use in coherent optical processing, rather than as displays and storage materials.

Several surveys of coherent spatial light modulators exist (Casasent, 1976, 1977a,b). Most are restricted to one class of device such as electronically addressed (Casasent, 1974b), noncoherent-to-coherent optical converters (Lipson, 1976), holographic recording materials (Bordogna et al., 1972), or mass digital storage materials (Tufte and Chen, 1973).

B. TERMINOLOGY

In the following discussions of transducer materials, various electrooptic, crystallographic, quantum electronic, and optical terms will be used. Since detailed treatments of these items are available (Billings, 1949; Carpenter, 1950; Adams et al., 1970), only the highlights and pertinent results are included in the appropriate sections. Many of the materials to be discussed are optically birefringent. This phenomenon is also known as double refraction. All optically transparent materials refract singly or doubly. Singly refracting crystals are distinguished by one index of refraction, while the doubly refracting materials exhibit two different principal indices. To describe the effects of a birefringent material on an incident light wave, the polarization of the input light must be considered.

For a plane light wave of a given wavelength and propagation direction incident on a birefringent material, there are only two input polarizations for which the material presents a single index of refraction to the light wave. For all other polarizations of the input light, the light will propagate as two independent waves each with the same frequency and direction of propagation but with different propagation velocities (indices of refraction n_0 and n_e). The difference $\Delta n = n_e - n_0$ is the material's optical birefringence. If Δn is the same for all propagation directions, the material is isotropic. All birefringent materials are anisotropic and are characterized by different Δn values for all propagation directions. Δn will be a minimum for one (uniaxial materials) or two (biaxial materials) directions of propagation. If the material is nonactive, the two preferred polarizations are linear and at right angles and the minimum $\Delta n = 0$. The directions of propagation for which the minimum Δn occurs are the material's optical axes. For optically active materials, the two polarizations are nonlinear for all propagation directions. Along the direction of minimum Δn, the polarization is circular, while it is elliptical with varying eccentricity for all other directions. Two general classes of transparent optical materials are thus the singly refracting media, which are isotropic and nonactive, and all other materials, which are doubly refracting.

C. STRUCTURES

Several general remarks concerning the structure of these devices and materials will place much of the following discussions in perspective. The basic structure of an optically sensitive spatial light modulator is shown in Fig. 3. Many other versions and more practical configurations exist. As noted earlier, electroded devices will not be considered. Thus, the electrodes shown on the modulating material are continuous and uniform and used only to apply a uniform voltage across the structure. The resistivity of the photoconductor is much larger than that of the modulating material, so that initially most of the applied voltage appears across the photoconductor. A spatial voltage distribution is developed across the modulating material by illuminating the structure with a spatially modulated light distribution. This causes photocarriers to be generated within the photoconductor, decreasing its resistance, and causing a spatial voltage distribution across the modulating material itself.

This field distribution can affect the amplitude, phase, or polarization of a uniform read light beam by a variety of electrooptic effects. If nondestructive readout is desired, the photoconductor must be insensitive to the wavelength of the reading light. For these reasons, different wavelengths of reading and writing light are normally used in all optically sensitive light modulators. Degradation of the recorded image, improved device lifetime, and other desirable features result if the photoconductor and modulating material are separated by a dichroic reflecting mirror. In these structures, writing light is incident on the photoconductor side while the reading light is incident from the opposite side and readout is in reflection (as shown in Fig. 2 for the material at plane P_1).

The structure in Fig. 3 can also be locally addressed point by point. The applied laser beam can also be used to heat locally regions of the material by thermooptic recording. In many of these cases, a photoconductor layer is not needed. In certain materials, the spatial field produced can be used to deform physically the material. In these cases, a flexible top electrode is required. Alternately, the top electrode can be omitted and the initial uniform field can be produced by corona charging or other methods.

Certain materials are both electrooptic and photoconductive. The structure of these devices requires insulating layers to enable the uniform applied voltage to be switched spatially across the material. If

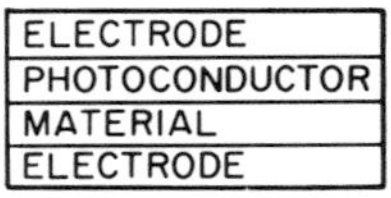

```
┌─────────────────┐
│ELECTRODE        │
│PHOTOCONDUCTOR   │
│MATERIAL         │
│ELECTRODE        │
└─────────────────┘
```

FIG. 3.   Basic structure for an optically sensitive spatial light modulator.

both the photoconductor and top electrode are absent, the structure is suitable for electron-beam addressing. The modulated electron beam deposits a spatially varying charge distribution across the material as the beam is scanned over the target.

IV. Deformable Devices and Materials

Most spatial light modulator devices and materials rely on various electrooptic effects to modulate the incident reading laser light. A large group of devices exist that physically deform in response to the incident writing signal. A uniform reading laser beam after transmission through such a deformed material can be described by

$$A(x, y) = T_0 \exp[j\theta(x, y)], \tag{4}$$

where T_0 is the constant transmission of the material and $\theta(x, y)$ is the spatial phase variation introduced by the deformations in the material. For the simple case of a one-dimensional sinusoidal deformation,

$$d(x) = d_0 + d_1 \sin f_x x, \tag{5}$$

the phase variation $\theta(x)$ can be described (dropping a constant term) by

$$\theta(x) = (2\pi/\lambda)(n - 1)d(x), \tag{6}$$

where n is the index of refraction of the deformed material. The output wave can then be expressed by

$$A(x) = T_0 \sum_{m=-\infty}^{+\infty} j^m J_m[k(n - 1)d_1] \exp(jW_x x), \tag{7}$$

where $k = 2\pi/\lambda$. The output due to a sinusoidal deformation is thus a series of plane waves whose amplitudes are proportional to Bessel functions.

A. General Considerations

Linear response requires that the deformations be kept below 0.2λ or so. For many deformable materials, the amplitude of the deformations has a $1/\omega^2$ dependence on the spatial frequency ω recorded. This often requires electronic or optical compensation. A unique characteristic of all deformable materials is the bandpass nature of the spatial frequency response. The central spatial frequency is inversely proportional to the material's thickness. When used in holographic recording, this central spatial frequency determines the optimum reference beam angle θ in Fig. 1 to be used. When images are to be recorded on these materials, the image must be coded with a grating whose spatial frequency is matched to the material's central spatial frequency.

While the central spatial frequency of some of these materials may be quite high, their bandpass will often be low and the response will decrease rapidly on each side of the central spatial frequency. Because of the dependence of performance on the material's thickness, this thickness must be accurately and reproducably predictable in advance. For many materials, this is not possible. One of the major items of concern in all deformable materials is reproducibility of results. Two other factors of major importance are the optical quality of a deformable material after repeated cycles of operation and the lifetime of these materials.

B. THERMOPLASTIC DEVICES

Low melting temperature plastics have seen considerable use as deformable recording materials in coherent optical data processing for many years by various researchers (Lee, 1974; Harris Semiconductor Div., 1974; ERIM, 1973; Doyle and Glenn, 1972). Polystyrene, chlorinated polyphenel, α-methylstyrene, Stayblite ester-10, Foral-105, and others have been the most used plastics. Both optically addressed holographic recording structures (Lee, 1974; Harris Semiconductor Div., 1974) and electron-beam addressed devices (ERIM, 1973; Doyle and Glenn, 1972) have been fabricated. A thin 0.4–1.5 μm thick thermoplastic layer is used in most cases.

The structure of the optically sensitive device consists of a photoconductor layer between the thermoplastic and a transparent grounded electrode. Since a second top electrode cannot be used, a uniform united charge layer is deposited on the free thermoplastic surface by corona (Lee, 1974) or parallel plate charging (Harris Semiconductor Div., 1974). This latter technique and the use of an aperture grid has produced more reasonable results and has decreased the thermoplastic damage and excessive heating that result from corona charging (Lee, 1974).

A typical operating cycle (Harris Semiconductor Div., 1974) is listed in Table I. Faster recording times have been demonstrated, but extending the device's lifetime and obtaining reproducible results have been issues of major concern with these materials. This particular cycle has been found to yield rather reproducible results. When the thermoplastic is operated in an argon atmosphere, the lifetime of certain samples has

TABLE I

REPRODUCIBLE THERMOPLASTIC RECORDING/ERASURE CYCLE

Uniform charging	300 V for 25 msec
Exposure to data	5–100 μJ/cm^2 for 100 msec
Heat development	4.5 W for 150 msec
Reverse charging	−300 V for 25 msec
Heat erasure	4.5 W for 450 msec

been extended to 1000 cycles by use of this and similar cycles (Lee, 1974; Harris Semiconductor Div., 1974).

Following the initial charging of the thermoplastic surface, the photoconductor is exposed to the input light distribution containing the desired information to be recorded. A 5–100 μJ/cm^2 exposure is required depending upon the photoconductor used. This exposure causes ionization and charge migration to the photoconductor–thermoplastic interface, however the surface charge density on the free thermoplastic surface remains uniform. Hence there is still a constant uniform electrostatic force on the thermoplastic. The uniform charging is continued during exposure to produce the desired field variations in the thermoplastic. To obtain actual deformations in the thermoplastic, it must be heated to its development temperature (50–70°C). This is accomplished by joule or rf heating. The required heat power varies considerably (Lee, 1974) with 30 W/cm^2 for 100 msec and 45 W/cm^2 for 4 msec used by some researchers.

During this development heating, the material deforms due to electrostatic forces. These deformations are "frozen in" by subsequent cooling of the material to room temperature. Precise control is needed during development to achieve long lifetime and reproducibility and because erasure is also achieved by heating the material to its softening temperature (70–100°C). During erasure by heating, the conductivity of the photoconductor and thermoplastic increase, the stored charge decays, and the thermoplastic softens and becomes flat. The optical quality of the surface of any deformable material after repeated cycles is not certain. In coherent optical processing, a surface flatness of less than $\lambda/4$ and excellent material uniformity and cosmetic quality are necessary. Thermoplastic devices require a rather complex support system for the precise control and monitoring of device parameters needed.

Device resolution is high (2000 lines/mm) but the bandwidth is generally only several hundred lines per millimeter. A particularly attractive feature of this material is the nondestructive readout (essentially unlimited) of stored data. The material has been used to record spatial imagery (focused onto the material using a 100 line/mm grating) as well as holographic matched filters of aerial imagery (using a reference beam angle determined by the material's thickness) and to perform real-time image correlations (Vander Lugt, 1974) using the material at planes P_0 and/or P_1 in Fig. 1.

Thermoplastic materials have also been electron-beam addressed (ERIM, 1973; Doyle and Glenn, 1972). One such device is known as the Lumitron (Doyle and Glenn, 1972). The target structure consists of a thermoplastic and transparent grounded electrode on a substrate. The surface charge distribution is produced by the electron beam. The high resistance of the thermoplastic results in storage of this charge at room temperature. When the material is heated to its development temperature (by a heating current pulse applied to the rear electrode on the thermoplastic), the material deforms in a pattern corresponding to the deposited charge distribution. When the heating current is removed, the thermoplastic returns to room temperature and the deformations can be stored. Erasure is also achieved by a heating current. As before, during erasure the surface tension forces exceed the electrostatic forces and the material flattens.

The time constant for deformations is tenths of a second while erasure requires over one second because of the thermoplastic's resistivity. Over 1800 line resolution over the 25×25 cm^2 target area and eight shades of gray have been demonstrated. The device's optical quality and lifetime are again limited. In an attempt to extend the device's lifetime, a system using a rotating 14-in. thermoplastic disk target has been fabricated (ERIM, 1973). Problems associated with the resultant polar data format, lifetime, and optical quality of this system are still under consideration.

One of the more dramatic demonstrations of the potential of the Lumitron is shown in Fig. 4 (Doyle and Glenn, 1972). A Fresnel hologram of a transparency of the word NEWS was imaged onto a high-resolution camera. The output video signal was used to modulate the electron-beam current for the Lumitron, and a charge pattern corresponding to the hologram was written on the thermoplastic target. Subsequent illumination of the Lumitron with coherent light produced the real-time, remote hologram reconstruction shown in Fig. 4.

C. RUTICON

A second type of deformable spatial light modulator uses a structure similar to that in Fig. 3. The deformable material used is an elastomer

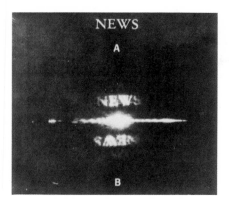

FIG. 4. Real-time reconstruction of a Fresnel hologram recorded on the Lumitron (Doyle and Glenn, 1972).

and the device is referred to as the Ruticon. Several types of Ruticons exist (Sheridon, 1972). They differ in the manner in which the electric field is applied across the structure. The most promising structure for coherent optical processing employs a flexible opaque metal electrode on the elastomer. This results in very effective isolation of the input and readout light. Readout is thus in reflection.

The operation of the device is similar to that of most deformable materials. Twenty to forty volts are applied between electrodes and the photoconductor is exposed to the input image light. Charge carriers are then generated in the photoconductor and drift to the elastomer/ photoconductor interface. This produces an electric field distribution across the elastomer causing it to deform in an imagelike pattern. Extended storage requires a photoconductor with low dark current decay (e.g., PVK). Exponential decay times of 5 min have been reported (Sheridon and Berkovitz, 1974, 1975). Device sensitivity is excellent (30 μJ/cm^2) and spatial frequencies as high as 100 lines/mm have been recorded. The spatial frequency response is again a bandpass with a peak typically at 40 lines/mm with the response dropping to zero near 20 and 60 lines/mm. These values are reported for a device with 6 μm and 4 μm thick elastomer and photoconductor layers, respectively. The peak spatial frequency response will increase as the thickness of the elastomer layer is decreased. This dependence of resolution on thickness holds for nearly all devices.

The resolution of the Ruticon is much lower than that of photothermoplastic, but no heat development is needed and erasure is faster (10 msec) and simpler (removal of the dc field between electrodes) than in thermoplastic devices. While its lifetime is limited (10,000 cycles has been quoted) (Bordogna *et al.*, 1972), it is much longer than that of thermoplastic devices.

The device has been used to perform high pass filtering in coherent light and other basic operations. Coherent correlation using a version of the system in Fig. 2 is also possible. A particularly interesting example of image subtraction is shown in Fig. 5 (Sheridon and Berkovitz, 1974, 1975). It was performed in noncoherent light but still demonstrates several interesting operations possible on this and similar devices. Because all deformable devices require the use of a grating to record imagery, a quasi-Schlieren readout optical system (Sheridon and Berkovitz, 1974, 1975) is needed to produce amplitude imagery.

By passing the central or side orders in the Schlieren readout system, a positive or negative of the input image can be produced. These features can be used to perform image subtraction. If image A (Fig. 5a) is written on the Ruticon and image B (Fig. 5b) is then reflected from the opposite surface of the Ruticon and focused in the output plane, the output images in Figs. 5c and 5d can be obtained by selecting the

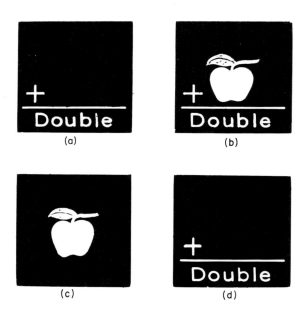

FIG. 5. Example of optical subtraction in noncoherent light using the Ruticon (Sheridon and Berkovitz, 1974). (a) Input image A, (b) Input image B, (c) subtraction of A from B, (d) similar parts of B and A.

appropriate sideband. The explanation of this form of subtraction is rather straightforward. Bright areas of image A cause appropriate areas of the Ruticon's surface to deform as a sinusoidal diffraction grating. If corresponding areas of image B are bright, diffraction occurs due to the recorded grating structure and no (or little) light is contained in the zero order sideband in the Schlieren readout system. The outputs in Figs. 5c and 5d thus correspond to those regions that are respectively different and the same in the two inputs. The data in Fig. 5c represents a reduction in the intensity of the common portions of the inputs by a factor of 20.

D. Oil Film Light Valve

In one of the most promising deformable devices, a dielectric oil film is used as the target for a scanning and modulated electron beam (General Electric Co., 1974). The charge pattern deposited by the electron gun causes the dielectric fluid to deform. This subsequently causes a spatial phase modulation in the readout laser beam as it passes through the target. The fluid's thickness is kept constant by a uniform, constant, electron-beam current raster on which the modulating signal is superimposed. The readout laser beam is passed through an input window beside the electron gun as shown in the schematic diagram of Fig. 6.

The rise time for the fluid deformation is rapid and is determined by the fluid's viscosity and surface tension. The deformation decay time

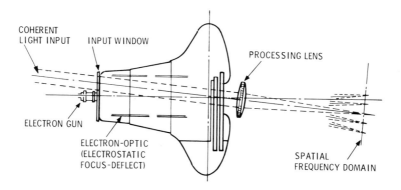

FIG. 6. Schematic diagram of the oil film coherent light valve (General Electric Co., 1974).

can be varied from 4 to 300 msec by varying the average beam current. Typical decay times are 10 to 20 msec. This lack of storage, its dependence on beam current, and the device's optical quality (Turpin, 1974) are the major device limitations and the subject of present research. At present 500 × 500 point resolution and 30 msec frame rates are obtainable. Resolutions of 1000 × 1000 are possible.

This device is a modified version of a noncoherent large screen projection television device. For applications using coherent light, higher quality optical windows are used, the maximum deformations in the oil are kept below $\lambda/10$, and the Schlieren projection optics are not present. The fluid is recirculated by a rotating glass disk target and the light valve is operated at 50°C. Seven bits of data can be resolved in each input cell element and the present bandwidth to the 3 dB points extends from 2–10 MHz. By tripling the horizontal scan rate, a 30 MHz upper cutoff can be realized and by aperture correction of the response the overall 3 dB bandwidth can be extended from 1 to 15 MHz.

The principal coherent optical processing application of the oil film light valve has been in wideband signal analysis (Thomas, 1966; Nobel, 1974; Markevitch and Rodal, 1975). In this application a one-dimensional time signal is written in raster format on the oil film. T seconds of data are recorded on p raster lines at a line scan rate f_h and at a resolution of n cycles per raster line. The maximum recorded frequency is thus $f_m = nf_h$ and the total number of cycles in the input $np = N$ is the input time- or space-bandwidth product. The optical two-dimensional Fourier transform of this input distribution is a frequency spectrum; but rather than a display of x and y spatial frequencies along each axis, the spectrum is folded. It consists of n loci lines with p points per line. Frequencies from 0 to f_h that are present in the input will appear along the first loci, frequencies from f_h to $2f_h$ will appear along the second loci line, etc. The coarse frequency resolution per line is f_h and the fine frequency resolution is $f_h/p = f_m/N = 1/T$.

With a 2500 cycle resolution per line and 1200 line resolution device, the spectrum associated with a 100 MHz bandwidth input signal will have a coarse frequency axis resolution of 40 kHz and a fine resolution along each line of 33.3 Hz. Thus if 30 msec of the input signal is recorded, a bandwidth of 100 MHz and a fine frequency resolution of 33.3 Hz can be obtained. Since the output format is square (or rectangular), this represents a very compact and efficient use of the available spectrum space. This folded spectrum analysis can be used with many of the devices reported on in this chapter.

Two examples of such an output spectrum are shown in Fig. 7. A wideband rf receiver (0.5–12 MHz) was used to record the signals in the

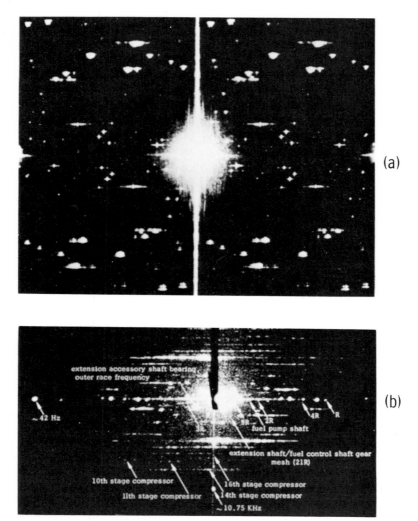

FIG. 7. Real-time optical folded spectrum outputs (Preston, 1972). Courtesy Department of Defense. (a) Wideband 0.5 to 12 MHz spectrum of rf signals in the San Francisco Bay area with a resolution of less than 0.5 Hz. (b) Spectrum of 12 sec record of the signal from an accelerometer mounted on a jet aircraft engine with a resolution of 0.1 Hz.

San Francisco Bay area. A photographic record of these signals in a raster format was then prepared, placed in the input plane of a Fourier transform lens and illuminated with parallel coherent light. The two-dimensional optical Fourier transform, produced in real time, is shown in Fig. 7a. It corresponds to the folded spectrum output pattern previously described. Upon closer examination, frequencies separated by less than 0.5 Hz can be distinguished and the entire spectrum of all radio broadcast stations as well as some of the shortwave stations can be seen in a single compact spectrum format (Preston, 1972).

Another example of a folded-spectrum output is shown in Fig. 7b. In this case, a full 12 sec record of the signal developed by an accelerometer mounted on a jet aircraft engine was recorded in a raster format at a 42 Hz sweep rate. The optical transform of a transparency of this input data is shown in Fig. 7b. Signals covering a dynamic range in excess of 50 dB can be located. Frequency components are visible corresponding to many vibrational modes that could not be readily observed using conventional electronic spectrum analyzers. The 12 sec time record resulted in an output frequency resolution of less than 0.1 Hz (Preston, 1972).

E. Membrane Light Modulators

Several other deformable devices have also been developed, such as the Ferpic PLZT device (Maldonado and Meitzler, 1974) and the membrane light modulator (Preston, 1972; Reizmann, 1969) which uses a deformable elastomer layer. The electroded and photosensitive membrane light modulators have been used in coherent optical processing (rather than as page composers) and are thus discussed briefly. The device structure consists of a thin dielectric on a glass substrate on which stripe electrodes are deposited. A regular array of 40 μm perforations (5 μm spacings are also possible) on 50 μm centers is made in the dielectric, and a thin 0.1 μm thick reflective membrane mirror is then stretched across the perforations and grounded. A 20–40 V signal applied to the electrodes can cause the membrane to deform and spatial phase modulation of a laser beam in reflection is possible.

The optical quality of the device is excellent ($\lambda/10$ flatness); its response time is fast (0.1–1.0 nsec) and its lifetime is in excess of 10^{12} cycles. However, its low 100×100 element resolution, the need for row addressing, its low optical efficiency, and the lack of storage appear to have limited extensive use and development of the device. The results of optically processing data from a frequency-hopping radar on a 100×100 element membrane light modulator are shown (Preston, 1972) in Fig. 8a. An electrical signal, proportional to the phase of 100 radar echoes (obtained by repetitively pulsing the radar at a single transmitted frequency) was applied to the 100 row electrodes on the membrane light

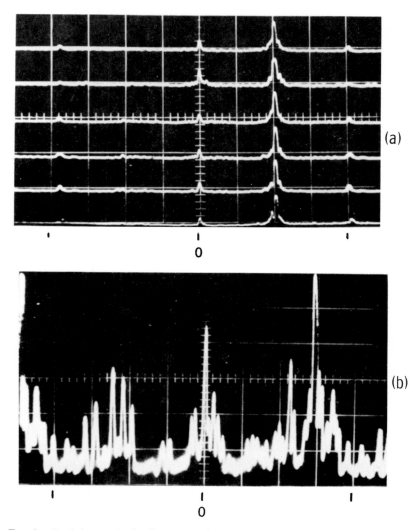

FIG. 8.   Real-time optically processed radar data using the electroded membrane light modulator (Preston, 1972). Courtesy the John Hopkins University, Applied Physics Laboratory. (a) Oscillogram display of the output for six successive sets of 100 echoes from a pulsed Doppler radar. The horizontal displacement of the peak pulse is proportional to the fine velocity of the target within a 62 m/sec unambiguous velocity interval. (b) Oscillogram display of output for 100 pulses from an FM stepped radar. The horizontal displacement of the peak pulse is proportional to the fine range of the target within a 100 ft unambiguous range interval.

modulators. The surface of the modulator was imaged onto an opaque mask containing 10,000 (100 × 100) circular apertures, each one-half the diameter of the corresponding membrane element. The optical Fourier transform of the phase modulated laser beam reflected from the device was formed. A one-axis oscillating mirror output scanner was used to connect this transform plane output to an oscillogram display. The output for six successive sets of 100 echoes are shown in the six oscillograph traces in Fig. 8a. The location of the pulse in each trace is proportional to the target's Doppler frequency and hence to its fine velocity. A fine velocity resolution of 0.62 m/sec in a 62 m/sec unambiguous velocity interval was obtained.

The results of the analogous processing of 100 pulses from an FM stepped radar are shown in Fig. 8b. The transmitted frequency was increased by 5 MHz for each pulse to cover a 500 MHz bandwidth. The same processor used in obtaining the data in Fig. 8a was again employed. The location of the peak pulse in the oscillogram output in Fig. 8b is now proportional to the target's fine range. A fine range resolution of 1 ft in a 100 ft unambiguous range interval was obtained. More details of these and other types of radar signal processing by optical techniques are available in the references (Casasent, 1975, 1977b; Casasent and Casasayas, 1975a,b).

A photo-activated spatial membrane light modulator has also been fabricated (Reizmann, 1969). It consists of p–n junction diodes (one per membrane element) diffused into the lower side of the device with a transparent electrode diffused below the diodes. A perforated resistive layer and collecting electrode are then deposited on the top and a metallized polymer applied over the entire structure. Operation of the device requires application of a voltage between the collecting and diffused electrodes to back-bias the junction diodes. When the spatially modulated light is incident on the device, hole-electron pairs are generated. This causes a potential to be developed between the p region of the diode and the collecting electrode causing the membrane to deform.

This device has been used to perform digital logic operations (Preston, 1972). Other phase modulating materials can also be used to perform similar operations. The optical configuration in Fig. 1 is used; the photo-addressed membrane light modulator is placed in P_0 and a Fourier hologram of various on-axis and off-axis excited membrane elements is formed at P_1 on film. By exciting specific membrane elements, a 0° or 180° phase shift can be introduced at discrete locations in the input laser beam. A detailed analysis of the contents of the output plane P_2 will show that the combinations of the in-phase and out-of-phase components of the light distribution can be combined to produce a field strength at P_2 that is the logical exclusive OR, the identity function, or other digital logic functions of the input used in P_0 and the input used to produce the hologram in P_1.

V. Liquid Crystals

Liquid crystals are a material intermediate between a solid crystalline and an isotropic liquid material. They exhibit the properties of fluids as well as the spontaneous anisotropy normally associated only with solid crystals. Large anisotropies with low voltages result from the orientational ordering of the liquid crystal molecules. Over 3000 liquid crystal references (Eastman Kodak Co., 1974) exist and over 15 electrooptic effects (Flannery, 1973) have been identified. Thus no survey can hope to be inclusive. Most of this research has concentrated on electroded devices and noncoherent projection display applications and is thus not appropriate for the present discussion. Only those devices and effects appropriate for coherent optical data processing are thus discussed.

Three liquid crystal phases occur. The nematic phase is characterized by a one-dimensional ordering of the liquid crystal molecules with the long axes of the molecules parallel. In the cholesteric phase, the molecules have a nematic alignment in each plane with the direction of alignment progressively changing from one plane to the next. In a smectic liquid crystal all molecules in all planes are aligned parallel.

The electrooptic effects in liquid crystals are due either to dielectric forces (field effects) or a combination of dielectric and conduction forces (current effects). The major field effects are: the twisted nematic effect, guest-host interaction (or electronic color switching), field-induced birefringence (or deformation of aligned phases), and the cholesteric-to-nematic transition. The major current effects are dynamic scattering and storage mode. Other effects such as thermooptic writing have also been demonstrated.

Most of the initial liquid crystal structures used the current effects, especially dynamic scattering. The very nature of this effect is to destroy the coherence of an incident laser beam. Its use has even been suggested (Bartolino, 1973) as a replacement for a ground glass diffuser. The halo effects, noise, and wide angle scatter that result are other reasons for not considering the use of the scattering effect for the present applications. The current effects involve the transport of charge and require setting a viscous liquid into motion. The lifetime and contrast of devices using these effects are typically lower than for devices using the field effects.

The response time of field effect devices is much faster than for devices using current effects, since the field effect involves only the turning or tilting of the liquid crystal molecules. The dielectric anisotropy of the material determines the effect of the applied field on the liquid crystal molecules. For a liquid crystal with positive (negative) dielectric anisotropy, the liquid crystal molecules tend to align parallel (perpendicular) to the field.

The basic device structure of Fig. 3 can be used to explain the operation of these devices. The initial molecular alignment is determined by the material's dielectric anisotropy and the preparation of the electrode surface. Ion beam etching, chemical treatment, thin film deposition, and proper rubbing can be used to control the alignment of the liquid crystal molecules at the electrode surfaces. A homogeneous or homeotropic alignment (molecules parallel or perpendicular, respectively, to the electrode surface) can be achieved. In the presence of a field between the electrodes in Fig. 3, the elastic forces tending to realign the molecules in their original orientation usually compete with the dielectric forces tending to reorient molecules in the electric field.

A. TWISTED NEMATIC EFFECT (Boller *et al.*, 1972)

The twisted nematic effect was devised for use in alphanumeric displays. If a nematic crystal with positive dielectric anisotropy is used, the molecules are aligned parallel to each electrode surface with no field present. In the conventional cell, the molecules exhibit a 90° twist (a quarter-spiral structure) between the electrodes, with all molecules parallel to the electrode surfaces. When a voltage above threshold appears across the liquid crystal, the molecules will start to align normal to the electrodes. With no field present, an incident reading light wave polarized along the preferred alignment direction associated with the incident electrode will have its plane of polarization rotated through the twist angle of the spiral (90° for the present discussion). When illuminated with reading light and with parallel input and output polarizers used, no output light will appear if there is no field present. Where a large field above threshold is present, the crystal appears isotropic to the input reading light. It exhibits no rotary power and the transmitted light is a maximum. Intermediate levels between complete homeotropic and complete homogeneous alignment produce intermediate transmitted light levels.

The twisted nematic effect is of great practical importance because the twist angle is essentially independent of the cell thickness and is determined by the surface preparation of the electrodes. As a result, thin cells with faster turn-on times can be produced with less care required in maintaining a uniform cell thickness. This effect is also rather independent of the wavelength of the light used as long as the wavelength remains less than or comparable to the cell thickness.

B. FIELD-INDUCED BIREFRINGENCE EFFECT (Soref and Rafuse, 1972)

The field-induced birefringence effect can also be explained using the device structure in Fig. 3. If a liquid crystal of negative dielectric anisotropy is used and the electrodes are properly prepared, the molecules can be aligned normal to the electrode surfaces with no field present. With a field present across the liquid crystal, the molecules will tend to align parallel to the electrodes. With no field present the liquid crystal appears isotropic, while with a field present it is birefringent. Large birefringences, $\Delta n = 0.2$ to 0.3, can be obtained with moderate voltages. The physical mechanism that produces the polarization rotation in the twisted nematic effect is also based on the birefringence of the liquid crystal molecules. The combination of the twisted molecular orientation and the uniaxial birefringence of the individual molecules causes the polarization rotation.

C. HYBRID FIELD EFFECT DEVICE (Grinberg et al., 1975)

A liquid crystal device structure suitable for use in coherent light and with many advantageous features has recently been demonstrated (Grinberg et al., 1975). The device structure is shown in Fig. 9. It uses a hybrid field effect in which the off-state condition for an elemental area of the cell is determined by the twisted nematic affect and the on-state by the birefringence effect. A thin 2 μm thick biphenyl nematic liquid crystal with positive dielectric anisotropy is used. The molecules are normally aligned parallel to the electrodes and have a 45° twist angle between the top and bottom electrodes. The structure consists of some 18 thin film layers and is typical of recent advancements in device fabrication. The dielectric reflecting mirror usually consists of 12 alternating quarter-wave thick ZnS and cryolite thin film layers formed by E-beam thermal evaporation. Broadband reflection over 400–700 nm is achieved by superimposing two mirrors, one centered at 488 nm and another centered at 632.8 nm.

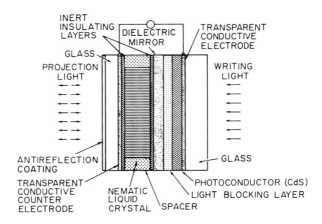

FIG. 9.   Multilayer structure of the hybrid field effect liquid crystal device (Grinberg *et al.*, 1975).

The writing light (typically 525 ± 25 nm) is incident from the right, while readout is in reflection at 633 nm from the left. The 2 μm thick CdTe light-blocking layer has a sheet resistance above 10^{11} Ω/square and an optical absorption of over 10^5. This isolates the writing and reading light. The CdS photoconductor and the CdTe form a p–n heterojunction that greatly improves photoelectric performance. Although other photoconductor layers are possible, a high resistance (above 10^{12} Ω/square) 12 μm thick CdS photoconductor is usually used. It is deposited by reactive rf sputtering in an H_2S atmosphere. Chemomechanical polishing of the CdS surface is needed to avoid performance degradation. Excellent surface and interface quality is essential in such a structure and can now be achieved rather consistently.

The electrodes are 30 Å thick E-beam deposited thin films of indium tin oxide with low 30 Ω/square sheet resistances. Good surface alignment of the liquid crystal molecules is critical for coherent optical processing applications. There must be little or no divergence in the orientation of the molecules across the electrodes, and the twist angle must be constant over the entire area of the cell. The required parallel alignment of the molecules is achieved by ion beam etching the 0.3 μm thick of sputtered SiO_2 insulating layers.

This structure allows simultaneous writing and reading at different spectral bands. The device requires only a low 6 V rms 10 kHz voltage between electrodes. The use of ac rather than dc excitation has been found to reduce greatly electrochemical deterioration of the structure.

The dielectric mirror further prevents the flow of dc currents through the liquid crystal and should result in a long lifetime device. The chemically inert SiO_2 layers further enhance device lifetime. The homogeneous alignment of the molecules results in faster switching times than for a homeotropic alignment. This and the thin 2 μm liquid crystal layer result in 10 msec rise times and 15 msec decay times.

Decay is automatic; the lack of storage is the one major drawback of the device. The device is thus normally used at plane P_1 in the optical system in Fig. 2. The input light is polarized along the preferred molecular alignment direction associated with the input electrode. The output light (viewed through a crossed polarizer) is zero with no field applied, since the polarization is rotated by 45° on traversing the cell from left to right and this rotation is subsequently canceled as the light wave exits the material after reflection from the mirror. The optical quality of present cells is 1.5 λ, but it is quite feasible than an optical flatness of less than $\lambda/4$ can be obtained.

D. OPTICAL PROCESSING APPLICATIONS (Grinberg et al., 1975)

Some of the more basic operations possible in an optical processor are simple low and high pass amplitude filtering. The optical system in Fig. 1 is modified as shown in Fig. 10 to allow the use of a device at P_0 that

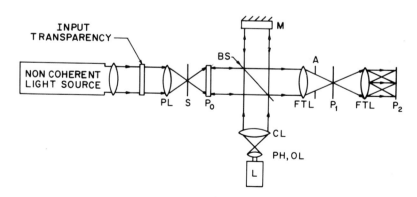

FIG. 10. Modified version of the optical frequency plane correlator of Fig. 1 to incorporate a reflex mode readout device in the input plane P_1. Code: L, laser; PL, projection lens; OL, objective lens; CL, collimating lens; FTL, Fourier transform lens; S, shutter; BS, beam splitter; M, mirror; A, aperture. P_0, P_1, and P_2 are the input, Fourier transform, and output or correlation planes, respectively.

requires different wavelengths for writing and reading and a reflex mode readout. As noted earlier, this device can also be used directly at P_1 in Fig. 2 in correlation experiments. A transparency of the Air Force resolution test chart was imaged onto the liquid crystal in noncoherent 525 ± 25 nm light. The reconstructed image in Fig. 11a was obtained in 633 nm reading light. A magnified version of the central portion of this image shows that the group 5–6 lines (corresponding to 114 lines/nm) are resolvable. With a simple point blocking aperture placed at the center of the transform plane P_1 in the optical system of Fig. 10, the high-pass filtered version of the image shown in Fig. 11b appeared in the output plane (P_2 of Fig. 10). This edge enhancement or differentiation of an image is useful in image analysis to emphasize image details of concern.

Several other operations are possible on images recorded on liquid crystals and other devices. These operations include contrast reversal, level slicing, and subtraction, and are especially useful in optical image analysis. In the case of the hybrid field effect liquid crystal, the effective birefringence of the device and hence its transmission can be controlled by varying the frequency or amplitude of the signal applied between the electrodes. If the output analyzer is rotated by 22.5° (one-half the twist angle), a small change in the applied voltage from 5.5 to 3.6 V rms will reverse the contrast of an image.

Contrast reversal is a necessary step in the subtraction of two images. If intermediate voltages (between 5.5 and 3.6 V rms) are applied to the hybrid liquid crystal device, intermediate levels of contrast can be obtained. The contrast and gray level of an image can be manipulated by varying the frequency of the applied voltage. This allows the threshold and slope of the liquid crystal's response curve to be altered electronically. In image analysis, this has the effect of making all intensity levels in the image below some threshold level black. The threshold can be adjusted by varying the frequency of the applied voltage. The device's gray scale response can then be shifted to different levels in the gray scale distribution of the input image. Examples of such image slicing using the hybrid liquid crystal cell are shown in Fig. 12. A total of 10 gray levels (based on 0.15 neutral density steps) have been demonstrated on this device.

The presently obtained specifications for this device are listed in Table II. As with all candidate devices and materials, these specifications represent presently obtainable values and are not the ultimate limits of liquid crystal technology. The lack of storage is probably the major deficiency of this device. However, both gray scale and storage are not presently simultaneously obtainable in any liquid crystal device.

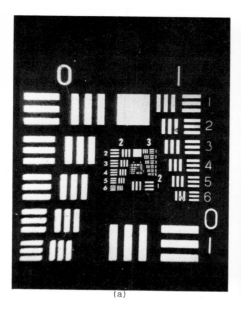 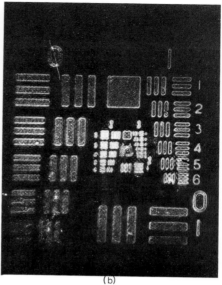

(a)   (b)

FIG. 11. Example of real-time high-pass spatial filtering or differentiation of an image recorded on the hybrid field effect liquid crystal device (Grinberg *et al.*, 1975). (a) Reconstructed image, (b) high-pass version of (a).

 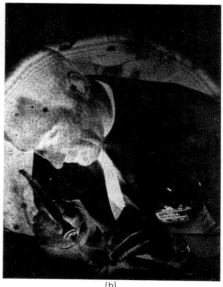

(a)   (b)

FIG. 12. Example of real-time level slicing of an image recorded on the hybrid field effect liquid crystal device, obtained by varying the frequency of the applied ac voltage (Grinberg *et al.*, 1975). (a) 10 kHz frequency, (b) 2 kHz frequency.

TABLE II

PRESENT HYBRID FIELD EFFECT LIQUID CRYSTAL SPECIFICATIONS

Write light	525 ± 25 nm peak
Read light	633 nm
Resolution	100 lines/mm
	60 lines/mm at 50% MTF
Contrast ratio	100:1
Sensitivity	10 μJ/cm^2 at full contrast
Applied voltage	6 V rms at 10 kHz
Turn-on time	10 msec
Turn-off time	15 msec
Gray scale	9 levels (0.15 N D per step)

VI. Crystals Exhibiting the Pockels Effect

Liquid crystal devices utilize many different electrooptic effects to produce spatial modulation of an incident reading laser beam. A group of devices also exists that uses crystals exhibiting the Pockels effect. In these materials, data are recorded as a spatial change in the crystal's refractive index. By the Pockels effect, these changes in the material's index of refraction can be used to modulate spatially the phase of a uniform reading laser beam. Many ferroelectric materials exhibit similar electrooptic effects. These materials can be distinguished by whether they are operated above or below the material's Curie point (Marie and Donjon, 1973).

In ferroelectric materials operated below the Curie point, electric field-induced changes in the orientation of domains can be used to scatter polarized readout light and thus amplitude modulate a laser beam. This property has been used in the Ceramic PLZT device (Smith and Land, 1972) and in other materials. However, as noted earlier, the scattering effect has severe drawbacks in applications involving coherent light. Anisotropic ferroelectric crystals such as $Bi_4Ti_3O_{12}$ have complex domain structures that produce electrically induced birefringence effects. Devices have been fabricated from such crystals (Cummins and Luke, 1971), however large samples are difficult to orient and grow and their use is thus limited. Many other candidate ferroelectric single crystals operated below their Curie points, such as gadolinium molybdate (Kumada, 1972) and lead germanate (Yamada et al., 1972), have been fabricated into optically sensitive devices. However, the motivation for most of this research has been the development of display devices

(Marie and Donjon, 1973; *IEEE Trans. Electron Devices,* 1973) and materials for mass optical storage of digital data (*Appl. Opt.,* 1974).

The second major classification of ferroelectric single crystal light modulators are those that are operated above the material's Curie point. This group of crystals consists primarily of KH_2PO_4 (KDP, potassium dihydrogen phosphate) and its isomorphs. One of the most promising materials is KD_2PO_4 (DKDP, deuterated KDP, or potassium dideuterium phosphate). It has been used extensively in coherent optical data processing; both optically sensitive devices (Grenot *et al.*, 1972; Donjon *et al.*, 1973) and many electron-beam addressed devices have been successfully fabricated. Data are stored in these crystals as a spatial variation in the material's index of refraction while reading light is phase modulated by the Pockels electrooptic effect.

A related class of optically sensitive crystal devices called the PROM (Pockels Readout Optical Modulator) (Oliver and Buchan, 1971; Vohl *et al.*, 1973) also use the Pockels effect for modulating readout light. These devices employ ZnS, ZnSe, and most recently $Bi_{12}SiO_{20}$ single crystals. These materials are both photoconductive and electrooptic and thus require different structures from the photo-DKDP devices. These materials are not ferroelectric and thus their electrooptic sensitivity and modulation efficiency are low (Marie and Donjon, 1973).

The remaining sections and hence the major portion of this chapter will be devoted to a discussion of the fabrication, operation, and performance of the $Bi_{12}SiO_{20}$ PROM device and the DKDP devices. These materials have probably been used more extensively in coherent optical data processing than any other devices. They are the most promising of the Pockels effect crystals and thus are extensively discussed.

A. POCKELS ELECTROOPTIC EFFECT

Detailed mathematical analyses of the Kerr and Pockels effects and the choice of crystal cut and input polarization direction exist in the literature (Billings, 1949; Carpenter, 1950). With the proper orientation of the crystal axes, the applied electric field, and the propagation direction for readout light, the crystal will exhibit two preferred propagation axes for incident polarized light. With no electric field present, the normal indices of refraction along these preferred axes are equal to n_0. When an electric field E is applied (in the direction of propagation of the readout light), the refractive indices n_1 and n_2 along these preferred axes are linearly related to E by a constant a,

$$n_{1,2} = n_0 \pm aE. \tag{8}$$

This causes a spatial modulation in the velocity of propagation of light through the crystal and hence a spatial variation in the phase of the transmitted light.

The electrooptic effect can be described with reference to Fig. 13. The crystal's axes of preferred polarization (X and Y) are orthogonal. The incident light E_i is polarized at 45° to X and Y, so that equal components of light travel along each axis. The refractive indices along X and Y are n_1 and n_2 and are given by Eq. (8). The amplitude of the light E_0 transmitted by the crossed output analyzer oriented at 45° to Y is related to the input amplitude E_i by

$$E_0 = E_i \sin[K(n_2 - n_1)]$$
$$= E_i \sin(\pi V/2V_{1/2}) \tag{9}$$

where K is constant, V is the voltage applied across the crystal, and $V_{1/2}$ is the material's half-wave voltage (at which the phase retardation between the two components of the input wave along X and Y differ by $\pi/2$).

Since the applied voltage V is in the direction of light propagation, this is a longitudinal rather than a transverse electrooptic effect. From Eq. (8), n is linearly related to the electric field present and hence the linear, longitudinal electrooptic effect (more commonly known as the Pockels effect) results.

As V is varied from 0 to $V_{1/2}$, the transmitted light amplitude (ignoring losses) increases from 0 to E_i. If the polarization of the input light is oriented along only one of the preferred axes and if the output analyzer is omitted, pure phase modulation of the input light occurs. For simplicity in this analysis a uniform voltage V across the structure was assumed (as indicated in Fig. 13). In the actual spatial light modulators

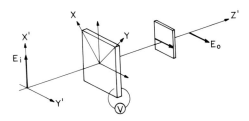

FIG. 13.   Schematic diagram used to explain the Pockels electrooptic effect.

using this electrooptic effect, a spatial voltage distribution $V(X, Y)$ is present and the amplitude of the transmitted light has a similar spatial variation.

The spatially varying potential $V(X, Y)$ required across the crystal for spatial light modulation can be produced by a scanning electron beam or by input writing light. In the latter case, several multilayer target structures incorporating photoconductor and blocking layers can be used. Since $Bi_{12}SiO_{20}$ is photoconductive while DKDP is not, differences in the structure and operation of devices fabricated from each material are expected. Devices using these two materials are thus considered separately.

B. PROM DEVICES

1. Operation and Performance

The three materials that have been considered for the PROM (Pockels Readout Optical Modulator) device are ZnS, ZnSe, and $Bi_{12}SiO_{20}$. The structure of the ZnS device (Oliver and Buchan, 1971) is shown in Fig. 14. An epitaxial layer of ZnS is grown on a GaAs substrate, and a parylene insulating layer and transparent Pt electrode are evaporated onto the top surface. The device is normally written and read in reflection from the same side since GaAs is opaque to visible wavelengths. Readout in transmission is also possible by selectively etching a window into the GaAs substrate and applying a thin transparent electrode at the ZnS/GaAs interface. The electrical connections shown in Figs. 14b and 14c correspond to two possible operating modes.

For the case shown in Fig. 14b, a voltage V_0 is applied before writing and $V_0 C_2/(C_1 + C_2)$ (where C_1 and C_2 are the capacitances of the ZnS

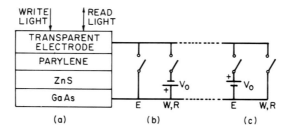

(a)   (b)   (c)

FIG. 14. ZnS spatial light modulator. λ_W and λ_R are the writing and reading light, respectively. (a) Device structure, (b) voltage connections for negative image readout, (c) preferred voltage connections for storage of a recorded image. E, W, and R refer to erase, write, and read modes, respectively.

and parylene, respectively) appears across the ZnS before writing. When the device is illuminated with UV write light, electron-hole pairs are generated at the ZnS/GaAs interface. The electrons flow through the ZnS and decrease the voltage across the ZnS layer. In this case, a negative image appears upon readout with visible light.

To erase the image, the electrodes are simply shorted. There is no need to flood the crystal with light as is often required in these devices. For long-term data storage, the operating mode depicted in Fig. 14c is preferable. A voltage V_0 is applied prior to writing; during writing and reading the electrodes are shorted. If a negative voltage is applied to the GaAs, the electron injection property of the ZnS/GaAs junction creates a uniform negative charge at the ZnS/parylene interface and erases any prior image. When the device is illuminated with spatially modulated UV light with the electrodes shorted, the structure is selectively discharged and data are stored as negative. The ZnS device has good sensitivity (10 μJ/cm^2), a dark storage of 100 hr, and storage under readout of 1 hr. Resolution is high (85 line pairs/mm in a 300 μm thick sample), but low diffraction efficiencies ($\eta = 10^{-2}$ to $10^{-3}\%$) result and contrast ratio is low (10:1).

$Bi_{12}SiO_{20}$ (Vohl *et al.*, 1973) has far superior electrooptic properties with a higher efficiency, large resistivity ($>10^{13}$ Ω-cm), large photocurrent to dark current ratio ($>10^4$), and lower half-wave voltage (3.9 kV) than Zns (13 kV). The basic structure of a reflex readout device is shown in Fig. 15. InO$_2$ electrodes are generally used at present. This reflex readout structure using reflection from the dichroic mirror is preferable since $Bi_{12}SiO_{20}$ is optically active and a reflex readout

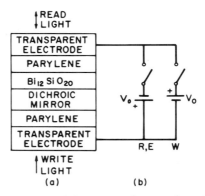

FIG. 15. $Bi_{12}SiO_{20}$ spatial light modulator. λ_W and λ_R are the writing and reading light, respectively. (a) Device structure, (b) electrical connections for write (W), read (R), and erase (E) modes of operation.

arrangement cancels the material's optical activity while doubling the effective phase retardation. This reduces the voltage required across the structure to approximately 2 kV. Various operating cycles are possible. The operating sequence depicted in Fig. 16 is normally used. A discussion of these steps is very instructive in demonstrating the operation of the device. The voltage division across the major layers (parylene and $Bi_{12}SiO_{20}$) are shown in Figs. 16a–f (Lipson and Nisenson, 1974) for various operating conditions.

A voltage $V_0 = 2000$ V $\simeq 0.5 V_{1/2}$ is initially applied across the structure. It is divided between the layers as shown in Fig. 16a with most of the voltage across the $Bi_{12}SiO_{20}$. The crystal is now flooded with UV or blue light. This creates mobile electrons in the $Bi_{12}SiO_{20}$ that drift to the crystal/parylene interface until the field across the crystal has been reduced to zero. This constitutes erasure as shown in Fig. 16b. One-half of the full V_0 potential is now across each parylene layer. This makes the fabrication of these insulating layers and the optical quality of the parylene interface surfaces very important. The holes in this crystal are essentially immobile and photoconductivity is due to electrons.

Data can now be written on the crystal. The erasing light is turned off, the applied voltage V_0 is reversed and the voltage distribution shown in Fig. 16c results. Nearly $2V_0 = V_{1/2}$ appears across the crystal. The exact voltage depends on the capacitances of the parylene and $Bi_{12}SiO_{20}$ layers. The crystal is now exposed to the writing, spatially modulated, blue light. This causes the field across the device to be reduced in bright areas of the input writing beam as shown in Fig. 16d. The blue writing light is strongly absorbed by the crystal and thus hole-electron pairs are generated close to the illuminated crystal surface. With the input side of the crystal negative (Fig. 16d), electrons will propagate through the crystal and decrease the voltage across it in illuminated areas, and the readout image (viewed through crossed polarizers) will be a negative, since no voltage is present in bright areas of the input and hence no phase retardation results in these areas.

If a positive voltage is applied to the illuminated side of the device during readout, a positive image results (contrast reversal) and the voltage division across the layers is as shown in Fig. 16e. With intermediate voltages applied during readout, the contrast of the recorded image can be arbitrarily modified as shown in Fig. 16f. This operation is known as baseline subtraction. Similar operations are possible on DKDP and on the hybrid field effect liquid crystal device. Various examples of these electronic contrast reversal and baseline subtraction operations on the PROM and DKDP will be presented shortly.

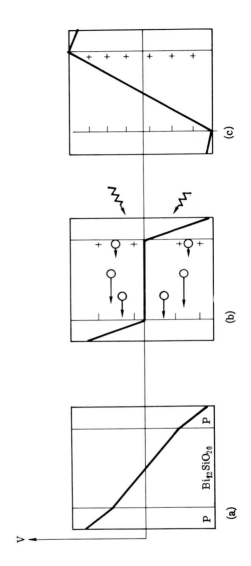

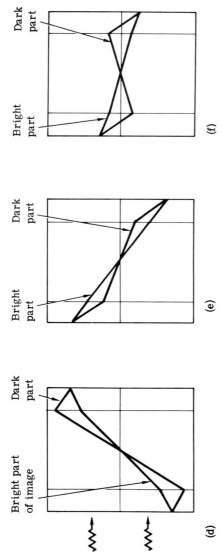

Fig. 16. Normal operating sequence for the $Bi_{12}SiO_{20}$ device. The division of the applied voltage V across the major layers of parylene (P) and $Bi_{12}SiO_{20}$ is shown at each step (Lipson and Nisenson, 1974). (a) Prime, apply V_0; (b) erase, flood with UV light; (c) reverse polarity of applied V_0; (d) exposure to input data with input side of crystal negative, readout resulting in a negative image; (e) application of $+V_0$ (input side of crystal positive) during readout resulting in a positive image; (f) baseline subtraction using intermediate applied voltage between $+V_0$ and $-V_0$ upon readout.

The device structure requires various precise fabrication steps. The importance of good surface quality and uniformity for the 3 μm thick parylene layers that must withstand 1 to 2 kV have been previously stated. The resolution in this and similar sandwich structures has recently been analyzed (Lipson, 1976; Sprague, 1975) and resolution elements smaller than one-half the crystal thickness have been obtained. This is attributed to the localization of the field near the crystal parylene interface at which the applied voltage is negative. These results can be seen in the PROM's superprime operating mode (Itek Corp., 1974) shown in Fig. 17.

The initial erasure and reversal of V_0 prior to illumination with the writing light are identical to the cases depicted in Fig. 16a–c. In the superprime mode, the writing illumination is incident on the side of the crystal that is positive. The PROM is very insensitive to light incident on this side. As a result, the field across the crystal will be reduced only near the parylene (Fig. 17a). If the polarity of the applied voltage is now reversed, the voltage division between the layers will be as shown in Fig. 17b. There is no field across the unexposed regions while the field for the exposed regions is now concentrated near the face of the crystal that is exposed. The writing exposure is continued with the voltage reversed. The crystal is now very sensitive to this light and the depth of penetration of the field will be reduced with continued exposure as shown in Fig. 17c. Care must be taken that this continued exposure reduces only the depth of penetration of the field and not the voltage drop across the crystal. While very precise control and timing of the applied

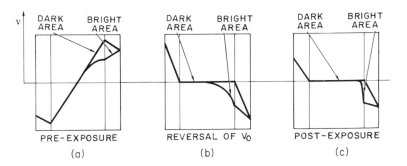

FIG. 17.   Superprime operating sequence for $Bi_{12}SiO_{20}$ device. The division of the applied voltage across the major layers of parylene (P) and $Bi_{12}SiO_{20}$ is shown at each step. The first three steps are identical to those in Fig. 16a to c. (a) Exposure to input data with the right side of the crystal positive; (b) reversed polarity of applied V_0; (c) continued exposure to input data with the right side of the crystal negative.

± 2 kV signals are needed in this operating mode, higher resolution images with better signal-to-noise ratios result because the field is confined to a thin region of the crystal.

The performance specifications of the $Bi_{12}SiO_{20}$ PROM depend on a number of factors (Itek Corp., 1974) and thus a single set of specifications is difficult to list. The typical PROM structure is 500–900 μm thick with 5 μm thick parylene layers. The material's sensitivity is optimum near 430 nm, thus writing is usually performed with a blue laser at 442 nm, although in most instances the input image is noncoherently imaged onto the device. An exposure of 5 μJ/cm² at 442 nm is required to reduce the voltage across the crystal (Fig. 16d) to the $1/e$ point. Readout is usually performed with 633 nm He–Ne laser light. The material is much less sensitive at this wavelength and a readout exposure of 100 mJ/cm² can be used before the recorded image will be degraded (voltage across illuminated areas decreased to the $1/e$ point).

As noted earlier, 2 kV is required for the reflex readout device and 4 kV for a transmission mode readout PROM (no dichroic mirror in Fig. 15). These relatively large voltages (compared to DKDP which requires 80 V for operation) are one disadvantage of the PROM. Another factor is that many of the fabrication steps involved in assembling the multi-layer structure are rather precise. Erasure is achieved by applying a voltage and flooding the crystal with blue light. The modulation transfer function (MTF) (Lipson and Nisenson, 1974) for one PROM device is shown in Fig. 18. It was obtained by recording an interference pattern

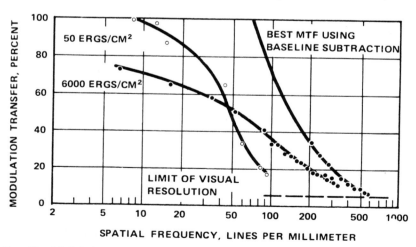

FIG. 18. Modulation transfer function (MTF) for the $Bi_{12}SiO_{20}$ device (Lipson and Nisenson, 1974).

and measuring the diffracted light intensities. In cases where fast imaging cone angles are used, the MTF response will be considerably reduced and each application will require a separate MTF measurement.

The MTF depends on the exposure level as shown in Fig. 18. Up to 50 lines/mm, a 5 μJ/cm^2 exposure is optimal; while beyond this spatial frequency, a 600 μJ/cm^2 exposure yields higher resolution. If the applied voltage is changed during readout (baseline subtraction), the zero-order term in the input can be removed or suppressed. For the data shown in Fig. 18, the modulation could be kept at unity out to 70 line pairs/mm by baseline subtraction. It is not certain whether the baseline level for the data in Fig. 18 was constant for the entire curve. However, in an image with a continuous range of spatial frequencies, the MTF can only be optimized at one spatial frequency by this technique (Lipson and Nisenson, 1974).

The optimum contrast ratio for the PROM is in excess of 5000:1. It is limited by crystal strain, scattering, and the efficiency of the polarizers. The optical quality of the device can be quite excellent with a surface flatness of $\lambda/10$ reported most recently. The crystal thickness, incident writing exposure, and wavelength greatly affect the sensitivity, MTF, and contrast of the PROM. Thinner PROMs are more sensitive at shorter wavelengths while the sensitivity of thicker PROMs is better at longer 442 nm wavelengths. The absorption and penetration depth of the exposing light produce these dependences. At 442 nm, sensitivity increases with thickness; at 365 nm sensitivity decreases with thickness, while for 404 nm exposure light no clear relationship exists. As the thickness of the crystal is increased from 400 to 1400 μm, the PROM's sensitivity to longer wavelength green or red light increases. The MTF appears to improve as the crystal's thickness is decreased from 1400 to 800 μm. The effect of the exposure level on the MTF was previously noted in Fig. 18.

2. Coherent Optical Processing Applications

As noted in the discussion of the normal operating mode shown in Fig. 16, the application of a uniform electric field across the PROM during readout can be used to add or subtract electronically a constant amplitude from a recorded image. This occurs because the PROM can store a recorded image and because, by the Pockels effect, the intensity of a readout image at any point is proportional to the voltage across the $Bi_{12}SiO_{20}$ at that point. If the recorded image has low contrast, it can be greatly enhanced by subtracting a constant voltage from the crystal. If the subtracted voltage is greater than or equal to the voltage corresponding to the maximum amplitude in the image, a contrast reversed image will result. With an intermediate voltage, all points on the image whose corresponding points on the crystal have that voltage across them will be dark. The effects of varying the amount of baseline subtraction for a gray scale image recorded on the PROM are shown (Iwasa and Feinleib, 1974) in Fig. 19. This operation, referred to as level slicing, has

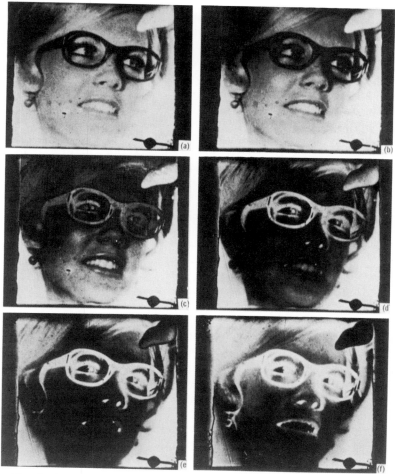

FIG. 19. Real-time level slicing (Iwasa and Feinleib, 1974) of a gray scale image (in noncoherent light) recorded on the $Bi_{12}SiO_{20}$ device. Progressively increasing amounts of baseline subtraction are applied to vary the original reconstructed image (a) to full contrast reversal (f).

also been demonstrated on the liquid crystal cell and on photo-DKDP and electron-beam addressed DKDP. This operation is performed in noncoherent light and is most useful in image analysis.

Baseline subtraction is also useful in coherent optical data processing. If the Fourier transform of data recorded on a device is viewed, the zero-order term is usually so large that it obscures weaker low spatial frequency signals. By baseline subtraction, the zero-order in the transform can be suppressed or removed. This can also be of use in reducing scattered light without affecting the intensities of important orders in the transform. Examples of such operations in coherent light using the DKDP device will be shown shortly.

The PROM has also been used to perform optical correlations (Nisenson and Sprague, 1975) using the optical system of Fig. 2. The two inputs were the letters O and S shown in the top portion of Fig. 20. The correlations O with O, O with S, and S with S are shown in the lower portion of Fig. 20. These output patterns were greatly overexposed to show that the resultant correlation plane pattern contained the proper data, e.g., the superposition of O and O with a central correlation spot (for the left-hand correlation in Fig. 20), etc.

C. PHOTO-DKDP (Marie and Donjon, 1973; Grenot et al., 1972; Donjon et al., 1973)

1. Operation and Performance

One of the most promising optically addressed ferroelectric crystal devices that uses the Pockels effect to modulate the reading light is shown schematically in Fig. 21. It consists of a DKDP crystal, a dielectric mirror, and a photoconductor sandwiched between transparent electrodes. It is referred to as Phototitus. It is structurally similar to many ferroelectric/photoconductor structures and others. Since DKDP is not photoconductive (as are $Bi_{12}SiO_{20}$ and ZnS), a separate photoconductor layer is needed. As will be shown shortly, the crystal is operated at its Curie point (-50 to $-60°C$) for optimum performance. At these low temperatures, photoconductors usually exhibit low efficiency and trapping phenomena. For this reason an amorphous selenium photoconductor is used. The transparent electrodes are conducting platinum films.

The approximate voltage division across the photoconductor and DKDP layers during the various write, read, and erase steps are shown in Fig. 22. A voltage $V_0 = 80$ V is initially applied across the device with

FIG. 20. Real-time coherent optical correlation (Nisenson and Sprague, 1975) of O with O, O with S, and S with S performed with the $Bi_{12}SiO_{20}$ device in plane P_1 of the joint transform correlator of Fig. 2.

the photoconductor side positive (see Fig. 21). Because of the high dielectric constant of the DKDP compared to the selenium (600 vs. 6), most of this V_0 initially appears across the photoconductor as shown in Fig. 22a. With V_0 present, the input data are projected or scanned onto the photoconductor side of the structure (see Fig. 21). The same basic principle used in other photoconductor device structures again provides the mechanism for developing a spatial voltage pattern across the modulating material. As the photoconductor is exposed, the applied V_0 will be partially or fully switched across the DKDP. During exposure, charges are created in the photoconductor and under the influence of the applied field drift to the DKDP–Se interface. The resultant field across

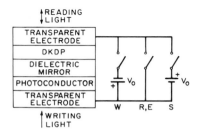

FIG. 21. Photo-DKDP device structure and voltage connections for write (W), read (R), and erase (E).

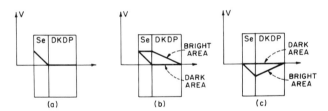

FIG. 22. Division of applied voltage across the selenium (Se) photoconductor and DKDP crystal during various stages of operation. (a) Application of V_0 across structure; (b) exposure to input light, (c) applied V_0 shorted during readout.

the DKDP is proportional point by point to the input exposure. The approximate voltage distribution across the structure is shown in Fig. 22b for the cases of dark and very bright regions in the input light distribution.

This voltage distribution produces a spatial variation in the crystal's index of refraction. By the Pockels effect, this can be used to modulate readout light incident on the DKDP side of the structure (see Fig. 21). Readout is in reflection from the dichroic mirror as it is in most practical structures. In this configuration, the effective birefringence is doubled, isolation of the photoconductor from the read beam is provided, and the crystal's optical activity tends to cancel.

Since an electric field can be capacitively coupled through the selenium layer, the electrodes are shorted during readout (see Fig. 21) to avoid a reduction in contrast ratio. The voltage across the DKDP is now zero in nonilluminated areas, while a voltage is present only across areas exposed to the input writing illumination as shown in Fig. 22c. A stored charge pattern can be erased by shorting the electrodes (see Fig. 21) and flooding the photoconductor with light.

The photo-DKDP device is practically symmetric with respect to the polarity of the applied voltage (the transit time for electrons is longer than for holes). Because of the thick photoconductor (the modulating material itself) in the PROM, its sensitivity is different for opposite polarities of the applied voltage. The photoconductor used in the photo-DKDP structure is thin and thus the device's sensitivity is the same for opposite polarities of the applied voltage. This feature can be used to subtract images by recording one image with $+V_0$ present (switch in Fig. 21 in position W) and the second image with $-V_0$ present (switch in Fig. 21 in position E). Subtraction is thus easier on DKDP than on the PROM. An example of this subtraction will be presented shortly.

A 170 μm thick DKDP crystal and a 10 μm thick selenium photoconductor layer are normally used. The resolution obtainable on such a thick material would not normally be comparable to that of other devices and the storage time of the structure at room temperature would only be tenths of a second. However, it has been shown (Casasent, 1973) that the effective crystal thickness d' is related to the actual crystal thickness by

$$d' = d\sqrt{\epsilon_{11}/\epsilon_{33}}, \tag{10}$$

where ϵ_{33} and ϵ_{11} are the longitudinal and transverse dielectric constants respectively, for DKDP. The value of ϵ_{11} is nearly constant with temperature with ϵ_{33} increases dramatically near the crystal's Curie point (Casasent and Keicher, 1974). Thus, by operating the device slightly above the crystal's Curie point, the effective crystal thickness can be reduced by over a factor of five (Casasent, 1973).

Other benefits result from Curie point operation. The time constant of decay for charge across the crystal is given by the product of the crystal's resistivity ρ and dielectric constant ϵ. Both of these parameters are temperature dependent and, in practice, storage times of hours have been observed at $-50°C$. These long decay times result in an increased resolution since the lateral spread of charge across the crystal is limited and the lines of force are effectively concentrated in narrow regions of the material. The half-wave voltage $V_{1/2}$ for DKDP is 3.7 kV at room temperature but is decreased to nearly 200 V at $-50°C$ (Casasent, 1973; Casasent and Keicher, 1974). KDP exhibits a similar decrease in effective crystal thickness, an increased time constant of decay, and a reduced half-wave voltage at decreased temperature. However, its Curie point is $-150°C$, whereas the corresponding transition temperature for DKDP is -50 to $-60°C$. This temperature range can easily be achieved by a simple Peltier cell cooling system. For these reasons DKDP is a preferable Pockels effect material. The exact transition temperature for DKDP varies with the crystal's deuteration level and this feature can be used to produce devices with very long storage times of days (72% deuteration) rather than hours (98% deuteration) if required. Another advantage of low temperature operation is an improved uniformity of response (Casasent and Keicher, 1974).

Resolutions in excess of 150 line pairs/mm and contrast ratios in excess of 100:1 have recently been demonstrated on this photo-DKDP device. Baseline subtraction was not used to obtain these values and the device had less than ideal selenium and DKDP thicknesses. Since DKDP is uniaxial in the absence of a field and has a natural birefringence, the contrast ratio of devices using such a material will depend on the cone angle ϕ of the readout light and thus the degree of collimation of the laser beam. For a 250 μm thick DKDP crystal operated at $-50°C$, the contrast ratio CR for 550 nm readout light has been shown to be

$$CR = 10^7/27\phi^4. \tag{11}$$

For an 8° cone angle, the theoretical contrast ratio is 100:1. For a 125 μm thick crystal and readout at 633 nm, the contrast ratio should exceed 250:1. With a smaller cone angle, even larger contrast ratios are possible.

The sensitivity of the device is excellent 10 μJ/cm^2 and comparable to most other optically addressed materials. The required voltage is only 80 V (the reflex readout mode reduces the required half-wave voltage to about 100 V, and by limiting V_0 to 80 V the device is operated in its most linear region). This voltage is considerably less than the 2 kV required in the PROM device.

The transit time for holes and electrons are 0.3 and 30 μsec, respectively (for a structure with 10 μm thick selenium layer). The exposing light is absorbed near the illuminated surface so that theoretical writing times of 0.3 or 30 μsec are possible if the selenium electrode is negative or positive, respectively. The practical erase time is 5 to 10 times the writing time since the field in the selenium layer is decreased during this operation. Light pulse durations less than these times are possible (writing and erasing has been performed with 10 μsec strobo-scope flashes) and frame rates of 1000 frames/sec are possible. Device lifetime appears to be excellent and several devices have been operated for over 3 years. The writing light can cover a rather broad band from the UV through the visible. Writing is normally performed at 440 nm and readout at 504 or 633 nm.

2. Optical Processing Applications

A dramatic example (Donjon et al., 1973) of both image addition and subtraction is shown in Fig. 23. The projected image in Fig. 23a was recorded on the photo-DKDP device by exposing it to a single image of the man, reversing the input image, and exposing the device a second time. This addition of images is a useful step in the integration of data for an improved signal-to-noise ratio. The voltage across the device was then reversed and the device reexposed to the left-hand image only. This effectively subtracts this image from the composite image in Fig. 23a as shown in the reconstructed image in Fig. 23b.

As the voltage across the crystal is varied, a constant field can be subtracted from a recorded image. This baseline subtraction can be used for contrast reversal, contrast enhancement, intensity contouring, level

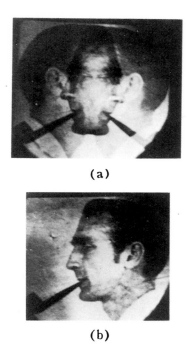

(a)

(b)

FIG. 23.   Real-time addition and subtraction of images using photo-DKDP (Donjon *et al.*, 1973). (a) Addition of a left- and right-handed image. (b) Subtraction of the left-hand image from the total image in (a).

slicing, and the suppression of the dc term in the Fourier transform. A uniform exposure, whose amplitude is equal to the average amplitude of a recorded image or pattern can be subtracted from the recorded data. In practice, the zero-order in the transform has been reduced by a factor of 1000 by this technique. This represents a large reduction in the scattered light and optical noise in coherent optical correlation and filtering experiments and can greatly increase the signal-to-noise ratio of the output.

Many interesting operations are possible on this and similar DKDP devices. If the original image used in Fig. 23 is recorded and a slightly shifted version of it is subtracted from this stored image, vertical or horizontal differentiation of the image can be obtained (Donjon *et al.*, 1973), as shown in Figs. 24a and 24b, respectively. For the output image shown in Fig. 24a, the subtracted image was shifted vertically from its original position, while for the case shown in Fig. 24b, the image was shifted horizontally. In the horizontal derivative of the image, horizontal

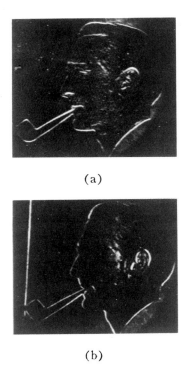

(a)

(b)

Fig. 24.   Real-time image differentiation using photo-DKDP (Donjon *et al.*, 1973). (a) Vertical differentiation, (b) horizontal differentiation.

features are attenuated (such as the top of the hair). In the vertical derivative of the image, the opposite is true. Omnidirectional derivatives of images are also possible and have been demonstrated by subtracting a defocused image from a focused one.

Many coherent optical processing operations have also been performed using two photo-DKDP devices, one in the input plane P_0 and another in the filter plane P_1 in a version of the optical system in Fig. 1 modified to allow the use of reflex-mode readout devices in the input and spatial filter planes. A typical example (Donjon *et al.*, 1973) in which the photo-DKDP device was used in the input plane is shown in Fig. 25. The words shown in the top of Fig. 25 were recorded on the DKDP in the input plane of an optical frequency plane correlator. When a holographic matched spatial filter of the letter A was formed and placed in the transform plane, the output shown in the lower portion of Fig. 25 was displayed from a thresholded camera placed in the output

FIG. 25.   Real-time optical correlation (bottom) of the words (top) recorded on DKDP with a holographic spatial filter of the letter A (Donjon *et al.*, 1973).

correlation plane. These bright output correlation peaks occur at positions corresponding to the locations of the letter A in the input image.

The recording of a holographic spatial filter on one DKDP device from an image recorded on another DKDP device has also been demonstrated and results similar to those in Fig. 25 obtained. The different sensitivity of the PROM and similar devices to the write and read wavelengths limits the practical implementation of operations such as this.

D. ELECTRON-BEAM ADDRESSED DKDP

The use of separate write and read wavelengths can represent a practical system implementation problem. One approach to this problem is the use of an electron-beam addressed device. Most data are available in electrical form at some point and, if not, can be obtained from an orthicon or similar image pick-up camera. In addition, much input data does not exceed the 1000 × 1000 point resolution possible with electron-beam addressed devices. Thus such devices are viable alternatives for many applications. Recall that transparencies of the input data are still needed for all optical-to-optical converters. This problem may be overcome by the use of image intensifiers and fiber optic coupling to a television monitor or scope display of the input data. However such systems are complex and will certainly suffer resolution losses. The only alternative is addressing by a point-by-point scanned and focused laser beam modulated by an electrical signal corresponding to the input data.

The existence of deflection systems capable of more than $10^3 \times 10^3$ point resolution at the 33 msec frame rates possible with electron-beam addressed devices are a major consideration in such a configuration.

1. *Operation and Specifications*

The most promising electron-beam addressed device uses a DKDP target crystal. Although the size and thickness of the DKDP crystal used varies with the specific device, target crystals as large as 5×5 cm^2 and as thin as 250 μm have been used (Casasent and Keicher, 1972). The crystal is usually operated at about $-50°$C. The schematic for one version of this device where readout is in transmission is shown in Fig. 26 (Casasent and Keicher, 1972).

The electron guns are off-axis but the scan and spot size are fully corrected for linearity and distortion (Casasent and Caimi, 1973). Two electron guns are used, one for writing and one for erasure. The target's electrode is grounded and both electron guns are operated in the suppressed cathode mode. With a high accelerating potential for the write gun, the secondary emission from the DKDP target is negligible and the data are written as a negative charge distribution on the front surface of the crystal by modulating the electron beam current with an input video signal. This causes a spatial variation in the crystal's index of refraction and a voltage-controlled induced birefringence to polarized input light that can be used to spatially modulate the amplitude (with a crossed polarizer and analyzer) or phase of an incident laser beam by the Pockels effect.

If the accelerating potential of the second electron gun is low (such that the secondary emission ratio of the target crystal is greater than

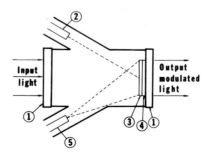

Fig. 26.   Schematic of transmission-mode electron-beam addressed DKDP device. (1) Optical windows, (2) write gun, (3) target crystal, (4) transparent conducting electrode, (5) erase gun.

one), a defocused spray or flood of electrons from this gun can be used to erase the charge distribution on the crystal by secondary emission. Typical accelerating potentials for writing and erasing in this mode are 6 kV and 500 V, respectively.

This device structure is the most used (Poppelbaum *et al.*, 1968; Pritchard, 1969; Salvo, 1971; Sand *et al.*, 1973), although several variations of the arrangement have also been considered. In one version of this device (Goetz, 1970), the cathode was grounded and a low 3 kV accelerating potential was used during writing. Those points on the target addressed during writing were charged positively by secondary emission. During erasure, low energy electrons were used so that the target gained electrons, decreasing its potential toward an equilibrium value equal to the zero volt cathode potential.

The above operating modes require separate write, read, and erase cycles. In coherent optical data processing applications this is acceptable since the optical transform cannot be produced (read cycle) or correlations performed until the complete input has been recorded (write cycle). Erase times of 0.5 msec are possible and these devices are usually operated at television frame rates (Poppelbaum *et al.*, 1968; Salvo, 1971; Casasent, 1971; Casasent and Keicher, 1972; Sand *et al.*, 1973) with writing occurring during the first 31 to 32 msec of the cycle and reading and erasure occurring during the last 1 to 2 msec (usually during vertical retrace time of television). Other frame rates are possible, but television frame rates have become an accepted norm for real-time devices and are thus commonly used.

Many of these electron-beam addressed DKDP devices were originally intended for use as large screen projection displays. In such applications, the flicker that would result if separate write and erase cycles were used is objectionable. To overcome this problem a third mode of operation has been used (Marie, 1967, 1969) in which a constant electron beam intensity and a low 500 to 1000 V accelerating potential are employed. A fine grid is placed in front of the crystal target and very close (40 to 50 μm) to it. In this case, the electron beam acts as a flying short circuit between the grid and a corresponding point on the target and the modulating signal can be applied directly to this grid. By secondary emission, the point on the crystal target addressed by the scanning electron beam will charge to a potential within a few volts of the potential on the grid.

This grid must be very transparent or a loss of beam current will occur. It must also be very close to the crystal's surface or secondary electrons emitted from the crystal will fall back on the target rather than be captured by the grid. These redistributed electrons can severely degrade the resolution and contrast of the device. To reduce this effect a second grid is used. It is spaced several millimeters in front of the first one and is held at 100 to 200 V above the first. This second grid will capture all secondary electrons not attracted by the first grid. The structure of the actual device fabricated is shown in Fig. 27. A 25 × 25 mm² target crystal is used and is addressed with the electron beam incident on the crystal on-axis from one side; the readout light is incident in reflection from the opposite side. While the input signal can be applied between the main grid and the transparent electrode, both grids are usually operated at fixed potentials and the input signal is applied to the transparent conductor to avoid defocusing of the electron beam. A flicker-free display results because the charge at each point on the surface of the target is constant between successive scans.

Devices of the three types indicated have potentially similar performance specifications. Resolutions in excess of 40 lines/mm at the 50% MTF point and contrast ratios in excess of 100:1 have been obtained. For the 5 × 5 cm² crystal, this corresponds to over 2000 × 2000 point resolution. With the use of thinner target crystals and improved electron guns, the resolution could theoretically be increased by a factor of five or more. These devices have been operated at a rate of 30 frames/sec. The target crystal can be fabricated flat to less than $\lambda/10$. This is of prime importance in coherent optical processing applications. The uniformity of response of the target is quite excellent. Crystals with less than 10 ppm of metal impurities have been fabricated. As noted earlier, operation at −50°C greatly improves the uniformity of response. Incomplete erasure and the breakage of targets that occurred in earlier devices have now been largely overcome. DKDP is stable in a vacuum and sealed devices have been operated for more than three years.

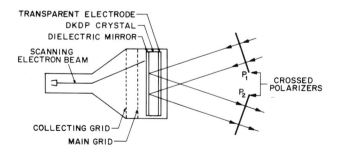

FIG. 27.   Schematic of reflex-mode electron-beam addressed DKDP device.

2. *Optical Processing Operations*

Numerous real-time coherent optical data processing applications using electron-beam addressed DKDP have been considered. Space permits only a brief explanation of selected applications. Further details can be found in the indicated references.

The amplitude transmittance T of the device between crossed polarizers (apart from a constant phase factor) is

$$T = \sin kV(x, y), \tag{12}$$

where $V(x, y)$ is the applied input signal and

$$k = 2\pi r_{63} n_0^3 / \lambda, \tag{13}$$

where r_{63} is a component of the electrooptic tensor. The amplitude transmittance can thus be positive and negative (Groh and Marie, 1970). It is thus possible to suppress the undiffracted light (the zero-order term in the Fourier transform) by removing the dc component from the input signal. In practice, considerable problems arise in optical correlation because the zero-order term is overexposed in the Fourier transform hologram used in pattern recognition applications. Considerable optical noise also results due to scatter from this intense light. If the dc component of the input signal can be blocked, the full Fourier spectrum including the low spatial frequencies can be recorded on ordinary photographic film with less stringent dynamic range requirements and with better fidelity.

This electronic suppression of the zero-order term is demonstrated in the reconstructed image (Groh and Marie, 1970) in Fig. 28. This is a real image reconstructed from a Fourier transform hologram made from an input recorded on the electron-beam addressed DKDP device. The dc level of the input signal and hence the zero-order term in the Fourier transform have been electronically suppressed as described above. The dark contour around the letter M is due to those points where the input voltage to the device was zero. The amplitude transmittance is positive inside this dark contour and negative outside of it. Since intensity is recorded in the image, these regions having negative amplitude transmission appear bright in the reconstruction. This bright region is confined to a relatively small area around the letter since there is still a slight attenuation of low spatial frequencies in the recorded hologram. Suppression of the zero-order by a factor of 10^3 has been demonstrated by this technique.

A print of a computer generated hologram (Lohmann and Paris, 1967) has also been recorded on electron-beam addressed DKDP. Conversion

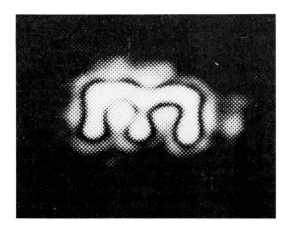

FIG. 28. Real-time reconstruction from a Fourier transform hologram made from an input recorded on electron-beam addressed DKDP with the dc level of the input signal (and thus the zero-order term in the Fourier transform) suppressed (Groh and Marie, 1970).

to the electronic signal required for modulation of the electron gun's beam current was achieved by focusing a television camera on the print. The subsequent reconstruction (Goetz, 1970) of the letters "ICO" is shown in Fig. 29. The quality of the television camera used was largely responsible for the degraded resolution in the reconstruction.

In yet another demonstration of holographic reconstruction in real-time on this device, a simulated time-varying acoustical hologram (Farrah et al., 1970) was viewed with a television camera. A print of a static hologram of the letter E was viewed by the camera as the print

FIG. 29. Real-time reconstruction of a computer generated hologram recorded on electron-beam addressed DKDP (Goetz, 1970).

was oscillated through 45° to simulate a moving image. The video output was used to modulate the electron beam incident on the DKDP crystal and thus produce a charge distribution on the crystal proportional to the simulated acoustical hologram. The reconstructed image is shown in Fig. 30 (Goetz *et al.*, 1972). Because of electronic limitations and to allow easier viewing of complex objects, the frame rate of the DKDP device was reduced to 5 frames/sec for this reconstruction.

A final example of real-time holographic reconstruction using electron-beam addressed DKDP is shown in Fig. 31 (Weiss, 1974). It shows the real-time reconstruction of various levels in a three-dimensional X-ray image, conventional methods of displaying the three-dimensional information used in X-ray diagnosis include tomography and tomosynthesis (Koch and Tiemens, 1972). These cannot image fast-moving objects such as the beating heart or fast-flowing contrast media injected into the brain, kidney, etc. The method of coded sources (Barrett *et al.*, 1972) using a Fresnel zone plate for the aperture or a nonredundant point distribution source seems to offer a solution to the X-ray imaging of fast-moving objects. The basic principles discussed in detail elsewhere (Weiss, 1974) require the recording of the object through an array of X-ray sources with point distribution P. This resultant image is denoted by s. A Fourier transform hologram P_0^* of the projection of this array of sources P with a pin-hole camera is then formed. If the Fourier transform S of the image s is then focused onto the plate on which the Fourier transform hologram P_0^* is stored, the resultant reconstructed image, viewed at the same reference beam angle at which the hologram was formed, will contain one of the layers in the original three-dimensional object in focus. As the position of the Fourier transform hologram filter is changed various layers in the three-dimensional depth of the original object can be focused.

To demonstrate the use of optical processing to implement this process in real-time, lead models of the numerals 0 to 3 separated from each other by 2 cm were fabricated and multiprojected by an X-ray tube

FIG. 30. Real-time reconstruction of a simulated acoustical hologram recorded on electron-beam addressed DKDP (Goetz *et al.*, 1972).

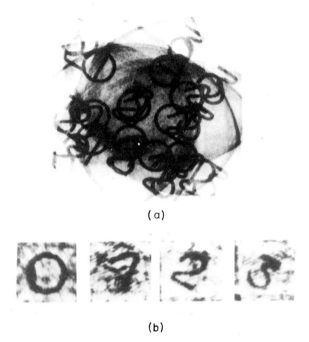

(a)

(b)

F_IG. 31.   Real-time reconstruction of various levels in a simulated three-dimensional X-ray image recorded on electron-beam addressed DK DP (Weiss, 1974). (a) Superimposed input X-ray image of lead models of the numerals 0 to 3, (b) reconstructed images of each of the four numerals.

onto an image intensifier tube. The video output was then used to modulate the beam current for the DK DP tube and a charge distribution corresponding to the superimposed image in Fig. 31a was deposited on the DK DP. The Fourier transform of this distribution was then optically produced. With the Fourier transform hologram P_0^* placed in this transform plane, the reconstructed images of the four digits at different depths in the input can be obtained by moving the P_0^* filter plate. The four reconstructed images (Weiss, 1974) thus obtained are shown in Fig. 31b.

One of the major data processing applications for the high-speed and parallel processing possible with coherent optics and real-time transducers is radar signal processing (Casasent and Casasayas, 1975a,b; Casasent, 1975). If the received signals from N elements of a linear phased array are written on N successive lines of the DK DP crystal, the

Fourier transform of this input pattern will consist of a central dc term and two first-order off-axis peaks of light. It can be shown (Casasent and Casasayas, 1975a) that the horizontal coordinates of these first-order diffraction peaks of light are proportional to the elevation or azimuth angle of the target within the radar's search space. For multiple targets, multiple first-order peaks of light occur. The optical output for a target at 15° from bore sight for a 100 element linear phased array with a ±30° beam forming cone is shown (Casasent and Casasayas, 1975a) in Fig. 32 as displayed by a thresholded pickup camera. The central dc term is not present (it can be electronically suppressed as indicated earlier) and only the first-order peaks appear. This radar data was processed in real-time on electron-beam addressed DKDP. Targets at various angles out to the full 30° beam forming area were successfully detected. The same processing principle has been applied to a 70 × 70 element planar phased array with a 13-bit Barker coded waveform (Casasent and Casasayas, 1975a). The received signals were written on the DKDP in the proper format and optically processed in real time. As before, targets out to the full beam forming area of the radar were successfully detected with the full resolution of the radar (Casasent, 1975).

The DKDP system has also been used to process real raw pulsed Doppler and FM step radar data (Casasent and Casasayas, 1975b). One hundred heterodyned returned signals from an FM stepped radar with

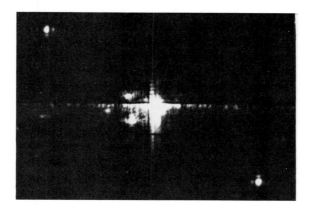

FIG. 32. Optically processed radar data from a 100-element linear phased array radar processed in real time using an electron-beam addressed DKDP input device. The target's elevation or azimuth angle can be determined from the location of the first-order diffraction terms (Casasent and Casasayas, 1975a).

an 0.2 μsec pulse width at f = 5.650 GHz with a Δf = 5 MHz step between pulses were recorded on successive lines on the DKDP. The Fourier transform of this distribution is shown in Fig. 33 (Casasent, 1975; Casasent and Casasayas, 1975b). The vertical coordinates of the first-order off-axis peaks of light (upper left quadrant and lower right quadrant) are proportional to the target's fine range (Casasent and Casasayas, 1975b). The data shown correspond to a target with a fine range of 128 m in the 300 m range bin in question. This data agree with the actual digitally computed values. It was possible to determine fine ranges to one meter for this radar.

A final dramatic example (Casasent, 1975; Casasent and Casasayas, 1975b) of real-time optical processing of radar data is shown in Fig. 34. Real pulsed Doppler radar signals from a Doppler radar with a pulse repetition rate of 1.25 kHz were used. One hundred returned signals were written on successive lines of the DKDP. In the Fourier transform, each target again produces two off-axis first-order diffraction peaks that are symmetric about the origin. The coordinates of these peaks are now proportional to the target's fine Doppler velocity in the 300 m/sec unambiguous velocity bin chosen (Casasent and Casasayas, 1975b). The actual optical output for one such set of 100 Doppler returns is shown in Fig. 34a. Two sets of symmetric first-order peaks are

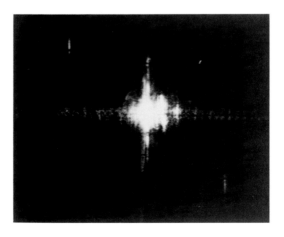

FIG. 33.   Optically processed radar data from an FM stepped radar for a target with a fine range of 128 m in a 300 m range bin, processed in real time using an electron-beam addressed DKDP input device. Fine target range resolution (proportional to the locations of the first-order off-axis diffraction terms) of 1 m was obtained (Casasent and Casasayas, 1975b).

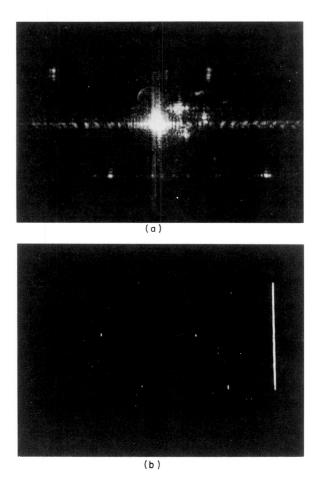

(a)

(b)

FIG. 34. Optically processed radar data from a pulsed Doppler radar for two aircraft crossing in the same bin, processed in real time using an electron-beam addressed DK DP input device. Fine Doppler resolution (proportional to the locations of the first-order off-axis diffraction terms) of 1 m/sec was obtained (Casasent, 1975). (a) Optical output, (b) thresholded display of data in (a) showing the diagonal pairs of peaks for both targets.

present. These correspond to two aircraft crossing in the same Doppler bin. The display of this data from a thresholded camera with the dc term suppressed is shown in Fig. 34b (Casasent, 1975). From the locations of the two pairs of points, the fine velocity of each aircraft within any Doppler bin can be determined to better than 1 m/sec.

The transform and correlation planes of a real-time optical processor using an electron-beam addressed DK DP input transducer have recently been interfaced to a digital computer (Casasent, 1971; Casasent and Sterling, 1975). The resultant hybrid optical/digital processor combines the best features of optical and digital processing.

The use of electron-beam addressed DK DP in the pattern recognition of image areas has also been considered (Casasent, 1974a). The side-looking radar input image shown in Fig. 35 was written on the DK DP crystal which was placed at the input plane P_0 of the optical correlator of Fig. 1. A holographic matched spatial filter of the landing field (shown in Fig. 35b) was formed at plane P_1 in Fig. 1. The resultant pattern in the output plane (P_2 in Fig. 1) is the correlation of these two images and corresponds to a single correlation peak of light as shown in Fig. 35c. This correlation peak was obtained in real time. Its position in the output plane corresponds to the location of the landing field in the input image.

An example of multiple pattern recognition in real-time using the DK DP light valve is shown in Fig. 36 (Casasent and Sterling, 1975). To demonstrate the parallel processing potential of a coherent optical correlator, a paragraph of text (Fig. 36a) with six occurrences of the word RADAR was written on the DK DP (placed in the input plane P_0 at Fig. 1). With a holographic matched filter of the word RADAR placed in the transform plane P_1, the pattern shown in Fig. 36b appears in output correlation plane. Rather than six simple correlation peaks (one for each occurrence of the word RADAR in the input), numerous strong cross-correlations characteristic of text correlations are present. Proper analysis by thresholding and integration in the digital section of the hybrid optical/digital system noted earlier yields the displayed output of Fig. 36c. The output is again available in real-time and the locations of the bright peaks in Fig. 36c correspond exactly to the six locations of the word RADAR in the input image. Extensions of these operations to many other applications are clearly possible.

VII. Summary and Conclusions

Many other potential real-time materials and devices applicable as reusable input and spatial filter transducers for a coherent optical processor exist. Available space has permitted a somewhat detailed view of those transducers that presently seem to be the most promising and those that have seen somewhat extensive use in coherent optical processors. Many materials and devices that have been used as large screen projection displays, page composers, and for the mass holo-

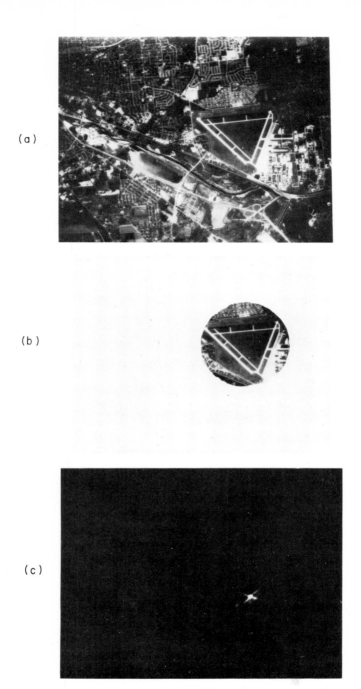

(a)

(b)

(c)

Fig. 35. Real-time optical pattern recognition using an electron-beam addressed DKDP device (Casasent, 1974a). (a) Input image, (b) portion of image from which holographic matched spatial filter was formed, (c) output optical correlation of (a) and Fourier transform hologram of (b).

(a)

THE DEVELOPMENT OF RADAR DURING WORLD
WAR II BROUGHT RADAR FROM A LABORATORY
CONCEPT TO A MATURE DISCIPLINE IN JUST
A FEW SHORT YEARS. SINCE 1945 RADAR
TECHNOLOGY HAS BECOME SO SOPHISTICATED
THAT THE BASIC RECTANGULAR PULSE RADAR
SIGNAL IS NO LONGER SUFFICIENT IN THE
DESIGN OF MANY NEW RADAR SYSTEMS.
MORE COMPLEX RADAR SIGNALS MUST BE
TAILORED TO SPECIFIC REQUIREMENTS.

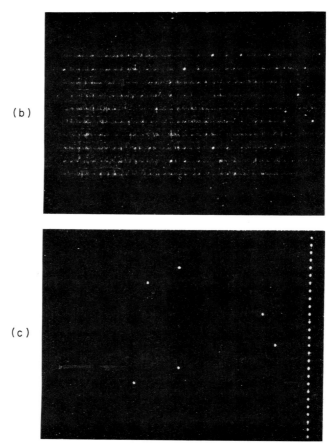

(b)

(c)

FIG. 36. Real-time optical pattern recognition using an electron-beam addressed
DKDP device (Casasent and Sterling, 1975). (a) Input image, (b) optical correlation of (a)
with a Fourier transform hologram of the word RADAR, (c) thresholded and integrated
display of (b) showing the six locations of the word RADAR in the input text.

graphic storage of digital data have not been included because they have seen no use or only limited use in coherent optical data processing.

The most promising devices appear to be the deformable oil film light valve, the hybrid liquid crystal, the PROM, photo-DKDP, and electron-beam addressed DKDP. Each device has its advantages and disadvantages and specific applications to which it is best suited. If a long lifetime is not required, thermoplastic devices are a possibility. The only two viable electron-beam addressed devices appear to be the oil film and DKDP light valves. The oil film device has no storage, and correction of its optical quality remains to be done. It is presently a more "hardened" device than the DKDP light valve, however. The liquid crystal device exhibits no storage while the PROM and photo-DKDP devices do. The resolution of the PROM apparently exceeds that of the other devices, but it requires large voltages for operation and many rather precise fabrication steps.

All these devices represent major achievements in crystallography, thin film technology, and electronics. They make many of the early dreams and promises of optical processing more realizable and are essential elements in any optical processor that is to achieve the parallel processing and high throughput possible. As stated at the outset, the specific application will determine the device to be used.

ACKNOWLEDGMENTS

The cooperation of the Department of Defense and many companies (Hughes Research Laboratory, Malibu, Calif.; Harris Semiconductor Division, Melbourne, Fla.; Ampex Corporation, Redwood City, Calif.; Xerox Corporate Research Center, Palo Alto, Calif.; General Electric Company, Syracuse, N.Y.), in providing imagery is gratefully acknowledged. The continued support of the Office of Naval Research on Contracts NR 048-600 and NR 350-011, the National Aeronautics and Space Administration and the Air Force Office of Scientific Research on Grant AFOSR-75-2851 for much of the author's work included in this chapter is also gratefully acknowledged.

REFERENCES

Adams, J. E., Haas, W. E., and Wysocki, J. J. (1970). "Liquid Crystals and Ordered Fluids." Plenum, New York.
Appl. Opt. (1974). 13. (Special Issue on Optical Storage of Digital Data.)
Barrett, H. H., Garewal, K., and Wilson, P. T. (1972). Radiology 104, 429.
Bartolino, R. (1973). Appl. Opt. 12, 2917.
Billings, B. H. (1949). J. Opt. Soc. Am. 39, 797.
Boller, A., Scherrer, H., and Schadt, M. (1972). Proc. IEEE 60, 1002.
Bordogna, J., Keneman, S., and Amodei, J. (1972). RCA Rev. 33, 227.

Carpenter, R. (1950). *J. Opt. Soc. Am.* **40,** 225.

Casasent, D. (1971). *Laser Focus* **7,** 30.

Casasent, D. (1973). *IEEE Trans. Electron Devices* **20,** 1109.

Casasent, D. (1974a). *Opt. Eng.* **13,** 228.

Casasent, D. (1974b). *J. Soc. Inf. Disp.* **15,** 131.

Casasent, D. (1975). *Dig. Int. Opt. Comput. Conf.* p. 5. IEEE Cat. No. 75CH0941-5C.

Casasent, D. (1976). *In* "Optical Information Processing" (G. W. Stroke *et al.*, eds.), pp. 13–46. Plenum, New York.

Casasent, D. (1977a). *Proc. IEEE* Jan. 1977.

Casasent, D. (1977b). *In* "Applications of Optical Data Processing" (D. Casasent, ed.). Springer-Verlag, Berlin and New York. Chap. 8 (In Press).

Casasent, D., and Caimi, F. (1973). *J. Vac. Sci. Technol.* **10,** 1102.

Casasent, D., and Casasayas, F. (1975a). *IEEE Trans. Aerosp. Electron. Syst.* **11,** 65.

Casasent, D., and Casasayas, F. (1975b). *Appl. Opt.* **14,** 1364.

Casasent, D., and Keicher, W. (1972). *Proc. Elec. Opt. Syst. Des. Conf.* 99.

Casasent, D., and Keicher, W. (1974). *J. Opt. Soc. Am.* **64,** 1575.

Casasent, D., and Sterling, W. (1975). *IEEE Trans. Comput.* **24,** 318.

Cummins, S. E., and Luke, T. E. (1971). *IEEE Trans. Electron Devices* **18,** 761.

Donjon, J., Dumont, F., Grenot, M., Hazan, J., Marie, G., and Pergrale, J. (1973). *IEEE Trans. Electron Devices* **20,** 1037.

Doyle, R., and Glenn, W. (1972). *Appl. Opt.* **11,** 1261.

Eastman Kodak Co. (1974). Publ. JJ-193.

ERIM (1973). Final Rep., Contract AFAL-TR-73-88.

Farrah, H. R., Maron, E., and Mueller, R. K. (1970). *Acoust. Hologr.* **2,** 173.

Flannery, J. (1973). *IEEE Trans. Electron Devices* **20,** 941.

General Electric Co. (1974). Tech. Inf. Ser. R7ELS-12.

Goetz, G. G. (1970). *Appl. Phys. Lett.* **17,** 63.

Goetz, G. G., Koppelmann, R. F., and Mueller, R. K. (1972). *Proc. Elec. Opt. Syst. Des. Conf.* p. 202.

Goodman, J. W. (1968). "Introduction to Fourier Optics." McGraw-Hill, New York.

Grenot, M., Pergrale, J., Donjon, J., and Marie, G. (1972). *Appl. Phys. Lett.* **21,** 83.

Grinberg, J., Jacobson, A., Bleha, W., Miller, L., Frass, L., Boswell, D., and Myer, G. (1975). *Opt. Eng.* **43,** 217.

Groh, G., and Marie, G. (1970). *Opt. Commun.* **2,** 133.

Harris Semiconductor Div. (1974). Final Rep., Contract NAS8-26360.

IEEE Trans. Comput. (1975). **24.** (Special Issue on Optical Computing.)

IEEE Trans. Electron Devices (1973). **20.** (Special Issue on Two-Dimensional Pictorial Displays.)

Itek Corp. (1974). Final Rep., Contract ETL-CR-74-18.

Iwasa, S., and Feinleib, J. (1974). *Opt. Eng.* **13,** 235.

J. Soc. Inf. Disp. (1974). **15.** (Special Issue on Optical Computing.)

Koch, M., and Tiemens, U. (1973). *Opt. Commun.* **7,** 260.

Kumada, A. (1972). *IEEE Trans. Sonics Ultrason.* **19,** 115.

Lee, T. C. (1974). *Appl. Opt.* **13,** 888.

Lipson, S. G. (1976). *In* "Advances in Holography" (N. H. Farhat, ed.). Dekker, New York. (In Press).

Lipson, S. G., and Nisenson, P. (1974). *Appl. Opt.* **13,** 2052.

Lohmann, A. W., and Paris, D. P. (1967). *Appl. Opt.* **6,** 1741.

Maldonado, J., and Meitzler, A. (1974). *Proc. IEEE* **59,** 368.

Marie, G. (1967). *Philips Res. Rep.* **22,** 110.

Marie, G. (1969). *Philips Tech. Rev.* **30**, 292.
Marie, G., and Donjon, J. (1973). *Proc. IEEE* **61**, 942.
Markevitch, R., and Rodal, D. (1975). *Proc. Elec. Opt. Syst. Des. Conf.* p. 101.
Nisenson, P., and Sprague, R. A. (1975). *Appl. Opt.* **14**, 2602.
Nobel, M. L. (1974). *AIAA Meet.*
Oliver, D. S., and Buchan, W. R. (1971). *IEEE Trans. Elec. Devices* **18**, 769.
Opt. Eng. (1974). **13**. (Special Issue on Optical and Digital Image Processing.)
Poppelbaum, W. J., Faiman, M., Casasent, D., and Sand, D. (1968). *Proc. IEEE* **56**, 1744.
Preston, K. (1972). "Coherent Optical Computers." McGraw-Hill, New York.
Pritchard, D. H. (1969). *RCA Rev.* **30**, 567.
Proc. IEEE (1977). Jan. (Special Issue on Optical Computing.)
RCA Rev. (1972). **33**. (Special Issue on Optical Storage.)
Reizmann, F. (1969). *Proc. Elec. Opt. Syst. Des. Conf.*
Roberts, H. N. (1972). *Appl. Opt.* **11**, 397.
Salvo, C. J. (1971). *IEEE Trans. Electron Devices* **18**, 748.
Sand, D., Faiman, M., and Poppelbaum, W. J. (1973). *IEEE J. Quantum Electron.* **9**, 708.
Sheridon, N. (1972). *IEEE Trans. Electron Devices* **19**, 1003.
Sheridon, N., and Berkovitz, M. (1974). *Eur. Elec. Opt. Markets Technol. Conf., 2nd* p. 354.
Sheridon, N., and Berkovitz, M. (1975). *Proc. Elec. Opt. Syst. Des. Conf.*
Smith, W., and Land, C. (1972). *Appl. Phys. Lett.* **23**, 57.
Soref, R., and Rafuse, M. (1972). *J. Appl. Phys.* **43**, 2029.
Sprague, R. A. (1975). *J. Appl. Phys.* **46**, 1673.
Stroke, G. W. (1972). *IEEE Spectrum* **9**, 24.
Thomas, C. E. (1966). *Appl. Opt.* **5**, 1782.
Tufte, O., and Chen, D. (1973). *IEEE Spectrum* **10**, 26.
Turpin, T. (1974). *Dig. Int. Opt. Comput. Conf.* p. 34. IEEE Cat. No. 72CH0862-3C.
Vander Lugt, A. (1974). *Proc. IEEE* **62**, 1300.
Vohl, P., Nisenson, P., and Oliver, D. (1973). *IEEE Trans. Electron Devices* **20**, 1032.
Weaver, C. S., and Goodman, J. W. (1966). *Appl. Opt.* **5**, 1248.
Weiss, H. (1973). *Proc. Int. J. Conf. Pattern Recognition.*
Weiss, H. (1974). *Dig. Int. Opt. Comput. Conf.* IEEE Cat. No. 74CH0862-3C
Yamada, Y., Iwasaki, H., and Niizeki, N. (1972). *J. Appl. Phys.* **43**, 771.

LASERS IN MEDICINE

R. M. Dwyer

Department of Gastroenterology
University of California, Los Angeles
Harbor General Hospital
Torrance, California, and
Center for Laser Studies
University of Southern California
Los Angeles, California

and

M. Bass

Center for Laser Studies
University of Southern California
Los Angeles, California

I. Introduction

The principal therapeutic uses of laser energy in medicine have been to cut, cauterize, or injure certain tissues (Goldman and Rockwell, 1971; Goldman, 1973a). Lasers have also been used for spectral analysis and tissue transillumination as diagnostic applications. In order to understand the use of lasers in medicine it is essential first to consider current treatment procedures.

A scalpel or surgical knife is the most common instrument used in surgical procedures. Cutting with a scalpel has been used throughout the history of surgery and is the method in which surgeons are trained. This type of cutting is easily and accurately controlled by the surgeon. The incision in the skin or other tissue is clean and is not surrounded by necrotic or burned cells as produced by electrosurgery. This makes it easier for scalpel-incised tissue to heal and improves the cosmetic quality of the healed wound. In addition, there is much less chance of wound infection when there is no necrotic tissue in which bacteria can multiply, and the excised tissue is preserved for pathological evaluation.

When a surgeon cuts with a scalpel, bleeding into the incision may impair the accuracy of his work by obscuring his view. Each bleeding vessel must be clamped and tied with sutures and the incision sponged dry to permit continued work. This obviously increases the duration and complexity of the procedure. It also means that foreign matter (the sutures) must be left in the wound after surgery. Sutures left in the closed wound may become a nidus for infection or foreign body reaction. If the bleeding becomes excessive, the quantity of blood loss may require transfusion, with the risk of hepatitis. In addition, there may be problems in maintaining adequate blood pressure and blood flow to such vital organs as the brain, heart, and kidneys.

Today, nearly all operating rooms are equipped with electrocautery units which can be used either to coagulate or cut tissue (Engel and Harris, 1975). These units deliver pulsed radio frequency (rf) electrical currents to coagulate tissue or continuous rf currents to cut tissue. Tissue cells are principally dissolved salts, water, and protein. They have a nonzero electrical resistivity and power is dissipated when a current is passed through them. This results in heating of the cells and the denaturation of protein which in turn produces a physical block to the passage of blood.

In the coagulating mode, the current-off time between pulses of rf energy permits the heat to be conducted away from the region treated. This distributes the induced heat so that the effect achieved is tissue coagulation rather than cutting. When a continuous current is delivered, the cells can get so hot that the water is vaporized and the cells rupture. By moving the point of application of the cutting current an incision is made.

Electrocoagulation and cutting are thus achieved by heating the tissue. One of the major disadvantages of this procedure is extensive subsurface damage. In addition, as the treated cells are dessicated the current may arc over to more moist tissue nearby. If the tissue is a modest sized blood vessel, the current may be conducted through the blood and produce damage to distant tissues. Thus, there is the risk of damage to tissues unrelated to the area of treatment.

The use of an electrical current is advantageous when a large mass of tissue with a rich blood supply must be incised. The current cuts and coagulates simultaneously and thereby speeds the surgeon's work.

The coagulation current can be used instead of sutures to stop bleeding from smaller blood vessels. This reduces the time required to stop bleeding and the amount of foreign material left in the wound. Bleeding that is heavier than a slow ooze frequently requires a suture tie because the clot formed by electrocautery may be sloughed off as it contracts, and bleeding may resume.

The cryosurgery probe is an instrument used to destroy certain tissue by application of extreme cold (Fusek and Kung, 1971; Raud et al., 1968). The probe is very small and is insulated so that only its tip becomes cold. This cold tip produces tissue damage by freezing the cells in the vicinity of the tip. Cryosurgery has been used to treat Parkinson's disease by destroying certain aggregates of nerve cells deep in the brain. It has also been used to destroy large cancerous tumors of the abdomen.

Laser phototherapy also produces coagulation and cautery by heating cells in the tissue (Goldman and Rockwell, 1971). The heating process is caused by the absorption of optical radiation by the cells. Since the optical absorptivity of most cells is very high, most of the incident energy is absorbed very near the surface (Kiefhaber et al., 1974). This means that with laser treatment few cells are affected and distant tissues are not damaged.

While the selected current and tissue resistivity determine the rate of electrocautery, the rate of laser cautery is principally determined by the incident optical power density and the optical absorptivity of the tissue. In both cases other thermodynamic properties, such as tissue heat capacity, cooling by blood flow, cooling by heat transfer to the air and other tissues, tissue density, are also important rate determining factors (Zacarian, 1969). Some important factors in the light–tissue interaction are listed in Table I.

At this point it is important to emphasize that in most literature on the

TABLE I

FACTORS IN LASER LIGHT–TISSUE INTERACTIONS

1. Wavelength of laser
2. Optical absorptivity of tissue at that wavelength
3. Intensity incident on the treatment site (W/cm^2)
4. Duration of the irradiation on the treatment site (sec)
5. Volume of tissue treated (spot size and penetration depth)

use of lasers in medicine, the characteristics of the irradiation are inadequately described. In order to specify laser irradiation properly one must give all of the following: (1) wavelength, (2) temporal waveform, (3) beam energy or power, and (4) spatial distribution of the light incident on the target. In this way the power density can be ascertained. It is useless to specify total power of a cw laser and not to give the area irradiated. It is similarly useless to specify pulsed laser outputs in energy density (J/cm^2) and not to explain the laser's waveform. In addition, it is often very useful to describe the laser beam delivery system and especially any final focusing lenses. Whenever possible in this article, we shall specify the irradiation as a power density (W/cm^2).

A laser beam can be accurately delivered to almost any site. Furthermore, by properly selecting the wavelength of the laser used, the beam can selectively affect different tissues at that site. Thus laser irradiation possesses properties that may make its use in certain applications particularly advantageous. It will not replace the scalpel entirely nor will it supplant electrocautery. It will, however, provide a treatment procedure for certain problems, which will result in improved patient care.

We shall discuss the use of lasers in medicine by considering the major areas of clinical treatment that have been investigated and applied to human subjects. In each section we shall discuss the medical problems, the current treatment procedures, the technique of laser treatment, the equipment, the results, and possible new areas of application.

II. Otolaryngology

Otolaryngology is a surgical specialty that deals with the treatment of disorders of the ears, nose, throat, and oral cavity. There is an extremely rich system of blood vessels in the area of the head and neck which creates a problem in standard surgical procedures. An excessive amount of bleeding may be encountered when a scalpel is used. This may extend the duration of the surgery because the bleeding vessels must be tied and may add to the difficulty of the procedure by impairing the otolaryngologist's view of the area of treatment. In certain problem areas such as the pharynx, larynx, trachea, and middle ear, treatment with conventional techniques is extremely difficult due to very limited accessibility (Paparella and Shumrick, 1973). These sites are small, hard to reach, and often very hard to see at any time.

The common technique employed today in head and neck surgery involves the use of a scalpel in conjunction with electrocautery and blood transfusions. In other areas with rich blood supplies or in procedures that cause an excessive amount of bleeding, it is often possible to use tourniquets to reduce blood loss. This, of course, is not possible in head and neck surgery. The presence of infection in the surgical field is a valid reason to delay surgery when only conventional tools and techniques are available.

In order to overcome the problems outlined above it is of some advantage in otolaryngology to develop new equipment and techniques. Equipment should be capable of being accurately manipulated in areas of restricted access. The degree of blood loss should be minimized to maintain an operative field free of debris. The procedure should neither be restricted by the presence of infection in the operated tissue nor should it result in the spread of infection. CO_2 laser light has been used to provide such a tool, and a variety of problems have been studied to develop the necessary techniques (Mihashi *et al.*, 1976; Jako *et al.*, 1973). The CO_2 lasers used in such surgery emit on the order of 50 W of continuous power at a wavelength of 10.6 μm. Since this is in the infrared and cannot be seen, a low power HeNe laser has been included to provide an aiming beam collinear with that of the CO_2 laser. Since no flexible fiber optics are presently available for use at 10.6 μm, an articulated arm optical system must be used to deliver the light from the laser to a surgical tool.

An articulated arm optical system is a series of mirrors mounted at 45° incidence angle to the beam axis and fitted into the ends of hollow tubes which can be rotated with respect to each other.[1] The laser beam is transmitted through the tubes by reflections from the mirrors and is aimed in any direction by rotating the tubes. The bearings on which these tubes rotate must be extremely accurate and free of slippage to maintain the required mirror alignment. With the addition of telescoping segments in the tubes the articulated arm makes possible the delivery of laser light to any target which can be visualized. On the other hand, articulated arm optical systems are delicate, expensive, and not as flexible as necessary in many surgical procedures.

The unfocused laser beam is ≈ 1 cm in diameter. In order to achieve the optical power density required for cutting or coagulation, the surgical tool (often a handpiece at the end of the articulated arm) can be fitted with a number of focusing lenses. These lenses permit the surgeon to obtain power densities from as low as that of the unfocused beam,

[1] One manufacturer of articulated arm light guides is Advanced Kinetics Inc., Costa Mesa, California.

~60 W/cm², to as high as ~7000 W/cm². In the latter case the focal spot diameter is ~0.5 mm.

When the area to be treated is accessible, such as the external areas of the head, neck, or the oral cavity, the surgeon manipulates the laser beam through a hand piece using a 14 cm focal length lens (Kaplan *et al.*, 1974). This tool can be gas sterilized and the articulated arm can be covered with sterile drapes when asepsis and a sterile field are needed. In these and most laser cutting and coagulating applications, it is necessary to provide a strong air suction near the operative field to remove vaporized tissue, steam, and smoke generated by the light–tissue interaction.

In order to deliver laser energy to sites with limited access, a surgical microscope with a laser beam micromanipulator is used (Jako, 1971). This device is essentially a long-focal-length microscope fitted with optics that permit the laser beam to be brought to a focus which is coincident with that of the microscope without harming the operator. In otolaryngology a 400 mm focal length surgical microscope permits accurate visualization of sites in the pharynx and larynx. The low power HeNe aiming beam and the CO_2 laser beam from the surgical unit are aimed at the site by auxiliary optics which the physician controls while viewing through the microscope. His controls provide micromanipulation of the laser beam on the target and permits him to select the tissue to be treated, the volume to be cut, and the rate of removal throughout the procedure.

If the physician must treat areas beyond the larynx a standard, rigid, hollow, ventilating bronchoscope can be fitted with a microscope attachment (Laforet *et al.*, 1976). The laser beam can then be focused on lesions in the trachea and the main stem bronchus with continuous monocular vision. The magnification in this device is 2×.

A wide variety of problems in the head and neck have been treated with laser radiation. In all these procedures it is essential to protect the patient's eyes from exposure to the intense laser light. Otherwise no unusual precautions have been found necessary.

Wet sponges or cotton swabs are used to protect certain vital structures, such as nerves or arteries, from undue heating during CO_2 laser treatment of nearby tissues (*Int. Conf. Laser Surg.*, 1975). Metal spatulas and other reflecting instruments have been used to try to reflect laser light away from vital tissues, but there is the concurrent danger of injury to the operating room personnel from the reflected beams. Some surgeons inject saline solution subcutaneously around the vital structures to protect them. This maneuver is effective because either water or saline, although able to absorb CO_2 laser energy, has a high heat capacity which prevents rapid overheating of the tissue structure.

In the oral cavity of humans superficial cancers, benign outgrowths of tissue (papillomas), and white patches of atypical mucosal cells caused by chronic irritation (leukoplakia) have been excised with a CO_2 laser surgical unit (Goldman et al., 1968). There are many blood vessels supplying the tissues of the oral cavity, and vessels greater than $\frac{1}{2}$ mm in diameter would have to be tied off if transected during surgery (Verschueren et al., 1975). The laser beam cuts and coagulates simultaneously, simplifying the procedure. Depending on the size of the treated area, complete healing was observed in 2 to 3 weeks. There was no evidence of local swelling after the operation and the pain experienced postoperatively was minimal. Strong et al. have observed the absence of contracture at the site of the healed wound (Strong, 1973). A contracture is caused by scar tissue buildup followed by shrinkage which deforms the treated area.

Localized lesions of the anterior nasal cavity, nasal vestibule, and septum have been successfully excised using laser irradiation (Int. Conf. Laser Surg., 1975). The lesions included papillomas, hereditary telangiectasia, and various cancers.

In the pharynx and nasopharynx, lasers have been used to perform tonsillectomies, adenoidectomies, the removal of carcinomas, and reconstructive plastic surgery (Kaplan et al., 1973a). Laser surgery of the larynx has been used to excise vocal cord nodules, polyps, cysts, and carcinomas (Jako, 1971). The larynx was visualized using a suitable suspension laryngoscope with the patient under general anesthesia. Lesions in all parts of the larynx can be treated with laser light provided they are satisfactorily exposed. They may be removed accurately, and by removing a succession of small layers, surface lesions as small as 1 mm in diameter can be removed without damage to the underlying muscle or elastic fibers of the vocal cord.

In order to deliver CO_2 laser light to sites in the trachea, the endoscopic attachment available with the CO_2 laser surgical unit is attached to a standard ventilating bronchoscope. With this equipment multiple recurrent papillomas have been removed (Jako et al., 1973). These growths interfere with normal breathing and can obstruct the trachea if allowed to grow too large. Blue-green argon ion laser light has also been employed to treat this problem by using the same optical system (Fiedler, 1973). To clear the operative field and protect the delivery system optics, the steam and smoke generated by the tissue vaporization was carried away by a tidal flow of oxygen and anesthetic gases, because if the tissue becomes overheated in a closed space, O_2 can reach a combustible temperature.

The inner ear cannot be approached by conventional surgical methods without causing a complete loss of function. Here the laser makes possible the controlled delivery of high levels of energy to a very small target area. Procedures that have been tried in middle ear surgery with argon ion laser radiation include the opening of a small hole in the ear drum for drainage. Stapedectomy has been performed on human cadavers. This is a procedure used in the treatment of certain types of deafness. Selective lesions have been created in the semicircular canals of monkeys in the treatment of nystagmus and vertigo without causing significant hearing loss (Wilpizeski and Sataloff, 1974; Sugar et al., 1974).

The future area of otolaryngologic laser use lies in the development of microsurgical techniques for middle ear surgery and continued development of already demonstrated procedures.

III. Ophthalmology

The main uses of lasers in ophthalmology are (1) the treatment of retinal detachment and (2) the photocoagulation of nonproliferative retinopathy. The use of laser light in diagnosis has been reviewed recently by Landers et al. (1976). Using a self-retinoscopy technique which is based on the patient's view of a laser speckle pattern, it is possible to measure separately the optical and neuronal portions of the optic pathway (Landers et al., 1976). This procedure can test for both spherical and cylindrical corrections to be included in prescribed eye glass lenses.

Let us first consider the history of the treatment of retinal detachments (Newell and Ernest, 1974). In the 19th century, retinal detachments were treated primarily with bed rest and by immobilizing the eyes. The latter, which was considered to be more important than restricting body movements, was achieved by bandaging the eyes and by placing sandbags on the sides of the head for many weeks. Surgical treatment consisted of drainage of the subretinal fluid. Temporary drainage involved a scleral puncture with a knife and was the first operation devised for retinal detachments. The operation was extended to include puncturing of the retina, thereby creating a second retinal hole so the retinal fluid could drain into the vitreous cavity.

Permanent drainage was accomplished by the use of multiple sclerotomies. This was achieved by drilling two holes into the globe of the eye and passing either a gold wire or a strand of horsehair in one hole and out the other. Permanent drainage was also attempted by irredectomy and choriodialysis. The latter is the process of opening the sclera, separating it from the choroid, and then perforating the choroid. Other forms of treatment such as subconjuctival injections and the creation of corneal retinal adhesions were used. In the early part of this century Gonin demonstrated that the cure of retinal detachment associated with retinal perforation or tear depended on obliteration of the perforation by sealing it to the choroid in scar tissue (McPherson, 1968). Today's successful treatment techniques were developed from this observation.

In 1949, light coagulation of a retinal tear was attempted by using focused sunlight to produce a burn in the retina. Then in 1954, Meyer-Schwickerath used a xenon arc lamp to produce thermal damage to the retina (McPherson, 1968). And in 1961, Zaret and his colleagues employed the compact and easily manipulated beam of a laser to photocoagulate the retina (Zaret et al., 1963). This therapy was explored further by a number of other workers (Zweng et al., 1966; L'Esperance, 1965).

The proper use of photocoagulation in the treatment of retinal detachment is as effective as primary penetrating diathermy and is safer (Landers et al., 1976). There is considerably less danger of hemorrhage with photocoagulation and it is much more easily applied. The incidence of the formation of initial or additional retinal breaks following either form of treatment is about the same, although retinal detachment more frequently results from a new break following diathermy treatment.

Xenon arc lamp photocoagulators emit in a broad spectral range from about 400–1600 nm. The emission is not spatially coherent and the retinal spot to which the arc can be focused is quite large. The spot size of the xenon light beam when focused in the eye is 500–1000 μm in diameter. Excessive heating also occurs in the ocular medium and the vitreous unless the xenon lamp system is specially equipped with infrared filters. Even with proper filtering the number of doses of flashlamp light that may be given in any treatment session is limited. Also, to achieve photocoagulation with the flash lamp unit, a relatively long exposure time (250–1000 msec) is required. Since retinal movements can occur in this long period, a general anesthetic is often required (L'Esperance, 1966).

Laser photocoagulation of retinopathies, especially those encountered in diabetic patients, has become very common (Patz et al., 1976). The lesions in the retina to which laser photocoagulation is particularly suited are proliferations of blood vessels. Regardless of the cause, these blood vessels are thin walled and fragile. They have a propensity to obscure vision locally by covering part of the retina and to rupture, causing an extravasation of blood in the vitreous, possibly obscuring all vision.

Optic photocoagulation requires a clear medium, maximum mydriasis (no photocoagulation should be attempted with a pupil that is smaller than 5 mm when exposed to a strong light), local anesthesia, and complete akinesia. Evaluation of the results of photocoagulations is complicated by the tendency of the retinopathy to fluctuate and of lesions to sometimes increase in one area of the retina while regressing in others. The Diabetic Retinopathy Study has undertaken a long-term evaluation of randomly selected patients with diabetic retinopathy. This disorder has become the leading cause of blindness in the United States. After two years, the study has reported that phototherapy as used in their protocol is of benefit in preventing severe visual loss in eyes with proliferative retinopathy (Patz *et al.*, 1976). Photocoagulation is used in proliferative retinopathy to destroy areas of new blood vessels and areas of hypoxic retina, which is believed to provide the stimulus for further blood vessel proliferation. In addition, photocoagulation is used in nonproliferative retinopathy in which there is vascular leaking as demonstrated by fluorescein angiography (Landers *et al.*, 1976).

The two lasers principally used in eye surgery are the ruby laser at 6943 Å and the argon laser which emits light at several blue-green wavelengths (its principal lines are at 4880 and 5145 Å). The ruby laser output used is a pulse of ≈ 1 μsec duration, focused on the retina to a spot of diameter between 100 and 700 μm (Cleary and Hamrick, 1971). With an argon ion photocoagulator the laser beam can be focused to spots as small as 50 μm and aimed at specific small lesions. The laser is often pulsed and each exposure causes a minute discrete retinal burn. As many as 400–500 bursts may be used in a single treatment and if necessary the treatment may be repeated or staged in a series (L'Esperance, 1969). Ruby laser light is not strongly absorbed in blood and so is not a good choice to achieve a direct coagulative effect on blood vessels in the eye. However, vessels may be indirectly affected by heat generated through absorption of ruby laser light in pigmented surrounding tissues. Absorption of the argon beam in blood vessels is approximately seven times greater than that of the ruby lasers. Therefore, the argon laser coagulates and obliterates blood vessels more easily. In the eye, argon lasers have been used to photocoagulate vessels of 30–50 μm (Wolbarsht, 1975).

Transmission of the laser beam to the ophthalmologic instruments has been accomplished by reflection off several mirrors as in an articulated arm light guide and, in more recent units, by the use of fiber optics. Laser photocoagulators may be used with direct or indirect ophthalmoscopes or with slit lamp units.

Laser-induced cataracts have been reported recently in rabbits (Lawwill, 1973; Priebe and Welch, 1973; Cain and Welch, 1974). This may be related to the increased temperature on the anterior surface of the lens during laser irradiation of the retina. The small miotic pupil of the rabbit's eye may aid in developing the cataract by concentrating the beam in one area. To examine the treatment of specific diseases with laser photocoagulation, one should refer to special journals and reference works on laser ophthalmology. The ruby laser, in the past, has been used to treat tears and postretinal detachments. The argon laser, on the other hand, is used currently for vascular disorders of the eye. Projected work in laser ophthalmology concerns the development of dye lasers and the determination of the exact wavelengths that are best absorbed in specific retinal layers. These data may well lead to treatments of specific layers of the retina for various kinds of disease (Wolbarsht, 1975).

Corneal ulcers have been treated externally with laser energy. This procedure employs an argon ion laser and fluorescein dye to treat ulcers caused by the bacteria *Pseudomonas aerugnosa* and the fungus *Candida albicans* (Wolbarsht, 1975). The infection site is dyed with the fluorescein dye by using antibodies specific for the infecting organism labeled with the dye. The labeled antibodies then attach to the ulcer-producing organism. Fluorescein strongly absorbs argon ion laser radiation and thus raises the temperature of the organism, destroying it without harming the surrounding tissue. This therapy can provide a treatment for a previously intractable eye disease.

Since lasers can be used to produce desired retinal burns they can also produce beams that cause unwanted retinal damage (Priebe *et al.*, 1976; Ham *et al.*, 1974). The issue of laser safety must be faced by the physician, the operating room staff, and the patient. The foremost rule is: Never look directly into a laser beam of any sort, even when wearing so-called laser safety goggles. Of course, when the patient's eye is being treated the area irradiated is selected by the physician and the burns are therapeutic, causing controlled damage. Though the direct beam must be avoided, a laser beam reflected from shiny metal objects (i.e., rings, tie clips, surgical instruments, etc.) or glistening wet tissues can also be dangerous. Laser safety goggles are effective in protecting one's eyes against scattered or reflected beams.

IV. Neurosurgery

The field of neurosurgery deals with the surgical treatment of various neural tissues in the skull, the spine, and elsewhere in the body. These areas have been approached in the past with standard mechanical instruments in combination with electrocautery. Ordinarily most neurologic lesions must be exposed in order to be treated. Exposing a lesion in the brain is achieved at the expense of cutting through good brain tissue which, if destroyed, might leave the patient either paralyzed or with some major neurological deficit. As an alternative, localized cryosurgical techniques have been developed to treat brain tumors or lesions (Raud et al., 1968). In this procedure, a long metal cryosurgical probe is inserted into the brain tissue to the location of the lesion. Liquid nitrogen at 77°K is pumped into the insulated probe to cool its tip. This makes it possible to treat tissue and areas deep within the brain without destroying all the tissue in between as in standard techniques. Cryosurgery of this sort is used to treat Parkinsonism, vascular lesions, and certain forms of tumors in areas that cannot be approached by conventional surgery. The operation is performed under local anesthesia so the therapeutic result and the patient's response can be carefully monitored.

The application of laser irradiation to neurosurgical problems has been studied extensively (Stellar, 1968, 1970). The laser can be used for incising tissue, boring holes in the skull, vaporizing lesions, and cauterizing blood vessels. The laser can convert neoplasms to vapor in a very short period of time. The extent of damage around a lesion that has been treated with a laser is less than a millimeter. This is an advantage in treating areas in the brain where it is essential that the least amount of tissue possible be destroyed. Blood vessels up to 1 mm in external diameter have been coagulated with a CO_2 surgical laser in neurosurgery. Disadvantages of laser surgery in the brain are that the area to be treated has to be exposed to the direct action of the laser beam, and the procedure duration may be prolonged over conventional methods.

Another application of CO_2 laser neurosurgery has been to perform laminectomies. This is the procedure for the removal of tissue from the spine of people who have disc disease. Further development of laser neurosurgery to create lesions called risorotomies is called for. This procedure causes disruption of the conduction pathway for pain in the spinal cord of patients having intractable pain. The lesions created by a laser can be precisely sized and extremely accurately positioned. The risk of side effects due to too large a lesion or due to a lesion being improperly placed is thus reduced.

V. Burn Surgery

Two basic functions of the skin or integument of the body are to protect the body from bacterial invasion and to prevent the loss of fluid and electrolytes from subcutaneous tissues. Both of these functions are disrupted by second- or third-degree burns. Let us first define what different degrees of burns are. A first-degree burn is simple erythema or redness of the skin; a second-degree burn is erythema plus the formation of blisters; and a third-degree burn is the through and through necrosis of the epidermis and the dermis of the skin. Third-degree burns are often charred black.

Ordinarily after a severe burn, the patient is brought to a hospital and the burned tissue is treated under the assumption that it is infected. Even if not initially infected the burned tissue is dead tissue and as such is a very likely place for an infection to start. To prevent this, the burned skin and any other damaged material on the surface of the body is removed by an initial debridement technique. Then various creams, salves, or chemical agents are spread over the burn to reduce bacterial colonization in the damaged tissue. However, in spite of these measures, systemic infection remains the principal cause of death in patients with extensive third-degree burns. An attempt to prevent fluid and electrolyte loss from the damaged tissue through vaporization, leakage, and dehydration is made by applying various forms of gauze and protective wrappings.

Barring infection, an area that has been burned will form an eschar (a scab) in a few days and this will spontaneously slough off between 21 and 35 days later. However, such unassisted healing usually leaves a cosmetically unacceptable and often physically disabling scar. Eventually the scar will contract and deform the surrounding areas. If enough contraction occurs around joints, then there can be permanent loss of function in certain parts of the body. To minimize these problems, the eschar that is formed is surgically removed sometime between one and two weeks after its formation. If there is enough undamaged tissue available either from the patient himself or from other donor sources (frozen pig skin and other allografts have been used), then a primary closure with a skin graft will be attempted. In order to prepare the site for the graft, the surgeon removes the eschar with a scalpel and, to the best of his ability, clamps, ties, or electrocoagulates any severed blood vessels. This procedure takes a fair amount of time and involves considerable blood loss. Blood transfusions are required with the concurrent risks of allergic reactions and hepatitis. Therefore, a technique for debridement of the burn site that would produce the least amount of blood loss and still provide an infection-free bed for the skin graft would be very beneficial.

Levine *et al.* used a CO_2 laser surgical unit for excision of burn eschars (Levine *et al.*, 1974). They found that the use of CO_2 laser light for the excision of third-degree burns resulted in a significant decrease in blood loss when compared to ordinary scalpel excision of the same areas. They also discovered that in the areas that were grafted, there was a marked decrease in the incidence of infection in the laser-treated area when compared to the scalpel-excised areas. Fiedler and others have used a high powered argon laser (over 15 W of total power) for resection of burn eschars (Fiedler et al., 1976). Fiedler conducted comparison studies by resecting half the burn eschar conventionally and the other half with the argon laser. His conclusion is that the laser treatment took 15–20% longer to perform than the conventional procedure. However, there was significantly less blood loss from the laser-treated area than from the scalpel-treated area. There was no difference in the rate of healing or the rate of infection in either area.

The concepts mentioned above can be extended to other areas where there is a break in the integument or covering of the skin resulting in a breakdown of the defenses against infection and leading to major fluid loss. One such problem area is that of bed sores or decubitus ulcers. Stellar reported excellent results using CO_2 laser light for resection and primary closure of oozing areas (Stellar et al., 1974). The patients, who until now would have required on the average 100 days in the hospital for a moderately severe bed sore to heal, required on the average only 28 days of hospitalization following laser resection and primary closure with a skin graft. Once again, laser treatment provides two major advantages over conventional treatments: (1) there is less blood loss and, (2) the area treated with the laser is sterile and thus is an ideal bed for immediate skin grafting.

Future developments in this area of treatment await further technological improvements in the equipment. However, laser resection of damaged skin is one of the few areas in medicine where there is presently a strong indication for its application.

VI. Gastroenterology

Gastroenterology is the study of diseases of the digestive system. It is a specialty in which recent technical developments have been adopted to improve diagnostic technique. The most important recent development has been the development of a fiber optic endoscope. Endoscopes are used to go down into the stomach or up into the colon for the purpose of obtaining a biopsy or observing a given anatomical abnormality. In the past, endoscopes were rigid hollow tubes containing a special optical system to enable the physician to view the region in the immediate area accessed by the device. The limitations of rigid endoscopes are obvious: (1) there is limited visibility, and (2) there is no flexibility, thus limiting the areas which can be inspected.

Modern fiber optic endoscopy came into being around 1968–1969, after the development of reliable fiber optics. With a flexible fiber optic endoscope, one may view almost all the gastrointestinal tract. If a particular lesion is seen, the visualization may help in determining the diagnosis. Biopsy samples may be taken through an endoscope so that one can tell if an ulcer contains cancerous cells and if it does, what kind of cancer it is. All these factors are important to the surgeon prior to operation if a curative surgical procedure is to be attempted.

Gastroenterology is a field of medicine that has used modern optics and so, much like opthalmology and dermatology, can be receptive to some form of therapeutics based on laser irradiation. If laser therapeutics are to be incorporated into gastroenterology then it has to fulfill certain needs and offer advantages over other methods.

Hemorrhage from various lesions in the gastrointestinal tract of humans often presents a difficult problem in either medical or surgical management. Previous treatments for upper gastrointestinal bleeding have included ice saline lavage, vasopressin infusion through an arterial catheter to the artery that is bleeding, and surgery. These methods have not met with total success and subsequently other therapeutic modalities have been attempted.

Electrocautery has been used in an attempt to control upper gastrointestinal bleeding (Papp, 1974; Sugawa et al., 1975). This modality has produced perforation and subsequently peritonitis in other thin-walled organs in the body besides the stomach. Even though the cost of the apparatus for this technique is reasonable, the risks involved are not.

When an electrocautery probe is used to coagulate a bleeding lesion in the upper gastrointestinal tract, a charred clot is formed at the tip of the electrode. As the electrode is removed from the lesion so is the charred clot. This phenomenon often produces further bleeding from the lesion now deepened as a result of the procedure. The tissue in the stomach is approximately 90% water and therefore is a good conduction medium for electricity. Enzyme histochemistry has shown deep cellular changes extending from the point of electrode application into the tissue in a triangular fashion. It was also noted that perforations at relatively long distances from the point of electrode application occurred when that point was very near arteries or veins. These conduits of blood contain sodium, potassium, and chlorine ions in solution and can act as a salt bridge to carry current to distant sites. Presently under investigational use in fiber optic therapeutics for gastrointestinal bleeding is a flexible needle which can be used to inject a vasoconstrictive drug directly into and around the bleeding lesion. This injection causes the vessels to contract and may temporarily stop the bleeding. The effect of the drug is not permanent and bleeding frequently resumes after a relatively short time.

With the advent of fiber optic endoscopy, the location and nature of bleeding sites are usually accessible for diagnosis. The logical extension of fiber optic endoscopy is to incorporate a system that permits treatment as well as diagnosis of bleeding lesions. This was accomplished by coupling a flexible fiber optic filament to an endoscope to deliver cauterizing laser light to the observed lesions (Dwyer *et al.*, 1975). CO_2 laser light previously had been used to achieve blood coagulation and, when passed through a rigid hollow endoscope, arrested bleeding from superficial stomach ulcers in dogs (Goodale *et al.*, 1970). Dwyer and Bass have since successfully treated bleeding lesions in humans (Dwyer *et al.*, 1976). The development of this concept by Dwyer *et al.* in the United States was paralleled by Kiefhaber and Nath in West Germany (Kiefhaber *et al.*, 1974, 1975).

A visible laser was chosen for this application because its output could be transmitted by the glass fiber. A continuous wave argon ion laser capable of a maximum of 4 W output power was focused with a 10× microscope objective lens onto the input end of a 200 μm-diameter, 150 cm long glass fiber optic filament. The amount of laser energy focused to a 2 mm spot required to achieve cautery corresponded to a power density between 11–40 W/cm^2 for varied time intervals.

The fiber optic filament, in its plastic sheath, was taped to the exterior of the endoscope, and its output end protected by a stainless steel cap with a glass window. The transmission of the fiber was about 80% and the output beam spread with a half-angle of approximately 4°. The input power was limited to around 2 W in order to avoid melting the fiber, although the manufacturer rated it for 5 W input. At approximately 14 mm from the output face of the fiber, the beam was about 2 mm in diameter, and rapid cautery could be achieved with a throughput power of 1–2 W.

Human beings have been treated effectively with this method and further development is underway. The fibers must be made physically more durable and able to fit down into the biopsy channels of currently available endoscopes. Laser cautery via fiber optics will not be the ultimate treatment for all gastrointestinal bleeding. However, it will offer a safe, effective alternative for some types of bleeding admitted to the hospital that would otherwise require surgery and/or multiple blood transfusions.

A major contribution was made by Kiefhaber and Nath when they measured the optical penetration in liver, skin, and stomach tissues for several lasers (Kiefhaber *et al.*, 1974). The penetration depth is the depth in which $1/e$ of the incident light is absorbed. Kiefhaber's and Nath's results are shown in Table II for CO_2, argon, and Nd:YAG lasers.

Initially Kiefhaber's group evaluated the cw argon laser for treating gastrointestinal bleeding and found the effect safe but superficial and limited to vessels $<1\frac{1}{2}$ mm in diameter. Kiefhaber *et al.* (1975) are now evaluating Nd:YAG laser irradiation using throughput powers >50 W with exposure time limited to <2 sec. The diameter of the irradiated area they use is ≈2 mm. The Nd:YAG laser light penetrates deeper into the moist tissue than argon laser light. This makes possible the treatment of deeper vessels; and the use of short time exposure limits, to some extent, the degree of temperature elevation in the surrounding tissue. The high power Nd:YAG beam was reported by Kiefhaber to coagulate effectively intact vessels up to 5 mm in diameter. Where higher powers of argon irradiation were tried, no coagulation of such vessels resulted. This information has caused the German group to start clinical trials with the Nd:YAG laser. Kiefhaber has demonstrated in a group of patients that this irradiation can stop arterial and high pressure venous oozing in acutely bleeding patients. The bleeding sites that Kiefhaber has successfully treated include high pressure esophageal varices and gastric and duodenal arterial bleeding.

It seems clear that laser irradiation of gastrointestinal bleeding to achieve cautery will soon be an important therapeutic technique (Silverstein *et al.*, 1975, 1976; Waitman *et al.*, 1975; Fruhmorgen *et al.*, 1975; Yellin *et al.*, 1976). The choice of laser optics and fiber optics for this application will be decided by the results of current clinical trials (Auth *et al.*, 1976).

TABLE II

PENETRATION DEPTH IN SKIN, LIVER, AND STOMACH TISSUE[a]

Laser	Penetration depth (mm)
CO_2 at 10.6 μm	0.05
Nd:YAG at 1.06 μm	0.8
Argon at 0.5 μm	0.2

[a] From Kiefhaber *et al.* (1974).

VII. Dermatology

Dermatology is the medical specialty concerned with diseases of the skin. Diseased or affected areas thus can be seen and in many cases treated with optical or other radiation. Dermatologists have utilized many different mechanisms for the treatment of the problems presented to them including: topical medications, systemic medications, optical radiation, ionizing radiations, and surgical procedures including electro-surgery and cryosurgery (Zacarian, 1969). Some dermatologists have, in addition, in some instances utilized psychotherapy. Let us first review the current techniques utilized by dermatologists. Then we will discuss existing and proposed laser treatments of certain skin problems.

Topical dermatologic therapy commonly in use includes various forms of creams, ointments and gels, powders, pastes, wet dressings and baths, destructive chemicals, and cleansing solutions. The purposes of some of these preparations include antibacterial, antifungal, and antiviral activities, along with disguising and covering properties. Oral systemic medications of many categories are also used to treat local skin diseases (Hall-Smith et al., 1973).

In this article we are primarily interested in the physical interventions available as treatments for skin problems. The tattoo is both a problem and a means of treatment in dermatology. Tattoos may be used to cover nevus flammeus (port wine lesion) and other benign skin discolorations. Tattoos can therefore be used for cosmetic effect in that they perma-nently camouflage certain areas and thereby improve the psychological and social adjustment of the patient. Frequently, however, the profes-sional or home-made tattoo becomes a liability and the patient wants it removed. The problem is often a psychological one stemming from the circumstances under which the tattoo was applied, and the social stigma surrounding its presence (Kitzmiller, 1970).

The physical difficulties encountered with tattoos usually depend on the methods employed in tattooing. One common complication is local infection stemming from the practice of some artisans to use their sputum to clean the tattooing needles. Diseases that have been transmit-ted by both the needle and unsterile tattoo dyes used include syphilis, tuberculosis, pyogenic infections, hepatitis, vaccinia, herpes zoster (shingles), leprosy, and tetanus. A person being tattooed also risks sensitivity reactions. For example, the red pigments, which are sulfides of mercury, may cause eczema-type reactions with swelling, itching, and local irritation. Green pigments, which contain chromium compounds, can produce reactions similar to mercury reaction. Yellow pigments, on the other hand, occasionally give urticarial reactions (hives) to the sun.

Blue pigments including cobalt compounds occasionally are capable of producing an allergic reaction. Foreign body reactions and keloids in the red area are common with tattoos, especially in Negroes. Sarcoidal reactions also have been described. Reticulum sarcomas have been described in one case with the use of blue pigment and malignant melanomas have been known to arise on the site of tattoos as have squamous cell carcinomas (Madden, 1970).

The (chemical methods) of removing tattoos involve treatment with a variety of acids, liquid ammonia, and silver nitrate solutions. Counter tattooing with zinc chloride, tannic acid, or silver nitrate has been attempted in the past. These techniques, however, can lead to sloughing of the skin containing the pigment and so must be used judiciously. Other previously used techniques for tattoo removal involve the injection of boiling water into the skin and scalding with steam. Newer techniques include liquid carbon dioxide applications and electrocoagulation. Surgical methods are most commonly used for excision with primary closure with smaller tattoos and also gradual and partial excisions with larger markings. Dermabrasion with sandpaper or revolving wire or diamond brushes, or salabrasion using table salt are commonly used to abrade tattoos (Epstein, 1970). Also, scars in these areas tend to be exaggerated and larger than in other areas of the body. Scars following various procedures in these areas are not uncommon and there is a tendency toward hyperpigmentation on the arm and forearms.

Heliotherapy, literally sun therapy, has been used for many centuries in the form of exposure to the sunlight for different skin conditions. More recently, dermatologists use ultraviolet lamps (Parrish et al., 1974; Mühlbauer et al., 1975). These have been applied for specific purposes such as antibacterial action, production of erythema, the action of synthesis on vitamin D in the skin, keratoplastic effects, development of pigmentation, and desquamation or peeling.

Dosage units are physiobiological and based on time, distance, and intensity needed for the production of erythema. Dermatologists must be knowledgeable in both the technical and medical aspects of the administration of ultraviolet light rays. Ultraviolet light treatment is contraindicated in certain forms of skin diseases and one must be able to make the diagnosis of such diseases as lupus erythematosis, xeroderma pigmentosum, and other diseases that may be produced or aggravated by light.

There are basically two main lamps used for phototherapy. One is called a hot quartz lamp which produces ultraviolet rays near 3000 Å. These are used to produce erythema and peeling and for antibacterial effects. The diseases most commonly treated with hot quartz lamp therapy include psoriasis, acne, and chronic dermatitis. Cold quartz lamps emit ultraviolet light near 2500 Å. These are used mainly to achieve peeling or exfoliation as indicated in the treatment of acne.

Another form of physical therapy used by dermatologists is ionizing radiation (Cipollaro and Crossland, 1967). Ionizing radiation derived from X rays or nuclear emissions constitutes one of the most effective methods of therapy in the practice of dermatology. However, X ray is actually used in a very small percentage of patients. This form of therapy must be employed only by those who are specially trained to recognize the conditions that call for its use and who understand the physical effects produced. These practioners must be aware of all the potential physiological effects that may follow its use. Ionizing radiations can produce unfortunate end results if they are misused or administered carelessly by improperly trained or ignorant personnel. In dermatologic practice, X rays are used almost exclusively as a source of ionizing radiations because of the ease of administration and the accuracy with which such ionizing radiations can be delivered. X rays are used for (1) to destroy malignancies, (2) to change the rate of growth of lesions such as granulomas and hemangiomas, and (3) to inhibit the activity of sebaceous glands in treating acne.

Surgical procedures for the purpose of obtaining biopsy specimens or removing small tumors of the skin are an integral part of dermatologic practice. Choice of the type of procedure depends on the pathological type, size, configuration, and depth of the lesion, and its anatomical position. With malignant or potentially malignant lesions the primary objective of surgery is to effect complete removal before the tumor metastasizes. If it is necessary to sacrifice the cosmetic appearance of the site to this end, it is justified. However, in premalignant or malignant lesions, the cure rate is often comparable using different therapeutic methods. In such cases, use of the least destructive or least deforming procedure is to the patient's advantage. Most skin tumors are benign and in the treatment of these lesions the emphasis is usually shifted toward the production of a cosmetically favorable end result. Incomplete or fractional treatment of lesions such as benign nevus hemangioma fibrous and sebaceous cysts entails no threat to the patient's health. The patient has the right to expect that the end result will be cosmetically acceptable.

A dermatologist has the choice of surgery using a scalpel, cutaneous punch, or electrosurgery as well as nonsurgical methods. Surgery in which the defect is closed by sutures has the advantages of rapid healing, a relatively small linear scar, and the availability of all tissue removed for pathological examination (Epstein, 1970). Electrosurgery in which the wound is allowed to heal gradually by re-epithelization or formation of granulation tissue has the advantages of simple technique, less danger of infection, no danger of dehiscence, and the production of a flat scar. The latter is particularly advantageous on weight-bearing surfaces. After the removal of superficial lesions by electrosurgery, re-epithelization without the formation of scar tissue is often possible. The following forms of electrosurgery are used: (1) fulguration, a mild terminal technique with high voltage, low amperage currents, called Oudin current, in which the active electrode is kept at a short distance from the lesion and the superficial destruction is caused by a spark jumping to the tissue; (2) electrodesiccation, similar to fulguration except that the active electrode is inserted into the tissue before the current is turned on; and (3) electrocoagulation, a biterminal technique. Active and indifferent electrodes with low voltage, high amperage currents are usually used as a cutting current for electrolysis.

The exposure of skin lesions to temperature below zero produces destruction through the vascular elements of the tissue being treated. Destruction of tissue by the application of solid CO_2 or liquid nitrogen is used in the treatment of verrucae, granuloma annulare, and solar keratoses (Zacarian, 1969). More superficial effects are produced by a carbon dioxide "slush," a mixture of powered CO_2 and acetone. This substance is occasionally used in the treatment of rosacea, telangiectasia, and acne.

The laser was easily introduced in dermatologic therapeutics because dermatologists have long been accustomed to using light treatments.

The types of laser equipment used in dermatology include ruby lasers with various output waveforms, Nd:YAG lasers, cw visible lasers, and CO_2 lasers. In dermatology the laser is often used to cause hemostasis, the cessation of bleeding. This, however, is limited to vessels less than 2 mm in external diameter. The reactions in the skin to laser therapy depend on the laser, the rate of light absorption, the anatomical area, the power density, and the duration of therapy. Of course, the thermal characteristics of the target area also play a major role. Clinically the reaction to laser therapy includes erythema, papules, vesicles (blisters), deep charring, crusting, eventual scarring, pigmentation and depigmentation (Goldman et al., 1969; Goldman, 1973b; Hall, 1971a). Microscopically, the reaction may vary from a minimal lymphocytic infiltration near the blood vessels to severe coagulation necrosis and thrombosis in some of the smaller blood vessels involved in the treated area. Chronic changes that have been described include nonspecific dermal fibrosis, and lymphocytic and plasma cell infiltration. It is extremely important in all areas of research including dermatology that proper data be taken. To date, many of the studies performed lack certain elemental data, such as time sequence, power densities, durations of exposures, spot sizes, etc. Only with proper documentation will it be possible to evaluate comparison studies between different forms of irradiation.

Today lasers are being used to treat port wine lesions, tattoos, seborrheic warty keratoses, basal cell carcinomas, warts, freckles, nevi, acne, and various growths both benign and malignant (Goldman and Rockwell, 1971). In general, the laser is used to remove some sort of growth or colored area in the skin, and in general the results are comparable to conventional modes of therapy. The advantage to using laser treatment is its speed and the superficial nature of the injury. There is also the potential advantage of using laser light that preferentially interacts with the desired tissue. The treatments have potential drawbacks in that some people will scar as much following laser treatment as following any conventional procedure. Also, people who are slightly pigmented will retain a vitiligo-like appearance in the area treated with laser radiation. This is a cosmetically unsatisfactory result.

Small lesions can be laser treated on an outpatient basis. However, if a larger area is to be treated the patient will require general anesthetic and hospitalization for the most part. Whenever possible, small increments of the lesion are treated during each session so that outpatient therapy can be used. This procedure has been used in treating port wine marks.

Special fibers have been used to deliver Nd:YAG laser light into comedonal cysts, such as seen in severe cases of acne. This procedure also works in the removal of hair.

CO_2 lasers have been used to treat skin tumors such as angiosarcomas where bleeding is involved. In fact, in any area to be treated where excessive hemorrhage can be expected or infection is present, laser treatment is strongly indicated.

Pulsed CO_2 lasers have been used in the removal of telangiectasia from different skin areas. The small broken blood vessels seen in the thighs of obese women in particular are eliminated painlessly because the stimulation is too short to register pain and the superficial bluish discolorations or veins can be removed with no residual scar tissue (Kaplan and Sharon, 1976).

Excisional biopsies can be performed very effectively with lasers because the microscopic detail is unaffected by the thin ($\sim$50 μm) (Fusek and Kung, 1971) margin of coagulation necrosis. On the otherhand, the use of a conventional electrosurgical unit to obtain a biopsy results in total coagulation necrosis of the entire specimen.

Lasers are also used for transillumination experiments. Other fascinating new diagnostic possibilities involve three-dimensional laser holography enabling one to study the presence and activity of varying densities in the skin and subcutaneous tissues. Some other diagnostic applications include microprobe analysis for cations in the skin and soft tissues. Analysis may be performed on tissue sections and on living skin. These have been used in the detection of calcium in the skin, gold, arsenic, and lead in the hair and skin of children with poisoning (Goldman and Rockwell, 1971).

VIII. Optical Design for Lasers in Surgery[2]

Laser light can be used to cut and to cauterize tissue. At the present time, CO_2 lasers at 10.6 μm, argon lasers at 0.48–0.51 μm, and Nd:YAG lasers at 1.06 μm have operational characteristics that make their use in surgery potentially valuable. In this section, the optics necessary to deliver safely the light from these lasers to surgical targets are described along with some suggested areas for improvements.

Surgery is a delicate and exact procedure. As we all know, surgeons spend many years learning how to perform operations effectively and with a minimum of risk to the patient. In most cases, an operation can be performed very well using a scalpel to cut and, where necessary, clamps or electrocautery to stop bleeding from blood vessels that have been cut. The laser scalpel which cauterizes as it cuts will therefore only be useful in a very few operations where heavy bleeding may occur. However, if its use involves only minor modification of procedure and, in addition, offers some benefits to the patient, laser surgery will become a part of surgical practice.

The laser light delivery system must end in a handpiece that the surgeon can manipulate in nearly the same manner as he would a scalpel. This means that the handpiece, which may include the final focusing optics, must be no longer than ~15 cm and no more than ~1 cm in diameter. In addition, the optics that couple the handpiece to the laser should not limit the surgeon's ability to manipulate the handpiece. Since the handpiece may be inserted into body cavities as part of the surgical procedure, it must either be autoclavable or so inexpensive as to be disposable.

When such a handpiece is transmitting intense laser light and blood or

[2] This section is taken from an invited talk presented by M. Bass at the 1975 SPIE Conference, Aug. 1975, San Diego, California.

debris is spattered onto its output surface, damage to the final optic will take place. It is therefore necessary to protect the output optic with an easily replaced protective cover or to continuously blow aside debris or ejecta moving toward the handpiece. The latter procedure must be accompanied by a vacuum system to remove the ejecta and prevent it from accumulating in the sterile surgical site.

The surgeon should be able to select the final focal spot size without halting his work by manipulating the optics in the handpiece or if necessary by rapidly switching handpieces. A foot switch to control the total laser power is also necessary.

Provisions for the eye safety of both patient and operating room personnel are essential. Dangerously powerful laser beams can be reflected from glistening moist tissue or other shiny objects in the operating room. While clear Plexiglas goggles are sufficient to protect against 10.6 μm irradiation, various colored filters are required to prevent Nd:YAG or argon ion laser light from entering the eye. These filters reduce the surgeon's ability to view the operative field and by altering the colors he sees, the filters may adversely affect his judgment or his ability to perform the operation. Thus, to make feasible the expanded use of Nd:YAG or argon ion lasers in surgery, filters for eye protection that do not seriously alter the surgeon's performance must be developed.

It is possible to use glass, quartz, or plastic core flexible fiber optics to transmit visible or near infrared energy from a source to a target. Until recently, however, it was not possible to transmit efficiently enough power through a fiber optic to be of use in surgery. The transmission was generally low (<25% for a 1 mm length), and the fibers had the unpleasant habit of melting when more than 0.2 W was incident.

Bundles of fiber optics cannot be used for high power applications because the incident light that does not enter the fibers enters the glue that bonds the fiber bundle together. The glue absorbs this energy and melts, leaving a useless bundle.

Today, fiber optics are available that can transmit >6 W at 10.6 μm for several meters with an efficiency of >95% (Crow, 1974). These fibers were originally developed for optical communications applications but can be obtained for other uses. In addition, the quality of less sophisticated fiber optics has improved to the point where powers up to 3 W can be transmitted over lengths of ~2 m with ≳80% efficiencies.

Since a bundle of fibers is inappropriate for high power applications, a single modern fiber is all that is necessary. The optics for coupling the light into the fiber should contain a beam splitter to reflect some of the laser light into a detector to monitor the laser's operation. It may also be useful to provide a variable optical attenuator in the coupling optics to protect the rest of the optics from too much power and to provide the surgeon a means of finely adjusting the power incident on the target.

The lens that focuses the laser light into the fiber optic core (typically 100–200 μm in diameter) should be mounted so that the fine x, y, z movements are possible. Its focal length should be such that the focal spot size is no more than one-half the fiber core diameter. Thus, the laser beam can be focused easily into the center of the fiber optic core. If the intense focused light is directly incident on the edge of the fiber, the fiber's entrance face will invariably be damaged due to the burning of the glue holding the fiber to the fiberoptic's termination.

Several separate fibers can be included in one jacket so that a rapid change can be effected if the one in use is damaged. The jacket should be so lined as to prevent kinking or stretching which could break the fibers.

Fiber optics are currently the delivery system of choice for ophthalmologic laser surgery. In this work ~3 W of laser power are all that is needed. Fibers as small as 60 μm in diameter are provided in these devices to permit the ophthalmologist to select the size of the lesion he will produce on the retina. For surgery involving larger targets, argon ion lasers with outputs of up to 20 W have recently come on the market. In addition, reliable cw Nd:YAG lasers with similar output at 1.06 μm are available.

If these devices must be used in pulsed modes of operation, then the possibility for pulsed laser damage to the fiber optic and the auxiliary optics must be considered. In addition, very high optical electric fields result when high power laser light is confined to a small cross-sectional area. Thus, in a fiber optic delivery system, the problem of transmission losses due to nonlinear optical processes may have to be faced by the system designer.

Since no flexible fiber optic is presently available for use at 10.6 μm, an articulated arm light guide must be used to make practical a CO_2 laser surgical unit. An articulated arm light guide with full three-dimensional beam steering capability must include six beam turning mirrors. For high power 10.6 μm applications, these should be metal mirrors. In some cases, provision must be made for cooling these mirrors. The spindles which permit the articulated arm full rotational freedom must be mounted in highly accurate and wobble-free bearings to assure that the optical alignment is maintained.

Small dust particles which settle on the mirrors in an articulated arm light guide can cause severe damage to the mirrors when the laser is turned on. Thus it is desirable to have the arm sealed or at least continuously flushed with a dry, filtered gas.

One simplification to the articulated arm for surgical use is the inclusion of the laser resonator in one of the segments of the light guide. This eliminates at least two of the mirrors but makes the laser design somewhat more difficult.

It should be clear that the articulated arm is not nearly as flexible as a fiber optic. It will, therefore, impair the surgeon's ability and limit access to certain surgical sites. However, at the present time it is the only available means to deliver 10.6 μm light for surgery.

Unless the use of laser light for cutting or cautery can be shown to be distinctly advantageous to the patient when compared to other means of surgery, it will not be adopted. So far, CO_2 laser treatment for the excision of vocal cord polyps (Jako et al., 1973), the debridement of decubitus ulcers (Stellar et al., 1974), the treatment of cervical erosions (Kaplan et al., 1973b), and the cautery of the liver and spleen (Hall et al., 1973; Hall, 1971b) has been demonstrated to be effective and advantageous. In fact, CO_2 cautery has also been found very useful in the preparation of burn sites for skin grafts (Levine et al., 1974). The CO_2 laser is advantageous wherever excessive bleeding is expected and the field of operation easily accessible. A recent and extensive overview of CO_2 laser surgery was published by Verschueren (1976).

The range of applicability of lasers in surgery can be explored and expanded by further research of the sort mentioned above. In addition, the development of more flexible fiber optic delivery systems for high power argon and Nd:YAG lasers will hasten the acceptance of laser surgery by the medical community.

ACKNOWLEDGMENT

The authors wish to thank Ms. C. Goertz for transcribing the text and typing this manuscript.

REFERENCES

Auth, D. C., Lam, V. T. Y., Mohr, R. W., Silverstein, F. E., and Rubin, C. E. (1976). *IEEE Trans. Biomed. Eng.* **23,** 129.
Cain, C. P., and Welch, A. J. (1974). *Invest. Ophthalmol.* **13,** 60.
Cipollaro, A., and Crossland, P. (1967). "X-ray and Radium in the Treatment of Diseases of the Skin," 5th Ed. Lea & Febiger, Philadelphia, Pennsylvania.

Cleary, S. F., and Hamrick, P. E. (1971). *Non-Ion. Radiat.* **2,** 1.

Crow, J. D. (1974). *Appl. Opt.* **13,** 467.

Dwyer, R. M., Haverback, B. J., Bass, M., and Cherlow, J. (1975). *J. Am. Med. Assoc.* **231,** 486.

Dwyer, R. M., Yellin, A. E., Craig, J., *et al.* (1976). *J. Am. Med. Assoc.* **236,** 1383.

Engel, T., and Harris, F. W. (1975). *J. Reprod. Med.* **15,** 33.

Fusek, I., and Kung, Z. (1971). *Proc. Eur. Cong. Neurosurg., 4th, Prague.*

Epstein, E. ed. (1970). "Skin Surgery." Thomas, Springfield, Illinois.

Fiedler, J. (1973). Personal communication.

Fiedler, J. P., Law, E., and MacMillan, B. G. (1976). *Ann. N.Y. Acad. Sci.* **267,** 254.

Fruhmorgen, P., Kaduk, B., Reidenbach, H. D., Bodem, F., Demling, L., and Brand, H. (1975). *Endoscopy* **7,** 189.

Goldman, L. (1973a). "Applications of the Laser." CRC Press, Cleveland, Ohio.

Goldman, L. (1973b). *Arch. Dermatol.* **108,** 385.

Goldman, L., and Rockwell, J., Jr. (1971). "Lasers in Medicine." Gordon & Breach, New York.

Goldman, L., Shumrick, D. A., Rockwell, J., Jr., *et al.* (1968). *Arch. Surg.* **96,** 397.

Goldman, L., Vahl, J., Rockwell, R. J., Jr., *et al.* (1969). *J. Invest. Dermatol.* **52,** 18.

Goodale, R. L., Okada, A., Gonzales, R., Borner, J. W., Edlich, R. F., and Wangensteen, O. H. (1970). *Arch. Surg.* **101,** 211.

Hall, R. R. (1971a). *Brit. J. Surg.* **58,** 222.

Hall, R. R. (1971b). *Brit. J. Surg.* **58,** 538.

Hall, R. R., Beach, A. D., and Hill, D. W. (1973). *Brit. J. Surg.* **60,** 141.

Hall-Smith, P., Cairns, R., and Beare, R. (1973). "Dermatology." Grune & Stratton, New York.

Ham, W. T., Mueller, H. A., and Goldman, A. J. (1974). *Science* **185,** 362.

Int. Conf. Laser Surg. (1975). *1st, Tel Aviv.*

Jako, G. J. (1971). *Laryngoscope* 2204.

Jako, G. J., Strong, M. S., Polanyi, T. G., *et al.* (1973). *Eye, Ear, Nose Throat Mon.* **52,** 36.

Kaplan, I., and Sharon, U. (1976). *Ann. N.Y. Acad. Sci.* **267,** 247.

Kaplan, I., Ger, R., and Sharon, U. (1973a). *Brit. J. Plast. Surg.* **26,** 359.

Kaplan, I., Goodman, J., and Ger, R. (1973b). *Obstet. Gynecol.* **41,** 795.

Kaplan, I., Gassner, S., and Shindel, Y. (1974). *Am. J. Surg.* **128,** 543.

Kiefhaber, P., Moritz, K., Nath, G., *et al.* (1974). *Program Int. Congr. Gastrointest. Endosc., 3rd, Mexico City.*

Kiefhaber, P., Nath, G., Moritz, K., *et al.* (1975). *Program Congr. Gastroenterol. Endosc., 7th, Vienna.*

Kitzmiller, K. W. (1970). *J. Med. Assoc., Ga.* Oct., 385.

Laforet, E. G., Berger, R. L., and Vaughn, C. W. (1976). *New Engl. J. Med.* **294,** 941.

Landers, M. B., III, Wolbarsht, M. L., and Shaw, H. E., Jr. (1976). *Ann. N.Y. Acad. Sci.* **267,** 230.

Lawwill, T. (1973). *Invest. Ophthalmol.* **12,** 45.

L'Esperance, F. A., Jr. (1965). *Arch. Ophthalmol.* **74,** 752.

L'Esperance, F. A., Jr. (1966). *Arch. Ophthalmol.* **75,** 61.

L'Esperance, F. A., Jr. (1969). *Am. J. Ophthalmol.* **68,** 264.

Levine, N., Ger, R., Stellar, S., *et al.* (1974). *Ann. Surg.* **179,** 246.

McPherson, A. (1968). "New and Controversial Aspects of Retinal Detachment." Harper, New York.

Madden, S. (1970). "Current Dermatologic Management." Mosby, St. Louis, Missouri.

Mihashi, S., Jako, G. J., Incze, J., et al. (1976). Ann. N.Y. Acad. Sci. 267, 263.
Mühlbauer, W., Nath, G., and Kreitmair, A. (1975). Int. Congr. Int. Confed. Plast. Reconstr. Surg., Paris.
Newell, F. W., and Ernest, J. T. (1974). "Ophthalmology Principles and Concepts." Mosby, St. Louis, Missouri.
Paparella, M., and Shumrick, D., eds. (1973). "Otolaryngology. Vol. 3: Head and Neck." Saunders, Philadelphia, Pennsylvania.
Papp, J. P. (1974). J. Am. Med. Assoc. 230, 1172.
Parrish, J. A., Fitzpatrick, T. B., Tanenbaum, L., et al. (1974). New Engl. J. Med. 291, 1207.
Patz, A., Fine, S., Pront, T., et al. (1976). Am. J. Ophthalmol. 81, 383.
Priebe, L. A., and Welch, A. J. (1973). Aerosp. Med. 1246.
Priebe, L. A., Cain, C. P., and Welch, A. J. (1976). Am. J. Ophthalmol. (Abstr.) (in press).
Raud, R., Rinfret, A., and von Leden, H., eds. (1968). "Cryosurgery." Thomas, Springfield, Illinois.
Silverstein, F., Rubin, C. E., and Auth, D. (1975). Gastroenterology 68, 1046. (Abstr.)
Silverstein, F., Auth, D., Rubin, C. E., et al. (1976). Gastroenterology 71, 558.
Stellar, S. (1968). Proc. Rudolf Virchow Med. Soc. City N.Y. 26 (Suppl.), 416 pp.
Stellar, S. (1970). Med. Biol. Eng. 8, 549.
Stellar, S., Meijer, R., Walia, S., et al. (1974). Ann. Surg. 179, 230.
Strong, M. S. (1973). Laser Surgery in Otolaryngology. Sir Wm. Wilde Lecture, Irish Otolaryngol. Soc.
Sugar, J. O., Stahle, J., Högberg, L., et al. (1974). Arch. Otolaryngol. 99, 330.
Sugawa, C., Shier, M., Lucas, C. E., et al. (1975). Arch. Surg. 110, 975.
Verschueren, R. (1976). "The CO_2 Laser in Tumor Surgery." Van Gorcum, Assen/ Amsterdam.
Verschueren, R. C. J., Kondstaal, J., and Oldhoff, J. (1975). Acta Chir. Belg. 74, 197.
Waitman, A. M., Spira, I., Chryssanthou, C. P., et al. (1975). Gastrointest. Endosc. 22, 78.
Wilpizeski, C., and Sataloff, J. (1974). Laryngoscope 84, 273.
Wolbarsht, M. L., ed. (1975). "Laser Applications in Medicine and Biology," Vol. 2. Plenum, New York.
Yellin, A. E., Dwyer, R. M., Craig, J. R., Bass, M., and Cherlow, J. M. (1976). Arch. Surg. 111, 750.
Zacarian, S. A. (1969). "Cryosurgery of Skin Cancer." Thomas, Springfield, Illinois.
Zaret, M. M., Ripps, H., Siegel, L. M., and Breinin, G. M. (1963). Arch. Ophthalmol. 69, 97.
Zweng, H. C., Flocks, M., and Peabody, R. (1966). Arch. Ophthalmol. 76, 11.

OPTICAL DATA STORAGE

H. Haskal
Department of Electrical Engineering
Tufts University
Medford, Massachusetts

and

D. Chen
Honeywell Corporate Research Center
Bloomington, Minnesota

I. Introduction

The past decade and a half has witnessed a widespread research activity in various aspects of optical data storage. Interest in optical storage was triggered by the discovery of the laser. A coherent beam of laser light can be focused to a high intensity diffraction-limited spot to effect a localized change in a medium and record a bit. Packing densities of 10^8 bits/cm^2 are possible by using a visible wavelength laser.

The promise of compact, large optical data stores (10^{11}–10^{13} bits) did not go unnoticed by the computer industry (Eschenfelder, 1970; Rajchman, 1970; Tufte and Chen, 1973). Other advantages were also perceived. The possibility of addressing the memory by deflecting the laser beam at very high speeds by purely electronic means and the combination of short access time, high capacity, no mechanical motion, and high reliability made the optical storage device an attractive alternative to conventional magnetic disk memories. However, to date, continued improvements in magnetic recording both in packing density and access time have made it difficult to justify the introduction of optical technology for data storage (Harker and Chang, 1972). Further improvements are necessary in the area of lasers, recording materials, and deflectors to realize the full potential of large-scale optical stores. Another factor of primary importance is the present cost advantage of magnetic disks over optical memories. Until both technical and economical problems are overcome, magnetic memories will continue to dominate the high capacity end of the memory hierarchy (Hoagland, 1974). The only laser storage device introduced in the market is the Unicon trillion-bit permanent memory (Gray, 1972). This device, while incorporating laser technology for recording and reading the information at very high packing densities, still relies largely on mechanical motion for the addressing.

Other commercial applications of optical storage techniques include the Holoscan (Sutherlin, 1973), a holographic credit card validation system, and the Megafetch (Strehlow et al., 1974), a random-access permanent holographic store. No alterable optical memory has been developed to date as a commercial product. Much more progress was achieved in the area of video recording, where laser technology plays an important role. The video disk player may soon become a common home entertainment device. Experience gained in optical memory research was an important factor that contributed to the success of the video disk. On the other hand, mass production of HeNe lasers for video players has already brought down their price by an order of magnitude and may thus contribute to making a future optical memory more economical.

The purpose of this paper is to describe the advantages and limitations of optical data storage and to review the status of research and development in the field. First the two basic approaches, bit-by-bit and holographic recording, will be described and the advantages of optical recording techniques outlined. Media and system components are reviewed next, followed by a detailed description of a number of recording systems that have been carried out to a very high degree of realization.

The emphasis will be on system requirements and actual components performance. In this way we will point out where further progress is necessary to make an optical storage device a reality.

II. Fundamentals of Optical Data Storage

A. ORGANIZATION OF OPTICAL DATA STORAGE

There are basically two different approaches that use an optical beam for addressing in a recording system. The bit-oriented recording stores data on a bit-by-bit basis. The information is generally stored sequentially in a uniform two-dimensional photosensitive or thermal-sensitive medium. The interaction of the optical source (in most cases a visible laser beam) with the storage material results in an alteration of the state of the medium at the storage bit location, with or without the assistance of an external electromagnetic field. During the readout operation, the same laser beam at reduced intensity or a different laser beam is deflected to the same storage location, and the intensity of the reflected or transmitted beam is detected by a detector. A suitable storage medium provides a difference in the intensity reaching the detector which depends on the state of the written bits, allowing the stored information to be read one bit at a time. Besides the laser source, the beam deflector for addressing, the beam modulator for intensity control, the detector for readout, and the material medium for storage, proper optical components are needed for directing, focusing, and relaying the optical beam, as well as electronic controls to direct the data flow and activate the beam addressing devices. A schematic diagram of a basic bit-oriented recording system is shown in Fig. 1.

With the availability of highly coherent laser sources, holographic recording technique is made possible. In this case, a block of information, in the form of a page, is recorded or read as one unit. The data input device is a one- or two-dimensional multielement modulator called the page composer. To record the data, the laser beam is split into a reference beam and a main beam. The main beam is directed to transmit through the page composer and interfere with the reference beams to form a holographic image of the input page on the recording medium. In

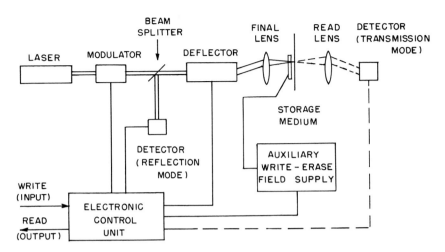

FIG. 1.   Schematic diagram of a bit-oriented optical recording system. Reflection (solid lines) and transmission (dashed lines) modes for readout are indicated. The auxiliary write–erase field is not always required.

the readout operation, the main beam is blocked by an optical shutter, and the recorded information is reconstructed on the plane of the detector array by diffracting the read beam (previously the reference beam) off the hologram. The detector array has the same format as the page composer and as many elements as there are bits in the page. In this manner, the entire page of data is available for electronic accessing, thus extremely high throughput can be achieved.

The optical system is arranged in such a way as to provide coincidence of the reference and the main beam on the storage medium, and the main beam always fills and pivots about the page composer for all address locations. Besides the more complicated optics required for this case, the page composer and the detector array are two additional essential components in the bit-oriented optical memory. However, since each deflected beam location is used to address an entire page, the deflector speed and capacity requirements can be greatly reduced.

A typical holographic recording system is schematically shown in Fig. 2.

Having defined the two types of optical storage, we can now relate the main features and requirements of optical storage to fundamental properties of an optical beam.

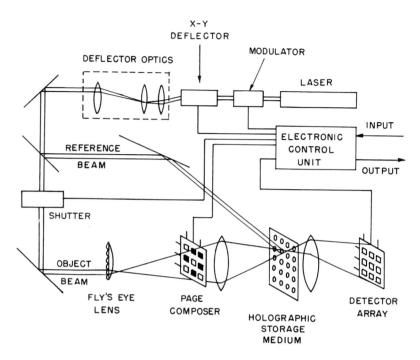

FIG. 2.   Schematic diagram of a holographic memory system. Only the transmission mode is shown. Writing operation is performed with the shutter open. During reading, the object beam is blocked by the shutter and the reference beam then becomes the read beam.

B. Fundamental Features and Requirements

This section discusses general optical and material considerations pertaining to the recording and retrieval of information by optical means. The high packing density of information afforded by optical recording imposes new system requirements on the bit-by-bit and holographic methods. In the bit-by-bit approach, tight mechanical tolerances must be maintained during writing and reading. The laser beam is focused by a lens to a microscopic spot on the recording medium. The steep focusing angle implies that only slight defocusing can be tolerated before writing becomes impossible or reading with a good signal-to-noise ratio becomes difficult. Numerical examples illustrating the depth of focus versus spot size are given. In holographic recording, mechanical tolerances are considerably relaxed at the expense of system complexity and higher laser power requirements.

1. *Resolution and Storage Density*

The fundamental limitation of resolution and depth of field for bit-oriented optical recording can be analyzed on the basis of laser beam optics. Following Kogelnik and Li's (1966) treatment, noting that the intensity distribution for the TEM_{00} mode of a laser beam is confined near the axis of propagation and the phase front is slightly curved, the field component u satisfies the wave equation

$$\nabla^2 u + k^2 u = 0 \tag{1}$$

For a beam propagating along the z direction, in a medium of refractive index n

$$u = \psi(x, y, z) \exp(-jkz) \tag{2}$$

where

$$k = 2\pi/\lambda \tag{3}$$

and λ is the vacuum wavelength. Since ψ is a slow varying function of z, $\partial^2 \psi/\partial z^2$ is neglected and the wave equation becomes

$$\nabla^2_{xy}\psi - 2jk(\partial\psi/\partial z) = 0 \tag{4}$$

A solution of this is

$$\psi = \exp(-j\{p(z) + [kr^2/2q(z)]\}) \tag{5}$$

where r is the radial coordinate, p the complex phase factor, and q the complex beam parameter, which can be written as

$$\frac{1}{q(z)} = \frac{1}{R(z)} - j\frac{\lambda}{\pi[w(z)]^2 n} \tag{6}$$

The first term is the real part of $1/q$, and $R(z)$ is the radius of curvature of the wavefront that intersects the axis at z. The second term gives the intensity distribution with a beam width of $w(z)$. The normalized intensity distribution of the beam is therefore given by

$$\psi \cdot \psi^* = \exp\{-2r^2/[w(z)]^2\} \tag{7}$$

Thus the beam intensity distribution is Gaussian with a $1/e^2$ point radius of $w(z)$. The z dependence of w can be obtained by noting that $\partial q/\partial z = 1$, therefore

$$q = q_0 + z = j\pi(w_0^2/\lambda)n + z \tag{8}$$

Substituting this into Eq. (7) leads to

$$w^2(z) = w_0^2[1 + (\lambda z/n\pi w_0^2)^2] \tag{9}$$

$$R(z) = z[1 + (n\pi w_0^2/\lambda z)^2] \tag{10}$$

It is seen that the beam amplitude profile is Gaussian everywhere, with a beam waist of w_0 and a far-field diffraction half-angle of

$$\theta_d = \lambda/\pi w_0 n \tag{11}$$

To achieve a high packing density in bit-by-bit recording one must reduce the size of the input beam by means of a focusing lens. We can determine the transformation effected by the lens using Gaussian beam theory and obtain the waist and position of the focused beam. This is illustrated in Fig. 3.

We assume here that the lowest order mode TEM_{00} of the laser is used for recording and also that the lens dimensions are large enough so that no truncation of the beam occurs. The lens transformation equations are (Kogelnik and Li, 1966)

$$(d_1 - f)/(d_0 - f) = w_1^2/w_0^2 \tag{12}$$

$$(d_1 - f)(d_0 - f) = f^2 - f_0^2 \tag{13}$$

where f is the effective focal length of the focusing lens and $f_0 = \pi w_1 w_0/\lambda$.

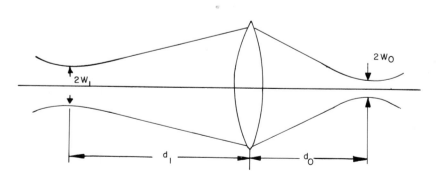

FIG. 3.   Focusing of a Gaussian laser beam.

From Eqs. (12) and (13) one can solve for the output parameters d_0, w_0 in terms of the input parameters d_1, w_1.

$$w_0{}^2 = \frac{f^2}{(\pi w_1 n/\lambda)^2 + [(d_1 - f)/w_1]^2} \tag{14}$$

$$= \frac{(f\lambda/\pi w_1 n)^2}{1 + [(\lambda/\pi w_1{}^2 n)(d_1 - f)]^2}$$

$$d_0 - f = \frac{(f\lambda/n\pi w_1)^2(d_1 - f)}{w_1{}^2 + [(\lambda/\pi w_1 n)(d_1 - f)]^2} \tag{15}$$

It is noted that if the input waist w_1 is placed at the front focal plane of the lens, i.e., $d_1 = f$, the output waist w_0 occurs at the back focal plane $d_2 = f$. The output waist is given by

$$w_0 = f\lambda/\pi w_1 = (2\lambda/n\pi)F \tag{16}$$

where $F = f/2w_1$ is the effective f-number of the beam. The radius of the recorded bit will be at the most equal to w_0. It is relatively easy to obtain w_0 values of about 1 μm. For example, by using an input beam with $w_1 = 1.5$ mm and a diffraction-limited lens with a focal length of $f = 4$ mm and $\lambda = 0.633$ μm one obtains from Eq. (14), $w_0 \simeq 0.5$ μm for $n = 1$. Thus a recording spot diameter of 1 μm corresponding to a packing density of 10^8 bits/cm^2 is in principle possible. In practice, an areal density of 10^6–10^7 bits/cm^2 is attainable. In considering the volume packing density, the medium thickness should also include the substrate thickness, which is generally of the order of 50–100 μm for flexible substrates and up to a few millimeters for rigid substrates. It is expected that a volume packing density of 10^7–10^9 bits/cm^3 should be attainable for bit-oriented recording with properly chosen recording materials and substrates.

In general the output waist position and magnitude vary somewhat with input waist position as seen from Eq. (15). However for short focal length systems used in optical recording the variations are negligible. It can be shown that the maximum deviation from focus is given by

$$(d_0 - f)_{\max} = f^2\lambda n/2\pi w_1 = w_0{}^2 n/\lambda \tag{17}$$

and occurs for

$$d_1 - f = \pi w_1{}^2 n/\lambda \tag{18}$$

Using the same example as before $w_0 = 0.5$ μm, $\lambda = 0.633$ m, $f = 4$ mm, $n = 1$, we obtain $(d_0 - f)_{\max} = 0.4$ μm and $d_1 - f = 11$ m. For all practical purposes the position of the waist is given by $d_0 = f$ and its magnitude by Eq. (16) regardless of the position of the input waist.

Holographic recording can be performed on a "thin" or a "thick" medium (Forshaw, 1974) depending on the ratio of medium thickness to spatial periodicity. The recording density on thin holograms is similar to that of bit-oriented recording (Chen and Zook, 1975). In a thick hologram (sometimes called "volume" hologram) individual holograms are recorded in the material by varying the angle or wavelength of the beam. An angular resolution of less than 1° per hologram was shown possible (Friesem and Walker, 1970) in a volume recording medium. A recording volume density of 10^8 bits/cm^3 is expected to be feasible in this case.

2. Depth of Field and Power Considerations

The depth of field in optical recording can be calculated from Eq. (9). If we can tolerate a spot diameter increase of 20%, we can calculate the distance from the Gaussian waist for $w^2(z) = 1.4w_0^2$ as

$$z = \pm 0.66 n\pi w_0^2/\lambda \qquad (19)$$

The total depth of field is

$$\Delta z = 1.3 n\pi w_0^2/\lambda \qquad (20)$$

As an example, if we make the bit or the spot radius equal to w_0, and if $w_0 = 0.5$ μm, $\lambda = 0.633$ μm, we have $\Delta z = 1.6$ μm for $n = 1$.

This example demonstrates one of the requirements for an optical recording medium; high packing density dictates a medium thickness of less than 1 μm. This requirement can be somewhat relaxed if there exists a writing threshold.

In a threshold recording process the laser beam affects the material only in the region in which the laser intensity I exceeds the threshold intensity I_{th}.

The intensity distribution of the Gaussian laser beam at the focal plane is given by

$$I(r, z) = (2P/\pi w_0^2) \exp(-2r^2/w_0^2) \qquad (21)$$

where w_0 is given by Eq. (16) and P is the total power in the laser beam. From Eq. (9) we have

$$\rho_0^2 = \tfrac{1}{2} w_0^2 \ln(2P_a/\pi w_0^2 I_{th}) \qquad (22)$$

where P_a is the absorbed power, and ρ_0 is the radius of the written spot. Substituting for w_0 from Eq. (16) we obtain after some algebra

$$P_a = \frac{2\lambda^2}{\pi n^2} F^2 I_{th} \exp\left[\frac{1}{2}\left(\frac{\pi n\rho_0}{\lambda F}\right)^2\right] \qquad (23)$$

From Eq. (23) we observe that for a given written spot size an optimum focusing system exists for which the power P_a is minimum. By differentiating P_a with respect to F^2 and equating it to zero, we obtain

$$F^2 = \tfrac{1}{2}(n\rho_0\pi/\lambda)^2 \qquad (24)$$

Substituting for F^2 from Eq. (16) and using Eq. (22) we obtain for the optimal case the simple relation

$$2P_a/\pi w_0^2 I_{th} = I_{peak}/I_{th} = e \qquad (25)$$

where I_{peak} is the on-axis intensity of the absorbed laser beam ($r = 0$). Thus for minimum power one must choose an optical system such that the threshold intensity I_{th} occurs at the $1/e$ points of the laser beam profile. For example in order to record a spot of radius $\rho_0 = 0.5\ \mu$m, $\lambda = 0.633\ \mu$m, one should choose an optical system with $F_{opt} = 1.75$ for minimum power requirements. However, choosing the optimal f-number also usually results in the minimum effective depth of focus for writing (Haskal and Rosen, 1971). The depth of focus is defined as the deviation from focus for which the nominal radius of the written spot does not change by more than $\pm20\%$. The normalized depth of focus is plotted in Fig. 4.

It is therefore advantageous at times to use a nonoptimal focusing system, in order to increase the depth of focus and thus relax the mechanical tolerance at the expense of increased recording power.

As an example let us examine thermomagnetic writing on MnBi. The Curie temperature of MnBi is 360°C and its decomposition temperature is 446°C. Therefore the peak to threshold intensity ratio cannot exceed

$$I_{peak}/I_{th} < 4.46/360 = 1.24 \qquad (26)$$

We must thus record on MnBi under nonoptimal power conditions. To record a spot of radius $\rho_0 = 0.5\ \mu$m, choosing a $I_{peak}/I_{th} = 1.2$, we obtain from Eq. (22) $w_0 = 1.65\ \mu$m at a wavelength $\lambda = 0.633$ m. The necessary F-number is then found from Eq. (24), $F = 4.1$. The result is that the power required for recording exceeds the minimum value (optimal case) by about a factor of 3. However, the depth of focus is increased to a value $\Delta z = 7.5\ \mu$m as compared to $\Delta z = 5\ \mu$m had it been possible to use $F_{opt} = 1.75$.

3. Writing and Materials Considerations

The optical properties of the material affect the writing and erasing requirements. Of special importance are the refractive index and the absorption coefficients at the operating wavelength. For a thin film

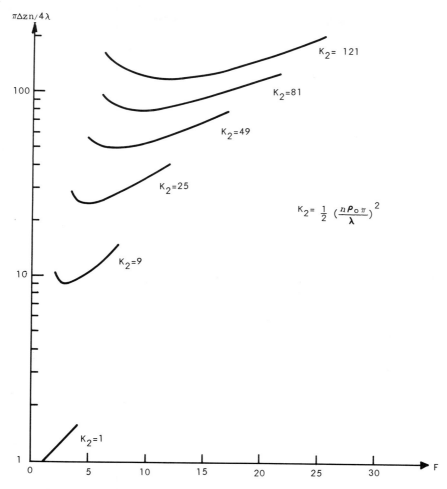

FIG. 4. Normalized depth of focus vs. F-number for constant spot size K_2.

medium, since the depth of field is directly proportional to the refractive index n, a high value of n is desirable. On the other hand, it is desirable to have a small n to achieve large angular separation of the stored holograms in a volume holographic medium. More importantly, the optical absorption characterized by the absorption coefficient α should be tailored according to the mechanism of read–write operation. For thermally induced recording, let us examine the case where the laser heating is achieved in short duration such that the thermal conductivity loss is negligible. The energy E_T required for heating a bit of radius ρ_0 and therefore of volume $V = \pi\rho_0^2 d$ (where d is the medium thickness) is given by

$$E_T = \pi\rho_0^2 d C_v \Delta T \tag{27}$$

where C_v is the volume heat capacity, ΔT the temperature rise required for writing. Since the energy converted into heat is equal to the energy absorbed, E_T can be related to the laser input writing energy E_W at the medium surface by

$$E_T = E_W(1 - e^{-\alpha d}) \tag{28}$$

Therefore,

$$E_W = [d/(1 - e^{-\alpha d})](\pi\rho_0^2)C_v \Delta T \tag{29}$$

To reduce E_W, it is desirable to make d small but $\alpha d \geq 1$ for efficient conversion of beam energy to heating. For $\alpha d \simeq 1$, d less than 1 μm, we need $\alpha > 10^4$ cm^{-1}. Most metallic media meet this requirement. When laser sources are used for optical recording, it is essential to reduce the writing power required by improving the material sensitivity. This is mainly due to the relatively low overall energy conversion efficiency of the visible lasers useful for optical recording. For the thermally induced effects, the writing energy as shown in Eq. (27) is proportional to V, C_v, and ΔT. For most solid materials C_v is in the range of 1–10 J/cm^3/°C. Therefore, $E_T/V\Delta T$ is about 10^{-2}–10^{-3} nJ/μm^3/°C. Besides making the bit dimensions small, it is also desirable to reduce the required ΔT. Most of the thermally induced materials have $\Delta T \sim 100$°C and an effective volume per bit (when the substrate is included for the thin film case) of 1 μm^3. Therefore the energy required per bit is about 0.1 to 1 nJ. For a 10 Mbit/sec recording rate, the laser power required is about 1 to 10 mW. Using a Gaussian beam with a radius of w_0 at $1/e^2$ point for heating a two-dimensional medium, the thermal decay time is approximately equal to $w_0^2/4K$, where K is the thermal diffusivity. Substituting typical values of K for metals and making $w_0 = 0.5$ μm, the thermal decay time is about 0.1 to 1 μsec. In a practical situation, the medium is supported or is thermally thick, therefore this time is reduced to 10^{-9} to 10^{-10} sec. The memory cycle time on a bit-by-bit basis, being of the same order of magnitude, is more than adequate for presently envisaged recording systems. In holographic recording the energy requirements are increased as compared to bit-by-bit recording since an entire page (~ 1 mm^2) is recorded at a time rather than a single bit (~ 1 μm^2). Thus, the required energy is in the range of 0.1 to 1 mJ for thermally induced holographic recording. Furthermore, the energy must be delivered in a short time

(~10 nsec) to avoid loss of resolution due to transverse heat conduction (Lee and Chen, 1972). The combined high power and short pulse duration requirements can be best met using Q-switched or cavity-dumped lasers (Maydan, 1970a).

To minimize writing energy it is desirable to use the energy in the photon rather than the converted heating effect for recording. In this case, it is appropriate to make $\alpha d \leq 1$ to insure uniform exposure. Photographic (P), photochromic (PC), and photorefractive (PR) media use the well-known photon-induced phenomena for recording. Alternatively, photon energy could be used to activate a recording medium. Typically a photoconductor layer is used over the recording material to block the electric charge flow except in the localized laser-illuminated region where the conductivity is drastically reduced. Either the charge distribution or the current flow as activated by the photoconductor layer is then used to achieve recording. Thermoplastic (TP), ferroelectric–photoconductive (FE–PC), and magnetooptic–photoconductive (MO–PC) are typical examples of this approach. The writing sensitivity for photon-induced effect varies over many orders of magnitude depending on the materials used. On the other hand, the sensitivity of photon-activated recording are all based on that of the conventional photoconducting material, in the region of 10^{-3}–10^{-4} nJ/μm^2. This represents about three orders of magnitude improvement over thermally induced recording techniques.

4. Readout Considerations

In any optical recording systems design, readout is an important aspect of the system performance. It is essential that the figure of merit for readout be optimized. This could involve the optimization of medium thickness, crystallographic orientation, antireflection coating, operating wavelength, and others. For each recording technique, a special optimization procedure applies. However, there are certain problems of general interest in readout. As in any detection problem, the object is to achieve a high signal-to-noise ratio. From the viewpoint of reducing noise, it is essential that the medium grain noise be kept low. This means that the medium should be essentially grainless, or with grains of dimensions much smaller than the bit size. The noise associated with the medium grain is known as the fixed-pattern noise. The origin of this noise depends on the materials used. It can arise from grain distribution, grain boundary scattering, strain-induced birefringence, domain wall scattering for magnetooptic and electrooptic materials, and other sources. Materials of the amorphous or glassy type are essentially grainless, but for most other media the fixed-pattern noise is an important contributor to noise, if not the dominant one. Consider the general case where the readout signal is derived from the state of the addressed bit location in the medium through a physical effect γ, i.e., $i(\gamma)$. The signal Δi for a binary case is given by the difference in reading a "1" bit and "0" bit. If there is a fluctuation in γ of magnitude $\Delta\gamma$ due to grains, and if the noise is medium limited, the signal-to-noise is simply given by

$$(S/N)_{\text{medium}} = \Delta i(\gamma)/[\partial \Delta i(\gamma)/\partial\gamma]\,\Delta\gamma \qquad (30)$$

Since $\Delta\gamma$ is observed from the statistically averaged fluctuation over the spot size, making the grain size small compared to the bit spot size will effectively reduce it.

For holographic recording, the fixed-pattern noise (due to dust and scratches, for example) is generally negligible because the information associated with each bit is spread out over the entire hologram, except in the case where the spatial frequency of the noise overlaps with that of the signal.

In most of the proposed optical recording schemes, a small laser beam is used for reading and writing. In materials with a writing threshold, it is important to realize that only regions in the medium in which the intensity of the writing beam exceeds the threshold are written and thus contribute to the readout signal. In the case of bit-by-bit recording with a Gaussian beam, the beam intensity profile at the focal plane is given by

$$I = 2P_0/\pi w_0^2 \exp(-2r^2/w_0^2) \qquad (31)$$

where P_0 is the read beam power, w_0 the beam radius at $1/e^2$ points, and r the radial coordinate. The fractional power P passing through a written bit of radius ρ_0 is

$$K = P/P_0 = (4/w_0^2) \int_0^{\rho_0} r \exp(-2r^2/w_0^2)\,dr$$
$$= 1 - \exp(-2\rho_0^2/w_0^2) \qquad (32)$$

where ρ_0 is given in Eq. (22). Therefore,

$$K = (I_{\text{peak}} - I_{\text{th}})/I_{\text{peak}} \qquad (33)$$

Since the available readout signal is reduced by a factor K, it is desirable to have materials that can tolerate without damage a large peak intensity compared to the threshold intensity. For MnBi films the peak to threshold intensity ratio must not exceed 1.2 and the resultant K factor is 0.17.

The readout efficiency of a holographic recording (i.e., the diffraction efficiency) is defined as the ratio of energy in the reconstructed image to that of the reconstructing beam. For low exposures, the diffraction efficiency η depends on the exposure E_0 in the following way (Lin, 1971; Collier et al., 1971)

$$\eta = SE_0V \qquad (34)$$

where S is the sensitivity of the material, and V the fringe visibility when a sinusoidal grating is recorded on the medium is given by

$$V = (I_{\max} - I_{\min})/(I_{\max} + I_{min}) \qquad (35)$$

As the exposure is increased, however, the value of η reaches a maximum which depends on the type of hologram. For a thin hologram in which the information is stored in the form of variations in the optical absorption, the maximum value of η is 3.7% (Kogelnik, 1969). A diffraction efficiency up to 100% is possible, however, in thick holograms.

III. Optical Recording Materials and Technology

The development of optical techniques for data storage hinges on the availability of suitable storage media. Many useful physical phenomena found in materials have been advanced for the intended application. Besides photographic film, photochromic media, and other well-known materials, a host of new optical storage techniques have been developed since the advent of lasers. The availability of coherent, monochromatic, collimated light sources makes it possible to achieve holographic storage and bit-by-bit storage at diffraction-limited density, and facilitates the beam steering, modulation, and detection for addressing and readout. The various recording techniques and materials together with the associated physical phenomena utilized are reviewed in this section. Because of the diversity of approaches, it is not possible to cover all optical storage materials with equal emphasis in this discussion. Instead, a few promising approaches are discussed in more detail, and the others are only briefly mentioned. However, an extensive bibliography is given to provide a source for further study.

A. Permanent Recording Materials and Effects

The foremost technology for high density permanent optical recording is the high resolution photographic emulsions in the form of films or plates. Both Kodak and Agfa have commercially available films capable of a linear resolution of 2000 lines/mm, at a writing sensitivity of about 10^{-4}–10^{-3} nJ/μm². The combination of high resolution and sensitivity makes them extremely attractive for recording applications. The readout is obtained from light intensity modification in exposed areas or by phase modulation. In the latter case, a chemical bleaching process is necessary to convert optical density pattern to a phase pattern (Collier *et al.*, 1971). The major drawback is the requirement of a wet chemical developing and fixing process following the exposure or writing operation. Thus, this material cannot be operated in real time. Some popular photographic films and their relevant properties are given in Table I. It should be noted that the Kodak 649 film has a broad spectral response whereas the Agfa films are of narrower spectral sensitivity. To convert the photographic density recording to phase hologram by bleaching, higher exposures are necessary. Other permanent recording materials are summarized in Table II and are reviewed in the following.

Photoresist is a popular material for holographic recording. The transparent polymer material is mixed with liquid monomer and catalyst solution to form the film medium. Upon illumination by UV light,

TABLE I

PHOTOGRAPHIC RECORDING MATERIALS

Material	Resolution (lines/mm)	Exposure (nJ/μm²)	Sensitive wavelength (Å)
Kodak			
649F	6000	7×10^{-4}	4000–6500
649F	6000	1.8×10^{-2}	4000–6500
649G, 6490	2000	10^{-3}	
SO-175		10^{-3}	
Agfa-Gevaert			
8E70	3000	2×10^{-4}	6328
8E75	3000	2×10^{-4}	6943
10E70	1500	5×10^{-5}	6328
10E75	2800	5×10^{-5}	6943
14C70	1500	3×10^{-6}	6328
14C75	1500	3×10^{-6}	6943
10E56	2800	5×10^{-5}	5145

TABLE II

PHYSICAL EFFECTS PROPOSED FOR NONPHOTOGRAPHIC PERMANENT OPTICAL MEMORY
APPLICATIONS

Physical effects	Typical materials	Resolution (lines/mm)	Sensitivity ($nJ/\mu m^2$)	Reference
Photopolymer (P.P.)	Monomer, dye, methylene blue mixture	1500	6×10^{-3}	Jenney (1970)
Photoresist (P.R.)	Shipley AZ-1350	1500	$\sim 10^{-2}$	Bartolini (1974)
Free radicals (F.R.)	Organic dye in polymeric binder	4000	0.1	Fotland (1970)
Dichromated gelatin (DCG)	$(NH_4)_2CR_2O_7$ or $K_2Cr_2O_7$ in gelatin	4000	$3-6 \times 10^{-2}$	Kosav (1965)
Metal engraving	Si	2500	0.5	Dalisa et al. (1970)
Metal film hole burning	Bi films, Rh films on Mylar	~ 1000	~ 1	Maydan (1971) and Gray (1972)

crosslinks are either formed (negative photoresist) or removed (positive photoresist). The region where there is no crosslink can be dissolved in the developing process, producing relief phase holograms. Shipley AZ-1350 positive photoresist has been extensively studied. Using AZ-303 developer, this material has a sensitivity approaching 10^{-2} $nJ/\mu m^2$ at 3–5% diffraction efficiency and a resolution exceeding 1500 lines/mm (Bartolini, 1974). In another photopolymer system, a dye and an initiator, usually methylene blue or thionine and p-toluenesulfinic acid, is mixed with the monomers before exposure (Jenney, 1970). This system has a sensitivity of 6×10^{-3} $nJ/\mu m^2$ at 6328 Å HeNe wavelength, a resolution of 1500 lines/mm, and is fixed by exposure to UV light. Other photopolymers that have been suggested for holographic recording are polymethylmethacrylate (PMMA) (Tomlinson et al., 1970), Dupont photopolymer (Booth, 1972; Colburn and Haines, 1971), and Opticon Chemicals UV57 and EMI-4128 (Forshaw, 1974). In yet another form of photopolymer, free radicals are used as initiators. Free radical films require dry processing. Organic dyes are used to dispose molecularly in a polymeric binder, providing a gain mechanism. Typical resolution of this type of material is 4000 lines/mm and sensitivity in the range of 0.1 $nJ/\mu m^2$. Exposure is in the blue or UV region; developing takes place when exposed to intense red or near infrared (Fotland, 1970).

Dichromated gelatin (DCG) films have also been used to record high quality holograms (Kosav, 1965; Shankoff, 1968). Dichromators such as $(NH_4)_2Cr_2O_7$ or $K_2Cr_2O_7$ when exposed to UV or blue light becomes insoluble in water whereas the unexposed region can be dissolved in water. More recently an improved method of chemically hardening of dichromated gelatin has been proposed (Lin, 1969). In this case, no gelatin was washed away during developing, but the amount of water absorption and therefore the expansion decreases with exposure. This step is followed by a rapid dehydration process in isopropanol to produce the phase hologram. The exposure sensitivity is about $3\text{--}6 \times 10^{-2}$ nJ/μm^2 at 5145 Å wavelength. The resolution is about 4000 lines/ mm.

Besides the photo-induced effect, thermally induced techniques were also suggested for permanent recording. Engraving of Si by a laser beam (Dalisa et al., 1970) is one example. But the most successful technique is hole burning in Bi films (Maydan, 1971) or Rh films (Gray, 1972). In these cases, the optical diffraction-limited resolution was usually obtainable, but the sensitivity is only about 1 nJ/μm^2.

B. ALTERABLE RECORDING MATERIALS AND TECHNOLOGY

There are many types of data recording that require various degrees of alterability, permanency, and other features. A large number of techniques have been proposed and studied for alterable recording in response to these needs. The materials and techniques generally fall in three categories: thermally induced, photon induced, and photon activated. The advantages and drawbacks of each technology are briefly outlined here. The physical effects and representative materials proposed for alterable optical recording applications are listed in Table III.

1. Thermally Induced Type Materials

The laser beam energy can be used to cause localized heating to effect write or erase in a memory medium. This is the thermally induced technique. A number of storage techniques have been proposed for thermally induced erasable optical memory applications. We will now review some of the proposed materials.

a. Thermomagnetic Media. Thermomagnetic effects in ferromagnetic or ferrimagnetic media were the first approach introduced for alterable optical data storage (Chen et al., 1968; Chang et al., 1965). The optical beam energy is used for heating a bit location to a temperature at which magnetization reversal can be effected, and the readout is based on the magnetooptic effect. Thus, this type of memory is often referred to as

TABLE III

PHYSICAL EFFECTS PROPOSED FOR ALTERABLE OPTICAL MEMORY APPLICATIONS

Category	Physical effects		Typical materials
Thermally induced	Thermomagnetic–magnetooptic (MO)	Curie point	MnBi, EuO, Gd–CO
		Compensation point	GdIG
		Coercivity reduction by heating	Co–P
			CrO_2
		Thermoremanent	
	Amorphous–crystalline (AC)	Phase transition	$Te_{88}Ge_7As_5$
	Semiconductor–metal (SM)	Phase transition	VO_2
Photon induced	Photochromic (PC)	F-Center	K Br
		F_A-Center	KCl with NaCl or LiCl doping
		M-Center	NaF
		Photo dimerization	Acridizimium, Toluene–sulfonate
	Photorefractive (PR)	Linear	$LiNbO_3$, BNN, SBN
		Nonlinear	$LiNbO_3$, KTN
	Photomagnetic		YIG:Si
Photon activated	Thermoplastic (TP)	Composite	TNF–PVC
	Elastomer (E)	Composite	Rution
	Ferroelectric–photoconductive (FE–PC)	Single layer	$Bi_{12}SiO_{20}$
		Two layer	$Bi_4Ti_3O_{12}$–ZnS
	Magnetooptic–photoconductive (MO–PC)	Composite	$Gd_{2.5}Yb_{0.5}Fe_{4.8}Al_{0.2}$–CdS

the magnetooptic memory. The magnetooptic effects utilized in readout are the Faraday or the Kerr effects, they refer to rotation of the polarization vector of light in transmission through (ϕ_F) or reflection from (ϕ_K) the medium, respectively.

Phenomenologically, for a beam transmitted through a medium of thickness **d**, the Faraday effect is often given by

$$\phi_F = \frac{K d \mathbf{M} \cdot \hat{k}}{\hat{n} \cdot \hat{k}} = F d \frac{\hat{m} \cdot \hat{k}}{\hat{n} \cdot \hat{k}} \tag{36}$$

where K is the Kundt constant, **M** the magnetization vector, $\hat{n}$ a unit vector perpendicular to the medium, $\hat{k}$ a unit propagation vector for the incident beam, F the specific Faraday rotation in degrees per centimeter, and $\hat{m}$ the unit vector of magnetization. Typical values of F in ferromagnetic media are of the order of 10^5 deg/cm.

It is seen from this that in order to achieve large ϕ_F, the easy direction of magnetization should be oriented parallel to the incident beam direction.

Similarly, Kerr rotation is also a sensitive function of the beam incidence angle, and the largest effect is the polar Kerr effect where the beam and the magnetization are both normal to the memory medium plane.

From a readout point of view the suitability of a material for magnetooptic applications is determined by the amount of magnetooptic rotation per unit optical loss. Therefore, transparency is an important consideration. Using the optical absorption coefficient α in cm^{-1}, defined by the Beer–Lambert law, in combination with the specific Faraday rotation, a material figure of merit may be defined as $2F/\alpha$ in degrees per neper optical loss. The factor of 2 accounts for the fact that the signal is derived from regions of opposite magnetization.

Reading of the magnetically stored information requires a polarized beam. Using a polarized laser beam of intensity I_0, in passing through or after reflection from the memory medium, the beam is analyzed by an analyzer with the axis of extinction rotated at an angle θ with respect to the original beam polarization direction. The difference in photodetector signal levels transmitted through regions of positive and negative magnetization is given by (Treves, 1967; Aagard $et\ al.$, 1972).

$$\Delta i = S_d I_0 \exp(-\alpha d)[\sin^2(\theta - Fd) - \sin^2(\theta + Fd)]$$
$$= S_d I_0 \exp(-\alpha d) \sin 2\theta \sin 2\phi_F \tag{37}$$

where S_d is the photodetector responsitivity, $\phi_F = Fd$ the Faraday rotation.

Optimizing Δi with respect to the medium thickness, and assuming $\phi_F \ll \pi$ we have $d_{opt} = 1/\alpha$ and

$$\Delta i(d_{opt}) = I_0 S_d e^{-1} \sin 2\theta (2F/\alpha) \tag{38}$$

For the case using Kerr effect, assuming $\phi_K \ll \pi$ we have

$$\Delta i = 2 S_d I_0 R \phi_K \sin 2\theta \tag{39}$$

where R is the surface reflectivity.

The readout signal is maximum for $\theta = \pi/4$. In this case, a differential detection system is used to cancel the large average signal. From this simple analysis, we see that the readout signal is linearly proportional to the figure of merit $2F/\alpha$ or $R\phi_K$ of the material used.

Magnetooptic materials can also be used for holographic storage. Taking the simple case of alternating strips of opposite magnetization, i.e., a magnetic grating of equal width, the first-order diffracted intensity for the transmitted beam is (Haskal, 1970; Mezrich, 1969).

$$I_1 = (4/\pi^2)I_0 \exp(-\alpha d) \sin^2 Fd \qquad (40)$$

Again optimizing with respect to the medium thickness and assuming Fd to be small, we have $d_{opt} = 2/\alpha$ and

$$I_1(d_{opt}) = (4/\pi^2)I_0 e^{-2}(2F/\alpha)^2 \qquad (41)$$

The diffraction from the magnetic grating is derived from the component of the field perpendicular to the original polarization direction. Therefore no analyzer is required. The readout signal in this case is proportional to the square of the figure of merit.

Referring to the discussion of medium fixed-pattern noise, it is easy to derive from Eq. (30) and (37) that the medium limited signal-to-noise is

$$\left(\frac{S}{N}\right)_{medium} = \frac{\Delta i}{\Delta i/\phi_F \Delta \phi_F} = \frac{\sin 2\phi_F}{(2 \cos 2\phi_F)\Delta \phi_F} = \frac{\phi_F}{\Delta \phi_F} \qquad (42)$$

where $\Delta \phi_F$ is the fluctuation of the Faraday rotation due to magnetic metallurgical inhomogeneity and other nonuniformity of the medium.

With this discussion in mind we will now examine the physical phenomena in thermomagnetic materials that have been suggested for optomagnetic recording (Chen, 1974).

1. Curie point writing (Mayer, 1958). Curie point writing is a recording technique in which the temperature rise in the heated spot exceeds the Curie temperature of the medium. During cooling from the Curie temperature, the combined field from the magnetic closure flux and an applied external field determine the direction of magnetization of the heated bit. In a medium in thin film form with the easy direction of magnetization perpendicular to the film plane, the closure flux is in a direction opposite to the magnetization direction. For this case, writing from the surrounding 0 level to a 1 level requires no external field. The erasure operation involves application of an external field to overcome the closure flux or the demagnetizing field to cause the written bits to be erased back to the 0 level. This is an example of threshold recording and is schematically shown in Fig. 5.

In order to be able to erase a spot effectively without affecting the unheated region, one condition must be satisfied: the demagnetizing field must be less than the coercive force of the medium. This condition is satisfied in some materials.

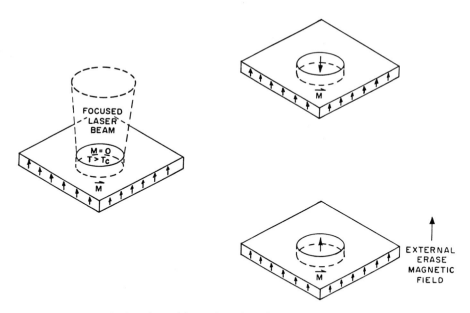

FIG. 5. Laser Curie point writing and erasing of a magnetic film with easy axis normal to the film plane. The diagrams on the right depict a written "1" bit due to the closure flux (upper) and an erased "0" bit by the application of an external magnetic field (lower).

Thin films of MnBi at room temperature (Chen *et al.*, 1968; Williams *et al.*, 1957; Feldtkeller, 1972; Unger and Rath, 1971; Ono *et al.*, 1972; Bernal, 1971) and EuO at cryogenic temperatures (Fan and Greiner, 1968; Ahn, 1970; Suits *et al.*, 1971) have been most extensively studied for this recording technique. Other materials including the amorphous films and other intermetallic compounds have also been proposed (Patajczak and Sczaniecki, 1970; Sherwood *et al.*, 1971; Shelton, 1973; Comstock, 1970; Sawatzky and Street, 1971; Stoffel, 1970; Sawatzky, 1971a,b; Güntherodt *et al.*, 1970; Suits *et al.*, 1966; Ahrenkiel and Coburn, 1973; Chaudhari *et al.*, 1973; Brown, 1974) for this technique.

2. Compensation temperature writing technique. In certain ferrimagnetic material such as gadolinium iron garnet (GdIG), the spontaneous magnetization is the sum of sublattice magnetizations. At the compensation temperature, the net algebraic sum of these sublattice magnetizations and the medium attains an extremely high coercivity H_c. A few degrees away from this compensation temperature the coercivity drops and magnetization switching becomes easy. By operating the medium at the compensation temperature, a switching field is applied in coincidence

with a laser heating pulse, which allows the heated spot to raise above a temperature at which the coercivity is below the applied switching field. The magnetization direction in the heated spot can therefore be switched. This method of writing has been demonstrated experimentally in single crystals (Chang et al., 1965; Coeure et al., 1971; Goldberg, 1967) and in thin films of gadolinium iron garnet (MacDonald and Beck, 1969). A variation of this technique based on the use of compensation domain walls in Ga-substituted YIG has been proposed and experimentally demonstrated (Krumme and Hansen, 1973), since the magnetooptic effect is attributed to the magnetization of the iron sublattice, which is not zero at the compensation temperature.

3. Temperature dependence of coercivity (Treves et al., 1969). There are a number of materials and techniques in which strong temperature dependence of the coercivity can be achieved for optomagnetic writing. One example is phosphorus-doped cobalt. At a temperature of about 150°C, the coercivity is decreased by a factor of 3 from that at room temperature. Therefore, switching can occur with a suitable field applied coincident with the laser heating pulse sufficient to raise the temperature of the heated spot to 150°C.

Another example is that of two-layer films such as palladium–cobalt alloys and permalloy composite films. The coercivity of the film lies in between that for the individual layers. When the medium is heated to a temperature above the lower of the two Curie temperatures of the individual layers and a suitable field is applied, localized switching can occur (deBonard, 1968).

4. Thermoremanent technique (Waring, 1971). Magnetization in a magnetic medium can also be altered at a temperature below the Curie temperature. The remanent magnetization M_R after a thermal heat cycle is usually reduced from the saturation value M_S. Under the influence of an external field, M_R can take any value between $+M_S$ and $-M_S$. In making use of this effect for digital recording, the minimum domain size must be much smaller than the bit dimension so that well-defined values for M_R can be assured for each write or erase. This is because M_R is derived from the statistical average of the ensemble of positive and negative domains within the heated spot. An added feature of this type of optomagnetic recording technique is the possibility for recording analog information. Since M_R is strongly dependent on the peak temperature and the applied field during cooling, precise control of these parameters are required to achieve reproducible results. Materials such as CRO_2 (Waring, 1971) and MnBi (Minnaja et al., 1973; Chen et al., 1973b) have been used to demonstrate this technique. Magnetooptic recording materials are summarized in Table IV.

TABLE IV

MAGNETOOPTIC MEMORY MATERIALS

Material	4 Ms(G)	$H_K = 2K$ / Ms(G)	Write–erase tech.	Write–erase temp.	Resolution (lines/mm)	Sensitivity (nJ/μm²)	Write–erase field (Oe)	Absorp. Coeff. $\alpha(10^5$ cm^{-1})	Fig. of merit $2F/\alpha$ (deg)	Operating wavelength (Å)	Oper. Temp.
MnBi (l.t.p.)	7,200	40,000	T_c	360°C	2000	0.3–1	600	5	3.6	6328	20°C
MnBi (h.t.p.)	5,500	>40,000	T_c	180°C	2000	0.1–0.3	600	5	1.4	6328	20°C
Mn₈Ti₂Bi (h.t.p.)	—		T_c	125°C	—	0.1–0.3	—	5.3	0.8	6328	20°C
Mn₅Ge₃	12,400	a	T_c	37°C	—	—	—	3.5	0.8	5500	0°C
MnAlGe	3,600	35,000	T_c	245°C	>40	3	500	4.7	0.54	6328	100°C
MnGaGe	4,170	9,500	T_c	185°C	—	—	500	5.8	0.28	6328	20°C
CrTe	1,015	a	T_c	61°C	—	—	—	2	0.5	5500	20°C
MnSb	9,600	a	T_c	300°C	—	—	—	7.5	0.8	5500	20°C
MnAs	7,900	a	T_c	45°C	—	—	—	4.5	0.2	6000	20°C
Fe₃Si₃	7,500	—	T_c	108°C	—	—	—	3.7	0.26	5500	20°C
EuO	23,700	a	T_c	70 K	1000	0.01–0.1	50	0.86	7.5	6000	20° J
EuO (Fe)	19,200	a	T_c	180 K	—	—	—	2.2	~3	7000	77 K
EuS	14,000	a	T_c	16 K	—	—	—	0.0008	58	6900	6 K
EuSe	13,200	a	T_c	7 K	—	—	—	2.2	3600	7500	4.2 K
CoCr₂S₄	2,300	—	T_c	225 K	—	—	~100	8	110	10000	200 K
GdCo	3,450	>300	T_{comp}	120°C	—	0.5	~500	0.06	0.45	4500–8200	20°C
GeIG	7,300	—	T_{comp}	25°C	50–100	0.1–0.8	~100	0.06	2.3	6328	15+3°C
GdIG (Film)	5,800	—	T_{comp}	−1°C	300	1.25	500	—	—	6000	(−1)+28°C
Co-P-(Ni-Fe)	—	a	$\Delta H_c(T)$	150°C	200	1	—	—	—	—	20°C
NeFe-PdCo-Co	—	a	$\Delta H_c(T)$	~140°C	40	0.5	20	—	—	—	20°C
CrO₂	1,600	a	$M_R(T)$	134°C	100	2.3	50	—	0.1	5000	20°C

^{a} In these media, the easy direction of magnetization lies in the memory plane. Therefore, full utilization of readout figure of merit cannot be realized.

b. Amorphous–Crystalline Transition (Neale and Aseltine, 1973). In certain amorphous semiconductors, the optical and electrical properties of the material are a function of the thermal treatment. The storage mechanism is based on the amorphous–crystalline transition that can be induced in thin films of this material by heating with laser radiation. The writing mechanism involves the application of a laser heating pulse to a film in the amorphous state, which causes crystallization of the material within the heated region. Application of a more intense laser pulse causes the medium to be heated to the melting point of the film and rapid cooling causes the material to revert to the amorphous phase (Ovshinsky and Klose, 1972). In another mode (the reverse mode), the material is prepared in mostly crystalline form and reverts to amorphous state by laser heating (Von Gutfeld and Chaudhari, 1972). Typical materials are chalcogenide films $Te_{81}Cd_{15}Sb_2S_2$. This class of materials has a relatively low writing sensitivity (10 nJ/μm^2) for the normal mode and 0.3 nJ/μm^2 for the reverse mode, and the writing mechanism requires pulses of approximately 1 μsec or longer for the normal mode and amorphizing pulses as short as 100 nsec from an injection laser were used for the reverse mode. Since the optical absorption and reflectivity of the medium is different for these two phases, detection of the written bits is possible. For example, typical reflectivity change for Te–As–Ge films is about 30% from crystalline to amorphous states (Feinleib and Ovshinsky, 1970) and absorption changes are shown in Table V. The material reversibility has not been extensively tested. There appears to be a fatigue effect on this type of medium. However, continued progress is being made to resolve this problem.

c. Semiconductor–Metal Transition. Certain materials exhibit a well-known defined phase transition from semiconductor to metal by heating, accompanied by an optical transmission or reflection change. This effect has been suggested for optical storage (Smith, 1973). For VO_2, the transition temperature is around 70°C. Films prepared by rf sputtering on quartz substrates were found to exhibit a hysteresis in transmission at

TABLE V

ABSORPTION COEFFICIENTS

State	Wavelength	
	6470 Å	9000 Å
Crystalline	3.4×10^5 cm^{-1}	2.5×10^5 cm^{-1}
Amorphous	2.5×10^5 cm^{-1}	1.0×10^5 cm^{-1}

the GaAs injection laser wavelength. The writing sensitivity was found to be about 0.03 nJ/μm^2, using 25–500 nsec laser pulses and minimum spot size was 2 μm limited by grain size. To erase the written information, the medium must be cooled by approximately 10°C. Thus, erasure cannot be performed on a bit-by-bit basis. This writing process is similar to the amorphous-to-crystalline transition in chalcogenides, but with improved writing sensitivity at the expense of tighter temperature control.

2. Photon Induced Technique

Physical effects involving change of states in a material due to the direct interaction between the photons and the material medium have been found useful for optical memory applications. As the beam energy is not converted to heat, some of the limitations in material sensitivity and response speed that apply to the thermally induced technique no longer hold and improved sensitivity is possible. There are however, other drawbacks in this approach.

In order to achieve a uniform effect in a photon-induced material, it is desirable to have the medium optically thin or $\alpha d \lesssim 1$, where α is the absorption coefficient and d the medium thickness. In certain cases, the absorption coefficient is so low that even when the memory medium takes a three-dimensional geometry, this condition is still satisfied. A three-dimensional memory medium is particularly suited for archival holographic storage.

Some of the major photon induced memory material and phenomena are now reviewed in the following.

a. Photochromic Materials. Photochromic materials undergo a change in their absorption spectra when illuminated with light of a certain wavelength. This color change results in an increase or decrease of absorption at another wavelength which coincides with the read beam wavelength. The induced color change may be erased by illumination with light of a longer wavelength or by heating. Alkalide halides such as potassium chloride and potassium bromide crystals are well-known photochromic materials (Reich and Dorion, 1965). Other materials include $SrTiO_3$ crystals doped with Fe–Mo and Ni–Mo (Faughnan and Kiss, 1969; Duncan *et al.,* 1970), CaF (Bosomworth and Gerritsen, 1968) and a variety of photochromic plastics and glasses (Megla, 1974). Also, some organic photochromic materials have been found useful for optical memory applications (Lo, 1974). Photochromic materials are of interest as volume holographic storage media. Photochromic materials are basically grainless. Resolutions greater than 3000 lines/mm have been achieved. The high angular discrimination allows a large number of holograms to be recorded in the same volume which can be selectively read out by angular rotation of the medium (Friesem, 1968). The disadvantages of photochromic media are: (1) Sensitivity for writing is relatively low. (2) They require beams of different wavelength for reading and writing in some cases. (3) Diffraction efficiency is usually low because this type of material is basically an absorption material. (4) Thermal stability is relatively poor. For most photochromic media, the stored information is rapidly bleached out at temperatures ranging from 50°–100°C. (5) Spectral response is poor. Most photochromics are only sensitive to one or two primary colors. (6) Some photochromic materials exhibit fatigue effects and cannot be recycled indefinitely. The physical process involved for writing may be described as follows: UV irradiation creates F-centers. Irradiating in the F-band with a suitable laser beam causes the F-centers to attain an excited state. The F-centers can then be destroyed thermally. Thus, selective heating by a laser at a high temperature has the effect of bleaching the F-band, causing the crystal to become selectively less opaque. During readout the crystal temperature must be maintained low enough that the efficiency of the optical bleaching process described above is negligibly small. Irradiation in the F-band at low temperatures does not destroy F-centers and thus causes no permanent change in the crystal. Alternatively, readout can be achieved using a beam of longer wavelength. Two methods can be utilized to record. In the first method the crystal is colored completely by X-ray or by γ-ray radiation, and then bleached optically at a selected point to correspond to the information. Alternatively, an uncolored crystal may be selectively colored. UV radiation is found to be effective for writing in this case.

Recent work at the Naval Research Laboratory (Schneider et al., 1970) has shown that M-centers in alkali halides can be used for optical memory. An M-center is a pair of nearest neighbor F-centers, which has two distinctly separate absorptions called M- and M_f-bands. The M-band is a single transition located in the visible or near infrared spectral regions, and the M_f band consists of two overlapping transitions peaking at shorter wavelengths. A distinct dipole moment is associated with each M-center absorption. One can align all M-centers along one preferred direction with a linearly polarized M_f light, thus making the M and M_f absorption bands strongly dependent on the polarization of light. These absorption bands are hence made dichroic. Information can be written or erased with polarized light in the M_f band and read through linear dichroic absorption in the M-band. It was found that the M-center can be reoriented with a 5145 Å wavelength Argon laser of 110 mW power.

The estimated number of read cycles before significant degradation of the readout signal occurs is at least 10^{10} cycles. The stability of the M-center alignment was checked at room temperature. Three months of life time was considered possible. This will be even better at lower temperatures.

One of the organic material suggested for optical recording is salicylideneaniline (Lo, 1974). This material has a writing sensitivity of 2 $nJ/\mu m^2$. It has been suggested for high speed (30 nsec) recording and holographic interferometry applications. However, the relatively low stability (fading within 30 hr at 25°C) makes it useful only for temporary storage.

More recently, photochromic glass has been used for recording (Megla, 1974). A resolution of 100 lines/mm and a sensitivity of 0.3 $nJ/\mu m^2$ was obtained.

Photodimer has also been suggested for optical memory applications (Tomlinson et al., 1972). The photodimers were formed by polycyclic aromatic hydrocarbons such as anthracene and their derivatives. These photodimers can be dissociated through a photodissociation process to the original monomers. When the photodimer is held in a rigid matrix, the dimer can be reconstructed efficiently because two monomers are held in the proper relationship for photodimerization. The absorption spectra of monomer and a dimer differs substantially, and associated with this is a difference in refractive index. These characteristics as well as the stability of both states at room temperature make such a system attractive for reversible phase holographic recording with nondestructive readout. Several photodimer systems as solution in rigid transparent polymer matrices as well as single crystals of photodimers were studied. It was found that repeated write–erase cycles produce no degradation in readout. The photosensitivity is in the neighborhood of 0.1 $nJ/\mu m^2$. A holographic grating diffraction efficiency as high as 5% has been reported.

b. Ferroelectric Photorefractive Effect. When a short wavelength laser light is illuminated over certain ferroelectric materials such as lithium niobate, the refractive index of the laser-illuminated region can be changed. This is called the photorefractive effect or the laser damage effect (Chen et al., 1968). This effect is especially suited for holographic recording because of its associated high resolution and high readout efficiency due to the fact that the information is stored in refractive index changes rather than absorption changes. Besides lithium niobate (Chen, 1969), this effect has also been found in lithium titanate (Ashkin et al., 1966), barium sodium niobate (Amodei et al., 1971), and strontium barium niobate (Thaxter, 1969; Thaxter and Kestigian, 1974). The mechanism responsible for this observed effect is believed to be the drift of carriers produced by photoionization due to the laser radiation. Carriers in the illuminated regions of the storage medium drift under the influence of an internal field and are trapped in immediately adjacent dark regions. The resultant charge displacements set up an electric field that modulates the index of refraction via the electrooptic effect. This index change may be erased by heating which then frees the trapped charges. Erasure is also possible using optical means since the displaced charge is still sensitive to light. Exposure of such holograms to a uniform readout beam tends to redistribute the charge leading to an eventual erasure of the written hologram. A novel method in which optically stable holograms can be produced involves heating the crystal to about 100°C for 30 min during and after the normal recording process (Staebler and Amodei, 1972). This mild heating allows ionic motion to take place which is entirely due to the electric field generated by the electronic displacement during the exposure or creation of the hologram. After the ionic pattern is created, the crystal is further exposed to intense light to erase the electric charge, but allowing the ionic charge pattern to remain. This produces a much more stable hologram because the frozen ionic charge pattern is not easily erased by the irradiation of the read beam. Orders of magnitude increase in stability to the read laser have been obtained. In experiments performed on lithium niobate and barium sodium niobate, the written hologram was read with a 500 mW/cm² laser intensity for hours with no degradation as compared to 500-sec read beam–induced erasure in a normal hologram. This ionic fixation process also improved the diffracting efficiency from 16% to 50%.

Another technique for fixing this type of written information is the application of an electric field (Micheron and Bismuth, 1972; Micheron et al., 1974b). The high mobility of the ions allows the written electronic pattern to be transformed into a stable ionic pattern by applying an external field slightly lower than the coercivity, for about 0.1 sec. To explain this fixation technique, we note that this applied field is not large enough to excite the trapped photoelectrons. As the spatial modulation of coercivity is created by the inscribed electronic distribution, this applied field allows the ions to redistribute along the c axis to cancel the spatial modulation. This spatial distribution will remain when the field is removed. After that a uniform illumination is applied to the storage medium, photoexciting the trapped electrons and leaving behind the uncompensated ionic pattern. Erasure is accomplished by applying an electric field higher than the microscopic coercivity.

The sensitivity of the photorefractive effect can be drastically enhanced by doping the ferroelectric materials with metallic impurities, notably Fe and Mo ions (Amodei *et al.*, 1972; Kurz and Kratzig, 1975).

Besides the linear laser damage effect discussed above, nonlinear damage effect has also been observed. In this case extremely short laser pulses were used to achieve high writing sensitivity. Two-photon photorefractive effects have been experimentally demonstrated in LiNbO$_3$ (Von der Linde *et al.*, 1974) and in KTN (Glass, 1974) with a writing power density as low as 10^{-3} nJ/μm^2.

The advantages of the ferroelectric type of holographic materials are: (1) High resolution—recording up to 4000 lines/mm has been achieved. (2) Reversibility—heating the material causes the recording to disappear. For the case of ionic hologram, heating for erasure will have to be performed at a much higher temperature or in an electric field for prolonged periods of time. Yet in a normal hologram heating above 170°C will cause the recording to disappear and the material can be recycled. Exact fatigue data are not yet available at present. (3) Stability of the ionic ferroelectric hologram is satisfactory. (4) Since this type of phase hologram is based on refractive index changes, high readout efficiency is attainable. (5) It lends itself to volume holography and has very high angular sensitivity for readout. The disadvantages are mainly in the relatively complex steps for fixation and the relatively high exposure energy requirement except for the two-photon laser damage effects in KTN.

3. *Photon Activated*

In the materials discussed above the media performed the combined function of response to the heating or photon energy in the beam as well as information storage. However, it is also possible to separate these functions through the use of a composite medium. The advantage of higher sensitivity in the photon-induced media can be combined with the advantages of improved stability or other features in selected storage media, making the composite photon-activated material very attractive for future recording systems.

a. Thermoplastics. Thermoplastics possess extremely high recording sensitivity as phase recording media and are considered the most advanced media for holographic recording applications (Colburn and Tompkins, 1974). The high sensitivity, comparable to that of photographic films, is made possible because of the inherent gain mechanism in the photoresponse by separating the exposure and developing stages. The recording process is demonstrated schematically in Fig. 6. The materials consist of a layer of thermoplastic in contact with a layer of photoconductor, coated over a transparent electrode which is supported by a

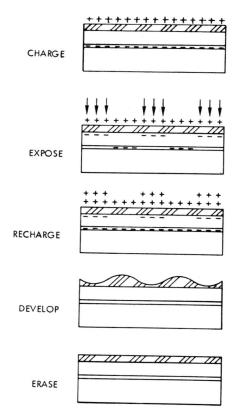

FIG. 6. The recording process of the thermoplastic composite material consists of (from top to bottom) a thermoplastic layer, a photoconductive layer, a conducting electrode, and a substrate. The operation for recording involves charging, exposure, recharge, and develop (heating) steps. For erasure, the material is heated to a higher temperature to remove the relief by surface tension as the thermoplastic softens.

suitable substrate. Using a corona discharge device, the thermoplastic is first charged uniformly over the surface. The optical information in the form of intensity variation is imposed on this sandwiched recording medium, causing the photoconductive layer to conduct, such that the intensity image is replicated into a special modulation of charge across the thermoplastic layer. After this exposure step, heat is applied to the medium to heat momentarily the thermoplastic layer to about its softening temperature. The electrostatic force causes the thermoplastic layer to deform and a relief image (modulation of the thickness) replicating the original image is obtained. To erase the written image, heat pulse is applied without exposure to light and charge. Surface tension of thermoplastic restores the smooth surface for the next exposure. The characteristics of some typical thermoplastic material is shown in Fig. 7. The recording sensitivity is about 10^{-4} nJ/μm^2. There are a few problems associated with this approach, notably the frost formation and degradation due to repeated write–erase cycling. Frost is the result of the spatial frequency associated with the natural wrinkling of the medium. This effect reduces the usable spatial bandwidth. The spatial bandwidth, however, should be adequate if the thickness of the medium is properly designed. There is a slow continuous degradation process during writing and erasing. Using stabelite ester 10 thermoplastic and poly-n-vinyl carbazole (PVK) photoconductive layers, repeated cycling exceeding 10^3 has been performed with tolerable deterioration of the readout signal (Lee, 1974).

  b. Ferroelectric–Photoconductive. The FE–PC technique refers to a composite material which consists of a photoconductive layer applied over a ferroelectric layer, sandwiched between conducting electrodes

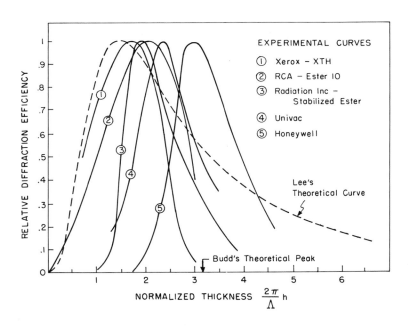

FIG. 7.   Relative diffraction efficiency as a function of the normalized thickness for various types of thermoplastics. The dashed line is based on an unpublished analysis by T. C. Lee.

with the electrode next to the photoconductor layer being transparent to permit light transmission.

With no light on the medium and a voltage applied to the electrodes, most of the voltage drop in the device is across the photoconducting layer, to inhibit switching of the polarization and the writing on the ferroelectric layer. However, when a selected spot on this structure is illuminated by a light of proper wavelength, the photoconductive layer is activated, allowing the voltage to be applied to the ferroelectric layer on this spot. In this manner, various regions over the two layer FE–PC device can be switched and polarized in the desired direction, with the light beam acting as an addressing link. The readout for the stored information may be based on the electrooptic effect or on a discharge of the stored electric charges at the position of each bit. In the latter case the readout is destructive.

Materials such as single-crystal bismuth titanate (Keneman et al., 1970), gadolinium molybdate (Kumuda, 1972), and ceramics such as PLZT (Micheron et al., 1974a) are well-known candidates for this type of storage. Typical photoconducting layer materials are cadmium sulfide and cadmium selenide films. Their dark resistivity of 10^8 Ω-cm is reduced by a factor of 10^4 during illumination by a visible laser. More recently, materials such as zinc sulfite and bismuth silicate ($Bi_{12}SiO_{20}$) have been found to be more suited for this FE–PC device (Feinleib and Oliver, 1972; Nisenson and Iwasa, 1972). These materials possess both photoconductive and ferroelectric properties; therefore, a single-layer device can be made, simplifying fabrication.

For a bit-to-bit oriented memory system, perhaps the most straightforward method for reading and writing on ferroelectrics is to bring a pair of electrodes across each bit location. This arrangement is not suitable for memories with large capacities because of the complexity in the interconnection to the bit location. However, there are certain unique advantages associated with this type of layout, making it particularly useful for image storage and page composer applications in the holographic memory. One of the most popular materials suggested for this application is the PLZT ceramic (Land et al., 1974). PLZT is capable of large refractive index changes due to the electrooptic effect. The switching voltage for a ceramic of a few tens of micrometers thickness is normally of the order of 100 V. A packing density of about 1.5×10^5 bits/cm², and switching speed of about 1 μsec have been experimentally demonstrated.

c. Magnetooptic–Photoconductive. One of the principal drawbacks of the magnetooptic recording technique is its relatively low sensitivity. A novel approach using a photoconductive layer with a transparent electrode deposited over a magnetooptic layer has been advanced by Philips workers (Krumme *et al.*, 1975). With an electric field applied to the transparent electrodes, localized heating on the magnetooptic layer is achieved through the ohmic loss in the laser-illuminated spot of the photoconductor. Using CdS for the photoconductor, InO as the electrodes, and epitaxially grown GdIG over GGG substrate as the magnetooptic layer, recording sensitivity as high as 2×10^{-4} nJ/μm^2 readout efficiency and a density of 10^6 bits/cm^2 have been achieved. The drawbacks of this technique include the need to isolate magnetically each bit location by ion etching, the slow decay time of the photoconductivity in CdS (10 μsec), and therefore relatively slow rate of writing and complexity in fabrication. Since this approach is relatively new, improvements in all of these areas are to be expected in the future.

C. SUMMARY AND COMPARISON OF RECORDING MATERIALS

Comparison of the recording materials cannot be adequately made without reference to the intended applications. Properties such as the storage life time, available signal-to-noise ratio, repeated cyclability, and complexity in fabrication are all important issues. However, as a general guide, the writing sensitivity and resolution play a dominant role in the selection of an optical recording medium, and therefore are specifically brought out in the present discussion.

In Fig. 8, we have plotted the required writing energy density in nanojoules per square micrometer and linear resolution in lines per millimeter for the various materials discussed in the previous sections. The diagonal lines indicate energy required on a per bit basis using the attainable resolution. On this scale, the photon-induced and photon-activated media fall in the range of 10^{-4}–10^{-2} nJ/bit and the thermally induced materials are between 10^{-1}–10 nJ/bit.

IV. Components for Optical Data Storage

In addition to the storage material, data storage systems require a number of other components, such as: modulators, deflectors, photodetectors, lasers, and page composers. The specific type of components and the requirements placed on them differ between the holographic and bit-by-bit systems.

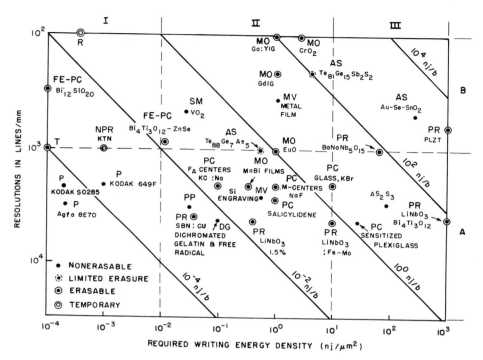

FIG. 8. Required writing energy density and achievable resolution for various types of proposed recording materials. The abbreviations referred to are: AS, amorphous semiconductor; DG, dichromated gelatin and free radical organic dye in polymer; FE–PC, ferroelectric–photoconductive; MV, metal vaporization; PR, photorefractive; MO, magnetooptic; NPR, nonlinear photorefractive; P, photographic; PC, photochromic; PP, photopolymer; SM, semimetal–metal transition; T, thermoplastic–photoconductor composite.

A. Modulators

The modulator is a component common to many electrooptic systems. It is used to superpose the information onto the optical carrier. For optical storage applications one is particularly interested in a number of its characteristics.

(a) Bandwidth, which is inversely related to the writing data rate, should be of the order of 1–20 MHz for the bit-by-bit system but less than 1 MHz for the holographic system.

(b) A large optical power handling capability is particularly important for holographic applications where a whole page is recorded at a time.

However, even for bit-by-bit operation peak optical powers of the order of 5–10 W may sometimes have to be handled by the modulator for high speed recording. The modulator occupies a position very close to the laser in the optical system, and the overall optical transmission of the train from laser to recording medium is typically the order of 10%. Therefore, the modulator has to handle considerably more power than is actually required for the recording process.

(c) Contrast or extinction ratio is the ratio between the optical powers transmitted by the modulator in the *on* and *off* conditions. Normally one uses the leakage light in the off condition for reading purposes and therefore that light level should be kept low in order not to affect the stored data upon repeated reading. Extinction ratios of 50–100 are desirable. Modulators that have been used extensively for data recording are of two types: electrooptic and acoustooptic.

1. *The Electrooptic Modulator*

The most popular electrooptic technique for beam modulation utilizes the linear electrooptic effect in optical crystals. The application of an electric field results in a change in the refractive index of the crystal proportional to the applied field. This is discussed in detail in the literature (Kaminow and Turner, 1966; Chen, 1970; Yariv, 1971). We consider here a transverse modulator as shown in Fig. 9.

In an electrooptic material such as KD^*P (KD_2PO_4) the modulating electric field is applied preferably along the z axis of the crystal, causing

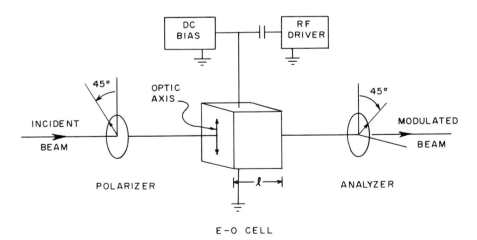

FIG. 9.   Electrooptic modulator.

the principal optical axes to rotate in the x–y plane by 45°; new axes are designated by x' and y'. The incident light propagates along the y' axis and is linearly polarized with its electric field at 45° with respect to the x' axis of the crystal. The applied electric field induces a net retardation between the x' and z polarizations in the crystal; thus, in general the light emerges elliptically polarized. A retardation of 180° ($\lambda/2$) produces linearly polarized light with the application of a half-wave retardation voltage, causing the beam polarization to be turned 90° with respect to the incident field. An analyzer oriented at 90° with respect to the incoming field follows the crystal; in that case on–off intensity modulation can be produced by applying the half-wave retardation voltage to the crystal.

In Jones's calculus notation we have for field components of the emerging beam

$$\begin{pmatrix} E_{x'}' \\ E_z' \end{pmatrix} = \frac{1}{2}\begin{pmatrix} 1 & -1 \\ -1 & 1 \end{pmatrix}\begin{pmatrix} e^{j\phi} & 0 \\ 0 & 1 \end{pmatrix}\begin{pmatrix} E_{x'} \\ E_z \end{pmatrix} \tag{43}$$

where $E_{x'} = E_z = E_0/\sqrt{2}$, $I_0 = |E_0|^2$ is the incident intensity, and the net retardation is given by

$$\phi = \frac{\pi n_0^3 r_{63}}{\lambda} L \frac{V}{b} - (n_0 - n_e)\frac{2\pi}{\lambda} L \tag{44}$$

where n_0 is the ordinary refractive index, n_e the extraordinary refractive index, V the applied voltage, λ the wavelength of light, and r_{63} the electrooptic coefficient.

The second term in ϕ is the natural birefringence. In the following we assume that the natural birefringence has been canceled out by means of a compensator which precedes the analyzer (Fig. 9) or by the technique of compensation using two crystals with their z axes rotated 90° with respect to each other. The light intensity emerging from the modulator can be obtained from Eq. (43)

$$I = |E_{x'}'|^2 + |E_z'|^2 = \tfrac{1}{2}|E_0|^2 (1 - \cos \phi) = I_0 \sin^2(\phi/2) \tag{45}$$

The modulation of intensity is not linear with applied voltage; to obtain linear modulation one could optically bias the modulator with a $\lambda/4$ plate and use only small modulation indices. For on–off applications, as in digital recording, the $\sin^2(\phi/2)$ characteristic presents no problems; in fact, it has the advantage that the rise time of the modulated light pulse is somewhat shorter than the rise time of the applied electric pulse.

The half-wave retardation voltage ($\phi = \pi$) is given by

$$V_\pi = (\lambda/n_0^3 r_{63})(b/L) \tag{46}$$

and thus V_π can be reduced by choosing a small geometrical factor b/L.

From a circuit viewpoint the electrooptic modulator can be represented as a lump capacitor with a high crystal resistance in parallel. For high speed modulation the circuit must be broadbanded by placing additional resistance R in parallel with the modulator.

The average power necessary to drive the modulator from the off to fully on condition is

$$P = V_\pi^2/2R \qquad (47)$$

For the modulator to be able to follow a pulse of width T we must make $T > 6RC$. The data rate is then given by

$$D = \frac{1}{6RC} \quad \text{(bits/sec)} \qquad (48)$$

where $C = K\epsilon_0 L$ is the modulator capacitance if a square cross section is assumed and the driving power

$$P = 3V_\pi^2 CD \qquad (49)$$

Typical values for a commercial modulator at $\lambda = 633$ nm are $C = 100$ pF and $V_\pi = 150$ V. The driving power for a 10 Mbit/sec data rate is about 67.5 W. The driving power can be reduced by optimizing the cross section to length ratio of the crystal.

For a crystal of square cross section the driving power can be written as

$$P = 3(\lambda/n_0^3 r_{63})^2 K\epsilon_0 (b^2/L)D \qquad (50)$$

To optimize the modulator design, the modulator crystal is placed between two lenses. Minimizing the cross section of the beam at the entrance and exit faces of the crystal also minimizes driving power. For a Gaussian beam the radius is given, as discussed in the Section II, by (Kogelnik and Li, 1966) Eq. (9). At the crystal faces, the beam radius w is given by

$$w^2(\pm L/2) = w_0^2[1 + (\lambda L/2n\pi w_0^2)^2] \qquad (51)$$

Taking derivatives of w^2 with respect to w_0 and equating it to zero, we have

$$\partial w^2(L/2)/\partial w_0 = 2w_0[1 - (\lambda L/2\pi n w_0^2)^2] = 0 \qquad (52)$$

The minimum values of beam radius are given by

$$w^2(L/2) = \lambda L/\pi n \qquad (53)$$

In practice one chooses the crystal cross section

$$b^2/L = S^2(4\lambda/\pi n) \qquad (54)$$

where S is a safety factor ranging between 3 and 5. Some sample designs are shown in Table VI.

The optimization procedure usually results in modulators with small optical apertures and may not be adequate for handling large optical powers. In particular electrooptic crystals such as $LiNbO_3$ and $LiTaO_3$ suffer from optical damage (photorefractive effect) at high laser power densities. This photorefractive effect, as discussed in the previous section, in turn decollimates the laser beam by wavefront distortion. To date most commercial electrooptic modulators that can handle suitable optical power for recording are made of ADP or KD*P which do not suffer from optical damage.

Another difficulty which arises in the operation of electrooptic modulators is the effect of power absorbed by the crystal. The loss factor tan δ for the modulating electric field and the optical beam absorption can cause small temperature rises. This is sufficient to cause significant changes in the natural birefringence of the crystal. As a result the extinction ratio of the modulator changes during operation. Elaborate servo loops or compensation techniques (Peters, 1965) are used to stabilize high speed modulators, unless the modulators are operated in tightly temperature-controlled ovens.

Modulators can be designed for minimum driving power for low optical power applications by using light waveguiding (integrated optics) techniques in electrooptic thin films (Hammer, 1975; Kaminow, 1975). The geometrical factors that dictate the bulk modulator design can be improved substantially because the optical beam is confined to the cross section of the waveguide modulator without diffraction. However, in

TABLE VI

COMPARISON OF ELECTROOPTIC MODULATORS[a]

	$LiTaO_3$	DKDP	$LiNbO_3$
Center frequency (GHz)	baseband	baseband	1.5
Δf (GHz)	1.3	0.22	1.5
b (mm)	0.25	0.75	0.5
L (mm)	10	57	5
S	2.9	4.3	11.6
$P/\Delta f$ (mW/MHz)	1.1	60	37

[a] Chen (1970).

general the power levels required for data recording are quite high, causing the optical power density in thin film modulators to be higher than comfortable; furthermore, at the present time the optical transmission of waveguide modulators is much lower than that of bulk modulators.

One can reduce the required optical power by allowing a longer dwell time of the beam during recording. By using a multichannel modulator one can record a word (several bits) at a time, thus no loss in throughput would result. Arrays of modulators lend themselves to fabrication by integrated optics techniques. Such arrays are also currently under consideration for use as one-dimensional page composers for holographic recording.

2. The Acoustooptic Modulator

The acoustooptic effect was first described by Debye and Sears (1932). In recent years it has generated increased interest for practical applications in laser modulation and deflection. New materials with excellent acoustic and optical properties have been developed. They have been the subject of several review articles (Pinnow, 1970; Spencer et al., 1967).

Basically the effect consists of a change in the refractive index of an optically transparent material in response to a mechanical strain induced by an acoustical wave via the photoelastic effect.

The change in refractive index can be related to the acoustic power, geometry, and material characteristics by

$$\Delta n = (M_2 10^7 P/2A)^{1/2} \tag{55}$$

where $M_2 = n^6 p^2/\rho v_a^3$ is a figure of merit for the material, p being the component of the photoelastic tensor, ρ the density in grams per cubic centimeters, v_a the acoustic velocity in centimeters per second, n the refractive index, P the acoustic power in watts, and A the cross-sectional area of the acoustic beam in square centimeters, M_2, the figure of merit, is frequently given relative to that of fused quartz. A list of representative acoustooptic materials and their properties is given in Table VII.

In an acoustooptic modulator a traveling acoustic wave induces in the material a sinusoidal phase grating of magnitude

$$\Delta \Phi = 2\pi l \Delta n/\lambda \tag{56}$$

and of period $\Lambda = v_a/f_a$ equal to acoustic wavelength, l is the interaction length, and f_a the acoustic frequency. The effect of the phase grating on

TABLE VII

ACOUSTOOPTIC PROPERTIES OF SELECTED MATERIALS[a]

Material	Range of transmission (μm)	λ (μm)	Refractive index	Acoustic wave	Acoustic velocity (10^5 cm/sec)	Acoustic attenuation (dB/cm GHz^2)	M_2 (10^{-18} sec^3/gm)	n at $P = 100$ W/cm^2
Water	0.2–0.9	0.633	1.33	Longitudinal	1.49	2400	126	2.5×10^{-4}
Fused quartz	0.2–4.5	0.633	1.46	Longitudinal	5.96	12	1.56	2.7×10^{-5}
Dense flint glass (SF-59)	0.46–2.5	0.633	1.95	Longitudinal	3.26	1200	19	9.7×10^{-5}
LiTaO$_3$	0.4–5	0.633	2.18	Longitudinal	6.19	0.1	1.37	2.6×10^{-5}
LiNbO$_3$	0.4–4.5	0.633	2.20	Longitudinal	6.57	0.15	7.0	6×10^{-5}
α-HIO$_3$	0.3–1.8	0.633	1.986	Longitudinal	2.44	10	86	2×10^{-4}
PbMoO$_4$	0.42–5.5	0.633	2.26	Longitudinal	3.63	15	36	1.3×10^{-4}
TeO$_2$	0.35–5	0.633	2.26	Shear	0.616	290	793	6.3×10^{-4}

[a] Pinnow (1970) and Uchida and Niizeki (1973).

an optical beam at normal or almost normal incidence to it is to diffract part of the light into higher diffraction orders.

Under the conditions of a long interaction length $l > \Lambda^2/\lambda$ one can operate in the Bragg scattering regime, in which it is possible to diffract the entire incident beam into one diffraction order as shown in Fig. 10. The Bragg angle is given by

$$\sin \theta_B = \lambda/2n\Lambda \tag{57}$$

and the intensity of light in the first order is

$$I = I_0 \sin^2(\Delta\Phi/2) \tag{58}$$

where I_0 is the incident intensity. For $\Delta\Phi = 2$ rad, approximately 70% of the incident light is diffracted into the first order.

From Eqs. (55) and (56) it is found that the acoustic power required is roughly proportional to the fraction I/I_0 of diffracted light up to about $\Delta\Phi = 2$ rad.

To insure good separation between the diffracted and undiffracted light beams we must make the Bragg angle larger or equal to the diffraction limited angle θ_d of the optical beam.

Thus $$\theta_B \gtrsim \theta_d \tag{59}$$

For a Gaussian laser and small beam angles we have, from Eqs. (11) and (57),

$$\lambda/2n\Lambda \gtrsim 2\lambda/n\pi w_0 \tag{60}$$

or

$$f_a \gtrsim 4v_a/\pi w_0 \tag{61}$$

The bandwidth of the modulator can be computed from the transit time of acoustic beam across the optical beam. The rise time of the

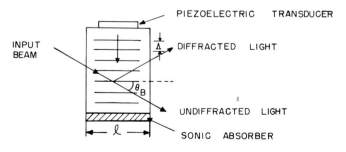

FIG. 10.   Acoustooptic modulator.

diffracted light pulse is given by (Maydan, 1970b)

$$t_r = 1.3(w_0/v_a) \tag{62}$$

for a Gaussian laser beam. Using the relation between rise time and bandwidth $\Delta f = 0.35/t_r$ one obtains

$$\Delta f_a = 0.27(v_a/w_0) \tag{63}$$

Combining Eq. (61) with (63) one has

$$f_a \simeq 5\Delta f_a \tag{64}$$

Thus the bandwidth of the modulator is limited to about 20% of the acoustic frequency. At the present time available acoustooptic materials and transducers allow operation at a maximum acoustic frequency f_a of about 1 GHz. It can be shown that under optimum conditions (Hammer, 1975) the theoretical driving power for the modulator for 70% diffraction efficiency is given by

$$P/\Delta f_a = 50.8\lambda_0^3/nv_a M_2 \quad \text{(mW/MHz)} \tag{65}$$

All quantities in Eq. (65) are in cgs units.

Table VIII gives values of acoustic drive power per unit bandwidth for modulators made with typical acoustooptic materials.

To compute the electrical driving power one must take into account the losses that occur in the piezoelectric transducer in the conversion of electrical to acoustic power. Transducer conversion losses of 1 dB have been obtained at 350 MHz, however at microwave frequencies conversion losses increase to 20 dB.

Acoustooptic modulators present great advantages for low bandwidth applications. They are easier to fabricate, are insensitive to temperature changes, require low drive power, and have very high extinction ratios

TABLE VIII

COMPUTED VALUES OF SPECIFIC ACOUSTIC POWER FOR ACOUSTOOPTIC BULK
MODULATORS AT $\lambda_0 = 0.633 \ \mu\text{m}$

Material	M_2 ($10^{-18} \ \text{sec}^3/\text{gm}$)	n	v_a ($10^5 \ \text{cm/sec}$)	$(P_a/\Delta f_a)$ (mW/MHz)
Water	126	1.33	1.49	0.5
Fused quartz	1.56	1.46	5.96	9.5
Dense flint glass	19	1.95	3.26	1.06
LiNbO$_3$	7	2.2	6.57	1.27
PbMoO$_4$	36	2.26	3.63	0.43
TeO$_2$	793	2.26	0.616	0.12

(up to 10,000). However, they introduce a higher optical insertion loss than electrooptical modulators.

B. DEFLECTORS

The light deflection system provides access to various storage locations of an optical recording. As such it must meet the requirements of large accessing capacity, speed, and low power consumption. These factors are not always compatible and in practice one must reach a compromise. Numerous schemes for light deflection are in existence; they utilize mechanical motion, the acoustooptic, or the electrooptic effect.

For bit-by-bit memories with capacities of the order of 10^8-10^{11} bits, one must rely largely on mechanical devices for scanning and/or some motion of the recording medium. Random access to a specific block of information in the memory is desirable for efficient interaction with the computer system. The random-access feature excludes to a large extent rotating mirror systems which scan the beam sequentially. However, combinations of random access and sequential beam deflection are possible to meet access time requirements.

For holographic memories with capacities of 10^8-10^9 bits one can utilize two-dimensional deflectors which can address 10^4-10^5 page locations with access times of 0.1–1 msec. This is now possible to achieve with acoustooptic or with digital electrooptic deflectors (Meyer et al., 1972). Commercially available one-dimensional acoustooptic deflectors can readily access one of 400 positions in 10 μsec.

To define the scanning capability of a deflector one introduces a quantity called the number of resolvable spots, which is invariant to size transformations the optical beam may undergo in an optical system without aberration and vignetting following the deflector. The number of resolvable spots N_R is given by the ratio between the maximum deflection angle ϕ_m and the diffraction-limited angle corresponding to the deflector aperture (Lee and Zook, 1968)

$$N_R = \phi_m W / e\lambda \qquad (66)$$

when W is the aperture of the deflector, λ the wavelength of light, and e a number of the order of unity which depends on the criterion used for resolution and the uniformity of illumination. A systematic survey of the present and anticipated performance of various light beam deflectors was undertaken by Zook (1974). A tutorial introduction to laser scanning systems was given by Beiser (1974). Mechanical deflectors such as rotating mirrors can be made to scan sequentially at very high speeds; the maximum rotational speed being limited only by the stiffness of the material. Mirrors made of beryllium with scan lines of 10,000 spots have been used in a scanner rotating at several hundred thousand rpm in low air pressure. Newer techniques utilize smooth cylindrical or spherical rotors on which reflective holograms (Beiser, 1973) are placed to serve the function of hololenses and focus the beam. Such hologram scanners can operate at normal air pressure at high speeds because they have extremely low aerodynamic drag. In general, to achieve a large resolution one must use large size spinning mirrors which must be accompanied by a reduction in mirror speed and a consequent increase in scan time.

Galvanometers are capable of random access. They can be programmed by suitable input signal processing to access a given position in minimum time with no overshoot (Brosens, 1971).

The access time for a moving-coil galvanometer can be minimized for a given resolution by varying the mirror dimensions. The final result given by Zook (1974) is

$$N_R \propto \tau_a^{168/143} \tag{67}$$

depends only on material parameters, magnetic field strength, and heat transfer parameter. In the above equation, τ_a is the access time.

Acoustooptic deflectors operate on the same principle as the modulators. To change the deflection angle one simply changes the acoustic frequency f_a.

The number of resolvable spots N_R for a given deflector of width W can be found as follows.

The Bragg diffraction angle for small angles is given by Eq. (57). The variation in θ_B due to a variable acoustic frequency is the deflection angle

$$\Delta\theta_B = -\lambda\Delta\Lambda/n\Lambda^2 \tag{68}$$

Assuming uniform illumination the diffraction angle for the optical beam is, from Eq. (11),

$$\theta_d = \lambda/nW \tag{69}$$

Thus the number of resolvable spots is

$$N_R = \Delta\theta_B/\theta_d \cong W\Delta f_a/v_a = \Delta f_a \tau_a \tag{70}$$

where Δf_a is the electrical bandwidth of the piezoelectric transducer, driver, and deflector.

Typically $\Delta f_a = f_0/2$ where f_0 is the center acoustic frequency of the deflector. To increase the number of spots one must use a material with low acoustic velocity. However, materials with low velocity have also high acoustic attenuation, thus only small apertures W can be used. It is found that an attenuation of 3–4 dB across the length W does not substantially affect the diffracted optical beam. Zook (1974) has computed the performance of acoustooptic deflectors assuming an aperture of 2 cm and an acoustic loss of 4 dB for a number of materials of importance in practice (Fig. 11). Materials with high figure of merit M_2 require low drive power. Typically, one requires several watts of electrical power for driving a deflector made of tellurium dioxide (TeO_2) or lead molybdate ($PbMoO_4$) and having $N_R \cong 100$.

Electrooptic deflectors based on the linear electrooptic effects are practical only for deflection over a small number of spots. This is mainly limited by power considerations and the high voltages that are needed to drive the deflectors (in the kilovolt range). The deflector consists of a sequence of prisms whose refractive index is controlled by the applied electric field. There are no transit time limitations for the electrooptical

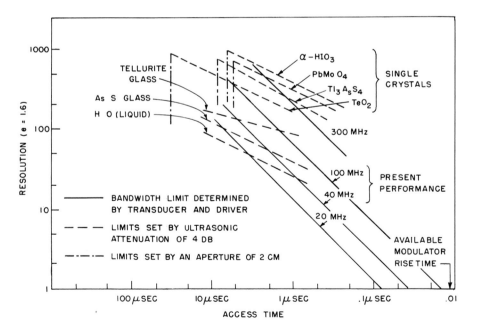

FIG. 11.   Resolution and access time of various acoustooptic deflectors. After Zook (1974).

deflector and the response is almost instantaneous, mostly limited by the current which can be supplied by the driver.

The resolution can be optimized by focusing the laser beam through the deflector to minimize the required drive power for a given resolution N_R. Zook (1974) has shown that this results in a relation

$$(N_R^{5/2}/\tau_a P) \propto (n^7 r^2 / \epsilon \lambda^3) \tag{71}$$

where P is the maximum available power from the power supply, r the appropriate linear electrooptic coefficient, and ϵ the dielectric constant. This relation is shown in Fig. 12 for a power $P = 1$ kW for a number of electrooptic materials KD_2PO_4 (labeled KD^*P), $LiNbO_3$ (labeled LN), and $Sr_{0.75}Ba_{0.25}Nb_2O_6$ (labeled SBN).

Another deflector of interest is the electrooptical digital deflector. The basic building block of this type of deflector is an electrooptic modulator followed by a birefringent crystal such as calcite. The light beam will exit the crystal at one of two possible locations depending on whether the electrooptic modulator is activated. Such a deflector, using liquid nitrobenzene as the electrooptic medium, has been thoroughly investi-

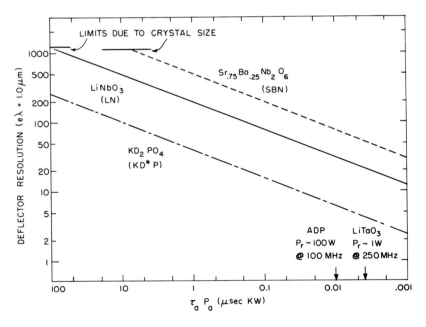

FIG. 12. Electrooptic deflectors performance. τ_a is the random access time and P_a is the total available power. After Zook (1974).

gated by Schmidt and Thust (1969). The quadratic electrooptic effect (Kerr effect) in nitrobenzene is used to switch the polarization. The switching electrodes and the calcite prisms are all immersed in nitrobenzene; because the refractive indices of calcite and of nitrobenzene are very close the reflection losses are very low. A 20-stage digital deflector has been recently described (Meyer *et al.*, 1972) with an optical transmission of 79% at a wavelength of $\lambda = 520$ nm. This deflector is capable of deflecting a laser beam into a raster of 1024 by 1024 positions at a deflection rate of 500 kHz. Switching voltages are of the order of 2–8 kV depending on the size and location of the state in the digital chain. Larger apertures are necessary in the later stages of the deflector.

C. Photodetectors

Photodetectors operating in the spectral range 0.3–1 μm (Seib and Aukerman, 1973) are of interest for optical storage applications. The requirements placed on the detectors are high sensitivity, fast response time, and low noise. Other practical considerations include small size, low power consumption, low voltage operation, low cost, and extended life.

The detectors that are applicable fall into three categories: photomultipliers, silicon photodiodes, and avalanche silicon photodiodes. Other detectors, such as photoconductors, phototransistors, and photofets, are either too slow or too insensitive to be of wide interest.

Photodetectors convert optical energy into electrical signals; they are square law detectors and respond to the intensity of light averaged over many optical cycles. The photocurrent generated at the detector can be expressed as

$$I_{ph} = \eta(eP/\hbar\omega) \tag{72}$$

where η is the quantum efficiency in electrons/photons, e the electronic charge magnitude, P the incident optical power, $\hbar = h/2\pi$ where h is Planck's constant, and ω the optical radian frequency.

In the detection of signals we are interested in a high signal-to-noise ratio in order to obtain a low error probability.

The noise sources are of several kinds: shot noise, thermal (Johnson) noise, and excess multiplication noise, besides the medium noise discussed in Section II,B,4.

The mean square value of shot noise current can be written as

$$\bar{I}_{sh}^2 = (2eI_{ph} + 2eI_D)\Delta f \tag{73}$$

where I_D is the dark current of the photodetector and Δf is the bandwidth. The mean square thermal noise current can be expressed as

$$\bar{I}_T^2 = 4kT\Delta f/R_{eq} \qquad (74)$$

where k is Boltzmann's constant, T the equivalent system temperature which takes into account the thermal noise from the detector and the following amplifier, and R_{eq} the equivalent load resistance consisting of detector internal resistance in shunt with the actual load resistance and amplifier input resistance.

If the detector has internal gain, such as in an avalanche photodiode or a photomultiplier, both the signal current and the shot noise current are amplified whereas the thermal noise remains the same.

The voltage signal-to-noise ratio at the output of the photodetector, rms signal voltage to rms noise voltage can be written as (Anderson and McMurtry, 1966; Melchior et al., 1970)

$$\frac{S}{N} = \frac{(\eta e/\hbar\omega)(P/\sqrt{2})}{\left\{\left[2e\left(I_D + \frac{\eta e}{\hbar\omega}P\right)\right]F + \frac{4kT}{M^2 R_{eq}}\right\}^{1/2} \Delta f^{1/2}} \qquad (75)$$

where M is the internal gain in the detector, and F is the excess noise factor which is the ratio of the signal-to-noise ratio at the input to that at the output of the multiplication process. The signal is assumed to be 100% sinusoidally modulated.

Silicon semiconductor photodiodes are an important class of detectors which are suitable for optical storage applications. In the following we will analyze the detection capability of a photodiode without internal gain ($M = 1$).

The equivalent circuit of the diode including the load resistor is shown in Fig. 13, where R_P is the internal resistance of the photodiode usually of the order of 1 to 100 MΩ, R_S is the series resistance of the diode and is generally less than a few tenths of ohms, C_P is the junction capacitance which is a function of bias voltage, and R_L is the load resistance, including the amplifier input resistance. In a complete circuit analysis one must also add to C_P the input capacity C_A of the following amplifier. The detection bandwidth Δf is a function of the product $C_T R_{eq}$, where $C_T = C_P + C_A$.

In an ideal case the dark current is zero and R_L can be made large enough in narrowband applications to make the signal shot noise predominant. In that case we have from Eq. (75)

$$\frac{S}{N} = \frac{(\eta e/\hbar\omega)(P/\sqrt{2})}{[2(\eta e^2/\hbar\omega)P\Delta f]^{1/2}} = \frac{1}{2}\left(\frac{\eta P}{\hbar\omega\Delta f}\right)^{1/2} \qquad (76)$$

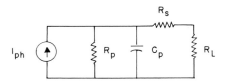

FIG. 13.   Photodiode equivalent circuit.

The rms power required for unity signal-to-noise ratio, called the noise equivalent power NEP, is given by

$$\text{NEP} = 2\sqrt{2}(\hbar\omega\Delta f/\eta) \tag{77}$$

and the ideal detectivity for a bandwidth $\Delta f = 1$ Hz and $\eta = 1$ is given by

$$D = 1/\text{NEP} = (2\sqrt{2}\hbar\omega)^{-1} \quad \text{W}^{-1}\text{Hz} \tag{78}$$

The quantity D for the ideal case is plotted in Fig. 14 along with the detectivity of a number of practical photodetectors.

The detectivity D for nonideal photodiodes falls short by about 6 orders of magnitude from the ideal case. The discrepancy is due to nonunity quantum efficiency and nonzero dark current.

Consider now the regime in which the dark current dominates. This is usually the case for real diodes operating in a relatively narrow detection bandwidth. The signal-to-noise ratio is given by

$$\frac{S}{N} = \frac{(\eta e/\hbar\omega)(P/\sqrt{2})}{(2eI_D\Delta f)^{1/2}} \tag{79}$$

The detectivity is now given by

$$D = (\eta e/\hbar\omega)/(2eI_D)^{1/2} \quad \text{W}^{-1} \text{ Hz}^{1/2} \tag{80}$$

The peak power required for a given signal-to-noise ratio is now found from

$$P = \sqrt{2}(\Delta f^{1/2}/D)(S/N) \tag{81}$$

As an example consider a commercial photodiode made by United Detector Technology, Inc., PIN-6D. Its detectivity at $\lambda = 0.85$ μm is equal to 1.5×10^{12} W^{-1} Hz$^{1/2}$ corresponding to a maximum dark current of 1 μA. To obtain a signal-to-noise ratio of 10 in a bandwidth of 10 kHz we must have a peak incident power P $\sim$ 9 $\times$ 10^{-10} W. The above analysis cannot be extended to a wide band system because of the assumption of negligible thermal noise.

To assess the relative weight of the thermal noise in a photodiode without internal gain we rewrite the noise term in the following form (at low incident power levels)

$$\bar{I}_n^2 = 2e[I_d + (2kT/eR_{eq})]\Delta f \tag{82}$$

At room temperature $2kT/e \sim 50$ mV, if the amplifier has a 3 dB noise figure we must take $2kT/e = 100$ mV. For the case of the PIN-6D photodiode the shot noise dominates as long as $R_{eq} > 10^5$ Ω. The equivalent resistance is largely determined by the load resistance. The bandwidth (3 dB point) is then given by

$$\Delta f = 1/(2\pi R_L C_T) \tag{83}$$

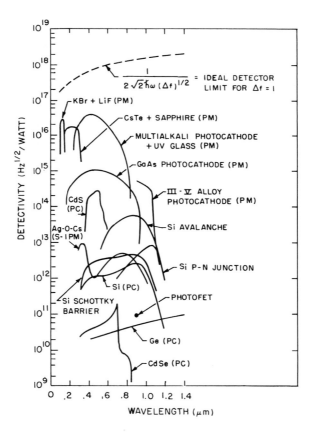

FIG. 14.   Detectivity of photodetectors. After Seib and Aukerman (1973).

The capacity of the photodiode is 28 pF at a bias voltage of 50 V; including the amplifier capacitance we assume $C_T = 40$ pF. To obtain a bandwidth of 10 kHz we require $R_L \leq 4 \times 10^5$ Ω, a condition which is consistent with our assumption that shot noise dominates.

If a broader band is required as in optical memory applications ($\Delta f \sim$ 10 MHz) one must reduce the value of the load resistance. This enhances the thermal noise component. For the same diode considered before with $\Delta f = 10$ MHz we obtain from Eq. (83), $R_{eq} = 400$ Ω. The equivalent thermal noise current $2kT/eR_{eq}$ is now equal to 250 μA which is much larger than the dark current. The peak power required for a $S/N = 10$ is equal to $P = 10$ μW. Thus even when one is thermal noise–limited the required power level at the detector is still quite low.

For MnBi with a $K = 0.17$ factor using differential detection with an analyzer angle $\theta = 45°$ we obtain the required power level for reading from Eq. (82), $P_{read} = 250$ μW. Thus the reading power level is not too high even for a bit rate of 10 Mbit/sec and will not affect the stored information upon repeated reading.

The signal-to-noise ratio computed in all cases above assumes good recording material uniformity. If substantial material variations occur on a scale comparable to the bit size, the signal-to-noise ratio is essentially given by Eq. (30) as described in Section II,B under readout considerations. Furthermore if a laser is used in the readout process, laser noise must also be included under the various noise sources appearing in the signal-to-noise computation. However, laser noise can be largely reduced by differential detection techniques (Treves, 1967; Aagard, 1973).

The silicon avalanche photodiode is capable of wideband detection as well as high sensitivity by virtue of the fact that it has an internal gain mechanism.

The avalanche photodiode operates at sufficiently high electric fields in the depletion region to impart an energy greater than the bandgap energy to the photogenerated carriers. This results in carrier multiplication or avalanche. The multiplication gain M is of the order of 10^2 to 10^4 in silicon diodes. In the multiplication process excess noise is generated described by the factor $F = M^x$ where x lies between 0 and 1. The advantage of the avalanche photodiode is in its ability to detect over a wide band signals with high sensitivity. This can be seen from Eq. (75) in which the thermal noise is reduced by a factor $1/M^2$ relative to the shot noise. An optimum multiplication factor exists for which the thermal noise about equals the shot noise; this is due to the fact that the shot noise rises with M^x. The signal-to-noise ratio rises with M first but begins to fall off after the optimum M is reached. It is seen from Fig. 14

that the detectivity of silicon avalanche photodiodes is about an order of magnitude higher than that of silicon junction photodiodes.

Avalanche photodiodes require tight temperature control because the avalanche voltage is temperature dependent.

Photomultipliers have high internal gain ($>10^5$) and very low dark currents, therefore their detectivity approaches the ideal detector limit. Their performance can be further improved by cooling to reduce the dark current. The excess noise factor F for a photomultiplier is very low, of the order of 1.5. Bandwidths of 100 MHz are readily attainable with commercial photomultipliers. The disadvantage of photomultipliers is their relatively large size and the high voltage required for operation.

For holographic applications one uses a photodetector array onto which a whole page of the memory plane is projected. Thus the number of elements in the detector array must equal the number of bits in a page ($\sim 10^4$). The required sensitivity for a signal-to-noise ratio of 10 is about 1 pJ per bit, corresponding to about 10^6 photons at a visible wavelength. It is possible to operate photodetectors in the charge storage mode (Weckler, 1967); in this mode of operation the detector such as a photodiode or a phototransistor is normally backbiased and thus is equivalent to a capacitor. During illumination an amount of charge is removed from the capacitor proportional to the integrated number of photons incident on the detector. All photodetectors are illuminated in parallel for an integration period of 1–10 μsec. Thus the amount of optical power per bit is 1–10 μW/bit or a total power per page of 0.01–0.1 W. To account for optical losses in the system, including the diffraction efficiency of the holograms, a read power of at least 1 W is necessary. To compute the data rate we note that in principle, one could read out all 10^4 bits serially within a few microseconds. However, that would correspond to 10 Gbit/sec which is hard to handle at the present time by logical circuits. Therefore, one addresses a word (16 to 32 bits) at a time with corresponding data rates of 16 to 32 Mbit/sec. Recently photosensitive arrays consisting of MOS photocapacitors electronically scanned by charge coupled devices (CCD) have been demonstrated to operate up to 40 Mbit rates (Gandolfo et al., 1975). The sensitivity of these devices is compatible with holographic memory requirements.

D. Lasers

Lasers have unique properties, such as high brightness, coherence, and narrow spectral width, which make them particularly suited for optical recording applications. Because the linear packing density which can be achieved both in bit-by-bit and holographic recording is directly proportional to the wavelength, one is only interested in lasers operating in the visible and near infrared part of the spectrum. Some of the important considerations in the selection of a laser are: spatial coherence (usually single-transverse mode), low noise, power stability, small size, weight, adequate life, and cost.

The useful lasers fall into four categories: gas, solid dielectric, semiconductor, and tunable lasers. Their important properties are summarized in Table IX.

Gas lasers are the best developed to date. In particular the popular HeNe laser emitting at $\lambda = 0.633$ μm is by far the best engineered laser and has a lifetime in excess of 10,000 hr. Its cw power level (up to 50 mW) is adequate for recording at high rates on a large number of the materials described in Section III. Argon or krypton ion lasers emit in the blue-green and red part of the spectrum and are capable of delivering very high powers (up to 15 W). Recent improvements have extended the lifetime of ion lasers to about 5000 hr.

In addition to cw operation both the HeNe and argon lasers can be internally modulated by cavity dumping (Maydan, 1970a) or mode-locking (Smith, 1970). A mode-locked laser provides a train of high power narrow pulses (<1 nsec) equally spaced in time. In a recording process one selects particular pulses out of the train by means of an internal or external modulator. The pulse width cannot be varied in a mode-locked laser.

In a cavity-dumped laser a fast acoustooptic modulator is used to dump out the power circulating inside the laser cavity. The pulse width can be varied in the range of 15 nsec to cw with the narrower pulses having considerably higher power. Both mode-locked gas lasers and cavity-dumped lasers have been used for thermally induced recording (Haskal *et al.*, 1974; Maydan, 1971). More recently a combination mode-locked cavity-dumped laser was developed (Roberts *et al.*, 1974) for use in very high speed recorders. The metal ion He–Cd laser can provide up to 50 mW in the near ultraviolet 0.325 μm. The disadvantage of all gas lasers is the relatively low efficiency with which they convert electrical to optical energy, typically 0.1 to 0.01% (Bloom, 1966).

Solid dielectric lasers include the ruby laser emitting at 0.694 μm, and the Nd:YAG and the Nd–glass laser emitting at 1.06 μm. Ruby lasers operate usually in the pulsed mode and can deliver very short pulses of high power by Q-switching. However the pulse repetition rate is limited to a few pulses per second. Single-mode Q-switched lasers have been used for holographic recording on MnBi where high power and short pulse (<20 nsec) duration are necessary (Mezrich, 1969; Lee and Chen, 1972). The peak power used for recording a page of 10^4 bits is about 10 kW when all losses in the system are accounted for. To achieve a data rate of 10 Mbit/sec a pulse repetition rate of at least 100 pps is necessary. This is beyond the capability of ruby lasers. Nd: YAG lasers can operate cw with a single mode output power of up to 50 W. They can also operate in the pulsed mode, the repetitively Q-switched, mode-locked, and the cavity-dumped mode. By Q-switching the laser with an acoustooptic switch one can achieve repetition rates of up to 50 kHz with pulse width of 0.2–2 μsec and peak powers of a few kilowatts. Thus Nd: YAG lasers appear attractive for holographic applications although the wavelength 1.06 μm is somewhat long. Frequency doubling of the Nd: YAG lasers has also been achieved by placing a nonlinear crystal inside a laser cavity. The efficiency of solid dielectric lasers is of the order of a few percent.

Semiconductor p-n junction lasers are currently undergoing very rapid development as potential light sources for optical communication systems. Semiconductor lasers made of a single material such as GaAs emit in the near infrared (0.9 μm) and are called homojunction lasers. Homojunction lasers operate cw only at 77 K or in the pulsed mode with very low duty cycle at room temperature due to the fact that they require very high current densities (~50,000 A/cm²). Single GaAs lasers and arrays of up to 20 lasers have been fabricated and used for thermomagnetic writing and reading on EuO at cryogenic temperatures (Fan and Greiner, 1968; Wieder and Werlich, 1971). This will be discussed in a later section.

Double heterostructure lasers (DH) consisting of $Al_x Ga_{1-x}A$–GaAs–$Al_x Ga_{1-x}As$ display an index of refraction profile junction which acts as an optical waveguide. As a result of a better definition of the active region of the laser the threshold current density required for lasing is greatly reduced (1000 to 6000 A/cm²) and the laser can operate cw at room temperature (Hayashi and Panish, 1970).

A typical cw power obtained with DH lasers is 100 mW with a current of 1–2 A (Panish, 1975). Laser diodes have many advantages: (1) they can be modulated directly up to a few hundred megahertz by pulsing the driving current, (2) their efficiency is very high, (3) they are physically small and can be integrated into laser arrays, and (4) their cost is very low (a few dollars). At the present, a lifetime of a few thousand hours at cw operation has been demonstrated. It is anticipated that the lifetime will be increased to at least 20,000 h. Some of the disadvantages of semiconductor lasers are: (1) relatively low output, (2) poor temporal coherence (10 Å spectral linewidth), (3) large beamwidth and generally

TABLE IX

CHARACTERISTICS OF SOME COMMERCIALLY AVAILABLE LASERS FOR OPTICAL RECORDING

Laser wavelength (Å)	Active medium	Output power (W) (pulse energy J)		Beam diameter (mm)	Beam divergence (mrad)	Pulse rep. rate (pps); pulse width (μsec)	Special features
		Single mode	Multi mode				
A. Gas Lasers							
3250	HeCd	0.050		1.5	0.5		
3371	N_2		(0.01)	3	5	100; 0.008	
3371	N_2		(0.006)	6	25	50; 0.01	600 KW peak power
3507–7793	Kr	0.75 All lines		1.6	0.6		
3511–5287	Ar	8 All lines	50×10^{-6}	1.4	0.5		100 W peak UV
3645	Xe			2.5	5.0	10; 1	
4420	HeCd	(10^{-3})		0.8	1.0	10^6; 0.5	A-O modulation
4420	HeCd	0.020		0.8	1.0		
4579–6764	Ar/Kr	0.75 All lines		1.5	0.6		
0.46–0.56 μm	He–Se	0.010		0.8	1.0		Multiwavelength output
4955–5393	Xe	(0.15×10^{-3})		2.4	1.0	60; 0.5	300 W peak power
6328	HeNe	0.050		2.0	0.7		
B. Solid Dielectric Lasers							
0.26 μm	Nd:YAG		0.1	4	6–8		0.2 KW peak, Q-sw frequency doubled
0.53 μm	Nd:glass		(2)	30	3	2/60; 0.03	3 KW peak, Q-sw.
0.53 μm	Nd:YAG		2	4	6–8		1.5 KW peak, Q-sw.
0.67 μm	Nd:YAG		1	4	6–8		
6943	Ruby	(5)	(50)	8	10	2; 1000	
6943	Ruby		(100)	18	5–7	6/60; 1500	

Laser wavelength (Å)	Active medium	Line width (Å)	Output power (W)	Driving current (A) threshold	Driving current (A) peak	Beam divergence (mrad)	Pulse rep. rate (pps); pulse width (µsec)	Special feature
6943	Ruby		(15)	18	0.9		20/60; 15–20 × 10⁻³	
6943	Ruby		(0.3)	18	0.9		1/60; 0.1 × 10⁻³	
6943	Ruby/glass		(6)	18	0.9		20/60; 3–5 × 10⁻³	3 GW peak
6943–1.06 mm	Ruby/glass		(200)	3	5		1; 5,000	
1.06 mm	Nd:YAG	10	200	2	1.5			
1.06 mm	Nd:YAG	50	500	6	10			Cascade amp.
1.06 mm	Nd:YAG	(2)	(15)	5			20,000; 0.2	
1.06 mm	Nd:YAG	6 GW peak	(100)	25	3–5		0.2/60; 0.015	
1.06 mm	Nd:YAG		1 GW peak				15 0.010	
1.06 mm	Nd:YAG			7			150 × 10⁶; 0.0008	Mode locked

C. Semiconductor Lasers

Laser wavelength (Å)	Active medium	Line width (Å)	Output power (W)	Driving current (A) threshold	Driving current (A) peak	Beam divergence (mrad)	Pulse rep. rate (pps); pulse width (µsec)	Special feature
8560	GaAs	.60	1.2	1.5	7	3° × 3°	cw; 1	
8560	Array GaAs	60	2200 peak	5	65		13 × 10³; 1	
8550 ± 50	Array GaAs	300	37 peak		7		10 × 10³; 0.2	
8525 ± 50	Modulus GaAs	100	28 peak		7	570	10 × 10³; 2	
9050	Stacked GaSa	20	300 peak	10	40	125	10³; 0.2	
9000	GaAlAs	3 µm	2 peak	10	30	5–10	00–10⁶; 10–500	
9040	Array GaAs	80	480 peak	8	25	420	10²; 0.2	

D. Tunable Lasers

Laser wavelength (Å)	Active medium	Pumping method	Power output (W)	Beam diameter (mm)	Beam divergence (mrad)	Pulse rep. rate (pps); pulse width (µsec)	Special feature
3700–6500	Organic dye	N_2 laser	4–7 × 10³	1	1	100; .001	
3800–7500	Organic dye	Coax flashlamp	10⁵	5	2	50; 0.25	
4400–6500	Organic dye	A_r laser	10% of pump	3.7	2		cw
5250–7000	Organic dye	A_r laser	1.5				cw
5300–6700	Dye	Nd:YAG laser	400	0.25	1.7	75; 0.1	
5800–6300	Organic dye	Ion laser	0.1	1	0.5		cw
6500–3400	$LiNbO_3$	Nd:YAG	400	0.5	4.6	75; 0.1	Parametric oscillation

elliptically shaped beam output requiring special optics for focusing the laser. It is expected that the rapid progress in semiconductor lasers will stimulate their use in future optical memories. Recent advance in the use of guided wave distributed feedback (DF) technique provide improved laser characteristics and is well worth noting (Nakamura and Yariv, 1976).

Tunable lasers are of two kinds: dye lasers pumped by argon or nitrogen lasers and parametric oscillators in which a nonlinear crystal such as lithium niobate $LiNbO_3$ or "banana" $Ba_2NaNb_5O_{15}$ are pumped by Nd:YAG laser.

The dye lasers use active fluorescent materials such as Rhodamine 6 G or B in a solvent. The pumping is optical and therefore the overall efficiency is low (< about 0.1%). With several dyes it is possible to tune over the entire visible range. The cw power of dye lasers is of the order of a few milliwats to 1 W. In pulsed operation one can obtain 100 W peak power and pulses in the picosecond range. Tunable lasers may be useful for optical storage materials which require several wavelengths in operation, such as photochromics.

For bit-by-bit applications gas lasers are adequate up to very high data rates (~10 Mbit/sec). With a typical sensitivity of the material of 1 nJ/μm^2 only 10 mW are required at the bit location; accounting for all losses in the system, 100 mW of laser power is sufficient.

For holographic applications one may require high peak powers to write a page if a thermal effect is used. However in photon-activated photorefractive materials more modest powers are required because the optical power is integrated over the exposure time to produce the recording effect. Thus in $LiNbO_3$ with 1 nJ/μm^2 one can use a 1 W pulse with a duration of 10 μsec for recording a page containing 10^4 bits. This is well within the capability of argon lasers.

The laser power outputs and wavelengths of some typical commercially available lasers are summarized in Fig. 15.

E. Page Composers

The page composer is a component specific to holographic memories; its function is to convert the incoming electrical binary signals into a one- or two-dimensional spatial modulation of the object beam used for holographic recording. In its simplest form the page composer consists of an array of electrically controlled light shutters with the number of shutters equal to the number of bits in a page of the hologram (~10^4).

There are many requirements imposed on page composers for large

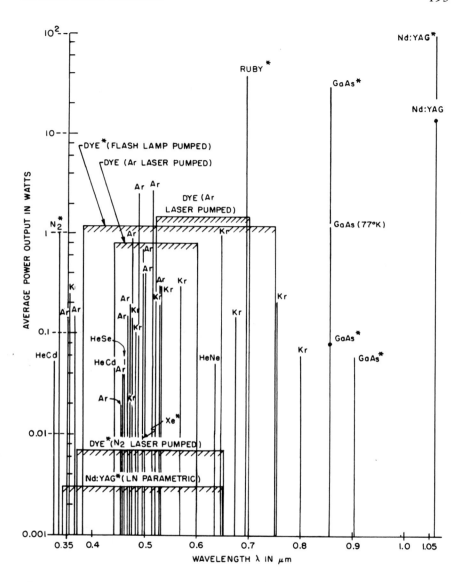

FIG. 15. Power and spectral characteristics of commercial lasers. Data taken from *Laser Focus Buyers' Guide* (1975).

capacity holographic memories. The most important consideration is speed; one must be able to introduce the data into the composer, perform the recording, and erase the data during 1 cycle time of the memory. Recording at a 10 Mbit/sec rate with 10^4 bits per page requires a page composer that operates in less than 1 msec. The data are usually introduced serially (possibly one line at a time), thus temporary memory must be provided by the composer until the whole page is filled and recorded; a storage time of a few milliseconds is sufficient. An optical angular aperture of the order of $\pm 20°$ is frequently required to accommodate nonparallel deflected light. The latter requirement excluded electrooptic crystals with anisotropic effects. It is also desirable to have an optical efficiency higher than 50% to reduce laser power requirements; this excludes thin magnetooptic films for this application because of low diffraction efficiency. Optical contrast (one to zero ratio) of at least 10:1 is also required. Finally, other desirable features are stability, lack of fatigue, and uniformity. Because of the numerous requirements the page composer must meet, no satisfactory solution exists at the present in spite of the large number of approaches pursued so far. Table X adapted from Roberts (1972) and Chen and Zook (1975) summarizes the various effects and materials considered for page composers.

One of the more promising approaches to date is that using PLZT ferroelectric ceramics. These ceramics are transparent materials which have very strong electrooptic properties. They are fabricated by hotpressing mixtures of lead zirconate, lead titanate, and lanthanum. These materials are easy to obtain and are inexpensive. They have been widely studied (Haertling and Land, 1971; Maldonaldo and Meitzler, 1970) and have been used for display (Maldonaldo and Anderson, 1971) and page composers (Roberts, 1972; Drake, 1974). The most popular mode of operation is the strain-biased mode. In this mode each of the elements of the array acts as an electrooptic amplitude modulator when the page composer is placed between crossed polarizers. The PLZT ceramics have a stress–optic property; a stress induces a strain along a particular direction and also a birefringence. The strain bias can be varied to change the birefringence and to make the 1 or 0 electrical state transmitting or opaque. Switching an element also changes its birefringence and its transmittance. Memory is built in the element with the 1 state corresponding to remanent polarization and the 0 state to the electrically depoled state. For a plate of PLZT 75–150 μm in thickness the typical half-wave "on" voltage is 50–100 V. The voltage is applied across the PLZT thickness by means of transparent electrodes. A page composer made of 128 × 128 elements with 0.125 mm elements on 0.250 mm centers was fabricated by Drake (1974) with strain-biased PLZT on

TABLE X

TYPES OF PAGE COMPOSERS

Page composer concept	Materials	Addressing techniques
Electric field induced birefringence (electrooptic effects)	PLZT (ceramic) $Bi_4Ti_3O_{12}$, KDP, KD*P, ADP	Electrode matrix, electron beam, light beam (with photoconductor)
Electric field induced optical scattering in partially poled ferroelectrics	Homeotropic liquid crystals, PLZT (ceramic)	Electrode matrix
Phase changes by variation of optical path length	Electrostrictive materials, PLZT (ceramic)	Electrode matrix, double hologram recording method
Birefringence switching in a ferroelectric–ferroelastic	$Gd_2(MoO_4)_3$	Electrode matrix
Reflection changes from thin, deformable membrane mirror elements	Metal films over a substrate support structure	Electrode feedthrough from transistor on back of substrate
Phase changes by formation of surface relief pattern	Thermoplastics, photoplastics, thin metallized membranes	Electron beam, electrode matrix plus charge
Phase disturbances by piezoelectric excitation of reflecting surfaces	Mirrored piezoelectric crystals	Individual switches to an rf driver
Optical density change by induced absorption	Photochromics, cathodochromics	Light beam (UV) plus flood illumination for erase
Optical scattering change by electrical excitation	Liquid crystals	Electrode matrix, light beam (with photoconductor)
Polarization rotation by magnetooptic effects	MnBi, EuO:Fe, Ni–Fe, $FeBO_3$, FeF_3	Light beam (absorption), conductor matrix
Traveling wave phase changes by acoustooptic interaction (Debye–Sears and Bragg effects)	Water (and other liquids), fused quartz (and other solids), $PbMoO_4$ (and other crystals)	Transverse interaction of coherent light and traveling acoustic waves
Thermally induced shift in absorption band edge	CdS, CdSe, As_2S_3	Electrode matrix for heating and heat sink substrate for cooling

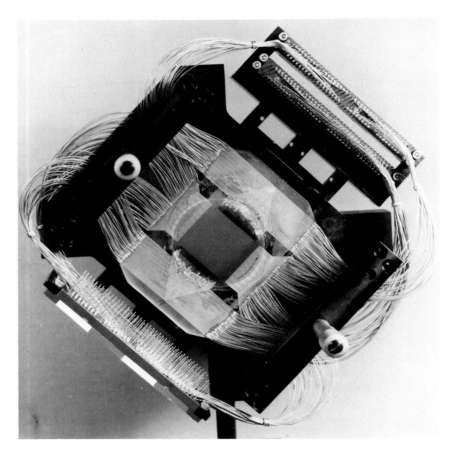

FIG. 16.   A page composer with 128 × 128 elements made of PLZT. Courtesy M. D. Drake (1974).

a Pyrex substrate as shown in Fig. 16. It was found that the contrast of the various matrix elements is highly sensitive to the local strain value. Because it is not possible to apply uniform strain over the entire matrix and because of thickness variations and material inhomogeneities one cannot operate the entire page composer at maximum contrast. The matrix can be made more uniform by reducing the strain-bias level. The switching time for the elements is of the order of 10 μsec. By activating one row at a time one can fully load a matrix of 128 × 128 elements in about 1.6 msec for a net data rate of 10 Mbit/sec.

To overcome some of the difficulties associated with the strain-bias mode other modes of operation have been studied by Drake (1974). In the differential mode the PLZT acts as a phase modulator; no strain bias is applied, no polarizers are required, and thickness and strain variations are canceled out. However, a lower contrast is obtained and a double hologram must be recorded. Other possibilities, such as a scattering mode and edge-effect mode, have also been considered.

Multichannel acoustooptical modulators have been used as one-dimensional page composers for high speed holographic recording on photographic film (Bardos, 1974; Roberts *et al.*, 1974). Linear composers with 64 channels operated well with crosstalk levels of less than 1:400 at 4 Mbit/sec rates per channel.

V. Optical Storage Systems

The main features of optical data storage, as was described in Section II, includes: (1) high packing density limited only by the diffraction of light, (2) high access time owing to the fact that inertialess beam addressing techniques can be incorporated, (3) improved reliability and flexibility obtainable because of the large working distance between the recording transducer and the medium, and (4) the possibility of high speed block-oriented holographic data storage. To design and implement an optical data storage system for the realization of many of these features is a complex and frustrating task. There has been a number of gallant efforts in the past years to construct optical recording systems to demonstrate the technology of optical recording. However, only a very limited commercial product has been introduced to date. It appears that at least for the immediate future, this technology will be more successful in the video recording than in the computer memory applications.

In this section, we will review a few representative optical recording systems advanced to date. The main purpose of this discussion is (1) to illustrate how these special features of optical recording can be implemented, and (2) to provide a brief overview of the status of the optical recording technology. We will first discuss a number of bit-oriented systems both permanent and alterable. This is followed by some examples of holographic recording systems. The optical video recording systems will be discussed last.

A. BIT-ORIENTED RECORDING SYSTEMS

1. *Permanent Bit-Oriented Recording Systems*

Many archival storage systems have been advanced in the past. The IBM 1360 photo store memory (Kuehler and Kerby, 1966) and NCR PCM1 bulk storage (Myers, 1964) represent earlier effort of optical readout of information stored in photographic plates. As lasers become available, recording by hole burning on metallic film was realized for real-time storage, as the slow wet chemical processing is eliminated. This is the basic storage technique utilized for the Unicon Mass Memory system.

The Unicon Mass Memory system made by Precision Instrument Company (Gray, 1972) is the first mass storage device based on laser technology to be introduced as a commercial product. The memory system provides an on-line storage capacity of 10^{12} bits at the price of 0.0002 cents per bit and unlimited off-line storage capacity at about 0.00002 cents per bit.

The recording medium consists of a thin layer of rhodium ($\approx$20 nm) deposited by rf sputtering on a polyester strip about 31 in. long, 4.75 in. wide and 0.007 in. thick. A focused argon laser beam is used to vaporize holes 3.5 $\times$ 4 μm in the metallic coating; a hole corresponding to a binary "1" and no hole to a "0." Each strip holds 11,600 tracks of data on 7.5 μm centers with a maximum of 197,000 bits per track. The capacity of a strip is about 2.3 $\times$ 10^9 bits; to achieve a capacity of 10^{12} bits, 450 strips are used. The strips are assembled into 18-strip packs with the packs mounted on a rotating carousel from which they can be unloaded automatically. During writing or reading the strip is mounted on a 10 in. drum rotating at 1500 rpm where it is held down by vacuum. To access the various tracks on the strip a carriage assembly containing a galvanometer and a focusing lens is moved along the axis of the drum; an optical encoder is used to position precisely the carriage. The galvanometer is used to access over $\pm$6 tracks from its center position and is also part of a servo loop which keeps the laser beam on track. The data are read by reflection with a contrast of about 10 to 1 between a "0" and "1" with the low light level (5% reflection) corresponding to a "1" bit. The light reflected from the bits passes through the focusing lens L_2 and is reflected by the beam splitter S_2 onto a dual photodiode (Fig. 17). The sum of the signals from the photodiodes is the value of the data bit being read; the difference between the signals provides a tracking error signal to the galvanometer servo. A complete Unicon memory system consists of two drums with two separate optical system

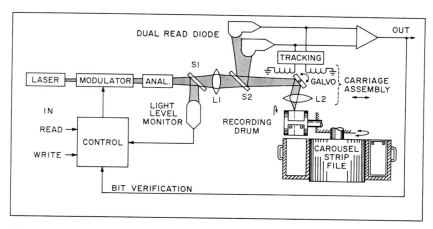

Fig. 17.   Read–write bit-oriented system of Precision Instrument. After Gray (1972).

sharing a 1 W argon laser. After the power is split between the two channels the beam passes through an electrooptic modulator which provides 100 nsec pulses at a 5 Mbit/sec pulse rate. The pulse width is chosen short enough so that only slight elongation of the bit occurs along the direction of rotation of the medium. To write a "1" bit about 250 mW of laser power are required at the medium location. The laser power is monitored via the beam splitter S_1 and a servo signal is derived to maintain constant laser power. The beam is then expanded by lens L_1 and directed onto the medium by the galvanometer mirror and the focusing lens L_2. The depth of focus, which is about 60 μm, is well within the mechanical runout and taper of the drum, strip thickness variation, and vacuum hold-down tolerance (total ~20 μm). The read power required is about 20 mW. Because dust particles and small defects in the coating or in the strip substrate result in reduced reflection and thus are interpreted by the photodetector as "1" bits, the coating process of the strips is carefully controlled. Furthermore, an internal air conditioning and filtration system is provided in the recorder unit to ensure constant temperature and clean air environment. In operation a new strip is first initialized; track headers and clock bits are recorded to identify the 11,600 tracks. Data are then inserted between the previously recorded clock bits. The data are then verified by reading; if an error is detected the word is repeated. Data redundancy is provided in the form of an error-correcting code. It was found that the raw error rate is about 1 in 10^6 bits; after correction the error rate is reduced to 1 part in 10^7 bits. A summary of the functional characteristics of the laser memory system is given in Table XI. The memory system consists of two parts: the laser recorder unit and the recorder control unit. The recorder unit contains the laser, the two drums, and the optical system as described above. The recorder control unit consists of a control computer, two word processors, two buffer memories, two read–write, and error control subsystems as well as the input–output control units.

The control unit provides direct interface with the host computer. Currently a Unicon laser memory interfaces with the ILLIAC IV computer as part of the ARPA computer network.

TABLE XI

FUNCTIONAL CHARACTERISTICS OF THE LASER MEMORY SYSTEM

Gross Capacity
      197,000 bits/track
  $\times$ 11,600 tracks/strip
  $\times$ 450 strips   = 1.03×10^{12} bits gross

Overhead Requirements (approximate)
    20% of gross capacity for error correction code bits (shortened fire code)
    4% for synchronizing clocks on each data track
    1% track identification
    4% for read-while-write correction data repeats
    3% for record headers and control marker words

Net Capacity
    $1.03 \times .68 = 0.7 \times 10^{12}$ net user data bits

File Access Times

Strip change time (worst case)	8 sec
Strip change time (min. adjacent slot)	6 sec
Average carriage movement	
1 track	1 msec
2–1000 tracks	220 msec
1000–11,000 tracks	340 msec
Drum revolution	40 msec
Average latency	20 msec
Sequential read time, full strip	8.6 min

Data Transfer Rates (per channel—user data bits)

Sequential read average	375 kbyte/sec
	3.0 Mbit/sec
Peak rate on track	425 kbyte/sec
	3.4 Mbit/sec

Error Rate
    Not more than 1 byte in error out of 10^8 read after application of internal error correction procedures

2. *Alterable Bit-Oriented Optical Memory*

Materials and techniques proposed for bit-oriented alterable optical memory applications have been discussed in Section III. We will review four different experimental systems, all based on the magnetooptic technology. With the exception of the polycube memory, all involve some degree of mechanical motion for addressing.

Ampex workers have constructed a tape system in which the storage medium is Co-P thin films, which utilizes the thermomagnetic coercivity change effect (Treves *et al.*, 1969). By means of localized laser heating to about 150°C, the coercivity can be reduced from room temperature value of 200 Oe to about 70 Oe. A coincident heating laser beam with a magnetic field of the order of 100 Oe can effect writing or erasing. The readout Kerr effect signal is obtained from a low coercivity Co–Ni–Fe film which is coated over the storage film. The experimental system involves a rotating mirror beam scanner that scans the focused spot transversely across the tape when it advances. Figure 18 shows a schematic diagram of this system (Hunt *et al.*, 1970). A technique called "medium modulation" was used to improve the signal. This involves the application of a small modulating magnetic field to perturb the readout layer. The presence or absence of the fixed modulation frequency in the Kerr signal is then detected at a "1" or "0" bit, respectively. The modulation carrier frequency was chosen to be outside the frequency spectrum of the medium noise and laser noise. For 5 μm spot sizes, using a 30 mW laser for reading, a signal-to-noise ratio of 30 at 6 MHz bandwidth was achieved. Based on the experimental results, the estimated performance of such a memory system is given in Table XII.

An erasable bit-oriented rotating disk experimental memory system using magnetooptic MnBi films has been constructed by Honeywell (Aagard *et al.*, 1972). The storage medium was prepared by vapor deposition techniques on glass or mica substrates (Chen, 1971). The easy direction of magnetization can be made perpendicular to the film surface. The magnetic hysteresis measurement shows an essentially square loop where the magnetization is independent of the applied field before reaching the coercive force.

In the design of the memory medium, we realize that the coercivity H_c, the closure flux $H_\perp$ at the center of a heat spot which determines the required erasure field, the laser writing power P, and the readout signal $\Delta I/I_0$ are all dependent on the film thickness t. These parameters are plotted in Fig. 19 as a function of the normalized film thickness $\tau = \alpha t$, where α is the absorption coefficient. Based on the requirements that (1) $H_\perp < H_c$, (2) the readout signal is optimized, and (3) the writing power is

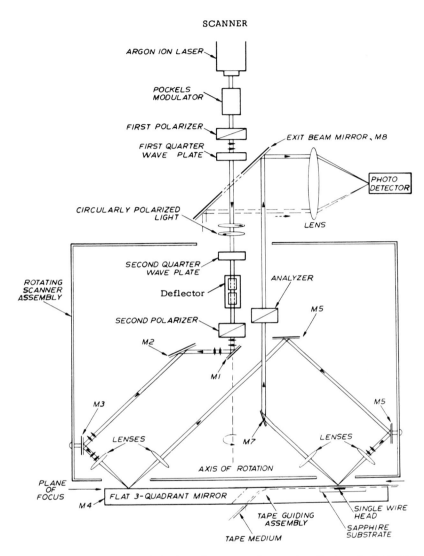

FIG. 18. The optical part of the laser-beam-record-magnetooptical readout system of Ampex. After Hunt *et al.* (1970).

TABLE XII

PERFORMANCE OF EXPERIMENTAL MAGNETOOPTIC MEMORY SYSTEMS[a]

	Ampex magnetooptic tape system	Honeywell MnBi rotating disk system	IBM cryogenic EuO disk system
Memory medium	Co-P with NiFeCo	MnBi films with SiO coating	EuO (fe) films
Medium dimension	3500-ft coating on 2-in. wide Mylar tape	6-in. diameter 1-in. band 400-Å thick film on glass	3-in. diameter disk 1750-Å thick film on glass
Areal packing density (bit/in.^{2})	6×10^6 (with redundancy)	10^8	10^7
Capacity (bits)	9.8×10^{11}	10^9	10^7–10^8
Bit dimension (μm)	4	1 (diameter)	5
Tack density (TPI)	2×10^3	10^4	3×10^3
Bit density (BPI)	3×10^3	10^4	3×10^3
Medium speed	10^3 in./sec	10 rev/sec	200 rev/sec
Writing laser power (mW)	1.5×10^3	5–10	70
Writing pulsewidth (μsec)	—	0.1–1	0.05
Erasure field (Oe)	100	700	200
Readout SNR (peak signal/rms noise)	32–35 dB	8	30
Readout bandwidth (MHz)	6	1	2
Access time (msec)	20 sec	50 (64 tracks)	2.5
Operating conditions	Room temperature in air	Room temperature in air	77 K in vacuum
Special remarks	Redundancy and error correction code used to get 10^{-9} error rate	$>10^7$ repeated cycles tested	10 element array GaAs laser transducers used

[a] From Chen and Zook (1975).

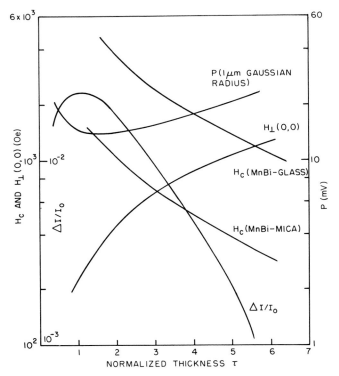

FIG. 19.   The dependence of coercivity H_c, demagnetizing field at the center of bit $H_\perp$ (0, 0), normalized readout signal $\Delta I/I_0$ and the required writing power for 1 μm Gaussian radius spots P, on the normalized film thickness τ of MnBi films.

minimized. The film thickness was designed to have a normalized value of $\tau = 2$, or an actual value of 400–500 Å. An experimental memory exerciser based on the bit-serial organization and rotating disk format was constructed. The medium was prepared on a 15.2 cm diameter glass disk, which was mounted on an air bearing and rotated at a speed of 10 rps. A schematic diagram of the experimental arrangement is shown in Fig. 20 (Chen *et al.*, 1973a). The laser beam is deflected to select one of the 64 tracks without moving the recording head. Beyond this limit, mechanical movement of the head is required. In this format, there are 10^5 bits for each track and 10^4 tracks for the 2.54 cm band on the disk, resulting in a total capacity of 10^9 bits per disk. The writing and erasing laser power is 10 mW delivered on the medium at a pulse duration of 0.1 μsec. In some experiments where the spot diameter is reduced to 1 μm,

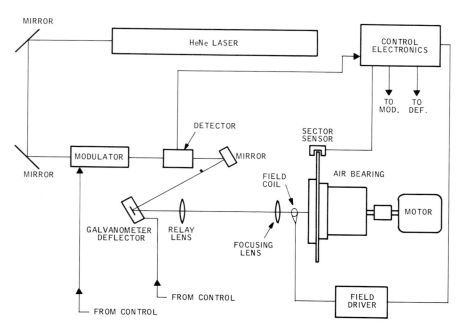

FIG. 20.   A rotating disk optical recording system using MnBi film as the recording medium.

a laser of 3 mW at 0.1 μsec is sufficient. The coercivity of typical film is about 1.5 kOe. The application of 700-Oe field in the unheated region has no effect on the stored information. The readout signal was derived from the reflected magnetooptic Kerr rotation in the medium, and a differential detection system was utilized. In Fig. 21, the upper trace shows a continuous readout signal from scanning along a track of written bits, four in a group, at a rate of 10 μsec/cm. The lower trace shows the readout signal from a virgin unwritten track. The fluctuation of the signal repeats itself upon repeated readout over the same track. We attributed this mainly to the film fixed-pattern noise. The readout signal-to-noise ratio (SNR) for this case is better than 8 to 1. Repeated cycling of write–erase–read has been performed up to 10^7 cycles with no detectable degradation of the memory performance if the peak power for writing is less than 10% above the threshold (Aagard, 1973). There is one particular aspect of this medium that should be mentioned. The Curie point writing temperature of 360°C is also the first-order transition temperature for the normal low temperature phase (l.t.p.). Above this temperature, there is a high temperature phase (h.t.p.), which is also

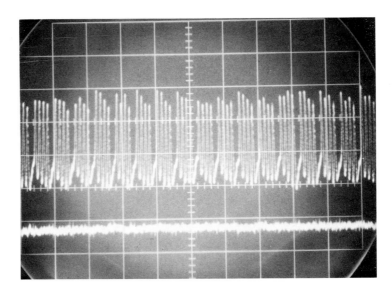

FIG. 21.   The readout signal of a written track (upper trace) and of a virgin unwritten track (lower trace). Time scale 10 μm/cm.

ferromagnetic with Curie temperature of 180°C. Because writing operation involves rapid cooling, the written region gradually transforms into the h.t.p. upon repeated cycling. The readout signal is approximately reduced by a factor of 2 for the h.t.p. However, as long as the laser power is sufficient for writing on a l.t.p. medium and the readout system is capable of reading off the h.t.p., the medium will be acceptable for the intended application. For the laboratory memory exerciser, this phase transition has not caused adverse effects, and the medium was proven applicable for the bit-serial memory application. The films, if protected with SiO coating, are stable and can operate in air at room temperature. The memory characteristics of this MnBi system are also summarized in Table XII.

Another experimental memory system of magnetooptic bit-oriented type is the cryogenic rotating disk data store using Fe-doped EuO films. This system was developed by workers at IBM (Fan and Greiner, 1968, 1970). The unique feature of it, besides the use of cryogenic environment, is the use of a GaAs laser array as a read–write source. The schematic diagram of the system is shown in Fig. 22 (Patlach, 1972; Brown, 1972). The film was coated on a 3 in. diameter glass disk. Since the easy direction of magnetization for this medium is in the plane of the

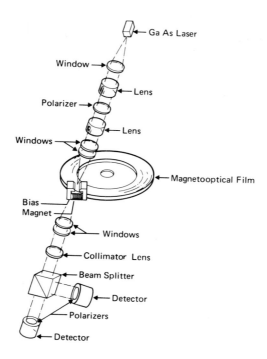

Ga As Laser

Window

Lens

Polarizer

Lens

Windows

Magnetooptical Film

Bias
Magnet

Windows

Collimator Lens

Beam Splitter

Detector

Polarizers

Detector

FIG. 22.   The optical arrangement of a beam addressable magnetooptic (EuO film) disk memory system by IBM. After Patlach (1972).

film, the read beam must be arranged to have an oblique incidence angle to the film surface. A bias magnetic field is required for writing or erasing in coincidence with the laser beam. The use of GaAs laser array of 10 individual elements allows parallel read–write operation. The energy density generated by each laser element at the storage plane was 0.07 nJ/μm^2 with an input current of 500 mA for 50 nsec.

The cryogenic environment of such a rotating disk memory system requires ingenious design and fabrication. As shown in Fig. 22, the rotating memory disk is attached to the rotor of the drive motor, supported by a dry-lubricated low temperature bearing, and enclosed in the He gas–filled (100 μm pressure) stainless chamber, maintaining at 77 K temperature. The stator of the drive motor is outside the chamber, and a rotating magnetic field is coupled through the chamber wall to drive the rotor. In this manner, low temperature vacuum seals are eliminated, and heat loss minimized. The large magnetooptic effect of EuO at this temperature together with the relatively large bit size contributes to the large peak signal to rms noise of 30 at 2 MHz bandwidth. The performance characteristics of this experimental bit-oriented system is also given in Table XII.

More recently, Philips Laboratory workers have constructed an experimental polycube memory using the nonvolatile magnetooptic photoconductive sandwich (MOPS) as the storage medium (Hill *et al.,* 1975). The system is block organized in blocks of about 10^3 bits, at a random access time of <500 sec. The total capacity is 6.5×10^7 bits. A sketch of this experimental memory is shown in Fig. 23. The system uses a 16-stage electrooptic digital deflector for addressing 256×256 positions, each with a spot diameter of 7 μm and a 10 μm center spacing. The 5 mW HeNe laser beam, after passing through the deflector, is split first into 8×8 beamlets using calcite prisms, and then into 4×4 beamlets using glass cube (polycube) beam splitters. The 16 memory planes are attached to the exit of the polycube beam splitters. Each memory plane consists of 64 memory chips with 65,536 cells each, making a total of 6.5×10^7 bits. The MOPS memory medium consists of a transparent electrode, a photoconductor layer, and a matrix of gadolinium-substituted iron garnet single-domain magnetic islands (cells) epitaxially grown on single-crystal substrates. Writing or erasure requires the coincidence of the laser beam (selecting one of 256×256 spots), the magnetic field (one field coil for each of the 16 planes), and the electric current pulse for heating (selecting one of the 8×8 positions). Readout is by the magnetooptic technique. The system offers a nonvolatile storage, with a random access time of 100–500 μsec, a data rate of 0.5–2 Mbit/sec, and 1024-bit parallel readout capability.

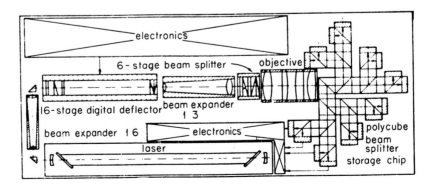

FIG. 23.   Sketch of polycube magnetooptic photoconductive sandwich (MOPS) memory unit. After Hill *et al.* (1975).

B. HOLOGRAPHIC RECORDING SYSTEMS

1. *Read-Only Holographic Recording*

A binary hologram digital read-only memory was devised by Shew and Blanchard (1969). In their system the information is stored on photographic film in the form of one-dimensional Fourier holograms. One byte of data (8 data bits and 1 clock bit) is encoded in each hologram; thus all data combinations are represented by 256 holograms. The holograms are computer generated and then recorded on photographic film by an electron beam. The binary holograms used in the memory consist of many parallel transparent apertures on an opaque background and are similar to diffraction gratings. To decode the hologram the first-order diffraction pattern is detected at the Fourier transform plane of a lens. The reader consists of a transparent drum on the inside of which the photographic film is wrapped, a 3-mW HeNe laser, a light deflector, and a nine-element photodetector array.

The experimental results demonstrated the insensitivity of holographic reconstruction to beam–hologram positioning error, film defects, and dust particles. For a hologram of 10 mils × 0.4 mils, a positioning tolerance of ±2.5 mils did not seriously degrade the signal-to-noise ratio at the detectors. For a drum of 4.75 in. inside diameter rotating at 3600 rpm, an average access time of 8.5 msec and a data rate of 2×10^6 bytes/sec was achieved. The detector array reads one byte at a time. The storage density is about 3.6×10^3 bits/mm^2, but results indicated that density could be increased to about 10^4 bits/mm^2 and the data rate by an order of magnitude.

The first complete optical read-only holographic memory system was investigated by Anderson *et al.* (1967) at Bell Telephone Laboratories. The concept of page-oriented random-access memory was introduced by these workers. The system consisted of a laser, an X–Y random-access acoustooptical deflection system, a hologram storage plane, and a photodetector array. The acoustooptical deflector directs the laser beam to any one of a large number of holograms arranged in a two-dimensional array. Each hologram contains a page of digital information, typically 4096 bits. The digital information is reconstructed at the position of the readout plane where it is detected by a photodiode or phototransistor array with one detector for each bit in the page. The recording medium was initially photographic film; later it was changed to dichromated gelatin to increase the diffraction efficiency.

The system (Fig. 24) which was implemented used a array of 32 × 32 holograms and a readout plane containing 5 chips of 8 × 8 phototransis-

Fig. 24. Photograph of the experimental read-only holographic recording system of Bell Telephone Laboratories. Courtesy L. K. Anderson.

tors, with the chips located so as to sample the center and the corners of the reconstructed data array. A random access of 2 μsec to any page in the hologram and a data rate of 50 Mbit/sec were experimentally demonstrated. The advantages of holography, such as, relative insensitivity to alignment and to scratches, were proved. However, difficulties were experienced in controlling the recording process performed in a special writing machine; as a result, variations in intensity as high as 5:1 for reconstructed "1's" were detected both within a single page or from hologram to hologram. The holographic read-only memory was not pursued further by Bell Telephone Laboratory workers because they felt that the lack of write and erase capability constitutes a severe limitation in most applications.

Another holographic read-only memory for the storage of digital information was investigated by Takeda et al. (1971) at Hitachi, Inc., in Japan. In order to increase the packing density they devised by computer calculations a random phase shifter plate that is introduced in the object beam during recording. The phase randomization reduces the dynamic range requirement on the storage medium for recording Fourier transform plane holograms of periodic objects and reduces the autocorrelation noise which is read out of the storage hologram near the reference beam (Burckhardt, 1970). The random phase shifter consists of a glass plate onto which numerous thin layers of cerium oxide have been deposited through random-pattern screens. In a digital hologram recorded with the random phase shifter in place a density of 10^5 bits/mm^2 was achieved, an increase of about an order of magnitude over previous holographic memories. The reconstruction of a 2×10^4 bit hologram is shown in Fig. 25 (Takeda, 1972).

A novel approach to address a large number of pages of holographic data has been advanced by the 3M workers (Tait *et al.*, 1967; Packard *et al.*, 1971). The heart of their read-only holographic data file is an electronically scanned CdS laser. The laser device consists of a scannable electron beam operating at 60 KV and at a beam current of 2 mA. The electron beam is focused to a spot diameter of 25 μm on a CdS target, causing it to lase at 5150 Å wavelength at a maximum pulse width

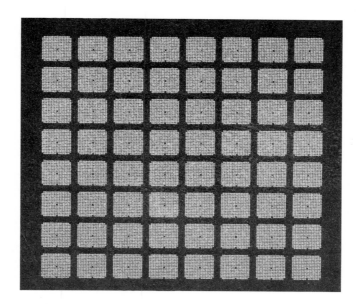

FIG. 25.   Photograph of the reconstructed 2×10^4 bits image of Hitachi experiment holographic memory using photographic plate from storage at a density of 10^5 bits/mm^2. [Courtesy Hitachi Laboratory, see Takeda (1972).]

of 50 nsec and peak power of 0.5–3.5 W. With a 26 mm × 26 mm target, over 10^6 lasing locations are possible. Using this electronically scannable laser, a randomly addressable holographic data file of 5×10^7 bits, called Megafetch data processor, was constructed. The system provides a random-access time of 10 μsec at a data rate of 1.5×10^7 bits/sec. There are 1024 × 1024 microholograms in the file, each containing 56 bits of data and 8 bits for parity check. The use of a photographic plate for storage medium makes this system archival in nature and is intended only for random readout of prerecorded information.

An interesting application of holographic recording is the high speed digital recorder. Holographic methods offer the potential of recording and reproducing data at several gigabits per second rates. A number of high speed digital recorders have been designed and partially implemented (Bardos, 1974; Roberts et al., 1974; Bardos et al., 1975). The first step in recording at high bit rates is the demultiplexing of data into a number of parallel channels. This allows the data to be fed to a multichannel acoustooptical modulator of reduced bandwidth. In the system described by Bardos (1974) the data are recorded on continuously moving photographic film in the form of one-dimensional holograms each containing 128 bits. Up to 1536 holograms can be recorded on a 35 mm film by scanning both the reference and object beam across the width of the film by means of a multifaceted rotating mirror. The dimensions of a hologram are 1 mm × 16 μm corresponding to an average packing density of 800 bits/mm^2. Recording rates of 400 Mbit/sec and readout rates of 40 Mbit/sec were demonstrated. The complete optical layout of the system is shown in Fig. 26. The laser beam from a cavity-dumped argon laser is split by means of an acoustooptic modulator (AOM1). The diffracted beam which is shifted in frequency by the rf frequency of the acoustic transducer is used as a reference beam. The undiffracted beam from the modulator is used as the signal beam and enters the multichannel acoustooptic modulator (AOM2) where it acquires the information to be recorded. Both modulators are driven at the same rf frequency; thus there is no frequency shift between the reference beam and the signal beam. This insures that well-defined fringes are recorded at the hologram plane. The two beams are then combined at Fourier transform plane at the lens L7 where a precision slit S5 is located. The lenses L8 and L9 and the scanner form a moving image of the slit at the film plane. For readout the diffracted light from the holograms is collected by the lens L10 and then reflected and Fourier-transformed onto a linear photodiode array. Only 20 channels of the page composer were demonstrated in the system, but page composers with up to 64 channels have been fabricated with good channel

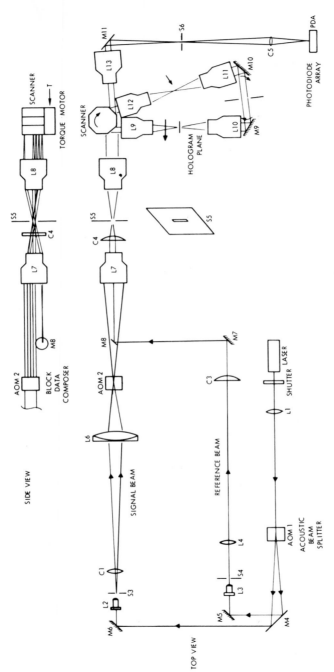

Fig. 26. Optical layout of a breadboard wideband holographic recorder of Harris Intertype. After Bardos (1974).

isolation. The holograms had a diffraction efficiency of 0.5% and a signal-to-noise ratio of 100:1 was obtained at 4×10^6 holograms/sec. Such a system can be extended (Bardos *et al.*, 1975) to record at 2 Gbit/sec rates and readout at 0.6 Gbit/sec rates by using a wider film, higher transport velocity for the film, and a higher power laser. Other possibilities exist for the design of multigigabit recorders, among them one using two-dimensional Fourier transform holograms, a cavity-dumped and mode-locked argon laser, and charge coupled devices for readout.

A storage system that combines alphanumeric and graphical data together with digitally encoded data on the same microfiche chip has been described by Kozma *et al.* (1971). Such a microfiche is called a Human Readable Machine Readable (HRMR) system. Information from it can be retrieved visually by the human operator or optically from the digitally encoded part for computer usage.

On a standard microfiche 4×6 in. card containing 60 pages of human readable information one encodes the same data in holographic form in the unused portion of the card which is about $\frac{1}{4} \times 4$ in. in area. The amount of data stored is about 2.5×10^6 bits at a density of about 4000 bits/mm². The data are stored in the form of one-dimensional Fourier transform holograms which are computer generated. The computer formats the data in blocks of 256 bits and performs a 512-point Fourier transform. A random phase is assigned to each bit in the computation. The digitized holographic signal is applied to a digital-to-analog converter which in turn controls an electrooptic modulator that modulates the recording laser. The recorded holograms are about 3.2 mm long with a track width of 10 μm. Two holograms are recorded along the $\frac{1}{4}$ in. dimensions and 6510 tracks are formed in the 4 in. dimension. The recorder unit is shown in Fig. 27. To read out the holograms one uses a special reader which contains a GaAs laser diode or a HeNe laser, a photodetector array, and an optical system for producing the inverse Fourier transform of the holograms at the plane of the photodetector array. A dual-channel hologram reader has also been designed. Experiments have been performed with the GaAs laser as a light source and a linear array of 42 photodiodes for reading. The alignment tolerance of Fourier transform holograms was demonstrated and a signal-to-noise ratio of better than 24 dB was obtained corresponding to an error rate of less than 10^{-7} when 4% of the holograms is obscured by defects.

HRMR systems have application in data bases that change slowly, such as, inventory accounts, personnel records, and insurance records. Other applications include mass memories for computers and archival data storage of seismic data.

A new approach to optical digital recording was recently described by

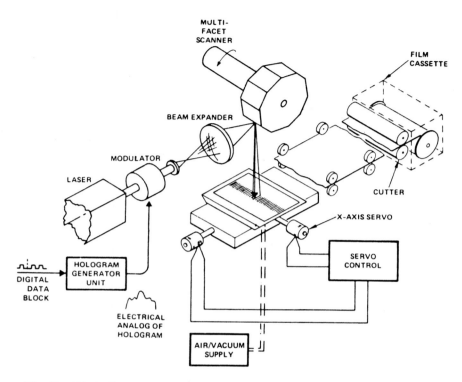

FIG. 27. Block diagram of a HRMR optical recorder unit of Harris Intertype. After Kozma *et al.* (1971).

Russell and Walker (1976). Information is permanently recorded on a photographic plate in bit-by-bit form. In contrast with previous systems the recording medium is held stationary during recording and playback, and a new type of mechanical scanner has been incorporated. The scanner has four microscope objectives mounted on a scanner wheel. The wheel rotates at 3600 rpm and the whole scanner assembly moves with a synchronously driven lead screw along the plate. As a result, the data are recorded as a series of arcs (Fig. 28). A four-facet mirror called the distributor is located on the end of the scanner shaft. Its function is to direct the input light beam to the proper objective during its active part of the scan. The light transmitted through the recorded bits is collected by a bundle of plastic fibers and lead to a photomultiplier.

Using a 10× microscope objective, one can record and play back recorded bits of 1 μm in diameter with a distance between tracks of 2 μm. This corresponds to a packing density of 5×10^5 bits/mm². A color

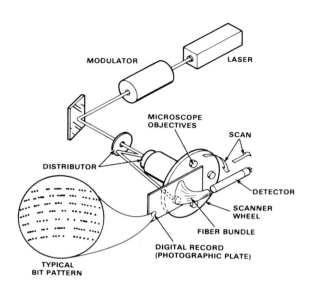

FIG. 28. Optical layout of a digital recording system of Battelle Pacific Northwest Laboratories designed for video playback. After Russell and Walker (1976).

television program including audio was recorded and played back off the photographic plate with no degradation. A 1 mW HeNe laser is required for playback. To keep the laser beam on track during playback a servo system is used. A digital signal of 1.6 kHz is applied to a galvanometer deflector to provide a deflection of the laser beam of about 0.25 μm. If the beam is centered on the data the light signal contains only a 3.2 kHz frequency. With the beam off track a 1.6 KHz signal appears with the phase indicating the direction of the error. The error signal is filtered and rectified to provide a correction dc current to the galvanometer deflector to keep the beam on track.

The photographic plate is covered by a transparent layer of sufficient thickness to keep dust particles out of focus. The system was primarily designed as a low-cost video player but can also be used as a large-scale data store for computer applications.

2. Read–Write and Alterable Holographic Recording

The first complete description of a read–write holographic memory was given by Rajchman (1970). In his paper Rajchman envisioned an optical memory replacing most of the computer memory hierarchy and thus having a revolutionary impact on computer organization. A large research effort to implement the holographic memory was initiated at RCA Laboratories. The optical configuration of such a memory is shown in Fig. 29 (Stewart and Consentino, 1970). To write at a given location of the storage medium the X–Y deflector is supplied an address to which both the reference and the object team are deflected.

A special component called a hololens is shown as part of the system. The hololens consists of an array of permanent phase holograms and serves as the beam splitter for recording on the medium. These holograms represent blank pages of information; the pages are copied onto the medium with the page composer supplying the digital pattern to be recorded. Hololenses have been made out of dichromated gelatin with a diffraction efficiency of 73%. During writing the electrooptic polarization switch is not activated and the object beam is transmitted by the polarizer to the page composer to acquire the information, after which it is reflected back onto the storage medium where it interferes with the reference beam. During readout the polarization switch is energized and turns the plane of polarization by 90°, thus the object beam is blocked by the polarizer. The reference beam addresses the desired hologram page and the reconstructed image of the recorded information is projected onto the sensor array. Initially the storage medium proposed by RCA Laboratory Workers consisted of thin magnetic films of MnBi (Mezrich, 1969) with a Q-switched ruby laser used for recording. Later on a thermoplastic–photoconductor sandwich was used as a storage medium and an argon laser was used for recording

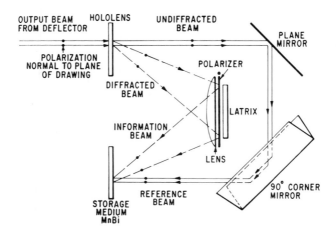

FIG. 29.   Illustration of an optical read–write holographic memory proposed by RCA. After Stewart and Cosentino (1970).

and reading (Stewart *et al.*, 1973). A 10^7-bit holographic memory using an acoustooptic beam deflector, a nematic liquid crystal page composer, a hololens, a thermoplastic storage medium, and a silicon photodiode array was implemented. The memory was partially populated in a way that made possible the assessment of a fully populated memory system. The page composer was fully built to provide the 1024 bits per page. Two spots per bit were used to provide additional immunity against image fluctuations from a variety of sources. The deflector was also fully built, but only 16 central holograms and 32 peripheral holograms were addressed. The photodetector array contained 20 photodiodes for sensing 10 bits out of 1024 bits on the page. The implemented system indicated that further effort was needed to improve both components such as the page composer and the erasable storage medium. Considerable effort was also dedicated by RCA Laboratories to the improvement of electrooptic crystals, such as lithium niobate, in which the photorefractive effect is used for holographic volume recording. A reconstructed image from a fixed hologram in lithium niobate is shown in Fig. 30 (Amodei *et al.*, 1971).

Thaxter and Kestigian (1974) proposed a layered optical memory for volume holography in which the recording material is $Sr_{.75}Ba_{.25}Nb_2O_6$ (SBN). This material has a very high recording sensitivity which can be enhanced by using an external electric field of a few kilovolts per centimeter. Another effect unique to SBN is the latent-to-active reconstruction property of the recorded phase hologram. In the latency condition an applied electric field antiparallel to the spontaneous polarization of the crystal prevents reconstruction. The proposed layered optical memory configuration is shown in Fig. 31. The medium consists of a stack of crystals with each layer not recording or not diffracting unless energized by a layer-select voltage. In operation a layer is selected for recording by the application of a voltage to it parallel to the *c* axis of the crystal. All unselected layers are transparent to the reference and object beams and recording takes place only in the selected layer. To read the hologram a readout beam oppositely directed to the reference beam illuminates the memory. Application of a negative voltage to a layer prevents reconstruction from that layer (latent state) while application of positive voltage (same polarity as in recording) activates the layer for readout. Thus to readout a particular layer one applies a positive voltage to the selected layer and negative voltages to all unselected layers. A two-layer model of SBN crystals was built, and discrimination between reconstructed patterns from the two layers was over 10 dB.

A digital holographic memory using two-dimensional storage is limited

FIG. 30. The reconstructed image of a scene holographically recorded at RCA in a crystal of $LiNbO_3$. (Courtesy R. D. Lohman.)

to a capacity of about 10^{10} bits if no mechanical motion is employed in the system (Anderson, 1971). Several approaches have been suggested for increasing the capacity to 10^{11} bits without sacrificing the fast random-access feature of an all-electronic addressing mechanism.

The approach suggested by D'Auria *et al.* (1973) at Thomson-CSF Laboratories uses the three-dimensional storage properties of a thick holographic material. By changing the angle of the reference beam with respect to the object beam it is possible to record a series of pages (e.g., 10^2) at the same location in the medium. The material can be a ferroelectric crystal such as lithium niobate using the photorefractive

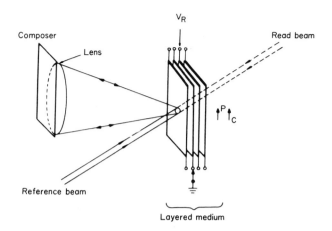

FIG. 31. Layered optical memory of Sperry Rand, using stacked layers of $Sr_{0.75}Ba_{0.25}Nb_2O_6$ crystals. Layer selected is achieved by the adjustment of V_R.

effect for recording. A detailed calculation shows that one can store about 10^{11} bits in a $LiNbO_3$ crystal 20 cm × 20 cm in cross section and 1 cm thick.

A read–write three-dimensional holographic system described by D'Auria *et al.* (1973) uses an acoustooptic beam deflector and translator (Fig. 32). The first $X-Y$ acoustooptic deflector D_1 selects the location for recording in the memory plane. The second deflector D_2 then selects the angle of incidence of the reference beam. Thus at the selected location

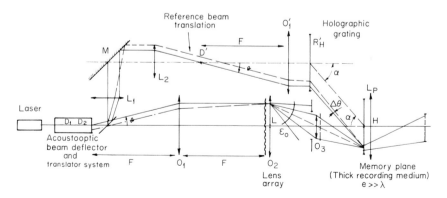

FIG. 32. Holographic memory system of Thomson-CSF using a rotating reference beam and thick holographic recording medium. After D'Auria *et al.* (1973).

random access to any selected angle between the reference and object beams is possible. To avoid a Doppler shift difference between the reference beam and the object beam the deflection system must be placed before the beam splitter in the complete optical system as shown in Fig. 32. The holographic grating in the system provides exact coincidence between the reference and the object beam at the memory plane. Among the components that dictate the capacity of the memory, lenses play an important role. For a given storage density D the required diameter Φ of the largest lens in the system can be written (D'Auria *et al.*, 1973)

$$\Phi = (2/\sqrt{\pi})(C/D)^{1/2} \qquad (84)$$

where C is the capacity of the memory. Assuming a density of 10^6 bits/cm² and a capacity of 10^{10} bits, a lens of 80 cm in diameter is necessary, which makes it difficult to realize with the necessary f-number and field angle. Such a lens could be replaced by an array of phase holograms (hololens).

Other approaches for increasing the capacity of a holographic memory were suggested by Kiemle (1974). Both mechanical and nonmechanical solutions were examined.

The mechanical approach proposed by Kiemle records narrow hologram tracks on a continuously moving photosensitive medium analogous to magnetic tape. The optical system used for recording is shown in Fig. 33. To record a bit one applies a pulse to the modulator and a hologram of the bit is recorded. The bit is stored in a hologram that is much longer than the distance between adjacent bits on a track; thus many holograms (≈ 100) are superposed. For readout only the reference beam illuminates the holograms; for every recorded binary 1 bit a bright point is reconstructed at the photodetector location. Densities of 500 bits/mm have been achieved experimentally. For good signal-to-noise ratio, a track width of 10 μm appears sufficient. Because of the symmetrical arrangement of the reference and object beams the loci of maximum and minimum of the interference pattern are perpendicular to the moving medium; thus depth of focus is not a problem. Similarly, small angular deviations of the storage medium have negligible effect.

Another solution for increasing the capacity of the optical memory without moving the medium was proposed by Kiemle and was termed the modular memory. In a modular memory a common laser and deflection system is shared by several modules. In this respect it is similar to the polycube memory discussed earlier. The laser beam is split among the various modules by a system of fixed beam splitters. A read–write module (Fig. 34) consists of a glass block containing a storage

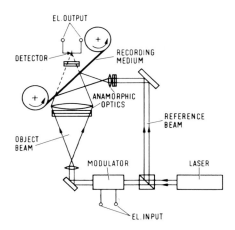

FIG. 33.   A moving medium holographic recording system of Siemens Laboratory. In the plane of the drawing, the object beam is convergent and the reference beam divergent. Normal to this plane, both beams are focused on the medium by anamorphic lenses to form a narrow line parallel to the direction of film movement. At readout, the reconstructed image points move past the detector with size matched to the point size. After Kiemle (1974).

plate, a page composer, a fixed array of holograms (hololens) for illuminating the page composer, and a detector array. It is seen that the read beam is always perpendicular to the storage plate; thus no loss of resolution occurs because of obliquity factors. To compute the memory capacity Kiemle assumes a system in which the laser beam is split by the beam splitters into 256 secondary beamlets with each beamlet accessing 4 modules arranged in an array. The capacity of one storage plate of

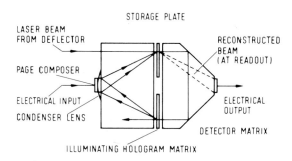

FIG. 34.   Read–write holographic recording module using reflection-type page composer by Siemens. Each module has a capacity of 1.7×10^7 bits. After Kiemle (1974).

dimension 25×25 mm^2 with a refractive index of 2, operating at a wavelength $\lambda = 0.488$ μm, is about 2×10^7 bits. The total memory capacity is about 2×10^{10} bits. The deflector must be capable of supplying 256×256 positions, well within the present state of the art. Larger capacities are possible when deflectors with more resolvable spots become available. The realization of the modular concept relies heavily on the availability of a sensitive recording material with high diffraction efficiency because of the rather inefficient utilization of available laser power.

C. OPTICAL VIDEO DISK AND OTHER SYSTEMS

It has long been recognized that optical recording techniques can be useful for the video recording applications. The realization of this approach, however, did not take place until recently. Although video recording does not demand extremely low error rate, its data rate and high packing density requirements are similar to those for the computer memory. Recording based on laser beam scribing or hole burning of a metallic coating over a suitable substrate, such as a glass or plastic disk, has achieved a track density of 5,000 tracks/cm. With a 30 cm diameter disk and a 10 cm band, using a one frame per revolution format, a total playback time of about 30 min of color video signal can be obtained from each disk surface. Currently, there are a number of competing optical video systems in the development stage. One interesting example is the video long play (VLP) system presently being developed by the Philips Laboratory which uses metal-coated plastic disks for the recording medium and a HeNe laser as the light source (Compaan and Kramer, 1973). A schematic diagram of the VLP is shown in Figure 35. The inset in the figure indicates the shape of the laser-recorded indentation on the disk: 0.16 μm deep, 0.8 μm wide, and 2 μm track spacing. The master is recorded with a 100 mW laser and plastic video disks are reproduced from the master similarly to the reproduction of phonograph records. The playback system uses a 1 mW HeNe laser with the readout signal derived from the laser beam reflected from the recorded pits. Ingenious optical track servoing (Bouwhuis and Burgstede, 1973) and focus control (Janssen and Day, 1973) as well as signal processing schemes (van den Bussche *et al.*, 1973) were incorporated in the VLP system to achieve the desired design goals. Similar video recording for master fabrication currently under development includes (1) the use of silver halide as the storage medium by I/O metrics (2) the HeCd laser recording on PVC flexible disk employing an aerodynamic stabilizer by Zenith and Thomp-

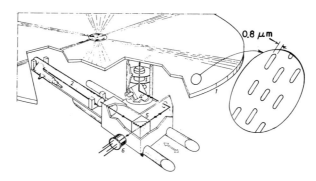

FIG. 35. Schematic diagram of the Philips video long play (VLP) playback unit. The record (1) is scanned from below by light from the He–Ne laser (2). The objective (3) is held focused on the record by a system based on a loudspeaker mechanism. The pivoting mirror (4) ensures that the beam remains centered on the track; the mirror is operated by a rotating-coil arrangement. Incident and reflected light are separated by the prism (5). The detector (6) converts the reflected light into an electrical signal. The inset depicts the format of the laser written data bits. After Compaan and Kramer (1973).

son-CSF, and (3) the Disco-vision system using metal film on plate glass disks by MCA.

The noncontacting readout by optical means for the video recording offers many important advantages over existing magnetic video recording techniques and contacting mechanical techniques being developed by RCA and also Telefunken/Decca. Besides the elimination of record and transducer wear, the optical beam can be dithered to play back one frame at a time allowing a storage of about 50,000 pictures per disk surface. In certain design, each track is labeled with an address code, permitting rapid search for a specific track and frame. This technique greatly increases the utilization of video recording. It was estimated that if ASCII code were used, each disk could store about 100,000 book pages of information.

VI. Conclusion

In the forgoing discussion we have attempted to present a brief review of the progress made in the field of optical recording during the last decade. The accomplishment of this effort, however, cannot as yet be measured by commercial success, but should be measured by the wealth of knowledge it has brought forth. This knowledge is the basis for future development, not only in the area of optical recording, but also in many related fields of endeavor. We may summarize the major findings in the following:

1. The expected high areal recording density of 10^8 bits/cm^2 offered by the optical recording technique has been demonstrated. It should be realized that in final analysis, the recording system must handle the weight and volume of the recording media. Therefore improvement of volume packing density is most important and offers new challenge for future research. A volume recording density of 10^{10} bits/cm^3 should be realizable in the future.

2. There are many new physical phenomena in material media that were found useful for optical recording. Continuing research effort is desirable in search for an ideal alterable recording medium, in spite of the fact that certain promising materials, such as the magnetooptic medium for bit-oriented and thermoplastic medium for holographic recording, appear to fulfill most of the requirements for the intended application.

3. In the area of components, it is clear that the availability of the semiconductor injection lasers with a cw power of 10 mW and a life time of 10,000 hr will have a major impact to the bit-oriented optical recording technology. For holographic recording, the beam coherence requirements dictate the use of gas lasers. The key component that needs immediate attention is the high speed high contrast and low attenuation page composer. The improved understanding of the limitations and advantages of the various deflection techniques indicates that the use of a hierarchy of deflectors for addressing will be essential to achieve optimum system performance.

4. There have been many impressive laboratory demonstrations of optical recording systems in the past, but only a limited number of read-only optical memories were produced. This is partly due to the high cost of the state-of-the-art components needed to construct an optical memory at the present and partly due to the continuing improvement of the magnetic recording technology. Utilization of the advantages of optical recording by innovative systems design, and recognition of new opportunities as the laser technology becomes mature and the competing recording technology reaches its limit, are the key elements of future success.

It should be emphasized that the knowledge accumulated in the course of the development of optical recording is applicable to many other related fields. Recent developments in the optical video disk technology is just one example of many that are sure to follow. Conversely, the experience acquired from these new technologies should be extremely useful for the development of the future optical recording systems.

ACKNOWLEDGMENTS

The authors gratefully acknowledge the many helpful discussions and suggestions of Drs. O. N. Tufte, J. D. Zook, and T. C. Lee of Honeywell Corporate Research Center.

REFERENCES

Aagard, R. L. (1973). *IEEE Trans. Magn.* **MAG-9,** 705.
Aagard, R. L., Lee, T. C., and Chen, D. (1972). *Appl. Opt.* **11,** 2133.
Ahn, K. Y. (1970). *Appl. Phys. Lett.* **17,** 347.
Ahrenkiel, R. K., and Coburn, T. J. (1973). *Appl. Phys. Lett.* **22,** 340.
Amodei, J. J., and Staebler, D. L. (1973). *RCA Rev.* **34,** 71.
Amodei, J. J., Staebler, D. L., and Stephens, A. W. (1971). *Appl. Phys. Lett.* **18,** 507.
Amodei, J. J., Phillips, W., and Staebler, D. L. (1972). *Appl. Opt.* **11,** 390.
Anderson, L. K. (1968). *Bell Lab Rec.* **46,** 319.
Anderson, L. K. (1971). *IEEE Trans. Magn.* **MAG-7,** 601.
Anderson, L. K., and McMurtry, B. J. (1966). *Proc. IEEE* **54,** 1335.
Anderson, L. K., Brojdo, S., LaMacchia, J. T., and Lin, L. H. (1967). *IEEE J. Quantum Electron.* **QE-3,** 245.
Ashkin, A., Boyd, G. D., Dziedzic, T. M., Smith, R. C., Ballman, A. A., and Nassau, K. (1966). *Appl. Phys. Lett.* **9,** 72.
Bardos, A. (1974). *Appl. Opt.* **13,** 832.
Bardos, A. M., Nelson, R. H., Roberts, H. N., and Shuman, C. A. (1975). *Proc. Electro-Opt. Syst. Des. Conf.* p. 45.
Bartolini, R. A. (1974). *Appl. Opt.* **13,** 129.
Beiser, L. (1973). *Electro-Opt. Syst. Des.* **5,** 33.
Beiser, L. (1974). *In* "Laser Applications" (M. Ross, ed.), Vol. 2, pp. 53–159. Academic Press, New York.
Bernal, G. E. (1971). *J. Appl. Phys.* **42,** 3877.
Bloom, A. L. (1966). *Proc. IEEE* **54,** 1262.
Booth, B. L. (1972). *Appl. Opt.* **11,** 2994.
Bosomworth, D. R., and Gerritsen, H. J. (1968). *Appl. Opt.* **7,** 95.
Bouwhuis, G., and Burgstede, P. (1973). *Philips Tech. Rev.* **33,** 186.
Brosens, P. J. (1971). *Electro-Opt. Syst. Des.* **3,** 21.
Brown, B. R. (1972). *IBM J. Res. Dev.* **16,** 19.
Brown, B. R. (1974). *Appl. Opt.* **13,** 761.
Burckhardt, C. B. (1970). *Appl. Opt.* **9,** 695.
Chang, J. T., Dillon, J. F., Jr., and Gianola, U. F. (1965). *J. Appl. Phys.* **36,** 1110.
Chaudhari, P., Cuombo, J. J., and Gambino, R. J. (1973). *Appl. Phys. Lett.* **22,** 337.
Chen, D. (1971). *J. Appl. Phys.* **42,** 3625.
Chen, D. (1974). *Appl. Opt.* **13,** 767.
Chen, D., and Lee, T. C. (1972). *Appl. Phys. Lett.* **19,** 62.
Chen, D., and Zook, J. D. (1975). *Proc. IEEE* **63,** 1207.
Chen, D., Ready, J. F., and Bernal, G. E. (1968). *J. Appl. Phys.* **39,** 3916.

Chen, D., Otto, G. N., and Schmit, F. M. (1973a). *IEEE Trans. Magn.* **MAG-9,** 66.
Chen, D., Tufte, O. N., Aagard, R. L., and Schmit, F. M. (1973b). *Proc. Joint Conf. Video and Data Recording.*
Chen, F. S. (1969). *J. Appl. Phys.* **40,** 3389.
Chen, F. S. (1970). *Proc. IEEE* **58,** 1440.
Coeure, P., Gray, J. C., and Carcey, J. (1971). *IEEE Trabs, Magn.* **MAG-7,** 397.
Colburn, W. S., and Haines, K. A. (1971). *Appl. Opt.* **10,** 1636.
Colburn, W. S., and Tompkins, E. N. (1974). *Appl. Opt.* **13,** 2934.
Collier, R. J., Burckhardt, C. B., and Lin, L. H. (1971). "Optical Holography," p. 15. Academic Press, London.
Compaan, K., and Kramer, P. (1973). *Philips Tech. Rev.* **33,** 178.
Comstock, R. (1970). *J. Appl. Phys.* **41,** 1397.
Dalisa, A. L., Zwicker, W. K., DeBitetto, D. J., and Harnack, P. (1970). *Appl. Phys. Lett.* **17,** 208.
D'Auria, L., Huigonard, J. P., and Spitz, E. (1973). *IEEE Trans. Magn.* **MAG-9,** 83.
deBonard, D. (1968). *IEEE J. Quantum Electron.* **QE-4,** 378.
Debye, P., and Sears, F. W. (1932). *Proc. Nat. Acad. Sci. Wash.* 409.
Drake, M. D. (1974). *Appl. Opt.* **13,** 347.
Duncan, R. C., Faughnan, B. W., and Philips, W. (1970). *Appl. Opt.* **9,** 2236.
Eschenfelder, A. E. (1970). *J. Appl. Phys.* **41,** 1372.
Fan, G. Y., and Greiner, J. H. (1968). *J. Appl. Phys.* **39,** 1216.
Fan, G. Y., and Greiner, J. H. (1970). *J. Appl. Phys.* **41,** 1401.
Faughnan, B. W., and Kiss, Z. J. (1969). *IEEE J. Quantum Electron.* **QE-5,** 17.
Feinleib, J., and Oliver, D. S. (1972). *Appl. Opt.* **11,** 2752.
Feinleib, J., and Ovshinsky, S. R. (1970). *J. Non-Cryst. Solids* **4,** 564.
Feldtkeller, E. (1972). *IEEE Trans. Magn.* **MAG-8,** 481.
Forshaw, M. R. B. (1974). *Opt. Laser Technol.* p. 28.
Fotland, R. A. (1970). *J. Photogr. Sci.* **18,** 33.
Friesem, A. A. (1968). Ph.D. Thesis, Univ. of Michigan, Ann Arbor.
Friesem, A. A., and Walker, J. L. (1970). *Appl. Opt.* **9,** 201.
Gandolfo, D. A., Boornard, A., and Nicastro, L. J. (1975). *Proc. Electro-Opt. Syst. Des. Conf.* p. 55.
Glass, A. M. (1974). *Conf. Proc., Photonique, Cadavoche, Fr.*
Goldberg, N. (1967). *IEEE Trans. Magn.* **MAG-3,** 605.
Gray, E. E. (1972). *IEEE Trans. Magn.* **MAG-8,** 416.
Güntherodt, G., Schoenes, J., and Wachter, P. (1970). *J. Appl. Phys.* **41,** 1083.
Haertling, G. M., and Land, C. E. (1971). *J. Am. Ceram. Soc.* **54,** 1.
Hammer, J. M. (1975). *In* "Integrated Optics" (T. Tamir, ed.), pp. 139–200. Springer-Verlag, Berlin.
Harker, J. M., and Chang, H. (1972). *Proc. Spring Jt. Comput. Conf.* p. 945.
Haskal, H. (1970). *IEEE Trans. Magn.* **MAG-6,** 542.
Haskal, H. M., and Rosen, A. N. (1971). *Appl. Opt.* **10,** 1354.
Haskal, H. M., Bernal, E. G., and Chen, D. (1974). *Appl. Opt.* **13,** 866.
Hayashi, I., and Panish, M. B. (1970). *J. Appl. Phys.* **40,** 150.
Hill, B., Krumme, J. P., Much, G., Pepperl, R., Schmidt, J., Schmidt, K. P., Witter, K., and Heitmann, H. (1975). *Appl. Opt.* **14,** 2607.
Hoagland, A. (1974). *IEEE Intercon. Tech. Papers* March 26–29.
Hunt, R. P., Magyary, A. K., and Dickey, B. C. (1970). *J. Appl. Phys.* **41,** 1399.
Janssen, P. J. M., and Day, P. E. (1973). *Philips Tech. Rev.* **33,** 190.
Jenney, J. A. (1970). *J. Opt. Soc. Am.* **60,** 1155.

Kaminow, I. P. (1975). *IEEE Trans. Microwave Theory Tech.* **23**, 57.
Kaminow, I. P., and Turner, E. H., (1966). *Proc. IEEE* **54**, 1374.
Keneman, S. A., and Taylor, G. W. (1970). *Appl. Opt.* **9**, 2279.
Kiemle, H. (1974). *Appl. Opt.* **13**, 803.
Kogelnik, H. (1969). *Bell Syst. Tech. J.* **48**, 2909.
Kogelnik, H., and Li, T. (1966). *Proc. IEEE* **54**, 1312.
Kosav, J. (1965). "Light Sensitive Systems." Wiley, New York.
Kozma, A., Lee, W. H., and Peters, P. J. (1971). *Proc. IEEE CLEA.*
Krumme, J. P., and Hansen, P. (1973). *Appl. Phys. Lett.* **23**, 576.
Krumme, J. P., Hill, B., Kruger, J., and Witter, K. (1975). *J. Appl. Phys.* **46**, 2733.
Kuehler, J. D., and Kerby, H. R. (1966). *Proc. Fall Jt. Comput. Conf.* p. 753.
Kumada, A. (1972). *Appl. Ferroelectr.* **3**, 115.
Kurz, H., and Kratzig, E. (1975). *Appl. Phys. Lett.* **26**, 635.
Land, C. E., Thacher, P. D., and Haertling, G. H. (1974). *Appl. Solid State Sci.* **4**, 137.
Lee, T. C. (1974). *Appl. Opt.* **13**, 888.
Lee, T. C., and Chen, D. (1972). *Appl. Phys. Lett.* **19**, 62.
Lee, T. C., and Zook, J. D. (1968). *IEEE J. Quantum Electron.* **QE-4**, 444.
Lin, L. H. (1969). *Appl. Opt.* **8**, 963.
Lin, L. H. (1971). *J. Opt. Soc. Am.* **61**, 203.
Lo, D. S. (1974). *Appl. Opt.* **13**, 861.
MacDonald, R. E., and Beck, J. W. (1969). *J. Appl. Phys.* **40**, 1429.
Maldonaldo, J. R., and Anderson, L. K. (1971). *IEEE Trans. Electron Devices* **18**, 774.
Maldonaldo, J. R., and Meitzler, A. M. (1970). *IEEE Trans. Electron Devices* **17**, 148.
Maydan, D. (1970a). *J. Appl. Phys.* **41**, 1552.
Maydan, D. (1970b). *IEEE J. Quantum Electron.* **QE-6**, 15.
Maydan, D. (1971). *Bell Syst. Tech. J.* **50**, 1761.
Mayer, L. (1958). *J. Appl. Phys.* **29**, 1003.
Megla, G. K. (1974). *Opt. Laser Technol.* **6**, 61.
Melchior, H., Fisher, M. B., and Arams, F. R. (1970). *Proc. IEEE* **58**, 1466.
Meyer, H., Riekmann, D., Schmidt, K. P., Schmidt, U. J., Rahlff, M., Schroder, E., and
    Thust, W. (1972). *Appl. Opt.* **11**, 1732.
Mezrich, R. S. (1969). *Appl. Phys. Lett.* **14**, 132.
Micheron, F., and Bismuth, G. (1972). *Appl. Phys. Lett.* **20**, 79.
Micheron, F., Rochon, J. M., and Vergnolle, M. (1974a). *Appl. Phys. Lett.* **24**, 605.
Micheron, F., Mayeux, C., and Trotier, J. C. (1974b). *Appl. Opt.* **13**, 784.
Minnaja, N., Boschetti, P. L., and Chen, D. (1973). *AIP Conf. Proc.* **10**, 1435.
Myers, W. C. (1964). NCR-Ed, Hawthorne, California (Internal report). ·
Nakamura, M., and Yariv, A. (1976). *Tech. Dig. Integrated Opt. Meet.*
Neale, R. G., and Aseltine, J. A. (1973). *IEEE Trans. Electron Devices* **ED-20**, 1957.
Nisenson, P., and Iwasa, S. (1972). *Appl. Opt.* **11**, 2760.
Ono, Y., Esho, S., and Nagao, M. (1972). *Proc. Intermag 72.*
Ovshinsky, S. R., and Klose, P. (1972). *J. Non-Cryst. Solids* **8–10**, 892.
Packard, J. R., Tait, W. C., and Dierssen, G. H. (1971). *Appl. Phys. Lett.* **19**, 338.
Panish, M. B. (1975). *IEEE Trans. Microwave Theory Tech.* **23**, 20.
Patajczak, H., and Sczaniecki, Z. (1970). *Phys. Status Solidi A* **1**, 171.
Patlach, A. M. (1972). *IBM J. Res. Dev.* **16**, 313.
Peters, C. J. (1965). *Proc. IEEE* **53**, 455.
Pinnow, A. (1970). *IEEE J. Quantum Electron.* **QE-6**, 223.
Rajchman, J. A. (1970). *Appl. Opt.* **9**, 2269.

Reich, A., and Dorion, G. H. (1965). *In* "Optic and Electrooptic Information Processing" (J. Tippet, ed.), p. 567. MIT Press, Boston, Massachusetts.

Roberts, H. N. (1972). *Appl. Opt.* **11**, 397.

Roberts, H. N., Watkins, J. W., and Johnson, R. H. (1974). *Appl. Opt.* **13**, 841.

Russell, J. T., and Walker, R. A. (1976). *Opt. Eng.* **15**, 20.

Sawatzky, E. (1971a). *IEEE Trans. Magn.* **MAG-7**, 374.

Sawatzky, E. (1971b). *J. Appl. Phys.* **42**, 1706.

Sawatzky, E., and Street, G. B. (1971). *IEEE Trans, Magn.* **MAG-7**, 377.

Schmidt, U., and Thust, W. (1969). *Opto.-electronics* **1**, 21.

Schneider, I., Marrone, M., and Kabler, M. N. (1970). *Appl. Opt.* **9**, 1163.

Seib, D. H., and Aukerman, L. W. (1973). *Adv. Electron. Electron Phys.* **34**, 85.

Shankoff, T. A. (1968). *Appl. Opt.* **7**, 2101.

Shelton, C. (1973). *IEEE Trans. Magn.* **MAG-9**, 398.

Sherwood, R. C., Nesbitt, E. A., Wernick, J. H., Bacon, D. D., Kurtzig, A. J., and Wolfe, R. (1971). *J. Appl. Phys.* **42**, 1704.

Shew, L. F., and Blanchard, J. G. (1969). *IEEE J. Quantum Electron.* **QE-5**, 333.

Smith, P. W. (1970). *Proc. IEEE* **58**, 1342.

Smith, A. W. (1973). *Appl. Phys. Lett.* **23**, 437.

Spencer, E. G., Lenzo, P. V., and Ballman, A. A. (1967). *Proc. IEEE* **55**, 2074.

Staebler, D. L., and Amodei, J. J. (1972). *Ferroelectrics* **3**, 107.

Stewart, W. C., and Cosentino, W. S. (1970). *Appl. Opt.* **9**, 2271.

Stewart, W. C., Mezrich, R. S., Cosentino, L. S., Nagle, E. M., Wendt, F. S., and Lohman, R. D. (1973). *RCA Rev.* **34**, 3.

Stoffel, A. M. (1970). *J. Appl. Phys.* **41**, 1405.

Strehlow, W. H., Dennison, R. L., and Packard, J. R. (1974). *J. Opt. Soc. Am.* **64**, 543.

Suits, J. C., Arzyle, B. E., and Freiser, M. J. (1966). *J. Appl. Phys.* **37**, 1391.

Suits, J. C., Lee, K., Winters, H. F., Phipps, P. B., and Kyser, D. F. (1971). *J. Appl. Phys.* **42**, 3458.

Sutherlin, K. K. (1973). *Dig. Tech. Pap., Top. Meet. Opt. Storage Digital Data, Aspen, Colo.*

Tait, W. C., Packard, J. R., Dierssen, G. H., and Campbell, D. A. (1967). *J. Appl. Phys.* **38**, 3035.

Takeda, Y. (1972). *Jpn. J. Appl. Phys.* **11**, 656.

Takeda, Y., Oshida, Y., and Miyamura, Y. (1971). *Dig. CLEA.*

Thaxter, J. B. (1969). *Appl. Phys. Lett.* **15**, 210.

Thaxter, J. B., and Kestigian, M. (1974). *Appl. Opt.* **13**, 913.

Tomlinson, W. J., Kaminow, I. P., Chandross, E. A., Fork, R. L., and Silfvast, W. T. (1970). *Appl. Phys. Lett.* **16**, 486.

Tomlinson, W. J., Chandrons, E. A., Fork, R. L., Prdye, C. A., and Lamola, A. A. (1972). *Appl. Opt.* **11**, 533.

Treves, D. (1967). *J. Appl. Phys.* **38**, 1192.

Treves, D., Hunt, R. P., and Dickey, B. (1969). *J. Appl. Phys.* **40**, 972.

Tufte, O. N., and Chen, D. (1973). *IEEE Spectrum* **10**, No. 2, 26; No. 3, 48.

Uchida, N., and Niizeki, N. (1973). *Proc. IEEE* **61**, 1073.

Unger, W. K., and Rath, R. (1971). *IEEE Trans. Magn.* **MAG-7**, 885.

van den Bussche, W., Hoogendijk, A. H., and Wessels, J. H. (1973). *Philips Tech. Rev.* **3**, 181.

Von der Linde, D., Glass, A. M., and Rodgers, K. F. (1974). *Appl. Phys. Lett.* **25**, 155.

Von Gutfeld, R. J., and Chaudhari, P. (1972). *J. Appl. Phys.* **43**, 4688.

Waring, R. K., Jr. (1971). *J. Appl. Phys.* **42,** 1873.
Weckler, G. P. (1967). *IEEE J. Solid-State Circuits* **2,** 65.
Wieder, H., and Werlich, H. (1971). *IBM J. Res. Dev.* **15,** 272.
Williams, H. J., Sherwood, R. C., Foster, E. G., and Kelly, F. M. (1957). *J. Appl. Phys.* **28,** 1181.
Yariv, A. (1971). "Introduction to Optical Electronics." Holt, New York.
Zook, J. D. (1974). *Appl. Opt.* **13,** 875.

SUBJECT INDEX

A

Acne
  laser treatment of, 128
  quartz lamp treatment of, 126
Acoustooptic deflectors, 178–182
Acoustooptic modulator, 174–178, 212
Acoustooptic properties, of selected
  materials, 175
Adenoidectomies, lasers in, 113
Adenosine diphosphate, 17
ADP, see Adenosine diphosphate;
  Ammonium dihydrogen phosphate
Alterable holographic recording, 216–222
Alterable recording materials
  in optical data systems, 152–168
  physical effects in, 153
  thermally induced, 152–160
  thermomagnetic, 152–158
Amino acids, in protein structure, 3
Ammonium dihydrogen phosphate
  in carbon monoxide binding studies, 15
  in optical recording, 173
Amorphous-crystalline transition, in optical
  data storage, 159
ATP, see Adenosine triphosphate
Autocorrelation function, 34

B

Bacteria, photosynthetic, 10–12
Bacteriochlorophyll
  absorption spectrum for, 10–11
  oxidation of, 38
Basal cell carcinoma, laser treatment of,
  128

Beam addressable magnetooptic disk
  memory system, 207
Bed sores, laser treatment of, 120
Beer's law, photomultiplier and, 8
Biopsy, lasers in, 128
Bismuth silicate ($Bi_{12}SiO_{20}$) crystal device,
  71–81, 167
  modulation transfer frequency for, 79–80
  superprime operating sequence for, 78
Bismuth titanate, 167
Bit-oriented optical memory, alterable,
  201–208
Bit-oriented recording systems, 198–208
Blindness, diabetic retinopathy in, 116
Blood coagulation, with pulsed rf currents,
  108
Bragg scattering, 176
Breadboard wideband holographic
  recorder, 213
Burn eschars, removal of, 119–120
Burns, degrees of, 119

C

Cadmium sulfide photoconductor, 66
Candida albicans, 117
Carbon dioxide laser
  in burn surgery, 119–120
  in cauterizing, 129
  in dermatology, 127–128
  in otolaryngology, 111
Carbon monoxide-photolysis systems,
  experimental, 14–16
Carboxylmyoglobin
  optical absorption spectra of, 13
  photolysis and, 16
  photodissociation of, 14